VISUAL LANGUAGES AND APPLICATIONS

LANGUAGES AND INFORMATION SYSTEMS

Series Editor: Shi-Kuo Chang
University of Pittsburgh
Pittsburgh, Pennsylvania
and Knowledge Systems Institute
Skokie, Illinois

*Series was formerly entitled
MANAGEMENT AND INFORMATION SYSTEMS

A Continuation Order Plan is available for this series. A continuation order will bring delivery of each new volume immediately upon publication. Volumes are billed only upon actual shipment. For further information please contact the publisher.

VISUAL LANGUAGES AND APPLICATIONS

Edited by

Tadao Ichikawa
Hiroshima University
Higashi-Hiroshima, Japan

Erland Jungert
Swedish Defence Research Establishment
Linköping, Sweden

and

Robert R. Korfhage
University of Pittsburgh
Pittsburgh, Pennsylvania

PLENUM PRESS • NEW YORK AND LONDON

Library of Congress Cataloging-in-Publication Data

Visual languages and applications / edited by Tadao Ichikawa, Erland
  Jungert, and Robert R. Korfhage.
      p.   cm. -- (Languages and information systems)
  Includes bibliographical references.
  ISBN-13: 978-1-4612-7871-9   e-ISBN-13: 978-1-4613-0569-9
  DOI: 10.1007/978-1-4613-0569-9

  1. Visual programming languages (Computer science) 2. Visual
programming (Computer science)   I. Ichikawa, Tadao. II. Jungert,
Erland. III. Korfhage, Robert R.   IV. Series.
QA76.65.V56 1990
006.6'6--dc20
                                                          90-35433
                                                          CIP

© 1990 Plenum Press, New York
A Division of Plenum Publishing Corporation
233 Spring Street, New York, N.Y. 10013
Softcover reprint of the hardcover 1st edition 1990

CONTRIBUTORS

ALLEN L. AMBLER • *Department of Computer Science, University of Kansas, Lawrence, Kansas 66045*

ENRICO BARICHELLA • *GMSVP—Gruppo Medico Sistemistico di Via Pace, Milan, Italy*

MAURIZIO BERETTA • *GMSVP—Gruppo Medico Sistemistico di Via Pace, Milan, Italy*

DAVE BRIDGELAND • *Artificial Intelligence Laboratory, Microelectronics and Computer Technology Corporation, Austin, Texas 78701*

SHI-KUO CHANG • *Department of Computer Science, University of Pittsburgh, Pittsburgh, Pennsylvania 15260*

WILFRED CHEN • *Computer Science Department, Cornell University, Ithaca, New York 14853*

DONALD B. CROUCH • *Department of Computer Science, University of Minnesota—Duluth, Duluth, Minnesota 55812*

NICOLA DIOGUARDI • *Institute of Internal Medicine, University of Milan, Milan, Italy*

ROBERT DUISBERG • *Computer Research Laboratory, Tektronix, Inc., Seattle, Washington, Present affiliation: School of Music, University of Washington, Seattle, Washington 98191*

JOHN FIELD • *Computer Science Department, Cornell University, Ithaca, New York 14853*

MICHAEL L. GRAF • *MCC Software Technology Program and NCR Corporation, Austin, Texas 78759*

ESA HELTTULA • *Department of Computer Science, University of Tampere, S-F33101, Tampere, Finland*

M. HIRAKAWA • *Faculty of Engineering, Hiroshima University, Higashi-Hiroshima 724, Japan*

CHARLES E. HUGHES • *Computer Science Department, University of Central Florida, Orlando, Florida 32816*

AULIKKI HYRSKYKARI • *Department of Computer Science, University of Tampere, S-F33101, Tampere, Finland*

T. ICHIKAWA • *Faculty of Engineering, Hiroshima University, Higashi-Hiroshima 724, Japan*

ERLAND JUNGERT • *Swedish Defense Research Establishment, S-581 11 Linköping, Sweden*

ROBERT R. KORFHAGE • *Department of Information Science, University of Pittsburgh, Pittsburgh, Pennsylvania 15260*

DEXTER KOZEN • *Computer Science Department, Cornell University, Ithaca, New York 14853*

TIMOTHY C. LETHBRIDGE • *Department of Computer Science, University of Ottawa, Ottawa, Ontario, Canada K1N 6N5*

KAZUO MATSUMURA • *Systems & Software Engineering Laboratory, Toshiba Corporation, Kawasaki 210, Japan*

FANYA S. MONTALVO • *DEC Cambridge Research Lab, Cambridge, Massachusetts 02139*

J. MICHAEL MOSHELL • *Computer Science Department, University of Central Florida, Orlando, Florida 32816*

MARK A. MUSEN • *Medical Computer Science Group, Knowledge Systems Laboratory, Stanford University School of Medicine, Stanford, California 94305-5479*

PIERO MUSSIO • *Department of Physics, University of Milan, Milan, Italy*

MARCO PADULA • *CNR-SIAM, Milan, Italy*

MAURIZIO PIETROGRANDE • *Institute of Internal Medicine, University of Milan, Milan, Italy*

MARCO PROTTI • *Department of Physics, University of Milan, Milan, Italy*

WILLIAM PUGH • *Computer Science Department, Cornell University, Ithaca, New York 14853*

KARI-JOUKO RÄIHÄ • *Department of Computer Science, University of Tampere, Tampere, Finland*

DAVID N. SMITH • *IBM T. J. Watson Research Center, Yorktown Heights, New York 10598*

M. TANAKA • *Faculty of Engineering, Hiroshima University, Higashi-Hiroshima 724, Japan*

SHUICHI TAYAMA • *Design Center, Toshiba Corporation, Tokyo 105, Japan*

TIM TEITELBAUM • *Computer Science Department, Cornell University, Ithaca, New York 14853*

BRAD VANDER ZANDEN • *Computer Science Department, Cornell University, Ithaca, New York 14853*

COLIN WARE • *School of Computer Science, University of New Brunswick, Fredericton, New Brunswick, Canada E3B 5A3*

PREFACE

The importance of visual languages—languages that incorporate nontextual elements—in the human–computer interface became clear some six or seven years ago. While the meaning of the term "visual language" was initially rather unfocused, as research continued and results were reported, the various components of the work bagan to take shape. The exact boundaries of the area of visual languages will always remain fuzzy, as they must for any work that interfaces with other disciplines; but we can now visualize the shape of this field more clearly.

The present volume is organized into six sections, the first three consisting of papers central to the theme of visual languages, with the last three sections concentrating on the use of visual languages.

The volume opens with a chapter that develops some of the theoretical underpinnings of visual languages. We follow this with three chapters related to the visual aspects of interface design. The third section presents developments in visual programming languages, an important subarea.

The second half of the book begins with two contributions on the problems of animating algorithms, followed by a section on simulation animation. The book closes with four chapters on miscellaneous applications, in medicine, geography, information retrieval, and spreadsheets.

Any compilation such as this is largely a historical record. While the book was in preparation, research on visual languages continued, more conferences were held, and a journal began publication. Yet these chapters present a focused view of the major themes that underlie current and future research.

The Editors

CONTENTS

VISUAL LANGUAGES
AND APPLICATIONS

INTRODUCTION

The interface between the user of a computer-based information system and the system itself has been evolving at a rapid rate. The use of a video screen, with its color and graphics capabilities, has been one factor in this evolution. The development of light pens, mice, and other screen image manipulation devices has been another. With these capabilities has come a natural desire to find more effective ways to make use of them. In particular, much work has gone into the development of interface systems that add visual elements such as icons and graphics to text. The desire to use these visual elements effectively in communication between the user and the system has resulted in a healthy competition of ideas and discussion of the principles governing the development and use of such elements. The present volume chronicles some of the more significant ideas that have recently been presented. The first volume in this series on the subject [*Visual Languages* (Chang, Ichikawa, and Ligomenides, eds.), Plenum, 1986] covered work done in the early days of the field of visual languages. Here we represent ideas that have grown out of that early work, arranged in six sections: Theory, Design Systems, Visual Programming, Algorithm Animation, Simulation Animation, and Applications.

THEORY

Fundamental to the concept of visual languages is the conviction that diagrams and other visual representations can aid understanding and communication of ideas. We begin this volume with a chapter by Fanya S. Montalvo that discusses some of the psychological concepts that are relevant to the production and use of meaningful visual constructs.

DIAGRAM UNDERSTANDING
THE SYMBOLIC DESCRIPTIONS BEHIND THE SCENES

Fanya S. Montalvo

1. Introduction

When two scientists talk to each other about their ideas, they typically do not restrict themselves to words; they also draw diagrams, label them, and tell each other what these diagrams represent. "Here's a ball rolling down an inclined plane," one scientist may say, for example, and simultaneously sketch a diagram such as that in Figure 1. In order to understand this kind of conversation, the scientists must recognize the circle as such and associate it with a ball, recognize the arrow and associate it with a vector, and recognize the triangle and associate it with a ramp. After these associations are made, the behavior of the objects in the diagram is then determined. The diagram is a kind of notation with which to solve simple physics problems. Alternatively, the scientists may use a standardized notation whose meaning is known by everyone in the culture, such as algebra. In either case, there is a specific association between visual objects and descriptions for these objects.

The conversation the two scientists are having is a kind of *diagrammatic conversation*. They are generating visual symbols that stand for the things they are talking about, and they are recognizing visual symbols as objects of discourse. The diagrams on paper are just as much a part of their conversation as the words they speak.

In order to make sense of this kind of conversation, we need to understand the visual vocabulary being used. In order to embody such a vocabulary in a conversation with a computer system, several conditions

---

FANYA S. MONTALVO • DEC Cambridge Research Lab, Cambridge, Massachusetts 02139.

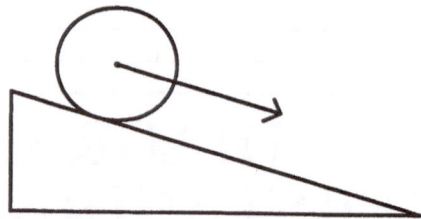

FIGURE 1. A sample diagram.

must hold. The system must have both *recognizers* and *generators* for the visual vocabulary and methods of associating it with the application domain vocabulary, physics in this case.

When captured by a system, the recognition component of the conversation is in the domain of computer vision. The *vision* problem is the process of going from a sequence of light intensity arrays digitized by a television camera to a symbolic description of a situation that can be used by a reasoner to solve a spatial problem, such as navigation or assembly. Aside from the procedural issues of *how* one solves this problem, the declarative part is one-half of the denotation relationship, that is, the relationship between the image and its symbolic description. (See Figure 2.)

The declarative part of the graphics problem is the opposite of the declarative part of the vision problem. It involves going from a user's symbolic description of a picture or diagram or sequence of these to the light intensity array typical of modern frame buffers. Currently available graphics systems do only part of the job. For one, such systems are largely procedural in nature. One can tell them *how* to draw in detailed procedural terms, but one cannot describe *what* one wants to draw in higher-level terms. For another, current graphics systems are limited in the number and types of objects to which a user can refer: for example, a user can represent *x*-, *y*-coordinates, polygons, and RGB values, but not properties such as *near, larger-than, inside, above, convex, color-by-name, contrast* and *squiggliness*. These are properties of diagrams that users want to manipulate while interacting with

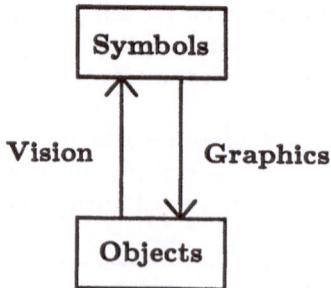

FIGURE 2. The denotation map for vision and graphics.

a graphics system. Some graphics experts devote much time and effort to programming these relationships, but in each case the relationship is custom-made to the application, with little room for flexibility by the user. Custom-made graphics are procedural rather than declarative: a user can get the system to do all kinds of interesting things but cannot graphically *refer* to component parts and properties, and therefore cannot easily change them. In order to refer more easily to objects in the graphical domain, one can be aided by symbolic descriptions and inference machinery applied to the graphics interface part of the system, as well as to the application part. The best way of capturing descriptions and reasoning is with knowledge representation systems. Although knowledge representation systems have been generally applied to specific application domains, they also need to be applied to the graphic component of systems. If the visual reasoning is described in the same higher-level language as the application domain reasoning, new ways of displaying complex ideas can be synthesized more flexibly and quickly.

We wish to call that part of the overlap between computer vision and computer graphics that has to do with the correspondence between symbolic descriptions and images *diagram understanding*. Computer vision and computer graphics, at least as originally conceived, were thought of as straight-through, batch processes, ones from image to description and vice versa, with little interaction with a user. But combining methods from the two fields can provide a framework for a system that can have a *diagrammatic conversation* with the user. The diagrammatic conversation paradigm, because of its tight feedback from a human, has a chance of validating the higher-level properties and operations implemented by the system. By "validation," we mean finding a way of testing that the conversation "sounds" right as in the natural language paradigm. Much work has been done in the area of natural language understanding.[1] We would like to further this work by including diagrams in natural dialogues. Zdybel *et al.*[2] and Friedell *et al.*[3, 4] have shown that including declarative knowledge about display in standard knowledge-based applications can increase their flexibility and power. The present study goes further to address the issues of validation of those descriptions and acquisition of natural, visual primitives and compositional operators for use in such systems.

An experimental paradigm for validating the association between symbolic descriptions and images is proposed in this chapter. It involves simultaneously presenting two sets of figures to a subject and asking the subject to describe the difference between them. These presentations are known as Bongard problems.[5] We then translate verbal descriptions into symbolic descriptions in computer systems' terms. Both recognizers and generators are implemented for each property gathered in this way. Subjects can then verify the map between descriptions and images by checking their correspondence in both directions: between graphic input and the system's subsequent symbolic description, and between symbolic input and a sample image produced by the system. By incorporating the range of visual properties gathered in this way into a graphics tool kit having mechanisms that allow attachment to a particular application domain, we can then verify how the properties fare as part of a full diagrammatic conversation in some application domain. By testing the set against a wide range of applications, we can get a measure of the degree of completeness and generality in the kit as well as of its utility. We describe an initial version of such a system in Section 6 and in Ref. 6.

2. Some Underlying Assumptions

Implicit in the view that graphic interaction is a diagrammatic conversation are the three underlying assumptions discussed in the following sections.

2.1. Intelligent Graphic Input Is a Computer Vision Problem

The first assumption is that graphic input can be viewed as a *recognition* problem. There are two aspects to recognition: the *how* and the *what*. We will concentrate on the *what* in this chapter. The *what* concerns the space of possible objects and properties a user can select and manipulate. For example, a paint program recognizes pixels in specific colors, bounded regions that can be filled, and frames as in a film. A draw program recognizes connected line segments, circles, rectangles, texture patterns, etc. This is apart from *how* they are recognized. Suppose that in an interactive graphics system, a user wants to select objects and properties of objects by pointing and input objects by drawing. The system has to have a very good idea of *what* constitutes valid objects in a given domain. For example, if one points to a set of squares (Figure 3a), is one selecting the set (Figure 3b), one of the squares (Figure 3c), one of the line segments in one of the squares (Figure 3d), the corresponding line segment in all of the squares (Figure 3e), or one vertex of one of the squares (Figure 3f)? The possibilities are endless. In order to constrain the pointing and drawing process to manageable proportions, it is necessary to know what the common objects of discourse are. This constraint on the domain of discourse is similar to that required in natural language. The process is constrained by the context, since denotation can vary over contexts.[7] For example, Ciccarelli's system[8] allows one to draw circles and ellipses around text or other objects. In Ciccarelli's

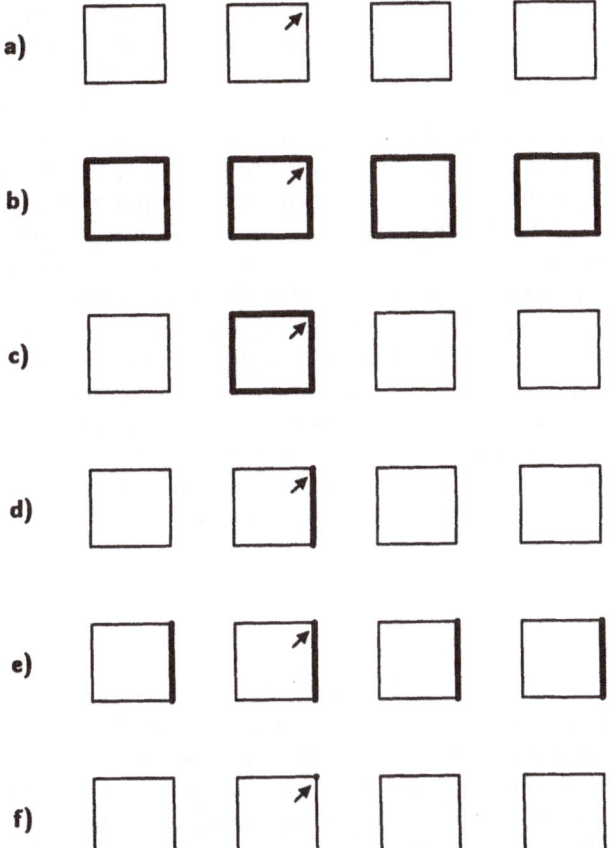

FIGURE 3. The ambiguity of pointing to a set of squares (a). The thicker contours in (b)–(f) represent highlighting of the potential referents of pointing in (a).

system, any sloppily connected curve will be recognized by the system as an ellipse in the most general case, or as a circle if the aspect ratio is close to one. Elements of computer vision are apparently unavoidable in the general graphic input problem: input must be *recognized* as being in a certain semantic category in order to be parsed correctly and must be disambiguated by context in order to be understood. In any case, graphic interaction restricts the nature of the vision problem to a more narrow one of finding a correspondence between the user's input gestures and the domain of visual objects in a specific application.

The observation that the input side of full graphic interaction is a vision problem has not been widely recognized among the graphics community because of the simple nature of graphic input thus far. However, if we are to advance to more complex diagrammatic systems, more sophisticated kinds of recognition are necessary because more flexible kinds of pointing are desirable. For example, in a text formatter, it would be nice to change the size of all the spaces between sentences by just pointing to one and stretching it rather than just being able to refer to a single space.

Thinking of the graphic input problem as computer vision helps in this regard, because knowledge of human vision can be brought to bear. Conversely, problems in vision can be simplified if they are, in turn, recognized as partially graphics problems in terms of echoing intermediate results of processing to the user as recognition proceeds, and thus allowing user guidance. In this way, rather than being a straight-through, batch process from picture to goal, the process becomes more of a conversation with the user. A user can help the system understand pieces of a picture and thus allow intermediate results in the vision process.[9] Using both the technology from computer vision in graphics and technology from computer graphics in vision allows us to concentrate on the structure and content of higher-level descriptions rather than on the computation-heavy, low-level parsing and generation.

2.2. Abstraction Exists in the 2-D Domain

A second assumption in this work is that even though lower-level issues of segmentation and contour extraction are bypassed with graphic input, interesting higher-level issues still remain. Even in the two-dimensional (2-D) domain of diagrams, higher-level issues such as layout and the composition of primitive properties into complex objects remain. For example, in Figure 4, a user may first input four squares in the configuration shown and may later wish to refer to the square in the center. A system with knowledge of potential ways of reconfiguring a figure is highly desirable, and such knowledge constitutes higher-level or symbolic sorts of operations. Having a reasoning system underlying graphic representations facilitates the expression of these kinds of operations.

In this inquiry, we are restricting ourselves to the kind of diagrams scientists sketch easily: 2-D, without occlusion ($2\frac{1}{2}$-D), without motion, and

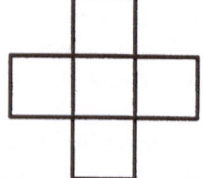

FIGURE 4. Even though the user may input four squares, the user may later wish to refer to the square in the center. Thus, graphic reference is a higher-level inference process.

without color. We do not intend to account for the full range of images common to computer vision and computer graphics—3-D, shaded, color images with motion—even though it appears that the paradigm will generalize to the 3-D, textured object domain.[10] Even given this restriction, the problems of discovering natural and flexible compositional and layout primitives and relating them in a meaningful way to linguistic symbols is challenging. However, it is a good place to start, because given these restrictions we can concentrate on how higher-level vision connects to the lower levels without diverting energy to lower-level parsing requiring massive amounts of computation, such as segmentation and contour extraction.

It is important to understand that "higher-level" does not equal "3-D." True, many interesting and complex issues exist in reconstructing a 3-D model from a 2-D image, but just the issue of which 2-D, symbolic descriptions correspond to which 2-D images is nonetheless abstract. How objects are inferred from groups of primitive properties and how diagrams represent complex domains are also difficult and interesting problems worth studying. There is some evidence that a 3-D description is not the only "highest-level" output of the human visual system.[11]

2.3. Some Form of Validation Is Essential

Finally, we have the assumption that human perception can be brought into the *conversational loop* in order to validate the correspondence between higher-level descriptions and lower-level image components. By the "conversational loop" we mean the tight feedback between a system and a user which continuously confirms what the user and the system are talking about. An example of this loop is the echoing of a rubber-band line when a user is drawing a line segment. After the first point is selected, the system continuously echoes a line segment from the first point to the current cursor position. This echoing gives the user feedback on what the line segment indicated by the current cursor position looks like. The loop signals a kind of agreement of reference between the user and the system: they both mean "this" line (the one currently being stretched). If the user and system "disagree," the discrepancy becomes immediately obvious.

The conversational loop in graphic interaction may provide a bridge between low-level and high-level visual representation by necessitating an intermediate vocabulary. At the low level, some validation for symbolic descriptions can be obtained through correspondence with single-celled feature detectors in biological vision systems.[12] At the highest levels, descriptions become more accessible to introspection. One way of discovering intermediate levels is by providing feedback that checks for the correspondence of reference between a user and a system as the user constructs complex objects from simple properties. Thus, the intermediate levels are spanned by echoing. Echoing is a kind of experiment in which the system continuously asks a user, "Is this what you mean?," and the user responds by continuing. If the echo is not what the user intended, the conversation will feel unnatural.

3. Steps Toward Diagrammatic Conversations

A diagrammatic conversation is not complete if we cannot break out of the application domain we are in and refer to the diagrams themselves in some way. The ability to refer to the diagrams themselves allows flexibility in the interface. Being able to refer to the diagrams and the application domain in the same statement is a meta-operation. This kind of reference requires a rich vocabulary for the diagrammatic domain as well as the application. Typically, the graphics interface builder and the application expert are different people. Because it takes so much time and effort to build a good graphics interface, the graphics interface builder must be an expert at graphics interfaces and is usually not an expert in the application domain too. The people most expert in visualizing the domain are the domain experts themselves, yet they do not have the time to become graphics experts to build good interfaces. So, users of the end products usually find the graphical interfaces inflexible and constraining. It would be better for domain experts to design, build, and modify the interfaces themselves. What domain experts need are domain-independent, graphical tools in which they can freely conceptualize how something should look without having to spend too much time getting it to look that way. They need a graphics tool kit with a rich enough set of visual primitives and operators in order to design and attach a graphical interface to a particular knowledge domain.

Before we can have a diagrammatic conversation with a system, we have to have a vocabulary in which to speak, one that is natural to people and understandable to computers. An example of the kind of vocabulary we would like to have is illustrated by the following example. Suppose we ask for a plot of three variables over time and we do not wish to specify exactly how to draw the $x–y$ axes. Graphics packages exist that do this, but typically the user has no direct control over layout except through coordinate-related input parameters. After the plot has been output, the user cannot then say "move the y-axis label a little to the right" or "color the wiggly line red." Interactions are not typically in terms of high-level descriptors such as "a little," "to the right," "red," or "wiggly." Pointing does not help very much by itself, because pointing is ambiguous, as we saw with Figure 3.

So we see that there are two conditions for a smooth diagrammatic conversation: (1) that the set of visual primitives be natural to humans and computable by machines, and (2) that the system have knowledge about visual properties as well as application properties so that manipulations will respect both visual constraints and application domain constraints. These two conditions could be characterized briefly as finding the right vocabulary and finding the right rules.

4. Finding The Right Vocabulary

In order to draw complex diagrams, or select visual properties from an existing set, we must have an extensive and flexible set with which to start. The constraints of a smooth diagrammatic conversation will help hone a system to a more natural set of diagrammatic concepts, but they will not help find such concepts in the first place. The starting point should be to capture some of the visual categories that humans have about the world. However, because most of the human visual system is not introspectable, the standard knowledge engineering paradigm of asking an expert will not do. Rather than being a drawback, we believe this lack of introspective ability to be a feature. It certainly prevents us from falling into the introspection fallacy: that people have direct access to their own computational processes. We do not have access to such knowledge without an experimental paradigm that will make the knowledge explicit.

The paradigm that we wish to introduce is just such an experimental paradigm. It takes advantage of the large set of visual puzzles composed by Bongard as problems for pattern recognition.[5] Figure 5 is an example of a Bongard problem. The problem posed by the figure is to find the minimal description that distinguishes the six figures on the left from the six on the right. In this case, the distinguishing property is that of being *filled* as opposed to *hollow*. The key idea to this paradigm is to make people's visual knowledge explicit by presenting Bongard problems to them. Unlike standard intelligence tests that involve visual analogy, Bongard problems are simpler. They require simple discrimination rather than analogy. Each of the sets of objects on either side of a center dividing line have the widest possible variability in all but the target property. The solution makes explicit only the one property that distinguishes all the elements on the right from those on the left. If there are alternative descriptions, it is easy to tell which is the most concise description given the whole set of Bongard problems (there are 100 Bongard problems in all). It is also easy to construct a variation of the property embodied by one of the distinguished sets that still fits the distinguishing description. Therefore, each explicit solution yields a visual property in symbolic form (a person has to state the solution in

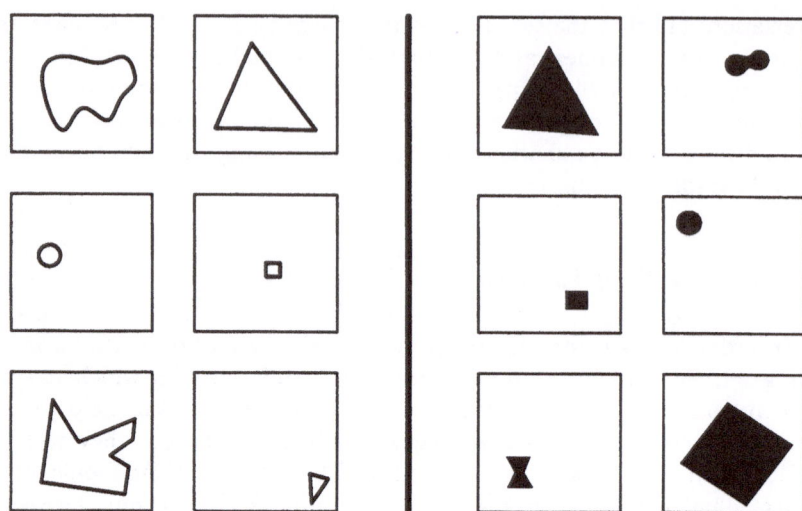

FIGURE 5. Bongard problem #3.

words) and a set of visible objects that embody the property and span a space of parameters within which the property can vary and still be the same identifiable property.

Thus, the first step in our paradigm is to gather sets of symbolic descriptions along with their corresponding images by presenting Bongard problems to people. The next step is to build computational recognizers and

FIGURE 6. Bongard problem #6.

generators for those properties. The third step is to build a system in which all the properties coexist and can be referenced, composed, and manipulated in objects embodying those properties. Given these three steps, users of the resulting system can then verify whether their input matches the symbolic description given by the system and whether a sample object produced by the system when given a symbolic property by the user does in fact embody that property. In other words, the system's recognizers and generators can be tested against human input at both the symbolic and the visual ends. In this way, a diagrammatic conversation can be used to verify the correspondence between symbolic descriptions and visual properties.

In addition to primitive properties, Bongard problems can also suggest operators for combining primitive properties. Typical solutions are compositions of several properties. For example, problem #6 (Figure 6) involves the ability to recognize a polygon and the *count* property of the number of sides of the polygon. In problem #10 (Figure 7), the situation is a bit more complicated: edges must first be filtered before the *sidedness* property can be determined. Finally, in problem #97 (Figure 8), the pixel array must be smoothed and thresholded in order to extract predominant contours. In many cases, it is not just the primitive properties that matter but how they are composed. It is through this explicit identification of the *relationships* between properties that we can recognize how higher-level descriptions are built up from lower-level primitives. Solutions to Bongard problems provide explicit examples of visual relationships and abstractions, as well as primitive properties.

FIGURE 7. Bongard problem #10.

To summarize, the experimental paradigm is this. First, a visual property is made verbally explicit by presenting a Bongard problem to human subjects. The system itself does not solve the Bongard problem. Second, the verbal descriptions are translated to symbolic descriptions in the system's terms. If there are alternative descriptions, the most concise and implementable is preferred. Third, the denotation map consisting of recognizer and generator is implemented for each property. Subjects can then verify the map by checking the correspondence between graphic input and the resulting symbolic description and, similarly, by checking the correspondence between symbolic input and a graphic object produced by the system. Finally, by incorporating the set of visual properties gathered in this way into a graphics tool kit having mechanisms that allow attachment to an application domain, we can verify how the properties fare as part of a full diagrammatic conversation in some application domain. By testing the set against a wide set of applications, we can assess the degree of completeness and generality in the kit as well as its utility.

Sometimes, the applicability of a certain property is not known in advance. The Bongard paradigm affords a certain amount of generality independent of particular application domains. We were at first concerned that a particular property, squiggliness of a closed curve, in problem #20, was not obviously applicable in some real graphics context. On showing it to Gene Ciccarelli, however, he immediately thought of computer networking examples in which the central node is represented by a cloud in order

FIGURE 8. Bongard problem #97.

to deliberately keep the process vague. It is not clear in advance how application experts visualize their domain. It is desirable to provide them with as wide a range of properties as possible and allow them to select and construct their own idiosyncratic presentations. Bongard problems provide a very rich vocabulary from which to choose.

In addition, new Bongard problems can be created as needed to verify new properties. We can throw out unused properties and create and test new ones. Douglas Hofstadter has invented 46 new Bongard problems that are much more abstract than Bongard's original 100. We need not restrict ourselves to Bongard's original properties once we have a good structure for embodying, manipulating, and testing visual properties. The overhead of building new presentations from scratch need not be paid for every time a user wants to create an entirely new visual property.

5. Elements Of Bongard Problems

Let us examine Bongard problems more closely in order to understand their advantages for extracting symbolic descriptions from human subjects. They have three important characteristics: (1) the solutions to the problems establish the correspondence between symbolic descriptions and image properties; (2) the problems provide vivid examples of the composition and decomposition of visual properties; and (3) vividness on the visual side and conciseness on the symbolic side are related.

5.1. Concreteness and Precision

The first characteristic makes symbolic descriptions more concrete. Descriptions alone are not very well grounded if not attached to visual examples that make the exact nature of the target property explicit and compelling. The set of figures in a Bongard problem do this in several ways. First, they show six positive examples—the figures on the left—of the target property embodied in objects having several variations. For example, in Figure 5 the property *hollow* on the left is varied in several different ways: *number-of-sides*, *size*, *curved/straight*, and *concave/convex*. Second, a problem presents six different examples of near missess—the six figures on the right— all of which similarly share properties of *three-* and *four-sidedness*, *large* and *small*, *curved* and *straight*, and *convex* and *concave* but do not exhibit the target property of being *hollow*. Symmetrically, positive and negative examples are also present for the property embodied by the six figures on the right. In this way the strictly *visual* properties of *hollow-ness* and *filled-ness* are unambiguously associated with the symbolic terms we have been using, that is, by the descriptive solution to the problem.

There are several advantages to this concrete association between descriptions and visual properties. Visual examples constrain the property being defined to a small concise example.[13] The set of six figures is actually an example of a *single* property, *not* just one object. In addition, the association of the property with a symbolic term, or set of terms, makes the target property explicit for both the left and right fields of the problem. The two target properties are points on a dimension. In this case, the dimension is just binary, *hollow/filled*; but in other cases it may be a continuous dimension, such as *size* or *orientation*; or it may be a many-valued discrete dimension, such as *sidedness*. So an experimental paradigm having only two sample objects to distinguish is not as precise because it does not narrow the target property sufficiently. A paradigm having only one set of objects as examples of the target property is also not precise enough, because it provides no negative examples, leaving the universe of potential properties unbounded. A paradigm like this one for distinguishing two sets of objects having variations over other common property dimensions does have the requisite elements of concreteness and precision.

5.2. Decomposition and Composition

Another advantage of Bongard problems is that they provide a test for clarifying the structure of the decomposition of objects into properties. There is no prescription for such a test, but if a decomposition exists, two Bongard

FIGURE 9. A problem in the style of Bongard.

problems that distinguish the two properties can be constructed and tested. Let us take the example in Figure 9. There are two equally good solutions to this problem. The figures on the left are all *closed* and the ones on the right are all *curved*. Thus, at least two solutions to the problem exist: *closed* versus *open*, and *straight* versus *curved*. If two solutions exist and can be found experimentally, the problem can be decomposed into two: one distinguishing the property *closed* from *open*, and the other distinguishing *straight* from *curved*. Figures 10 and 11 are tests for this decomposition.

Treisman and co-workers[14, 15] also have designed a paradigm which produces decomposition of objects into primitive properties, but the target properties in each case are represented by only one object or are replicated exactly by several identical objects with no variations. In effect, there are not enough positive and negative examples of the target property to sufficiently narrow its visual definition. The output of the experiments is not a symbolic description in all cases. The paradigm supports findings of the decomposition of some properties, but the emphasis is on finding "illusory conjuncts" rather than on validating symbolic descriptions and finding a complete set of primitives and compositional operators.

The set of Bongard problems goes further to embody compositional relationships of complex objects as well as primitive properties. One finds properties applied to relationships between objects and properties of properties of objects. Figures 12 and 13 show examples of properties of properties of objects. Figure 12 illustrates the property of *inside* versus *outside* applied to

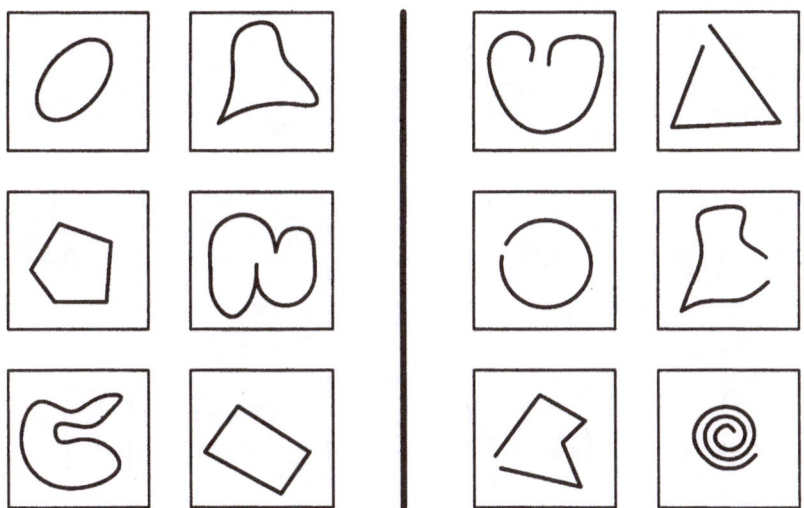

FIGURE 10. Bongard problem #15.

FIGURE 11. Bongard problem #5.

the relationship of *distance* among the small circles. Figure 13 again illustrates the *inside/outside* property, this time applied to the *sidedness* of polygons. Thus, properties gathered from Bongard problems can be viewed as compositional operators that can be applied recursively to primitive objects to form more complex objects and relationships. Properties isolated in this way clarify the structure of composition producing higher-level visual properties.

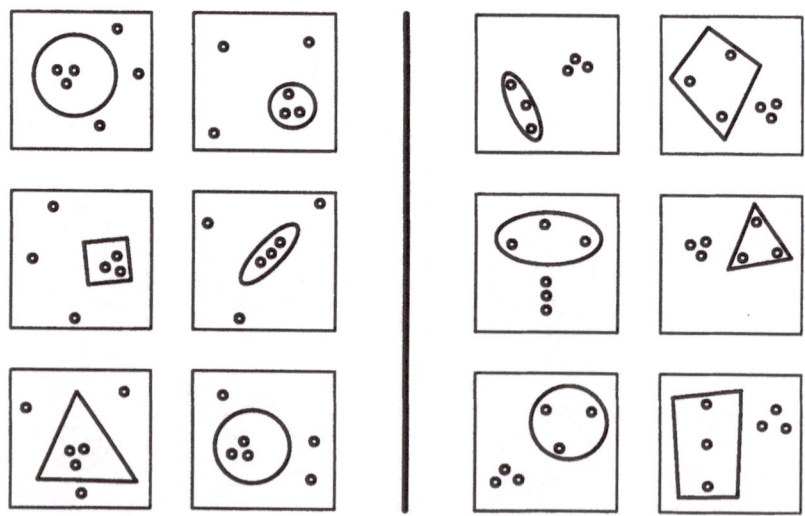

FIGURE 12. Bongard problem #49.

FIGURE 13. Bongard problem #53.

5.3. Vividness and Conciseness

Just as solutions to Bongard problems associate symbols with images, the identification of visual properties can be influenced by *vividness* in the visual domain and *conciseness* in the symbolic domain. Vividness determines which of the potential properties will be seen first and how fast it will be seen. Conciseness determines which description will be more easily remembered and expressed. It appears that the two criteria interact, although the exact nature of their interaction is not clear. Following are two examples of interaction.

In the first example, the only difference between the objects in Figure 14[16] is the line orientation of the diagonal line. However, the fact that one object is *closed* and the other *open* stands out more vividly than the difference in line orientation. The *closed/open* feature is also the more concise description of the two, because even though line orientation is the more primitive and concise feature of the diagonal line by itself, the description of the line in the context of the right-angle vertex is longer when one includes the relationship of the diagonal lines' endpoints to the other two lines. It is in the whole context that the *closed* versus *open* description becomes the more concise one, because it includes the relationships between the three lines, not just the

FIGURE 14. Example demonstrating that there is a difference between a primitive property and a vivid one.

properties of the diagonal line. So here the more vivid feature in the image domain is also the more concise feature in the description domain. Vividness appears to influence conciseness.

The second example involves a brief experiment. Glance at Figure 15 on the next, covered, right-hand page for about a second, cover it, and then try to describe it before reading on. About half of the people to whom we have informally shown this figure (as well as the author), when constrained by a short glance, described the figure as two overlapping pentagons (or regular polygons), each with different width outline. As you can see on closer inspection, there are indeed two overlapping pentagons, and two different weight outlines, but their weight does not correspond one-to-one with pentagons. The pentagons each have thick and thin segments, and the polygons of uniform weight are irregular and six-sided.

Our interpretation of this result is that subjects only have time to parse properties—*weight* and *five-sidedness*—and that the process that associates properties with single objects for the purposes of description happens after viewing and without the chance to verify the objects for discrepancies. A description, in turn, must be concise in order to be remembered. Building a description of these irregular polygons is difficult and presumably requires more than one second of scrutiny. A pentagon is much more concise. One is forced to construct a plausible object to account for the simple properties already parsed, because properties do not exist by themselves. So an object with five sides and thick borders is inferred even though one does not exist in the figure. The lack of conciseness of the description of the actual figure appears to influence the way we see, that is, its vividness. Again, vividness and conciseness seem to go hand in hand, but in this case conciseness seems to be influencing vividness.

6. KnowViz

We have designed a general-purpose, graphic-interface-building tool kit, called KnowViz for knowledge visualizer,[6] based on the diagram understanding principles discussed above. When its development is completed, designers, not necessarily programmers, will use it to design and attach graphic interfaces to applications. The system consists of a semantic network of properties for interactively designing a graphic interface and a set of methods for attaching visual properties to application domain properties.

Properties, objects, and relations found in Bongard problems are represented uniformly as frames[17, 18] in the semantic network. Properties, represented on the screen by prototypes, are incrementally combined to

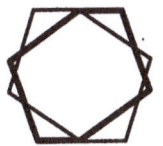

FIGURE 15. Test figure.

form more complex properties, objects, and displays. Relations act as both descriptions and compositional operators on properties and objects to form more complex properties and objects. Each property represented by a frame has a slot for the value of the property itself and slots for a *generator* function, a *recognizer* function, and an *echo* function. (See Figure 16.)

The slot with the same name as its frame is used for inheritance down to any subclasses of the property. Thus, combining properties will incrementally specify more details of a property, as will be illustrated further below. The *generator* function generates a prototype of an object having the target property. The *recognizer* function is a predicate that determines whether or not a property is present in a given object. We are not turning all recognizer functions loose on all objects uniformly but are using them in constrained situations in which domain knowledge can guide which recognizers are triggered for a given input or pointing situation. The *echo* function is used for interactive manipulation when a user selects a property and modifies it. Just as standard *move* operations continuously display the results of moving an object across the screen, echo functions applied to specific scalar properties display changes in the given property continuously as the mouse moves. Thus, any property can be modified directly using the mouse. Binary properties are toggled, and symbolic-valued properties pop up a menu of selections whenever the user chooses to modify them.

Figure 17 shows how simple properties can be combined to produce

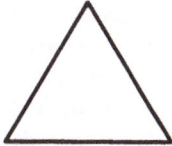

SIDEDNESS
 Recognizer: < function >
 Generator: < function >
 Echo-Function: < function >
 Sidedness: 3

FIGURE 16. A sample unit with an example prototype.

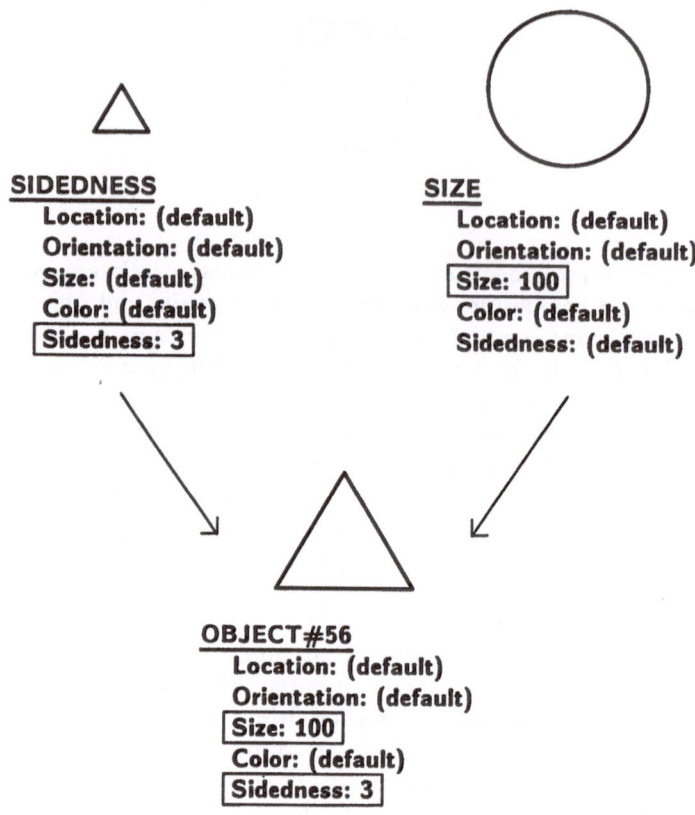

FIGURE 17. Combining properties to form more constrained objects.

more specifically constrained objects. Each property prototype, such as the triangle which represents *sidedness* with value *3*, must have other default properties in order to be drawn. So somewhere the system must specify default *locations, orientations, sizes, colors,* and *sidedness* for each prototype. However, the target property, the slot with the same name as its frame, overrides any default values in slots of equal name whenever prototypes are combined. So in the figure showing two properties being combined, the *sidedness* value of the *sidedness* prototype overrides the *sidedness* value of the *size* prototype. Similarly, the *size* value of the *size* prototype overrides the *size* value of the *sidedness* prototype. In this way a composite figure inherits the target property of a prototype representing that property. These inherited values are specified by user input or manipulation rather than defaulted.

In general, not all instances of property combination have been considered in detail, but we plan to experiment with this paradigm in order to discover combination rules that are as abstract as possible and use specific rules for combination only where necessary. The abstract rules will be pushed up in the hierarchy as much as possible so that we do not have to build 2^N combination rules for N properties. Most combinations will be impossible, such as combining *touching* with *above*. Objects will be combined only with a corresponding relation, and only when the arity of the relation matches the number of objects being combined.

Although much of the design of KnowViz has been specified in detail, it is only partially implemented. The subsystem that attaches visual properties to application domain properties and thus allows application manipulation *through* its graphics is specified only in its broadest form. A more detailed description of the design of KnowViz can be found in Ref. 6.

7. Conclusion

We have introduced the area of diagram understanding, analogous to natural language understanding. Although previously not named as such, it concerns the issues of both the recognition and the generation of visual objects by a computer system. Traditionally, these areas have been called computer vision and computer graphics, respectively. But there is a core issue in this area: the symbolic description of visual objects and their correspondence to concepts natural to people. In an interactive system, the user can have a diagrammatic conversation when the right sorts of associations are provided. The requirements of a smooth conversation drive the representational associations toward more natural, human-based concepts. The need for human interaction motivates a test-bed system having both recognition and generation of visual objects, for the purposes of studying higher-level representation. There is no guarantee that the denotational loop will converge unless we have humans somewhere in the loop. There are two ways of providing feedback. One is to test entire systems for smoothness of interaction, as has been done with natural language understanding. Another is to build systems out of small modules that have been tested individually and whose compositional operators have also been tested against human perception.

With such a system, denotation itself is illusive and ambiguous. It is necessary to have a system that can at least represent these various possibilities of reference in order to have it do the necessary level switching.

A method of visual knowledge acquisition has also been presented. It involves an experimental paradigm that makes descriptive properties explicit. Compositional operators can also be explored and isolated with this paradigm. Properties are seen as more basic than objects in a vocabulary for diagram understanding.

We describe a kit of visual properties and operators to be used by domain experts to design and attach graphic interfaces to specific domains. We argue that static graphic interfaces cannot work for everyone at all times. The best solution is for domain experts to design and modify their own interfaces. They are the most proficient in visualizing their own domain, and, as need varies, their visualizations change. It is impossible for graphics designers to keep up with changing visualizations of abstract concepts dreamed up by domain experts. Graphics interfaces should be as flexible and versatile as paper and pencil, and as easily used. In order to provide such generality, descriptive primitives specific to human vision should be provided. The implementation of recognizers need not be the same as in human visual systems, but the correspondence between human descriptions and visual objects must be the same.

8. Acknowledgments

Many thanks to Gul Agha, Phillip Apley, Michael Brady, Donald Byrd, Muriel Cooper, Randall Davis, Carl Hewitt, Douglas Hofstadter, Henry Lieberman, Ronald MacNeil, Marvin Minsky, Alex Pentland, Thomas Reinhardt, Aaron Sloman, Richard Weyhrauch, and Patrick Winston for inspiration, guidance, and helpful criticism.

We would also like to thank Macmillan Publishers Limited for permission to publish the Bongard problems appearing in this chapter.

The research described in this chapter was done at the Artificial Intelligence Laboratory and Media Laboratory of the Massachusetts Institute of Technology. Support of the A. I. Laboratory's artificial intelligence research is provided in part by the Digital Equipment Corporation and in part by the Defense Advanced Research Projects Agency of the Department of Defense under the Office of Naval Research contract N00014-80-C-0505.

References

1. T. WINOGRAD, *Language as a Cognitive Process, Vol. I: Syntax*, Addison-Wesley, Reading, Massachusetts, 1983.
2. F. ZDYBEL, N. R. GREENFELD, M. D. YONKE, AND J. GIBBONS, An information presentation system, Proceedings of the Seventh International Joint Conference on Artificial Intelligence, IJCAI-81, Vancouver, British Columbia, Canada, August, 1981, pp. 978–984.
3. M. FRIEDELL, J. BARNETT, AND D. KRAMLICH, Context-sensitive, graphic presentation of information, *Comput. Graphics* **16**(3), 181–188 (1982).

4. M. FRIEDELL, Automatic synthesis of graphical object descriptions, *Comput. Graphics* **18**(3), 53–62 (1984).

5. N. BONGARD, *Pattern Recognition*, Macmillan, London 1970.

6. F. S. MONTALVO, Knowledge Visualizer: A Graphic Interface-Building Tool Kit, MIT Media Laboratory Technical Report, Cambridge, MA (1988).

7. C. N. LABOV, The boundaries of words and their meanings, in *New Ways of Analyzing Variation in English*, C. N. Bailey and R. W. Shuy (Eds.), Georgetown University Press, Washington, D.C., 1973.

8. E. C. CICCARELLI, Presentation based user interfaces, Ph.D. dissertation, Massachusetts Institute of Technology, Cambridge, Massachusetts, 1984.

9. J. GLICKSMAN, A Cooperative Scheme for Image Understanding Using Multiple Sources of Information, Department of Computer Science Technical Report 82-13, University of British Columbia, Vancouver, November, 1982.

10. A. P. PENTLAND, Shading into texture, Proceedings of the National Conference on Artificial Intelligence, AAAI-84, Austin, Texas, August 1984, pp. 269–273.

11. A. SLOMAN, What are the purposes of vision?, Presented at the Alvey Vision Conference at Sussex University, September, 1985.

12. F. S. MONTALVO, Aftereffects, adaptation, and plasticity: a neural model for tunable feature space, Ph.D. dissertation, University of Massachusetts, Amherst, 1976.

13. F. S. MONTALVO, Diagram Understanding: The Intersection between Computer Vision and Graphics, A. I. Memo No. 873, MIT Artificial Intelligence Laboratory, Cambridge, Massachusetts, November, 1985.

14. A. M. TREISMAN AND G. GELADE, A feature-integration theory of attention, *Cognitive Psychology* **12**, 97–136 (1980).

15. A. M. TREISMAN AND H. SCHMIDT, Illusory conjunctions in the perception of objects, *Cognitive Psychology* **14**, 107–141 (1982).

16. J. R. POMERANTZ AND W. R. GARNER, Stimulus configuration in selective attention tasks, *Perception and Psychophysics* **14**, 565–569 (1973).

17. I. GOLDSTEIN, FRL: a Frame Representation Language, A. I. Memo No. 333, MIT Artificial Intelligence Laboratory, Cambridge, Massachusetts, 1976.

18. M. STEFIK, An examination of a frame structured representation system, Proceedings of the Sixth International Joint Conference on Artificial Intelligence, IJCAI-79, Tokyo, Japan, August, 1979, pp. 845–852.

DESIGN SYSTEMS

A strong motivation behind the development of visual languages and environments is their applicability to the design and development of various systems. David N. Smith's chapter focuses on a simple "toolbox" interface that permits construction of models of interactive devices. VERDI, which Michael L. Graf presents, provides an environment in which distributed systems can be designed and simulated. Mark A. Musen describes PROTÉGÉ, a visual tool for the development of knowledge-based systems, and illustrates its use in a medical context.

THE INTERFACE CONSTRUCTION SET

David N. Smith

1. Introduction

The Interface Construction Set (InterCONS) contains both a visual data flow language and an environment for building data flow programs and presentation views of such programs. These presentation views are interactive computer interfaces which model applications, implement functions directly, or interface to external devices.

The data flow language is implemented using direct manipulation techniques. The data flow primitives (blocks) are dragged into a work area from a tool kit and then connected by wires to form circuits. The circuits can be executed immediately. Primitives include arithmetic functions, comparisons, flow control, visual output, program control, and interactive input.

Once a circuit is built, all but selected components (and all wires and connections) can be hidden. The visible components can then be resized and repositioned to form a presentation view. Presentation views can be executed in presentation windows which do not have the ability to edit the programs or presentation.

1.1. Related Work

1.1.1. Construction Sets. InterCONS was influenced by the *PinBall Construction Set.*[1]* In PinBall, the right part of the screen is a tool kit containing pictures of pinball-related components: balls, flippers, holes, bumpers, etc. Using a pointing device, a copy of a component is moved to a work area on

---

* Trademark of Electronic Arts.

DAVID N. SMITH • IBM T. J. Watson Research Center, Yorktown Heights, New York 10598.

© 1988 IEEE. Reprinted from the 1988 Workshop on Visual Languages, October 10–12, Pittsburgh, Pennsylvania, pp. 109–120.

© 1988 ACM. Reprinted from the 1988 SIGGRAPH Symposium on User Interface Software, October 17–19, 1988, Banff, Alberta, Canada, pp. 144–151.

the left. Many components can be moved over, and the components can be rearranged as desired. No wires connect components, but alternate views do allow for some behind-the-scenes tweaking of component interconnectivity for game scoring. Upon command, the pictures come to life and become a fully functional pinball game.

Trillium[2] is an environment for simulating and experimenting with interfaces for simple machines such as copier control panels.

1.1.2. Visual Programming. Several highly visual visual-programming systems also provided inspiration. In *Programming By Rehearsal,*[3] programs are developed using a theatrical metaphor. Users audition players to see what they do, and build programs by rehearsal of the players on a stage (or in the wings). In *The Alternate Reality Kit,*[4] an environment is provided in which various laws of physics can be seen, experimented with, and changed. Objects follow the laws in a particular "reality" (environment), and these can be readily changed. New laws and objects can be built from others; wires are used to show relationships.

A number of systems provide some interactive means of building control flow diagrams or N–S Charts of one type or another. These include BLOX,[5] Pict,[6] the program design system of Matsumura and Tayama,[7] the PIGS system of Pong and Ng,[8] and the GRASP system of Workman.[9]

For surveys of the visual programming field, see Refs. 10–12.

1.1.3. Data Flow. Data flow can be high level, in which program blocks are tied together with connections that carry high-level data collections, or low level, in which blocks are more primitive and the connections carry simple elements. High-level systems with interactive program editing include HI-VISUAL,[13] the visual software design system of Kobayashi,[14] and the LabVIEW system.[15] Lower-level systems include a systems programming language proposed by Kosinski.[16]

Somewhat related to data flow are constraint systems such as ThingLab,[17–19] in which constraints between objects are connected visually and solved interactively.

1.1.4. User Interface Elements. Borning and Duisberg use a constraint-based system to build user interface components.[19] Jacob uses state transition diagrams.[20] Brad Myers' Peridot system[21,22] infers what interface elements are to do from what is demonstrated interactively by the designer.

2. The Construction Set

InterCONS presents a set of tools and a workspace. Tools can be "grabbed" with a mouse, and a copy of the tool can be moved over to the workspace. Figure 1 shows a simplified tool kit and the associated work area. The Appendix contains a description of the tool kit.

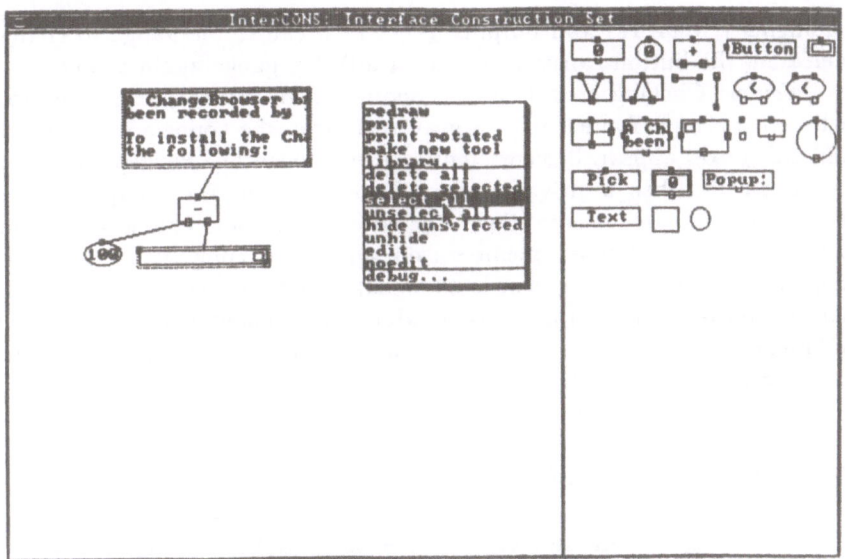

FIGURE 1. An InterCONS editing window. The right pane holds components which can be dragged to the left pane, the workbench. The components shown in the workbench have been connected with wires. The workbench main menu is also shown.

Wires carry integers and the flow is in one direction only. Tools have zero or more input connecters, shown as hollow boxes, and zero or more output connecters, shown as solid boxes. Dragging on a connecter causes a wire to appear; the wire can be carried to any unconnected connecter of the opposite type and dropped on it to form a connection. Upon connection, the circuit is executed.

Circuits can be run in other ways: by interacting with a control such as a button or slider, by changing the value of a component such as a constant, and by disconnecting a wire. (In this last case, the newly unconnected input connecter is treated as if it had a zero for an input; more on this later.)

For example, a button and a gauge are dragged over (circuit 1a), then connected (circuit 1b). When the button is depressed (by placing the mouse pointer over the button and pressing on a mouse button), the button

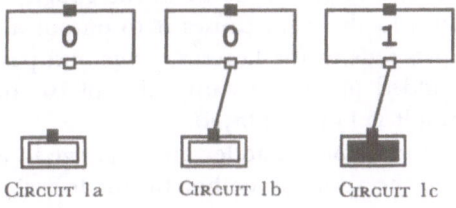

CIRCUIT 1a   CIRCUIT 1b   CIRCUIT 1c

highlights (circuit 1c) and outputs a 1, which causes the gauge to change. Releasing the button causes it to output a 0; the gauge again changes.

Editing. Clicking on a tool (or choosing a menu item) selects the tool. Selected tools are framed with a gray rectangle, the connectors disappear, and edit boxes appear. Selected tools can be moved and resized.

Each tool has a private menu. Depending on the component, the workbench private menu allows for altering values, changing options, and/or selecting a different member from a family of components. In revaluing, the value of a component is changed; constants take on new numeric values, and text takes on new string values. Some components are members of families; the adder can be changed into a multiplier, divider, subtracter, or other arithmetic function.

3. The Data Flow Language

The tools, the interactive components, and the execution model of InterCONS were designed to implement interactive interface components. A data flow model is used, with execution details oriented toward this interaction goal.

Circuits. Wires carry integers. Although the execution model can readily have other numeric types in the wires (as well as other kinds of objects), the needs of the current set of interactive components are well met by integers.

An execution of a circuit is quite simple. Starting with a specific component, it and all components that accept inputs from it are executed until all downstream components have been executed once.

In the earlier button and gauge example, pressing the button caused the button to execute; then the gauge executed. Releasing the button caused the button to again execute; then the gauge executed.

As a more complex example, consider a slider that has been edited to make it long and flat that is hooked to a gauge, then that to an adder (which adds a constant), and finally to a second gauge. First, the circuit with the constant not yet connected is shown as circuit 2a. The first visible execution occurs when the constant is connected in circuit 2b. The constant is executed; it outputs its value to the adder, which adds a zero (the current output from the slider) and passes the 10 to the gauge, which displays it.

Sliding the slider to the right causes it to output a new value (11) in circuit 2c. The 11 proceeds to the bottom gauge and passes through to the adder, where it is added to the constant value of 10, and then to the top gauge, where the result (21) is displayed.

Loops. Circuit 3a contains an adder and a gauge in a loop. A button is hung on one input of the adder. A tie bar (at the left edge) aids in connect-

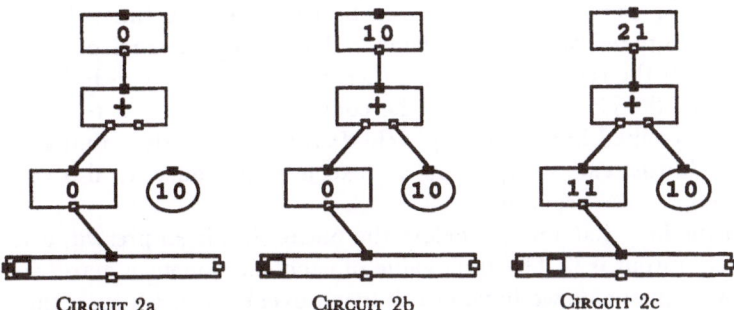

CIRCUIT 2a   CIRCUIT 2b   CIRCUIT 2c

ing the gauge output to the adder input; the tie bar simply passes along its input. Pressing the button once and releasing causes the gauge to display a 1 (circuit 3b). Pressing again and releasing causes the gauge to display a 2. Holding down the button causes the circuit to run and the gauge to continuously increment.

Note that a loop holds a value. This is an important property and is used extensively when programming with the data flow language.

4. The Execution Model

InterCONS circuits are interpreted. Data flow is conceptually parallel; on a serial machine, this parallel property has to be simulated. This simulation can cause problems with the definition of multiple-input devices. This section describes the execution model and how multiple-input devices are handled.

4.1. Time, the Clock, and Execution

Execution of a circuit is governed by a master "clock" with a "time" value. The clock value is incremented by 1 before starting to execute. Each component remembers the time at which it last executed.

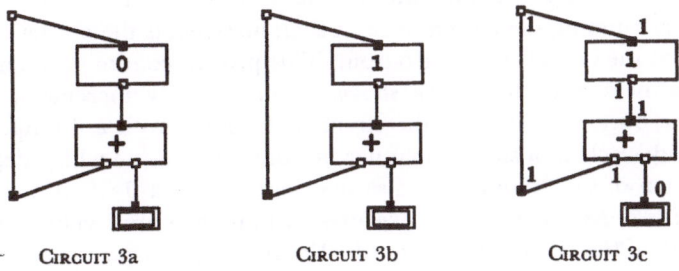

CIRCUIT 3a   CIRCUIT 3b   CIRCUIT 3c

When a component is about to be executed, the time of the master clock is compared with the remembered time. If the time of the clock is greater than the remembered time, then the component can be executed. If the time of the clock is equal to the component time, then the component has been executed in the current cycle. It is this comparison that guarantees that the downstream components are executed just once. It also guarantees that a loop stops executing.

In the loop (circuit 3a), before the button has been pressed, each input and each output is 0. The time value of each component is zero (since they are new components we have just dragged over). Now, we press the button. The master clock is incremented. The button outputs a 1 to the adder. The adder adds the 1 to its other input (a 0) and passes the result to the gauge. The gauge displays the 1 and passes it along to the tie bar. In each case so far, the time values of the components have been less than that of the master clock. However, when the tie bar outputs the 1 to the adder (and places the value into one of the adder's input "registers"), the adder cannot execute since its time is not less than that of the master clock. Meanwhile, the button has been released. The button then increments the clock, sets the button output to 0, and reexecutes the circuit.

The button output of 0 is passed to the adder. The adder adds the 0 to its other input (a 1) and passes the result to the gauge. The gauge displays the 1 and passes it along to the tie bar (circuit 3b). However, when the tie bar outputs the 1 value to the adder, the adder cannot execute since its time is not less than that of the master clock. The values at each input and output connection are now as in circuit 3c.

Note that this second execution does not change the visible state of the circuit. The gauge still shows a 1. However, this 1 is from the left input of the adder, and not from the button. The loop has thus "remembered" the value.

If the button is momentarily pressed again, the same process happens except that the button output (1) is added to the remembered adder input (also a 1) to produce a 2.

If the button is held down, the first execution is the same except that the gauge shows a 2. But the button semantics notices that the button is still down after running the circuit once; it then increments the master clock and again runs the circuit with a 1 output. This process continues so long as the button is held and the gauge shows a continuously incrementing value. When the button is released, the circuit is executed with a 0 output.

A slider acts in a similar manner but outputs a value which depends on the position of the "thumb." It also does not output a 0 when done.

Registers. As a component executes, it puts its output values into input "registers" of the components connected to it without regard to time or clock values. These values stay in the input registers until changed; they potentially stay forever if the part of the circuit that presented the value never executes again.

4.2. Multiple-Input Components

Devices with two inputs have been described as executing whenever any input is ready. This is a simplification that worked for the circuits described so far. However, consider circuit 4a. The button output (1) is sent along two paths by the splitter. The two middle gauges show the splitter outputs. The adder adds both values and produces a 2, which is shown in the top gauge as long as the button is held down (circuit 4b). Although this is the intuitively correct result, this would not be achieved in practice without special handling of multiple-input devices.

The following would happen if such devices were not handled specially:

- The button would output a 1.
- The fan-out would send the 1 along both paths; since parallel processing is simulated by a serial machine, one of the paths would really be first, and one of the paths would execute the adder.
- The adder would take the 1, add it to the 0 from its other input, and output the 1 to the gauge.
- Now the other path would be executed with the gauge passing the 1 to the adder. However, the adder would have already executed in the same time cycle, and execution would stop with the gauge showing a 1.

To prevent this, execution of multiple-input devices is deferred until all reachable single-input devices have been executed. Then one multiple-input

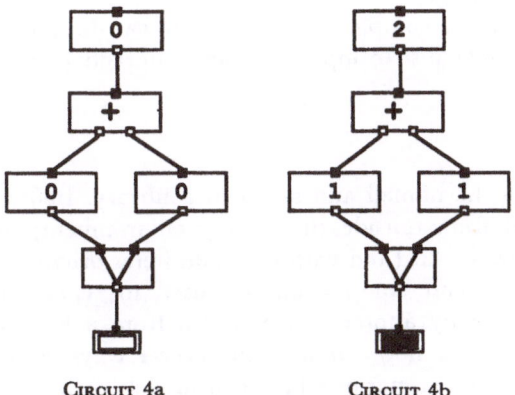

CIRCUIT 4a   CIRCUIT 4b

device for which all inputs have been presented is executed, and the process is repeated for new single-input devices. (This takes care of the case above.)

Finally, if execution of any multiple-input devices are still pending and none have both inputs ready, then one is arbitrarily chosen and executed, and the process again repeats for single-input devices. (Adders in some earlier examples are executed this way since the input from a constant will never occur in the same clock cycle as input from any interactive component.)

5. Building Interactive Components and Models

In circuit 5a, a button to count down is added to circuit 3a. Text buttons, which are functionally identical to the buttons used so far, are used here and have been labeled to indicate their functions.

Now, if this is to be used in a user interface, somehow the wiring needs to go away, as do those components which the user need not see. This is done by first selecting those components that are a part of the desired presentation; selection happens either by clicking on the component or with a menu option. The buttons and the gauge are shown selected in circuit 5b.

A main (pop-up) menu item *hide unselected* hides all but the selected components (and then unselects those) in circuit 5c. Now, only the components that the end user need see are visible. They can again be selected, the moved around and resized until there is some pleasing representation (circuit 5d).

Selecting *unhide* in the main pop-up menu allows further editing of the circuit. The initial circuit, with all components where they were, is shown. Each component thus has two positions and sizes, one for presentation and one for circuit editing.

After a circuit is complete, editing mode can be turned off so that the component responds just to inputs through interactive components.

5.1. Libraries

Circuits can be named and saved in a library. Items from the library can be invoked from outside the editing environment; they appear in a window with no tool kit (and with no menu items oriented toward editing).

Additional circuit components are used to replace one presentation view in a window by another view (taken from a library) or to pop up presentation views in new windows in several ways. Screens can thus be hooked together into scenarios which can model interactive programs.

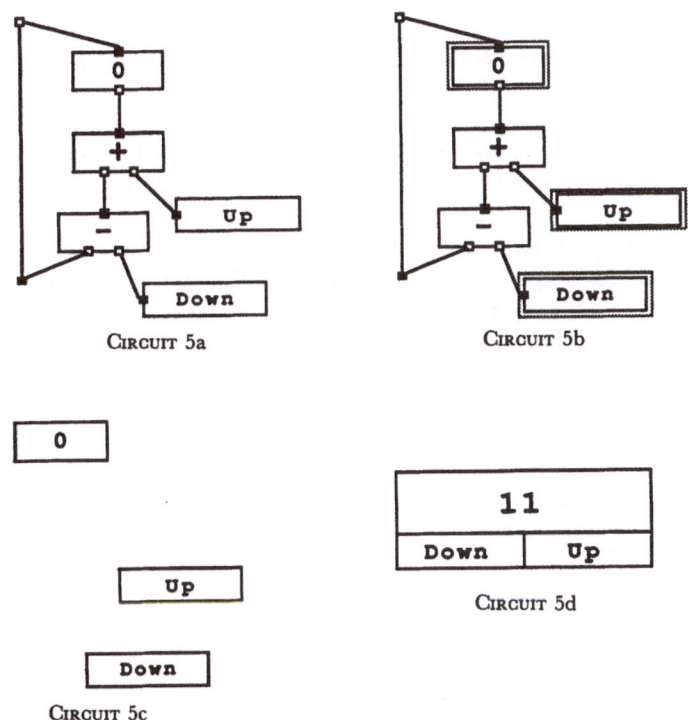

CIRCUIT 5a   CIRCUIT 5b

CIRCUIT 5d

CIRCUIT 5c

5.2. Example: Scroll Bars

Scroll bars, including buttons at the ends to scroll by increments, are easily made. A viewport component simulates an application window by displaying a bitmap containing an arbitrary image. (New images can be created or modified with an external picture editor; a menu item selects from a library of such images.) The viewport takes two inputs, for each of x and y directions, and echoes its inputs as outputs.

A simple arrangement might be as shown in circuit 6a. Moving the slider causes the viewport image to scroll. Sliders are scaled so that the output value at the far left is a 0 and at the far right is 100. Viewports are scaled so that the left edge of the bitmap is at the left of the viewport when the input is 0 and the right edge of the bitmap is at the right edge of the viewport for an input of 100. As a result, any slider can be hooked to any viewport, regardless of the size of either, and the maximum available movement, and no more, occurs.

A more complex arrangement (again only for the x-direction) is shown in circuit 6b.

The slider, subtracter, adder, viewport, and tie bar constitute a loop similar to earlier examples. The gauge is replaced by a viewport, a slider is inserted into the loop, and multipliers and constants are added to cause the buttons to change the loop value by $+4$ or -4.

The buttons increment or decrement the value in the loop, causing the viewport image to scroll left or right and the slider thumb to also move right or left.

If the viewport were a real application that could scroll its own data around, it could output the new position of the data, and the scroll bar would automatically update. Other interactive devices could be added to the loop and each would update the others as well as scroll the data.

The presentation view (in circuit 6c) shows this circuit with scroll bars and buttons for the y-direction as well.

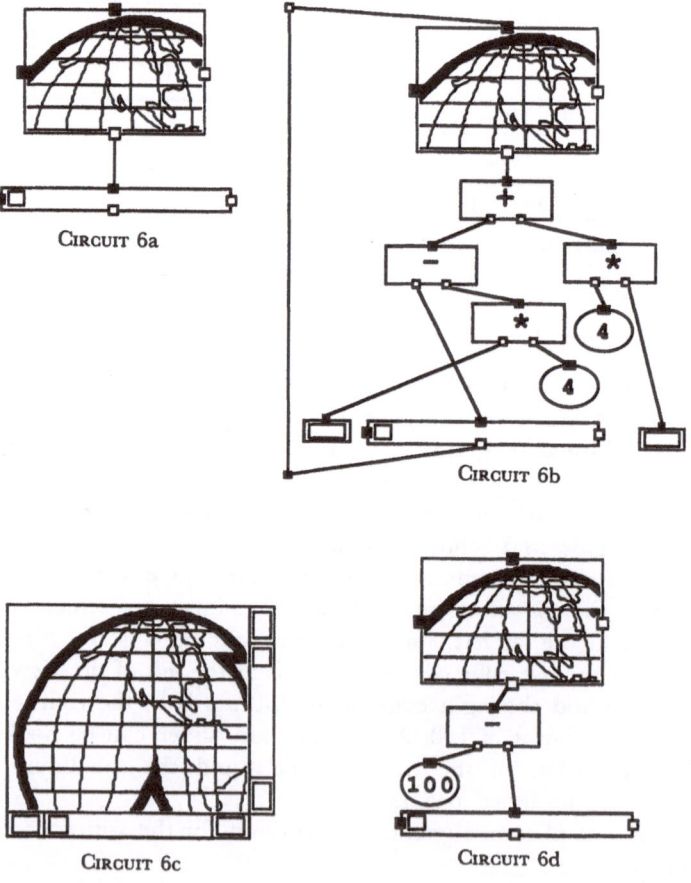

Circuit 6a

Circuit 6b

Circuit 6c

Circuit 6d

5.3. Example: Drag Bars

The scroll bars above are conventional; many systems have similar controls. InterCONS allows exploration of different ways of controlling things. What if the thumb on a slider *dragged* along the data in the viewport? The thumb and the data would move the same direction, rather that different directions.

Circuit 6d takes the output of the slider, "inverts it" (that is, subtracts it from 100), and inputs that to the viewport. The left edge of the data is thus visible when the slider is at the far right. Dragging the thumb seems to drag the data along.

6. Using InterCONS

6.1. Execution Windows and Chaining

After a circuit is complete, editing mode can be turned off so that only interactive components respond to user inputs. The circuit can then be saved in a named library of circuits.

Circuits in the library can be fetched and executed by name by a special circuit component. When this component receives a nonzero input, it fetches a circuit from a library and executes it. The execution can be in the same window (chaining), in a new automatically sized window (a pop-up), or in a window sized by the user.

Circuits executed from a library run in windows that contain just one pane; there are no editing tools present, and the menu items for development and debugging are missing.

6.2. Building New Tools

New tools can be built in the workbench and added to the toolbox. These tools are composite tools, made up of one or more primitive tools, wired together, and retaining values from having been executed.

While in the toolbox, the accumulation acts like a single component; copies can be dragged over to the workbench as often as needed. When the copies are dropped on the workbench, they expand back into individual components. In effect, the composite tool is a macro rather than a new primitive.

6.3. Interfacing to Other Code

Other code can interface to InterCONS by accessing variables which can be set from within a circuit. InterCONS programs can be invoked from other Smalltalk programs, interact with the user, and return some other values.

Also, InterCONS programs can invoke other Smalltalk programs and can reference values that those other programs make available.

6.4. Debugging

Several facilities are provided to assist with debugging. First are gauges: they can be placed in the path of any connection to see a value. This has been done several times in the examples above. Second is a trace mode which accumulates information about each component executed, its inputs and outputs, and the current time of execution. The quantity of data, and the visual distance of the data from the actual circuit, keeps this from being used frequently. The third facility is most useful for following the actual flow in a circuit. It executes the circuit slowly and uses reverse video to highlight the executing components, providing an animated view of the paths that execution takes. Last is a local menu item that displays various data associated with a component. Included are the input value(s), output value(s), and the time.

7. Additional Components

This section describes additional components used for merging values from two wires, logical control, program control, and selection of text and numeric values.

7.1. Fan-In

Circuit 7a is a different modification of the loop circuit (circuit 3a); it allows the remembered value to be reset to zero.

The new component is a fan-in. It takes an input from one (and only one) path and passes it to the output. It is an error to have two inputs in the same clock cycle. If the button on the adder is pressed, the loop acts as before, but with the fan-in passing the value through unchanged. If the button hooked to the fan-in is pressed, the 1 value passes into the circuit, resetting the remembered value to 1; this is a side effect which can be ignored since releasing the button sends a 0 in and through the circuit, resetting the remembered value to 0.

7.2. Logic Devices

InterCONS provides several logic devices. One takes two inputs, compares them according to a selectable relation, and outputs a 1 or a 0.

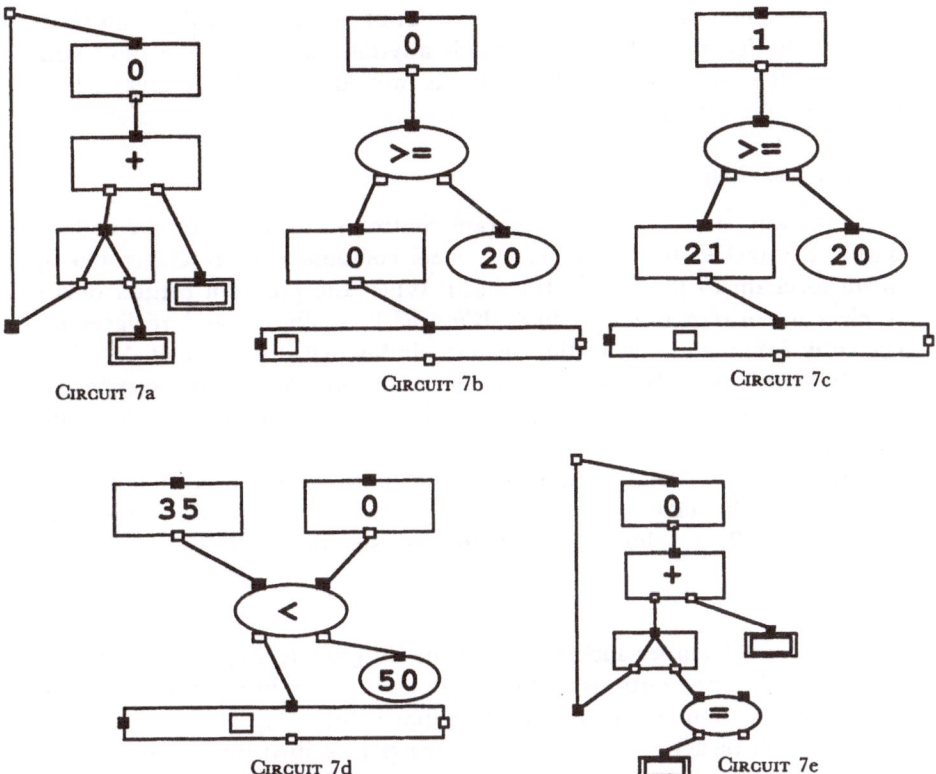

CIRCUIT 7a   CIRCUIT 7b   CIRCUIT 7c

CIRCUIT 7d   CIRCUIT 7e

In circuit 7b, the constant is compared with the output of the slider. (The gauge on the slider output shows the value.) If the slider value is less than the constant, the output of the comparator is 0. If not less, it is 1, as in circuit 7c. This output is useful as input to a number of devices, such as a trigger (see the Appendix) or a multiplier (where the 0 or 1 is multiplied by some "n.")

A second component (the path splitter) looks similar (and also has selectable comparisons) but has two outputs. If the relation is true, the *left* input goes out the *left* output; if false, the *left* input goes out the *right* output. In circuit 7d, the slider output shows in the left gauge when it is less than 50 and in the right gauge otherwise.

Note that all unconnected inputs are considered to have a constant 0 attached and that all unconnected outputs are considered to be attached to a component that absorbs the value.

A path splitter can be used to filter out the initial 1 from a button, causing it-to output a 0; this improves the reset button, described earlier (see circuit 7e). The circuit compares the output of the button with 0 and sends it along the left path if it is 0; it sends anything not 0 out the right path (and into the bit bucket). If the button is pressed, the 1, being greater than 0, goes out the right path. When it is released, the 0 will go out the left path.

7.3. Program Control

Program control is under program control, so to speak. In circuit 8a, a button is attached to the program control component (here configured by menu to chain to the circuit *Window2*). When the program control device receives a nonzero input, it finds *Window2* in a library and replaces the currently running circuit in the current window with that circuit.

In circuit 8b, a button is attached to the program control component configured for the exit function. It terminates the circuit and closes the window.

In circuit 8c, the button will pop up a new window containing the circuit *Calculator* taken from the library *Demos*. Not shown is the New function, like Popup, but which lets the user size the window.

7.4. Text and Number Pickers

Text and Number Pickers are essentially table lookup functions. Each takes a number and outputs a number. Each looks up in a list, based on the input number, some value and displays that value.

The text picker takes an array of strings (specified by a menu option) and displays the Nth one, given N as input. In circuit 8d, the loop holds a 5 and the text picker is configured with abbreviations for the names of the months.

In circuit 8e, the loop contains a fan-out which feeds the value to the number picker. It has been configured with the number of days in each month. Given an input of 2, it displays and outputs a 28.

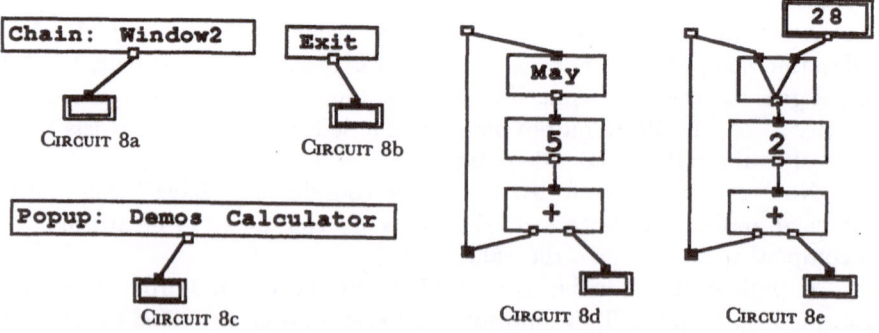

CIRCUIT 8a   CIRCUIT 8b

CIRCUIT 8c   CIRCUIT 8d   CIRCUIT 8e

8. Interface Example: A Calculator

The presentation view of the calculator is shown in Figure 2, and the internals are shown and described in Figure 3.

Presentation View of the Calculator. The calculator has two displays. The numeric keypad has a display for the current number; it is cleared with the "C" key. Pressing one of the large keys at the right adds or subtracts that value to/from the value in large display at the top, and the "CT" key clears the accumulated total.

Calculator Internals. The lower left quadrant contains the numeric keys; these are buttons with numeric labels that output the value of the label as an integer. The button outputs are cascaded together, using fan-ins, to a path switcher which only passes through nonzero values. The zero button is connected to a path switcher which filters out all but the zero. All the keys pass into a loop (top left quadrant) which adds the key to the accumulated result (initially zero), displays the sum, and loops around to multiply the accumulated value by 10 and then wait for the next key press.

The sum also passes out the fan-out at the top to the display and to the operation circuit at the right, where it is multiplied by zero and added to the display loop. When a + or − button is pressed, the 1 it outputs causes the accumulated number to be multiplied by 1 and added to the display loop. The zero from the + or − (or "C" key) is passed to the accumulator loop to clear it.

Two inactive components (rectangles) which form the case of the display are omitted from this view.

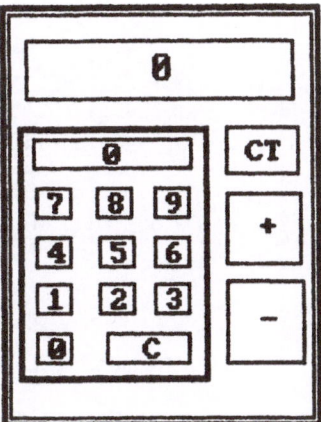

FIGURE 2. Presentation view of calculator.

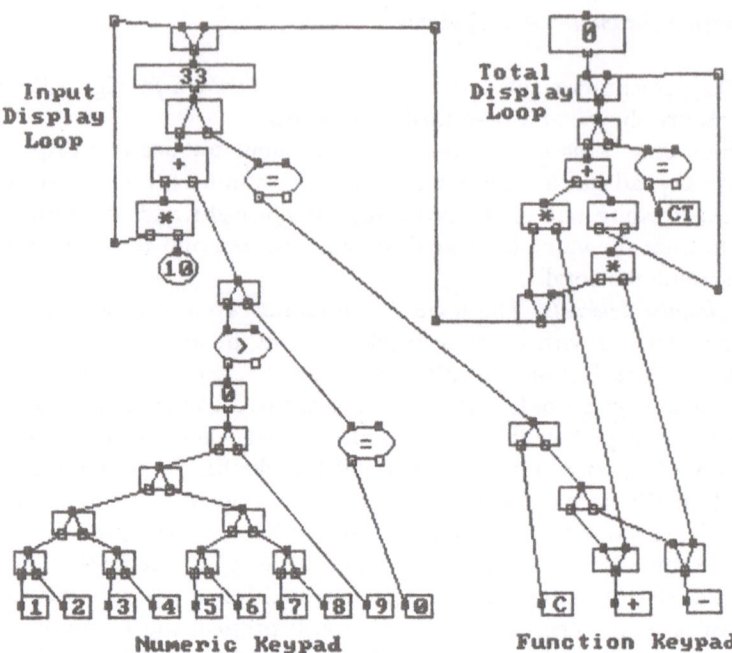

FIGURE 3. Calculator internals.

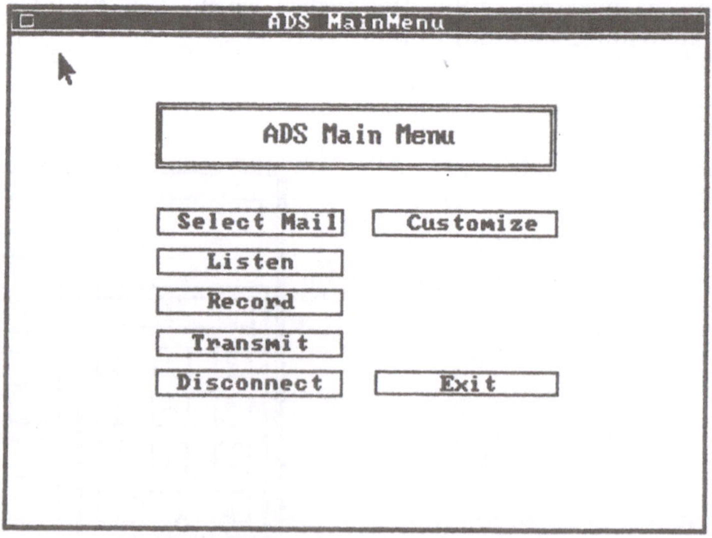

FIGURE 4. PhoneApp main menu screen.

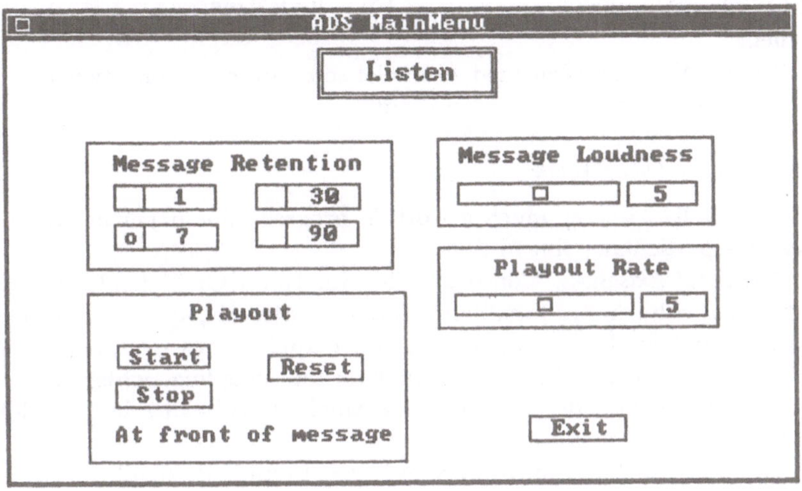

FIGURE 5. PhoneApp listen screen.

9. Interface Example: An Application

A proposed product might couple a telephone, an answering machine, and a personal computer. Proposed control screens could be modeled with InterCONS, as in Figure 5.

In the main menu (Figure 4), a user selects *Listen*. The screen in Figure 5 then appears. Controls are active. The *message retention* radio buttons are live, and the sliders work and show the value currently set. Selecting *Start*, *Stop*, or *Reset* simply displays a message, however, since there is no telephone really attached.

Using such models of an application, a designer can try out an application interface and iteratively improve it. The designer also might try out the interface with some novice users and see where they get into trouble.

10. Status and Future Work

InterCONS was implemented in about six months using Smalltalk/V.*
On an IBM PC/AT class machine, it performs more than adequately. On an

* Smalltalk/V is a trademark of Digitalk, Inc.

IBM PS/2 with a 80306 processor and Smalltalk/V286, the performance is excellent.

InterCONS has been used to model some simple applications and for building various interactive components.

10.1. Areas for Future Work

InterCONS is very much a work in progress; this paper describes the ideas at a particular point in time.

Functional Extensions. Controls built with InterCONS should be usable as controls within other Smalltalk windows; currently, they must run in a separate window. The coupling with other applications is currently loose; more thought needs to be given to making that coupling tighter and more useful. It would also be useful to have Smalltalk subpanes in InterCONS windows.

In addition, the primitives are expected to undergo significant revision as they are extended, merged with others, dropped in lieu of yet other primitives, and so on.

Fundamental Questions. Each of the primitives was written by hand. Although it is easy to add new primitives, it requires knowing a programming language and some part of the structure of InterCONS itself.

Interactively building new primitives would bring up several new questions. One is how to specify how interaction is done. For example, we might want a slider that is round and with a round thumb that moves inside the slider body. How do we specify the limits of motion of the thumb? How do we specify the range and scaling of output values? What happens when we resize the new slider? Does the thumb scale up or not?

If a composite object such as a scroll bar could be made into a new primitive, how can the following be specified: the buttons do not resize, the sliders stretch along their long dimensions but not their short ones, and the viewport stretches in all directions (but its contents do not)?

What does it mean to have a loop inside of a composite primitive? Does the primitive contain its own execution model? If so, how does it know when to stop? If not, how can the loop possibly execute? (Is it possible that the execution model does not extend well to composite primitives? If so, what model will extend well?) What does the new primitive look like? How might its presentation be changed from the presentation of the composite primitives?

These questions, among others, remain open, and are the subject of follow-up work.

Appendix: The Tools

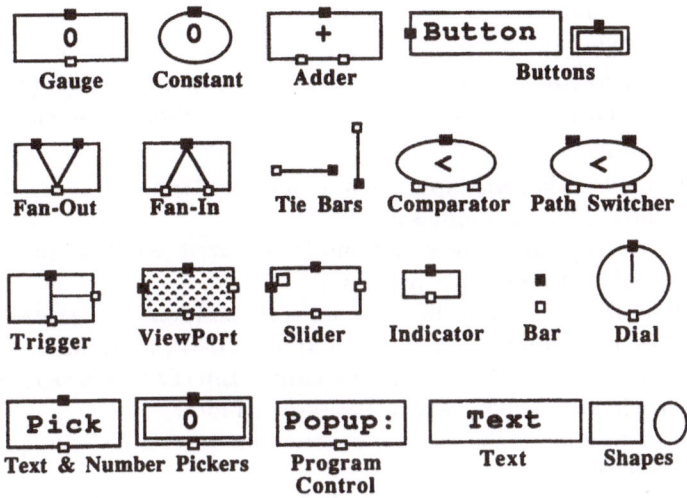

Gauge: Displays input and passes it to output.

Constant: Holds a constant value.

Arithmetic Ops: Takes two inputs and performs an operation.

Buttons: When pressed, outputs 1 and starts execution; when released, outputs 0.

Fan-Out: Passes the input along two output paths.

Fan-In: Takes an input in either input path.

Comparator: Compares inputs; outputs 0 if false, and 1 if true.

Path Switcher: Compares inputs; outputs the *left* input to the *left* output if true, else to the *right* output.

Trigger: Takes two inputs. If the side input is nonzero, the bottom input is passed out the top; otherwise, nothing is passed out the top.

View Port: Displays a (selectable) bitmap which represents an application's data. Scrolls the bitmap according to the input values. Outputs the input.

Slider: Moving the thumb outputs values which represent the thumb position in the slider body. Inputs reposition the thumb.

Indicator: Turns on (becomes dark) when the input is nonzero; passes the input to the output.

Histogram: Displays a black bar, with the length depending on the input.

Dial: Moves the needle 360 degrees for each increment of 100 given as input; passes the input to the output. Acts on negative as well as positive values.

Text Picker: Takes small integers in the range 0 to *n*; selects the *n*th string from an array of strings and displays that string in the box. (The initial array contains the string "Pick.") Passes the offset of the chosen value to the output.

Program Control: Takes an input; if it is nonzero, some program action is performed. The possibilities are:

Popup: to pop up a new automatically sized window containing a specified InterCONS program;

New: to interact with the user for the position and size of a new window containing a specified InterCONS program;

Chain: to replace the currently executing InterCONS program with a specified new program in the same window;

Exit: to terminate the currently executing InterCONS program, and close the window; and

Expr: to evaluate a given Smalltalk/V expression.

Number Picker: Takes small integers in the range 0 to *n*; selects the *n*th number from an array of numbers and displays that number in the box. (The initial array contains only a zero.) Passes the result to the output.

Text: For labeling; the enclosing box can be omitted.

Rectangle: Has no function; provides a shape for decoration of a screen. Can be drawn with a variety of thicknesses of pens, and with pairs of pens.

Oval: Has no function; provides a shape for decoration of a screen.

References

1. W. BUDGE, PinBall Construction Set, Electronic Arts, 1985.
2. D. A. HENDERSON, JR., The Trillium user interface design environment, Proceedings of the 1986 ACM SigCHI Conference, April 1986, pp. 221–227.
3. L. GOULD and W. FINZER, Programming by Rehearsal, XEROX Palo Alto Research Center, SCL-84-1, 1984.
4. R. B. SMITH, The alternate reality kit: an animated environment for creating interactive simulations, IEEE Computer Society Workshop on Visual Languages, 1986, pp. 99–106.
5. E. P. GLINERT, Towards "second generation" interactive, graphical programming environments, IEEE Computer Society Workshop on Visual Languages, 1986, pp. 61–70.
6. E. P. GLINERT and S. L. TANIMOTO, Pict: an interactive graphical programming environment, *IEEE Comput.* 7–25 (1984).
7. K. MATSUMURA and S. TAYAMA, Visual man–machine interface for program design and production, IEEE Computer Society Workshop on Visual Languages, pp. 71–80, 1986.
8. M. C. PONG and T. NG, PIGS—a system for programming with interactive graphical support, *Software Practice and Experience* **13**, 847–855 (1983).

9. D. A. Workman, GRASP: a software development system using D-charts, *Software Practice and Experience* **13**, 17–32 (1983).

10. B. A. Myers, Visual programming, programming by example, and program visualization: a taxonomy, ACM SIG-CHI Conference, pp. 59–66 (April 1986).

11. G. Raeder, A survey of current graphical programming techniques, *IEEE Comput.* 11–25 (1985).

12. N. C. Shu, Visual programming languages: a perspective and a dimensional analysis, pp. 11–34 in *Visual Languages*, S. K. Chang, T. Ichikawa, and P. A. Ligomenides (Eds.), Plenum Press, New York, 1986.

13. I. Yoshimoto, N. Monden, M. Hirakawa, M. Tanaka, and T. Ichikawa, Interactive iconic programming facility in hi-visual, IEEE Computer Society Workshop on Visual Languages, 34–41, 1986.

14. K. Kobayashi, Direct manipulation and a multi-dimensional Approach to Visual Software Design, IBM Tokyo Research Laboratory, TR87-1013, 1987.

15. LabVIEW: laboratory virtual instrument engineering workbench, (84–92) *Byte* 1986 (September).

16. P. Kosinski, A Data Flow Programming Language, IBM, RC4264, March 1973.

17. A. Borning, ThingLab—A Constraint-Oriented Simulation Laboratory, XEROX PARC, SSL-79-3, July 1979.

18. A. Borning, Defining constraints graphically, Proceedings of the 1986 ACM SigCHI Conference, 137–143, April 1986.

19. A. Borning and R. Duisberg, Constraint-based tools for building user interfaces, *ACM Trans.* **5**(4), 345–374 (1986).

20. R. J. K. Jacob, A visual programming environment for designing user interfaces, pp. 87–107 in *Visual Languages*, S. K. Chang, T. Ichikawa, and P. A. Ligomenides (Eds.), Plenum Press, New York, 1986.

21. B. A. Myers, Creating highly-interactive and graphical user interfaces by demonstration, Proceedings of the 1986 ACM SigCHI Conference, 249–258, April 1986.

22. B. A. Myers, Creating dynamic interaction techniques by demonstration, ACM SigCHI Conference Proceedings, 271–278, 1987.

3

A VISUAL ENVIRONMENT FOR THE DESIGN OF DISTRIBUTED SYSTEMS

Michael L. Graf

Abstract

MCC's Software Technology Program is developing technologies for the design and specification of distributed computer systems. This chapter presents VERDI, a visual environment for distributed systems designers. The environment uses a visual language as the expression of design. The visual language is based on the syntax and semantics of Raddle, a textual distributed system specification language concurrently under development at MCC. VERDI provides a powerful work environment which encourages initial use of a high level of abstraction and successive, simultaneous refinement of design segments. In this chapter, we describe VERDI visual language syntax and semantics, give examples of its use, and describe the VERDI workspace and tools for creation, simulation, and analysis of distributed system designs. Some areas of future work are listed.

1. Introduction

The design and specification of distributed computer systems is emerging as one of the most important problems facing the computer industry. In response, academic and industrial research is expanding and organizing to

MICHAEL L. GRAF • MCC Software Technology Program and NCR Corporation, Austin, Texas 78759.

attack this problem. At MCC's Software Technology Program, the focus on the design of large distributed systems is being addressed by a series of projects organized about the distributed system specification language Raddle, developed by Forman and formalized in Ref. 1.

The expressiveness and understandability of Raddle and other attempts to specify distributed systems with essentially textual languages (for example, Hoare's CSP[2] and Chandy and Misra's Unity[3]) suffers from a mismatch in the use of a linear technology (text) to describe nonlinear phenomena (distributed and parallel computation). Practicing designers using these textual representations must maintain their conceptual understanding of distribution and parallelism outside the expression of the design. This is usually accomplished by mental skills or use of some ad hoc adjunct representation, often diagrammatic. MCC's empirical studies of expert designers[4, 5] indicated a dependence early in the design process on visual representations. These usually begin with the higher levels of abstraction and reappear iteratively throughout all stages of design.

The MCC Software Technology Program has the objective of providing LEONARDO, a comprehensive software design technology which will significantly improve the productivity and quality of software development. A constituent of any such technology must be an environment for designers to exercise their craft. In the same spirit that Smalltalk and Lisp environments have been provided to programmers, we are providing systems design environments.

This chapter discusses VERDI, a visual environment for the design of distributed systems. The iconic primitives of VERDI are presented, the new communication primitive, N-party interaction, is introduced, and some simple example designs are developed. Finally, the overall environment and its animation, editing, and analysis facilities are discussed. The chapter concludes with a discussion of the future research directions for this project.

2. An Overview of VERDI

VERDI, the Visual Environment for Raddle Design and Investigation, is a distributed systems designer's working environment. The focus of the system is to provide a highly productive environment for designing complex, distributed systems. VERDI encourages the use of a high level of abstraction in the early design phases, allowing simultaneous incremental development of design fragments and supporting "what-if" experimentation within these incremental steps. In later phases of design, the designer may add detail as needed to express the design to implementors. The design development model favored for working with VERDI is Wirth's stepwise refinement.[6]

Currently, we are defining an extended methodology which provides for proof of correctness of high-level designs, combined with a transformation technique which preserves correctness as greater detail is achieved.

A design session using the VERDI environment takes the form of a series of iterations through three sets of activities:

- *Graphic editing* builds up the design from the available lexicon of visual icons and iconic design artifacts. This phase may include the acquisition of previously prepared design artifacts from a design library. Textual editors are also provided for those components of design specification where text is more appropriate, such as naming and specification of arbitrary computation.
- *Execution* of a design causes the graphic expression of the design to be executed and animated.
- *Analysis* of the design detects syntactic and semantic errors in design specification. Deadlocks are detected during execution. Under development currently is the integration of real-time performance modeling and analysis.

3. The Visual Language

A VERDI design consists of a set of graphs, each graph representing a connected set of *local actions*, *interactions*, and *compound actions*. The separate graphs are called *roles*. Roles are the processes and procedures of VERDI. Cooperating, communicating roles are gathered into nonintersecting subsets called *teams*.

4. Actions: Local Actions and Interactions

The visual language is based on the four basic structures:

- *Boxes* are the specific representation of the partners in an N-Party Interaction (the communication primitive of Raddle). An interaction (in the static sense) is a set of N boxes, all with the same name, located in N separate roles. Interaction names appear within the boxes. During execution, interactions are the locus of synchronization, communication, and data transfer among the roles in a team. Boxes also contain assignment statements in the embedded textual language.
- *Blocks* contain executable executable statements in the embedded language which do not require interaction with other sub-nets. These

FIGURE 1. VERDI actions: box, block, cast, return.

may include statements other than assignment statements (for example, file access). During execution, blocks are handled as 1-party interactions, that is, interactions which have no partners. They are equivalent to unlabeled boxes in Raddle.
- *Casts* are the mechanism by which control is passed from one role to another.
- *Return* structures appear in roles and cause control to be returned.

These four structures, boxes, blocks, casts, and returns, are referred to as actions, the latter three being *local actions*, the first a party of an *interaction* (see Figure 1).

Sequences and *choices* are structures which combine actions and reflexively sequences and choices to form more complicated structures. In a VERDI design, time is denoted by left-to-right orientation and thus so are sequences. Choice is represented vertically. (See Figure 2.)

5. Roles and Teams

In VERDI, each separate expression of sequential process is called a *Role*. It is through the interaction of these roles that VERDI addresses the issues of distributed systems. Roles which communicate are gathered into sets called *Teams*. In this section, we describe the syntactic elements of roles and teams. We also introduce the mechanism for creating teams, instantiation, and the

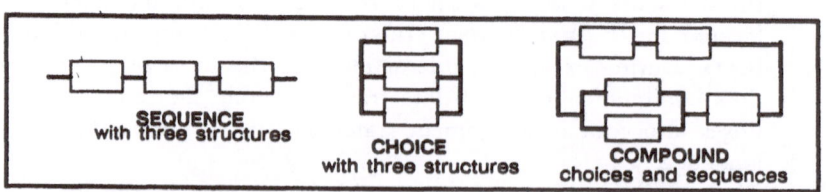

FIGURE 2. VERDI compound actions: sequence, choice.

method for communicating between teams, *token-casting*. Communication between roles in a single team, *N-Party Interaction*, the Communication Primitive, is discussed later.

5.1. Roles

Visually, a role is a simple action or a compound action with two circles attached at the left and right ends. Execution of a role begins at the left, travels from left to right, and loops back to the left circle when the right circle is reached. There are two types of roles: marked and unmarked (Figure 3).

A *marked role* begins execution as soon as it is created. This is denoted by a token (a large solid dot) in the starting (left) circle of the marked role. During execution, movement of the token through the role denotes the flow of control.

The starting place of an *unmarked role* is represented by a target. An unmarked role is created with no token in its starting place. Unmarked roles can be thought of as procedures awaiting execution. Execution of an unmarked role begins when a token is cast to the role from a role in some other team. The token may carry parametric information (passed data) with it. When the token is cast, it hits the target in the unmarked role and execution begins. When the token reaches a return structure, execution stops and the token with the current values of its parametric data returns to the caller.

5.2. Teams

Teams are the structures which group roles together. Interactions occur only between roles within the same team. The minimum set of roles to form a team is the closure with respect to interaction, but a team may contain disjoint sets of communicating roles (see Figure 4).

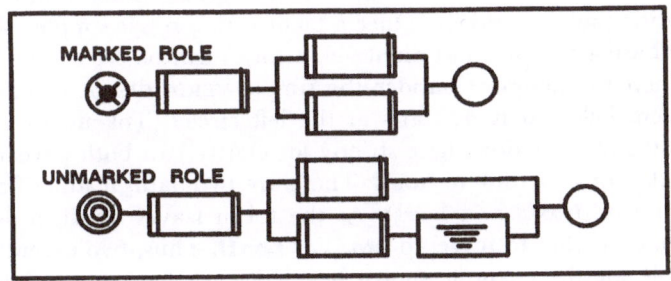

FIGURE 3. VERDI roles.

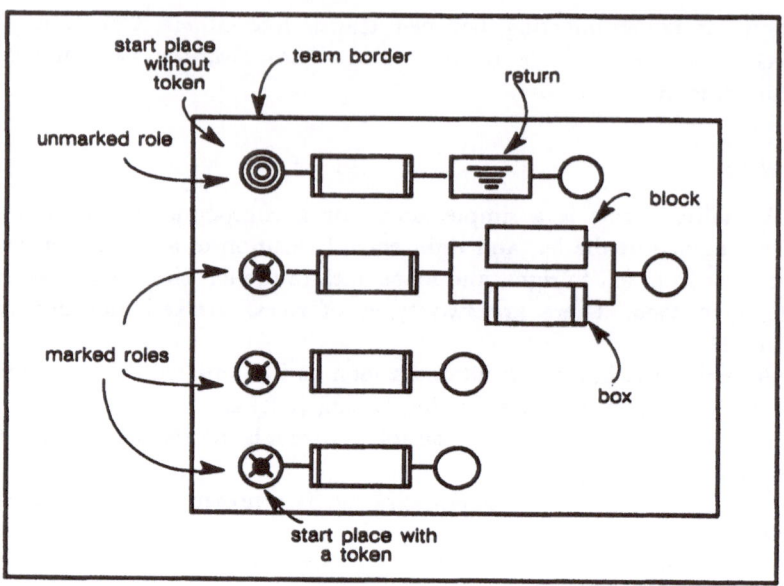

FIGURE 4. A VERDI team with four roles.

Having developed the structural representation of a VERDI design, we turn our attention to the issues of computation and communication in the Sections 7 and 8, discussing the embedded procedural language and N-party interaction, respectively.

6. Adding Motion to a Simple Design

A *token* is a marker, something like a program counter, which follows the execution path of a design. Once a team with a single simple role is built using the basic structures just discussed, a token can be used to trace execution through the design. Consider the simple VERDI design in Figure 5. A single token, let's call it **A**, starts at the left circle. (Tokens are not given names in VERDI. It is done here strictly for clarity.) In both parts of Figure 5, **A** travels along the link to **boxB**. There are two paths leading from **boxB** to, respectively, **boxC** and **boxD**. As the token leaves **boxB**, a decision is made about whether to travel to **boxC** or **boxD**. Thus, two execution paths are possible for the example shown here. The mechanism for determining which path to follow will be explained in later sections.

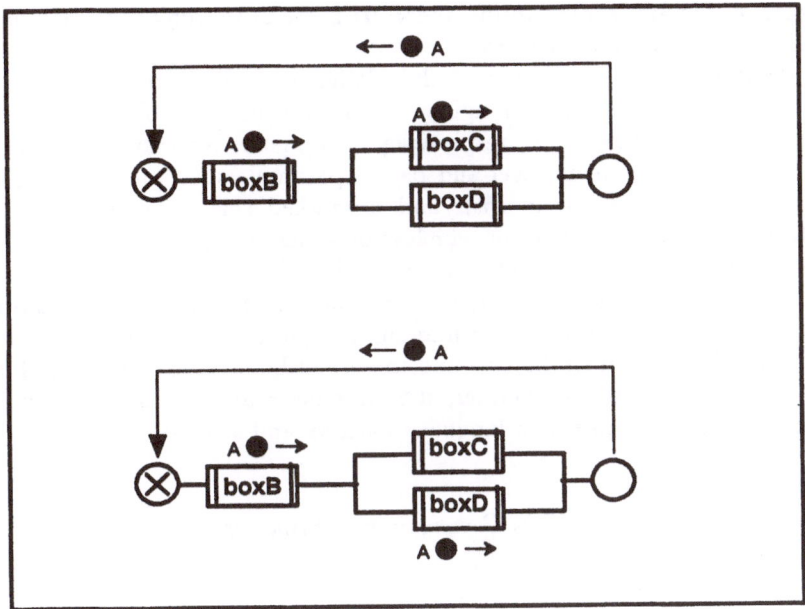

FIGURE 5. Execution paths.

7. The Embedded Procedural Language

We use textual components which add meaning to VERDI designs such as names, declarations, expressions, assignments, and conditions. These are all components of the procedural language embedded in VERDI. The actual selection of the embedded language in VERDI is largely arbitrary. The language must, however, support assignment statements, Boolean expressions, and simple extensions for team instantiation, structure replication, and token passing. VERDI's embedded language could be selected from such languages as C, Pascal, or Fortran or a functional language such as Lisp. The embedded languages used in the first two VERDI prototypes were a C/Pascal hybrid and Lisp, respectively. The third prototype (the current one) uses Pascal, with ADA and C under consideration as alternatives. Longer-range considerations include the possibility of multiple embedded languages in a single VERDI design.

Guards appear before every action and appear as Boolean expressions in the embedded language. Usually, the guard is the default Boolean constant *true* and is invisible in the VERDI design. Otherwise, the guards appear on the arc leading to the action. It is useful to think of the language as a language of guarded actions.

Within boxes and blocks, the designer may include assignment statements in the embedded language. Constants and variables are declared at the team and role levels, respectively. Parameters for team instantiation are declared at the team level and passed parameters for token casting are declared and referenced in casts and unmarked roles. VERDI includes an embedded language text editor which allows these textual components to be added. Syntax is checked and errors are rejected.

Looking ahead to Figure 7, we see examples of team and role naming, variable declaration, interaction naming, assignment statements (in boxes), procedure invocation (in blocks) and the use of Boolean expression on links. For the purposes of this chapter, it is not necessary to make an explicit description of the embedded language's syntax and semantics.

8. N-Party Interaction—The Communication Primitive

An *N-party interaction* consists of a set of N boxes in N separate roles of a single team instance. All boxes in an interaction share the same name. In the following example (Figure 6), there is a 3-party interaction, **ping**, and a 2-party interaction, **pong**.

An interaction executes when N separate tokens move simultaneously into all N members of the interaction. Before this happens, the parties of the interaction must first become *ready* and then *enabled*.

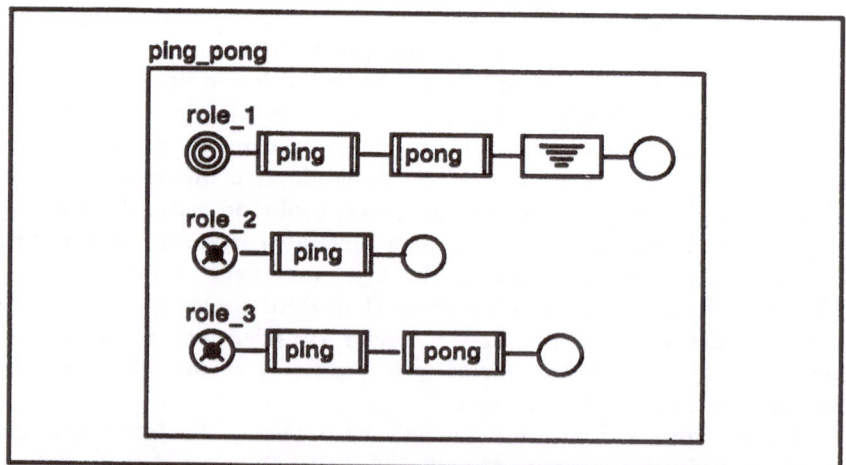

FIGURE 6. The **ping_pong** team.

A box is *ready* when there is a token waiting to enter it. This means that a token is waiting to traverse a path to the box and the box's guard evaluates to *true*. The token may be causing more than one box to be ready at the same time. Notice that the boxes **ping** in the marked roles **role_2** and **role_3** are readied in the **ping_pong** team. The box **ping** in the **role_1** can only become ready when a token is passed to that role.

Every box involved in an interaction must be ready for the interaction to become *enabled*. When a token from some other role in the system hits the target in **role_1**, the **ping** interaction is in that role *readied*. Because a box of the interaction **ping** is now *ready* in each role of the **ping_pong** team, the 3-party interaction is *enabled*.

When one or more interactions are enabled, the execution process of VERDI guarantees that at least one enabled interaction *fires*. By firing we mean that the tokens enter each box in the readied interaction simultaneously. Any assignment statements appearing in the boxes are performed. When this is completed in all the boxes, the interaction returns to the passive state and the tokens are able to move on. From a conceptual perspective, the firing of an interaction (including any assignments made) is a single atomic action. The changing status of boxes, the firing of interactions, and the movement of tokens are animated during VERDI simulation of designs.

9. The Scoping of Constants and Variables

Constants are always declared at the team level and are scoped over all the roles in the team. Variables are always declared at the role level and, except for interactions, are scoped only over the role in which they appear. Teams cannot access data within other teams except by parameter passing (which is really token casting in VERDI).

During an interaction, roles have read access to the variables in other roles which are involved in the interaction but can never make assignments to variables which are not their own. Assignments can only be made in the role where the variable is declared. As mentioned earlier, interactions are atomic actions. The effect of a variable assignment does not take place until after the interaction.

10. An Example

In order to demonstrate the concepts developed thus far, we use the following **ball_painting** example. The problem is to develop a team which

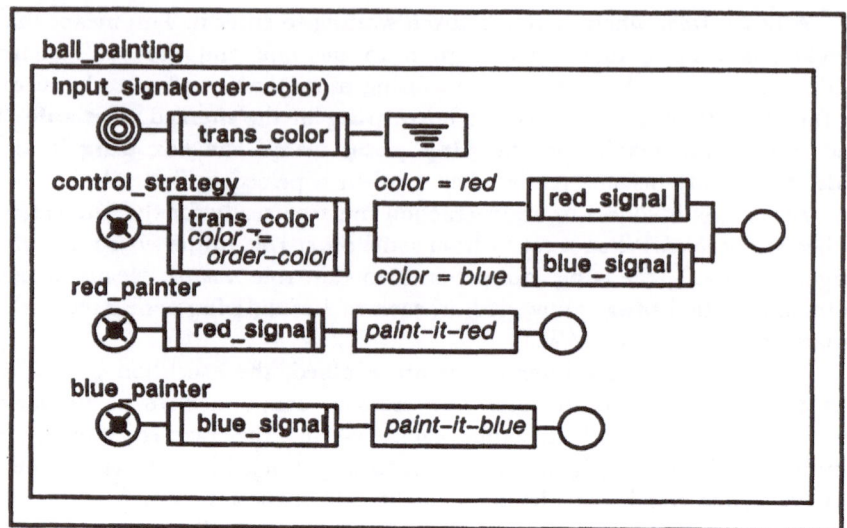

FIGURE 7. The **ball_painting** team: deterministic selection of color.

receives a token into an unmarked role, indicating a ball is ready to be painted. The token carries the data value *red* or *blue*. This causes a routine *paint_it_red* or *paint_it_blue*, respectively, to be run. Figure 7 represents a VERDI design solution to this problem.

When instantiated, the team **ball_painting** has boxes **trans_color**, **red_signal**, and **blue_signal** in a readied state in various roles, but no interactions are enabled. A token must be sent to the unmarked role **input_signal** in order to enable interaction **trans_color**. Upon receipt of the token, the interaction becomes ready and the variable *ball_color* is assigned the value brought by the token. When **trans_color** fires, the value of *ball_color* is assigned to the variable *color* in role **control_strategy**.

Upon completion of the **trans_color** interaction, if the value of *color* is *red*, the interaction **red_signal** is enabled. If the value of *color* is *blue*, the interaction **blue_signal** is enabled. When the appropriate **_signal** interaction fires, the token then advances to the subsequent process and cause the correct routine to be invoked. If *color* has a value other than *red* or *blue*, the team is deadlocked because the token in **control_strategy** is not able to proceed.

11. Resolving Conflict

Transitions do not automatically fire just because they are enabled. A conflict may occur, meaning that a single token is readying boxes in more

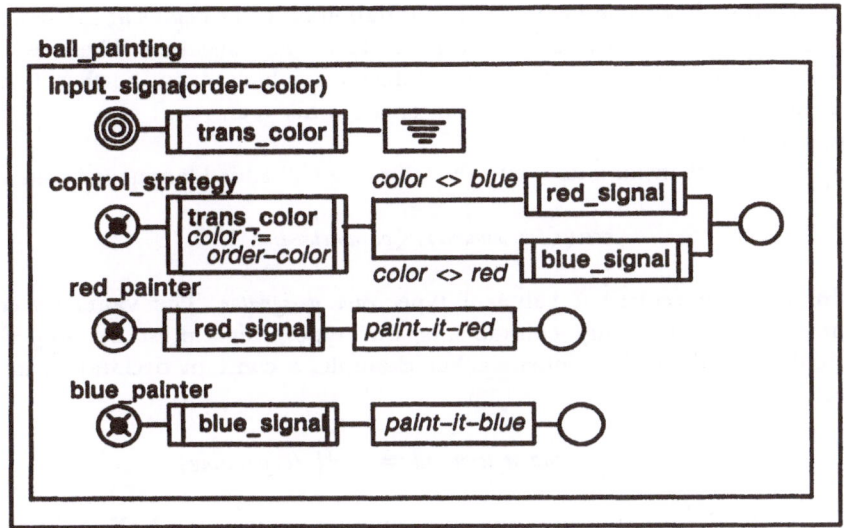

FIGURE 8. The **ball_painting** team: mixed determinism in selection of color.

than one enabled interaction. Since tokens are strictly conserved, the token can only proceed to at most one of the boxes. Conflicts are resolved non-deterministically by VERDI's underlying execution mechanism. In VERDI, when one or more interactions are enabled, at least one will immediately fire.

To illustrate this, consider altering the original design by simply changing the conditions on the links in **control_strategy** from *color = red* and *color = blue* to *color < > blue* and *color < > red*, respectively (Figure 8). With this change, if *color* is *blue*, the path to **blue_signal** is taken, and if *color* is red, the path to **red_signal** is taken as in the original design. But if *color* is something other than *red* or *blue*, we no longer have the fatal blockage seen in the first example but instead have a conflict, that is, whether to proceed to **red_signal** or **blue_signal**. The decision of which color to paint the balls is made nondeterministically by the underlying system.

12. Team Instantiation and Token Casting

A team design that is created in VERDI is really a design artifact or object. An instance (copy) of this object must be created for execution. This notion is particularly important when multiple instances executing concurrently are called for. When a team is instantiated, execution of all its marked roles begins immediately. Instantiation of teams begins at the system level, with the designer selecting a set of teams for execution. These teams may contain constant assignment statements which cause further team instantiation. In this way, teams can create other teams and cast tokens to roles in these teams.

Teams are instantiated with the following embedded language function:

$$new(\langle\, team\text{-}name\,\rangle,\ \langle\, parameter\text{-}list\,\rangle)$$

This function returns a value of type *team_designator*. The VERDI system currently supports only constants of this type which must be properly initialized with the *new* function. For example, a constant declaration in a team might be

$$team\text{\_}designator\ \ team\text{\_}id := new(ball\text{\_}painting)$$

which would cause instantiation of a running copy of the **ball_painting** team.

Once a team has been instantiated, it may contain unmarked roles. To execute, these unmarked roles must receive a token from another role. Any role which has a token and can reference the value of the *team_designator* of a team containing the target role can cast its token to that role. Using the embedded language editor to edit the contents of a cast structure, the designer specifies the *team_designator*, the target role name, and the set of parameters to be passed.

13. The Designers' Environment

As stated at the opening of this chapter, the intent of VERDI is to provide an environment for distributed systems designers to practice their craft. The assumed methodology of these designers is incremental progress, bounded by some form of test (mental or actual), and further progress or backtracking. The new design will be a combination of reused design artifacts and newly created designs.

The VERDI environment supports this methodology by allowing designers to use a graphic editor to build up partial designs, to execute them, and to add structure and computational detail as appropriate. An associated library facility allows for saving and reuse of designs.

The current VERDI user interface is a SunView application. Upon invocation, the Verdi Tool window appears. This window is a single graphics canvas with a mouse-driven cursor. A set of menus are used to direct the editing of the visual language design. When textual editing of names on embedded language components is needed, an overlapping window containing a text editor and the current value of the text appears.

14. Executing a Design

In executing VERDI designs, team borders turn gold as they are instantiated for execution. Tokens appear as red disks, visible as they move through the design. Paths and boxes change color with status change of ready (blue), enable (green), and fire (gold). During firing, all boxes involved in an interaction are connected by gold lightening bolts.

Execution run options include:

- Setting or clearing breakpoints.
- Examining the current status of data.
- Single_Step: Execution is advanced step by step.
- Multiple Steps: Continuous running until the specified number of steps have been executed, an error detected, or a breakpoint encountered.
- Free_Run: The simulation process is begun and continues until it terminates or is halted by an error or a breakpoint being encountered.

15. Analysis

VERDI performs analysis of static designs and provides diagnostic aids for analysis of the dynamic properties of designs. When problems (or possible problems) are detected, they are reported but not corrected.

Static analysis ensures that:

- Structures are syntactically correct.
- Embedded language statements are syntactically correct.
- Data declaration and usage is semantically correct.

Reachability analysis is often mentioned to us. Because of the use of dynamic guards, this is an essentially intractable problem with respect to offering analysis of large designs in a reasonable time. If there is sufficient demand, we will investigate the addition of this feature.

There are run-time features that assist analysis:

- Blocked tokens, ones which have all false guards ahead of them, are detected and announced.

- Deadlocks, where no token can move, are detected and announced.
- Mismatched parameters on token casts are detected. The user is immediately offered the opportunity to edit the cast command and then continue the run.
- Improper embedded language usage (e.g., arithmetic operations on a string) are detected. Again, the user has the opportunity to edit the faulty statements and continue.
- Faulty attempts to cast a token are detected and announced. These may include the cast to a nonexistent role or mismatched parameters.

During execution, when errors are detected, the system often allows the user to correct the error on the fly. The corrections are saved.

16. Future Work

The future work planned for VERDI includes:

- *Performance analysis*: When we introduced VERDI into our shareholders' sites, we were met with praise for the functional design capabilities of VERDI, immediately followed by demands that the package include performance-estimating capabilities. This demand has moved real-time modeling capabilities to the top of our priority queue.
- *Robustness*: The current version is a prototype. At the time of this writing, the transfer of VERDI to the shareholders has just begun. We will make substantial improvements in functionality, performance, fault tolerance, and user interface as a result of this experience. There will also be improvements and additions to the diagnostic and analytical features in the system.
- *Compatibility with Raddle-87*: Raddle-87 is the theoretical foundation of VERDI. The internal representation of design and the execution semantics are a nearly complete implementation of the Raddle-87 specification. We will soon complete full implementation of this specification.
- *Expression of large designs*: A common criticism of graphic expressions of programming languages and designs is that they do not scale up to large designs. To the author, this criticism is spawned by minds steeped in a long history of paper. In such a static, write-only medium, issues of geometry (placement, space allocation, etc.) dominate the designer's expressiveness. In a logical design, the design's topology should be the salient issue. We will experiment with dynamic graphics methods such as Furnas's fisheye concepts[7] to free

ourselves of these layout problems. We are also investigating the opportunities to manage complexity offered by hypermedia technology.[8]

Acknowledgments

The VERDI system is the result of the highly compatible and productive interaction of the author with some very talented people. To Ira Forman for Raddle, to Mike Evangelist for design methodology, to Vincent Shen for his relentless demands for improvements in functionality and performance, and especially to Les Belady for his unswerving support of this project, Thank you.

References

1. P. C. ATTIE, A Guide to Raddle87 Semantics, STP-340-87, Microelectronics and Computer Technology Corp., Austin, Texas, January 1988.
2. C. A. R. HOARE, *Communicating Sequential Processes*, Prentice-Hall International, London, 1985.
3. K. M. CHANDY AND J. MISRA, Parallel Programming Design: A Foundation, draft version, September 1986.
4. R. GUINDON, H. KRASNER, AND B. CURTIS, Breakdowns and processes during the early activities of software design by professionals, in *Empirical Studies of Programmers*, G. Olson, E. Soloway, and S. Sheppard (Eds.), Ablex, 1987, Norwood, N.J., pp. 65–82.
5. R. GUINDON AND B. CURTIS, Control of cognition during software design: what tools would support software designers?, Proceedings of CHI'88, Washington, D.C., 1988.
6. N. WIRTH, Program development by step-wise refinement, *Commun. ACM* **14**, 221–227 (1971).
7. G. W. FURNAS, The FISHEYE View: A New Look at Structured Files, Bell Laboratories Technical Memo, Murray Hill, New Jersey, October 1985.
8. J. CONKLIN, Hypertext: an introduction and survey, *Computer* **20**(9), 17–41 (1987).

4

GENERATION OF VISUAL LANGUAGES FOR DEVELOPMENT OF KNOWLEDGE-BASED SYSTEMS

Mark A. Musen

1. Introduction

Computer programs that contain the knowledge of human experts and that offer advice on the basis of that knowledge (*expert* or *knowledge-based* systems) are assuming increasing importance in commercial and industrial settings. From programs that configure complex electronic instruments to programs that supervise oil drilling to programs that perform risk analysis for insurance underwriters, knowledge-based systems have been created for myriad application tasks. Such systems typically contain large amounts of application-specific expertise encoded as a *knowledge base.* A generic, application-independent program (an *inference engine*) uses the knowledge base to generate situation-specific recommendations.

Expert systems are large computer programs. Thus, software engineering principles that apply to the construction of conventional computer programs also should apply to the development of expert-system knowledge bases. Yet the computer scientists who build expert systems (*knowledge engineers*) view *knowledge acquisition*—the process of interviewing application experts and encoding their expertise in machine-understandable format—as a problem that is qualitatively different from that of standard programming. In this chapter, I explore some of the difficulties of knowledge acquisition and demonstrate how the use of visual languages can ease the development

MARK A. MUSEN • Medical Computer Science Group, Knowledge Systems Laboratory, Stanford University School of Medicine, Stanford, California 94305-5479.

of certain classes of expert systems. I concentrate on PROTÉGÉ, a tool that constructs visual languages that are tailored for specific knowledge-acquisition tasks. First, however, it is necessary to describe the problem of knowledge acquisition in more detail.

2. The Knowledge-Acquisition Bottleneck

Workers in artificial intelligence (AI) frequently identify the process of knowledge acquisition as the principal bottleneck in the development of expert systems. Indeed, the word *bottleneck* appears in the AI literature so often that the metaphor almost has become trite—yet any overuse of the phrase is simply a reflection of the seeming relentlessness of the problem. Production-quality expert systems, quite simply, are associated with enormously long development times. Despite the wide range of tools that are commercially available to help system builders to encode expert knowledge (*expert-system shells*[1]), eliciting and structuring the knowledge often takes months or even years. For example, the expert systems that are now marketed by many AI start-up companies typically have required between 20 and 50 person-years to develop.[2]

2.1. The Communication Barrier

Much of the knowledge-acquisition problem can be traced to difficulties in communication. Knowledge engineers often lack the background in the application area that is needed to pose optimal questions, whereas the experts whose knowledge is to be encoded often have no idea how their knowledge is to be represented in the computer. Numerous workers in AI have suggested that if application specialists could somehow enter their knowledge directly without relying on programmers as intermediaries, the creation of expert systems might be expedited greatly.[3–5]

Because it is generally unrealistic to expect collaborators to learn traditional programming languages and knowledge-representation techniques, many workers have advocated the use of computer-based *knowledge editors* as a means to reduce dependence on computer scientists during knowledge-base construction.[3, 6–8] Most knowledge-editing tools require their users to define new knowledge bases using textual specifications that often are equivalent to the representations that a knowledge engineer might use to encode the same knowledge.[9] Davis' landmark knowledge editor TEIRESIAS,[3] for example, asked its user to type in new production rules for the MYCIN expert system[10] in the form of text strings that had a syntax close to that of natural language. TEIRESIAS' processing of entries in pseudo-English, however, did not obviate the need for the user to understand how MYCIN rules were programmed; conceptually, the user was still composing production rules.[9] The text-based approach in TEIRESIAS contrasts with that of the tools that I shall describe in this chapter, which use *graphical* knowledge-entry languages that are more abstract and, consequently, more intuitive to application experts. More important, users can *custom tailor* both the syntax and the semantics of these visual languages for particular application areas. As I shall describe in Section 4, this customization is achieved using a higher-level program, called PROTÉGÉ (Figure 1).

2.2. The Introspection Barrier

Although providing special-purpose graphical knowledge-entry environments reduces dependence on knowledge engineers, this approach addresses only part of the problem. Even when we give application specialists the necessary tools, it is unrealistic to expect them to create useful knowledge bases completely on their own. As with the construction of any large software project,[11] the development of an expert system requires significant creativity and invention on the part of system builders. Creativity is essential because the experts whose knowledge is to be encoded often cannot verbalize how they actually solve problems. The inability to explain

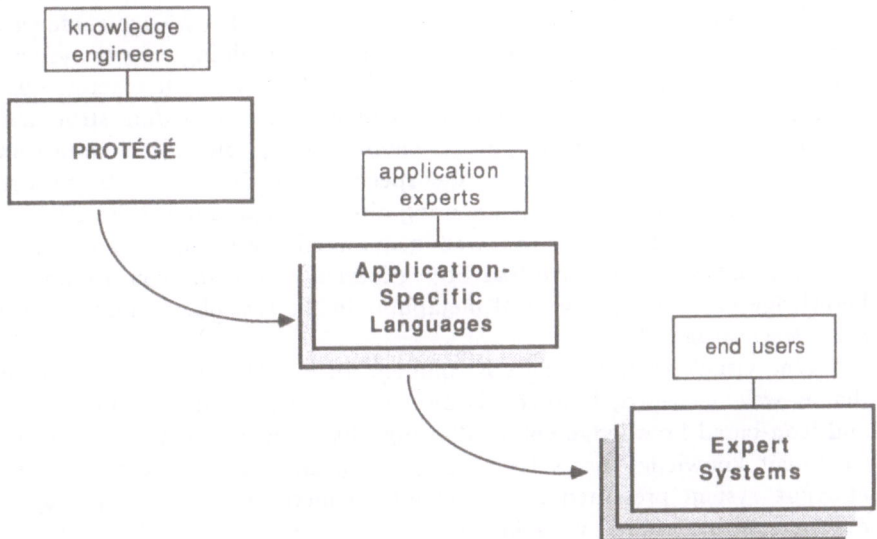

FIGURE 1. PROTÉGÉ generates visual knowledge-acquisition languages that are custom-tailored to specific application areas. Application experts use these languages to create and edit the knowledge bases of expert systems.

their problem solving does not occur because the experts are necessarily inarticulate, but because *all* trained professionals perform skilled tasks so proficiently that they do not consciously think about what they are doing in routine situations.[12] Like the father who struggles to tell his daughter how to ride a bicycle—and who witnesses the inadequacy of his instructions each time his daughter falls off—experts cannot simply introspect and tell a knowledge engineer (or a computer-based knowledge-editing tool) everything that they know that might be relevant in a particular situation.

Knowledge engineers serve the important functions of detecting gaps in the knowledge that domain experts volunteer and of helping the experts to fill those gaps by defining plausible sequences of actions that can achieve the necessary results. Despite popular notions, it is incorrect to view an expert system's knowledge base as a software embodiment of some expert's problem-solving acumen. Knowledge bases instead represent *models* of expert behaviors—models that attempt to approximate, but that cannot reproduce, the actual problem-solving steps used by application specialists.

2.3. The Modeling Barrier

Because the models that knowledge engineers help to create are particularly complex and broad in scope, development of such models is difficult. Graphical representations that help to organize and to summarize complex interrelationships are thus of great benefit to knowledge engineers. Accordingly, most commercial environments for building expert systems (such as KEE,[13] NEXPERT,[14] and many others[1]) incorporate extensive use of graphics to facilitate the visualization of programs and data structures (Figure 2). In such development environments, users can construct knowledge bases by entering textual specifications and then can browse through and inspect the knowledge using direct-manipulation techniques.[15] Knowledge engineers thus are well acquainted with the advantages of *program visualization* but have had little experience with the construction of knowledge bases using graphical metaphors in the first place—that is, with *visual programming*.[16]

One visual programming environment for expert-systems development that is well described, however, is OPAL.[17-19] OPAL combines forms-based and icon-based knowledge entry, allowing physicians to create new cancer-treatment knowledge bases for an expert system called ONCOCIN.[20] The PROTÉGÉ system presented in this chapter generalizes many of the ideas explored in the original work on OPAL.

The capacity of computer graphics to present multidimensional information in a comprehensible manner, coupled with the abstractive power offered by graphical languages, makes visual programming well suited for

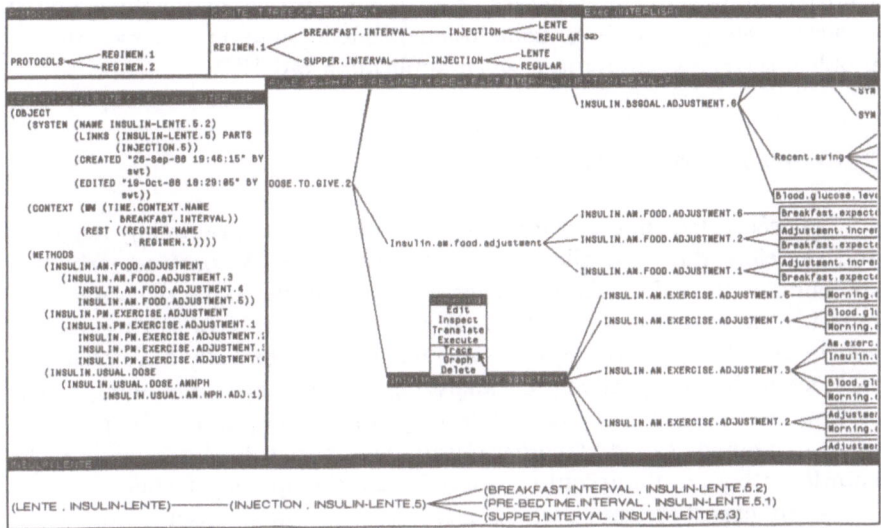

FIGURE 2. Visualization of data structures in a typical expert-system *shell*. Knowledge engineers enter descriptions of knowledge-base components via a standard text editor (left). The system then graphically displays portions of these data structures and the relationships among them (right).

the construction of intricate computational models. Knowledge engineers can view the entities and relationships in their evolving models pictorially and can enter and manipulate the models' components directly. The PROTÉGÉ system, which generates application-specific knowledge-acquisition languages, itself incorporates a visual language that assists knowledge engineers in the initial model-building activities. Once a knowledge engineer has used PROTÉGÉ to create a model of a set of application tasks, PROTÉGÉ automatically constructs a custom-tailored knowledge-entry tool that incorporates a visual language fashioned for the application area based on that model.

In this chapter, I shall describe how a knowledge engineer and a specialist in the treatment of hypertension used PROTÉGÉ to create an abstract model of how drug therapy may be administered to patients with high blood pressure. I then shall discuss how PROTÉGÉ automatically created a custom-tailored visual language from this abstract model that was specialized for the hypertension domain—a language that allowed physicians to work alone to enter knowledge about specific antihypertensive drug treatments. The emphasis will be on the role of visual languages in the knowledge-acquisition process. A detailed description of PROTÉGÉ and the knowledge editors that PROTÉGÉ generates has been presented elsewhere.[7]

Understanding PROTÉGÉ, however, requires an appreciation for the notion of a *problem-solving method*—a domain-independent solution strategy that a problem solver can apply to a given application task.[21]*

3. General Problem-Solving Methods

PROTÉGÉ does not provide a general-purpose programming language and therefore does not allow knowledge engineers to construct arbitrary computational models. Rather, PROTÉGÉ restricts the tasks that users can model to those that can be solved via a particular problem-solving method known as *skeletal-plan refinement*.[23] Workers in AI historically have identified such methods retrospectively by analyzing one or more functioning expert systems. For example, Clancey[24] developed his description of the problem-solving method called *heuristic classification* primarily by studying the knowledge base of the MYCIN program for the therapy of infectious disease.

Early expert systems, such as MYCIN, had unstructured knowledge bases consisting of scores of production rules. The developers of such systems originally considered these rules to be modular and independent. The rules were thought to lack relationships with other rules in the knowledge base and were considered to be devoid of any preordained role in problem solving.[10] Yet MYCIN used a subset of its rules only to derive *abstractions* from primary input data. For example, one such MYCIN rule concluded that patients with low white-blood-cell counts are immunosuppressed. The program used another subset of its rules only as *heuristics* that defined associations between these abstractions and potential solutions to the current problem. For example, another MYCIN rule concluded that immunosuppressed patients often are infected with certain bacteria. The identification of these different *roles* in which knowledge might be used during problem solving provided a useful framework for understanding how MYCIN arrived at its recommendations and allowed researchers to discuss the actions of MYCIN (and those of other systems) without needing to refer to the specific data structures with which the knowledge base was programmed. Clancey[24] showed how knowledge engineers could describe MYCIN's behavior, not in

---

* Terminology in the AI literature is not standardized. Chandrasekaran[22] uses the term *generic task* to connote what other researchers refer to as *problem-solving method*. Unfortunately, most authors use the word *task* (without the *generic* modifier) to refer to an application problem to be solved; a (nongeneric) *task* is thus inherently domain dependent. Because the distinction between a *task* and a *generic task* may lead to confusion, I shall consistently use the term *problem-solving method* when referring to a solution strategy and shall use the word *task* only when referring to an application problem requiring some solution.

terms of the seemingly random effects of one "modular" rule causing the invocation of another, but in terms of a coherent, domain-independent problem-solving method.

Clancey's heuristic-classification method retrospectively assigned a purpose to each fragment of information in the MYCIN knowledge base. Viewing each knowledge fragment in terms of its contribution to heuristic-classification problem solving imposed a structure on the knowledge base—a structure that made the expert system as a whole more understandable and more maintainable. Increasingly, interactive knowledge-acquisition tools have used models of problem-solving methods (such as that of heuristic classification) *prospectively* as the foundation for a knowledge-entry dialogue with their users. Rather than asking the user to type in individual production rules and other data structures as TEIRESIAS did, such tools ask the user to enter, for example, the ways in which a problem solver should condense input data into abstractions and how those abstractions might suggest solutions to the task at hand.[8, 25] The tools then translate the user's specifications of problem-solving behavior into a functioning knowledge base. Knowledge engineers consequently can think in terms of the explicit problem-solving methods presupposed by the tools, rather than in terms of the individual knowledge-base components needed to implement the methods.

Knowledge engineers use the PROTÉGÉ knowledge-acquisition tool to build special-purpose knowledge-acquisition tools that domain experts can use. The experts use the PROTÉGÉ-generated tools to develop knowledge-based systems that arrive at recommendations using the problem-solving method of skeletal-plan refinement. With this method, an expert system decomposes a problem's abstract (skeletal) solution into one or more constituent plans that are each worked out in more detail than the more abstract plan. These constituent plans, however, may themselves be skeletal in nature and may require further distillation into subcomponents that are more fleshed out. The refinement process continues until a concrete solution to the problem is achieved.[23]

ONCOCIN,[20] an expert system that advises physicians on the treatment of cancer patients, is an example of a system that solves problems by skeletal-plan refinement (Figure 3). ONCOCIN first establishes that a given patient is to be treated according to a particular plan (or *protocol*), then determines the individual X-ray treatments and chemotherapies (drug combinations) that must be administered in accordance with the protocol's predefined guidelines. ONCOCIN then refines its plans to give each of the chemotherapies into more detailed plans to administer a number of individual drugs. Thus, in the course of filling out (*instantiating*) its skeletal plan, ONCOCIN establishes *planning entities* such as the protocol according to which the patient should be treated, the X-ray treatments and chemotherapies to be given, and the

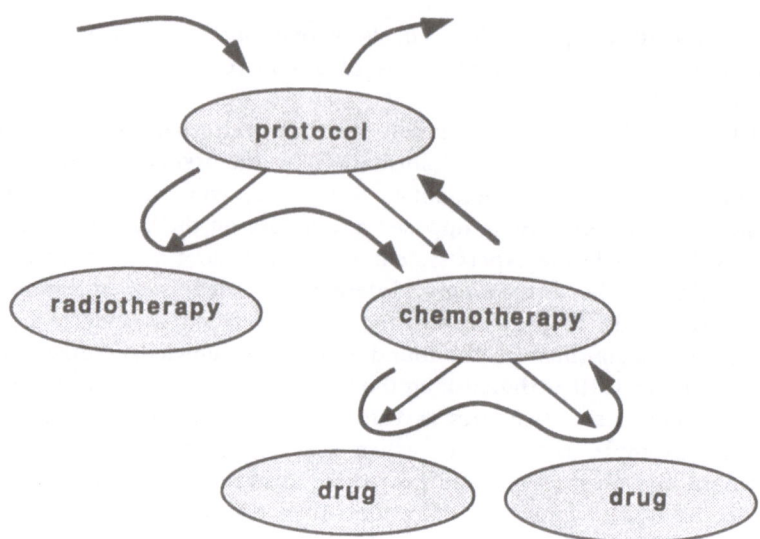

FIGURE 3. Use of the method of skeletal-plan refinement in the ONCOCIN expert system for cancer therapy. *Protocols* are resolved into their constituent *radiotherapies* and *chemotherapies*; chemotherapies are, in turn, resolved into component *drugs*.

drugs to be administered. At the same time, the instantiation of the skeletal plan may be affected by certain *input data* (such as laboratory test results or drug-induced side effects) that may cause ONCOCIN to take unusual *actions* (such as omitting a drug, substituting one drug for another, or postponing the administration of chemotherapy). The notions of *planning entities*, of *input data*, and of *actions* form the foundation of the model of skeletal-plan refinement that drives PROTÉGÉ. Like other knowledge-editing programs that are based on models of problem-solving methods, PROTÉGÉ asks its users to enter knowledge in terms of the predefined concepts in its model.[9] PROTÉGÉ differs, however, because of the graphical nature of the interaction.

4. *The PROTÉGÉ System*

PROTÉGÉ is a knowledge editor based on a forms-oriented visual language. Knowledge engineers use PROTÉGÉ to construct *models* of application areas that involve tasks that an expert system such as ONCOCIN can solve using skeletal-plan refinement. (For example, knowledge engineers have used PROTÉGÉ to create a model of how cancer therapies are administered.) PROTÉGÉ, in turn, automatically constructs a visual-programming environment that application experts can use alone to enter the details of individual tasks. (For example, PROTÉGÉ used the cancer-therapy model to generate

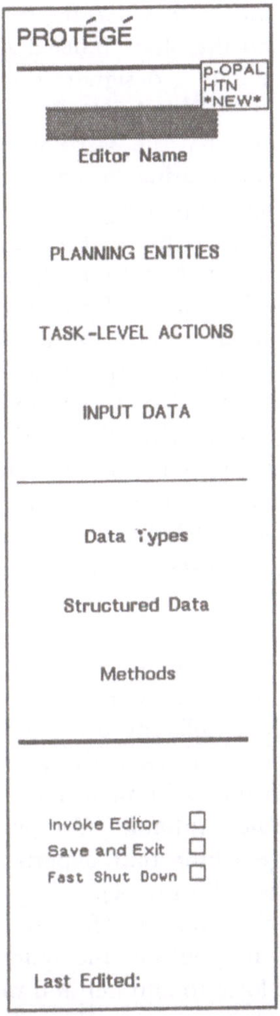

FIGURE 4. PROTÉGÉ main-menu form.

p-OPAL, a program that allows cancer specialists to enter knowledge of specific cancer-treatment plans for ONCOCIN.[7])*

Although knowledge engineers must enter some textual information into PROTÉGÉ from the keyboard, most interactions involve selecting "blanks" in the graphical forms on the workstation screen using a mouse pointing device and then "filling in" the blanks by making choices from pop-up menus. Figure 4 shows the main PROTÉGÉ form that appears on the

---

* The p-OPAL system has much the same functionality as does OPAL, the hand-crafted tool that physicians have used for several years to maintain the ONCOCIN knowledge base.

workstation screen when the system is first activated. In the figure, the user
has selected the blank labeled *Editor Name* and is about to make a selection
from the menu to designate the name of the task-oriented knowledge editor
that PROTÉGÉ is to be used to construct. (In the examples that follow, we
shall assume that the user has selected HTN, the name of a knowledge editor
that was built using PROTÉGÉ for entry of treatment plans in the area of
management of patients with hypertension.) The other "blanks" on the form
(PLANNING ENTITIES, TASK-LEVEL ACTIONS, INPUT DATA, and so on) do not
accept input values from the user but instead cause PROTÉGÉ to display
other, special-purpose forms each time the user toggles one of these blanks
with the mouse. Note that the first three of these toggle blanks correspond
to the three main components of the model of the skeletal-planning method
discussed in Section 2. Selecting the blank labeled PLANNING ENTITIES, for
example, displays on the workstation screen the form shown in Figure 5.
This form allows knowledge engineers to enter the names and hierarchical
relationships of the entities that compose skeletal plans in the application
area being modeled. Before we discuss the user's entries in the hypertension
example, however, a few general comments about the process of creating
models with PROTÉGÉ are in order.

The PROTÉGÉ system consists of 13 graphical forms. Each form is
devoted to a different topic and has a predefined layout. The knowledge
engineer builds a model of an application area by requesting the system to
display these different forms and by filling in the blanks appropriately. After
entering into PROTÉGÉ the model of the domain, the knowledge engineer
returns to the main-menu form (see Figure 4) and selects the blank labeled
Invoke Editor. Automatically, PROTÉGÉ verifies the model and constructs a
knowledge editor that experts can use to enter the details of individual
applications (Section 4).

PROTÉGÉ imposes few restraints on the order in which knowledge
engineers may fill out the system's graphical forms. Users may move freely
from one form to another and may fill in the designated blanks in any order.
PROTÉGÉ, however, contains safeguards that ensure the semantic consistency
of its users' entries. Thus, although most blanks can be filled in at random,
the system prevents a user from selecting a blank if additional information
must be entered elsewhere before the contents of that blank would have
unambiguous meaning. A user therefore cannot define an instance of some
component of the model being entered (for example, the input datum *white-
blood-cell count*) before describing the general class of which that instance is
a member (for example, *hematology data*). The system also prevents the user
from entering data that appear to conflict with previously specified information. Thus, if the user has declared that one entity is a component of another
(for example, that a *drug* is a constituent of a *chemotherapy*), that component

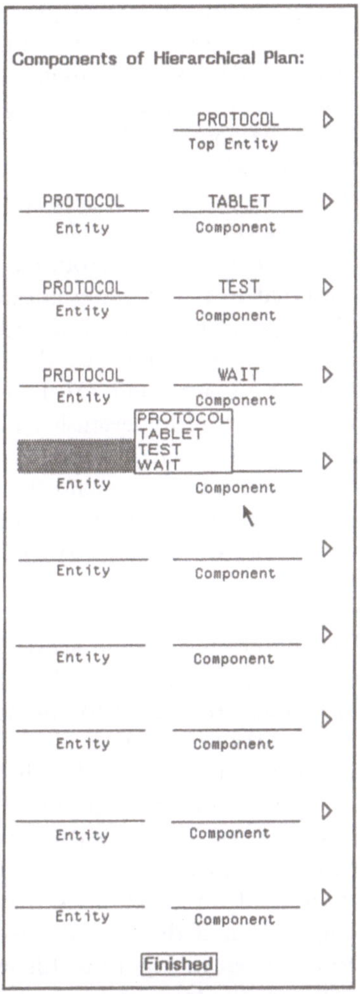

FIGURE 5. PROTÉGÉ form for entering *planning entities*, filled out for entities in the hypertension-therapy domain. The knowledge engineer has specified that PROTOCOLS comprise the administration of TABLETS, TESTS, and WAIT periods.

cannot also be defined as part of some additional entity (for example, that a *drug* also is part of a *radiotherapy*). Each blank verifies the semantic consistency of the input that it receives from the user in an ad hoc manner. PROTÉGÉ, however, cannot always guarantee the consistency of each item as it is entered, as the program has no way of determining in advance whether the user will fill in additional blanks and, if so, what those blanks' contents will be. The forms-based language in PROTÉGÉ does tend to prevent such errors from occurring in the first place, however. In addition to making blanks selectable only when it is appropriate for the knowledge engineer to access them, the system generates menus that restrict the user's entries to values that are consistent with prior data. The PROTÉGÉ language also makes it easy for knowledge engineers to know when specifications are incomplete; when data are missing, the corresponding blanks are empty.

The form in Figure 5, for example, allows knowledge engineers to model the constituents of skeletal plans in a given application domain. Whenever the user selects one of the blanks in the column on the right side of the form, the name of a new planning entity can be typed in. (In Figure 5, for example, PROTOCOLS, TABLETS, TESTS, and WAIT periods all are declared to be planning entities.) The user can select one of the blanks on the right of the form, however, only if the corresponding blank on the left side of the form indicates the name of the planning entity of which the new entry is a component. (In Figure 5, TABLETS, TESTS, and WAIT periods all are components of hypertension PROTOCOLS.) As can be seen in the figure, each time the user selects a blank on the left of the form, PROTÉGÉ dynamically constructs a pop-up menu that contains the names of those planning entities that have been entered into blanks on the right side. It is therefore impossible for the user to enter the name of a nonexistent entity in the left column of blanks.

PROTÉGÉ groups related information on each graphical form and encourages the user to create the model of the application area in a structured, top-down fashion. For example, when the knowledge engineer selects the small arrow next to one of the blanks in the form shown in Figure 5, a new PROTÉGÉ form is displayed on the screen, allowing the user to model the *attributes* of the indicated entity. Selecting the arrow next to the word TABLET in Figure 5 thus opens up the form shown in Figure 6. The knowledge engineer then can use this new form to enter and review the attributes of TABLETS and can select any of the arrows in the form in Figure 6 to open additional forms to enter and review the properties of each attribute. In Figure 5, had the user selected the arrow next to the word PROTOCOL, the form shown in Figure 6 still would have been displayed, but the attributes listed on the form in Figure 6 would have been those for PROTOCOL entities. Throughout the PROTÉGÉ system, the structure of the various forms is predefined, but the system determines the specific contents displayed on the screen by the context in which the user selects the forms.

PROTÉGÉ comprises a number of other forms, all of which are designed to assist knowledge engineers in the construction of general models of application tasks that can be solved using the skeletal-planning method. Figure 7, for example, shows a graphical form that solicits the names of *actions* that can be taken in a given application area. In the domain of administering therapy for hypertension, these actions include such notions as ending the protocol or changing the dose of the tablet prescribed for the

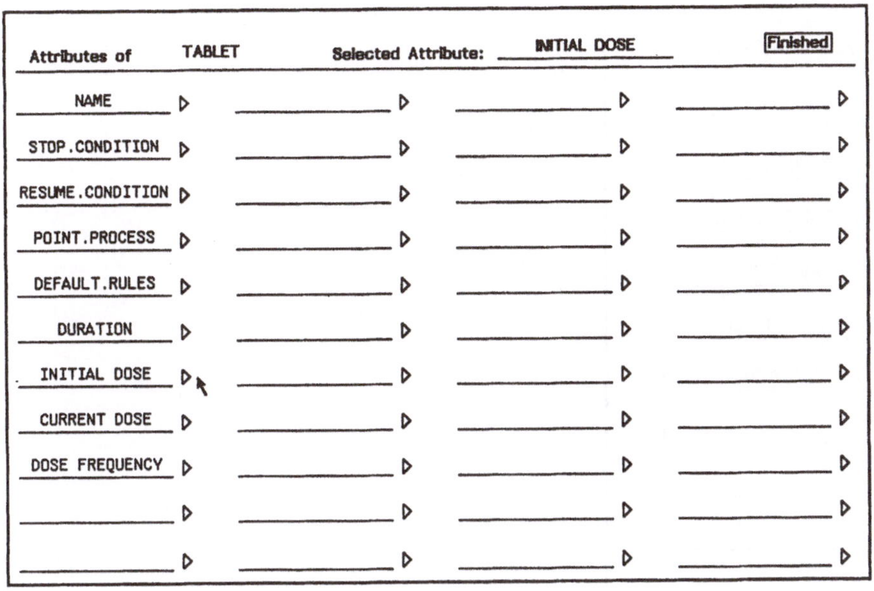

FIGURE 6. PROTÉGÉ form for entering *attributes of planning entities*. The form is filled out for attributes of TABLETS in the hypertension-therapy domain.

patient. Additional forms (invoked when any of the arrows in Figure 7 is selected) allow the knowledge engineer to specify, in domain-independent terms, how each action should be brought about by the expert systems for which PROTÉGÉ ultimately will generate the knowledge base.

The graphical forms in PROTÉGÉ group together related data and emphasize the relationships among the specifications entered by the user. Each transition from one form to another moves the user's view of the domain model that is being created to a different level within an abstraction hierarchy. The user first considers the entities of the skeletal plan, then the attributes of those entities, then the properties of those attributes. The forms help to break up a knowledge engineer's entries into manageable portions, and the relationships among the forms emphasize the relationships among the components of the user's specifications. The visual metaphor in PROTÉGÉ provides abstractive power that facilitates both building intricate models of new application domains (such as hypertension therapy) and displaying those domain models in a comprehensible manner.

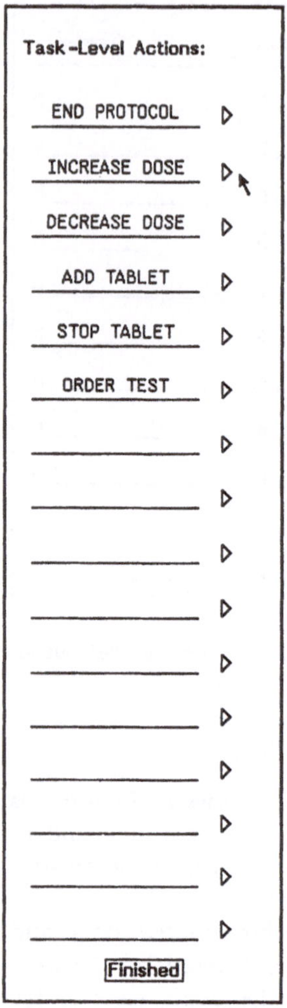

Task-Level Actions:

    END PROTOCOL   ▷

    INCREASE DOSE   ▷ ↖

    DECREASE DOSE   ▷

    ADD TABLET   ▷

    STOP TABLET   ▷

    ORDER TEST   ▷

    _____   ▷

    _____   ▷

    _____   ▷

    _____   ▷

    _____   ▷

    _____   ▷

    _____   ▷

    _____   ▷

    _____   ▷

    _____   ▷

    _____   ▷

        [Finished]

FIGURE 7. PROTÉGÉ form for entering *actions* that can modify
the refinement of a skeletal plan. The particular actions that
a user enters depend on the application area being modeled.
Here, the form is filled out to list actions that are relevant
for the task of hypertension management. Additional forms
allow the user to define the semantics of these task-level
actions in domain-independent terms.

5. Custom-Tailored Visual Languages

The approach taken in PROTÉGÉ assumes that system builders are working in application areas in which there is a need to create multiple, related
knowledge bases. Thus, for example, once a user has used PROTÉGÉ to create
a model of the hypertension-therapy domain, PROTÉGÉ uses that model to
produce a custom-tailored visual language that physicians can use to
describe individual hypertension treatment plans. Each of these treatment

plans necessarily will be somewhat different, but each will conform with the general model of high-blood-pressure therapy entered into PROTÉGÉ.

The visual knowledge-entry languages generated by PROTÉGÉ include both iconic and forms-based components. Although much of the languages' visual syntax is independent of the application area that has been modeled, the specific forms and icons in these languages are established by the domain model entered into PROTÉGÉ. Thus, whereas all PROTÉGÉ-generated languages include forms for entering values of the attributes of planning entities (for example, forms for defining how to administer TABLETS in the hypertension domain), the contents of such forms (that is, the particular attributes of TABLETS for which users must define values) and the interactive behavior of the forms' blanks (that is, the particular menus or other input mechanisms required) are derived solely from the domain model entered into PROTÉGÉ.

5.1. Forms-Based Knowledge Entry

The forms created by PROTÉGÉ have much the same style of interaction as do the forms in PROTÉGÉ itself and rely on the same user-interface management system.[26] Users select blanks one at a time with the mouse and make most entries directly from menus that are generated dynamically based on previously specified information. A form from the knowledge editor HTN, generated by PROTÉGÉ from the model of hypertension therapy discussed in the previous section, appears in Figure 8. The form contains three active blanks, permitting physicians to specify the following three concepts: (1) the starting dose of a tablet, (2) the frequency with which the patient should take that tablet, and (3) the recommended interval between visits to the physician. Each blank corresponds to an attribute of the TABLET entity that was described previously by the knowledge engineer using PROTÉGÉ (see Figure 6). The choices shown in the pop-up menu in Figure 8 correspond to the values for the attribute called DOSE FREQUENCY that were declared by the knowledge engineer using PROTÉGÉ.

The visual language in HTN includes a number of such domain-specific forms. Figure 9, for example, shows a graphical form that physicians use to enter the relationships between certain *input data* (in this case, vital-signs measurements) and corresponding *actions* to take. The application-specific components of the HTN form are all derived from the domain model entered into PROTÉGÉ. The fixed menu of possible vital-signs measurements at the top of the HTN form represents *data items* in the hypertension model; the blanks in the middle portion of the form (used to enter information about the context in which designated actions should be performed) refer to instances of the planning entities entered in the PROTÉGÉ form in Figure 5;

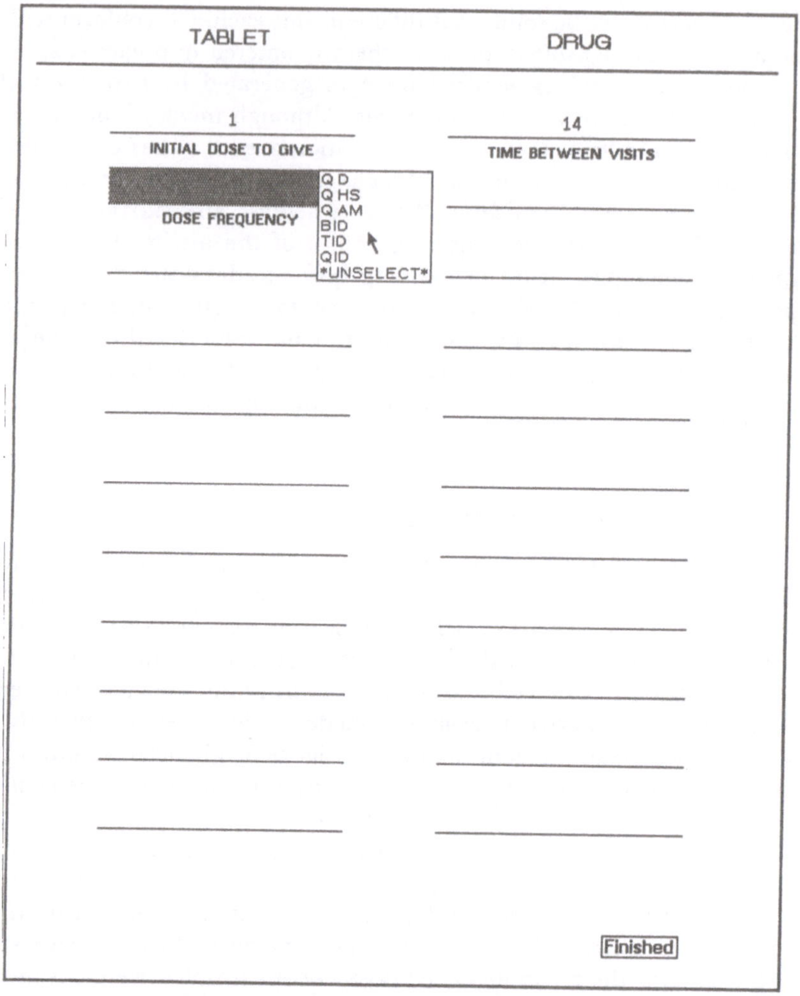

FIGURE 8. HTN form for entering information about TABLETS. The pop-up menu lists possible frequencies with which physicians can prescribe tablets. For example, *q d* is a Latin abbreviation that means "every day"; *q hs* means "at bedtime."

the entries in the pop-up menu of potential therapeutic actions are derived from the PROTÉGÉ form in Figure 7. After the HTN user has filled out the program's various forms, HTN transparently converts the user's graphical statements into sequences of production rules that then are incorporated within the incipient expert system's knowledge base. The translation of two-dimensional form entries into production rules is possible only because the

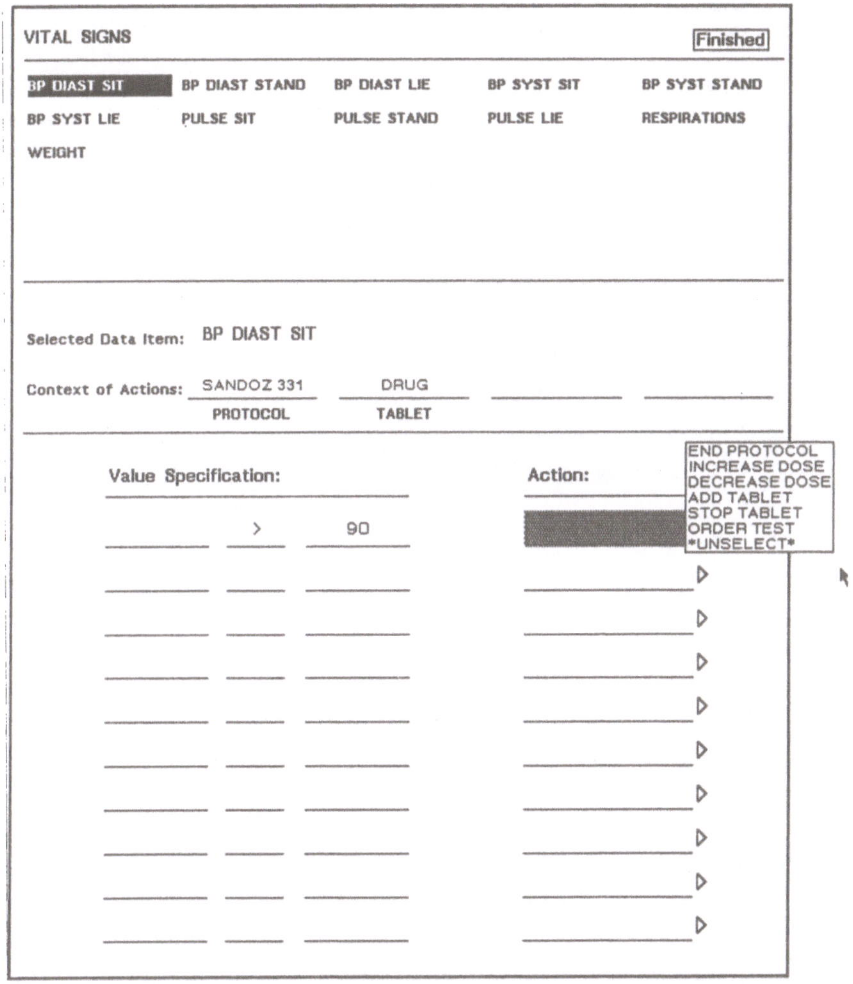

FIGURE 9. HTN form for entering actions to take that are predicated on vital-signs measurements. The user is about to specify what the expert system should recommend if a patient's diastolic blood pressure when measured in the sitting position is greater than 90 mmHg.

semantics of each of the blanks in HTN is established by the domain model that the knowledge engineer entered into PROTÉGÉ.

When knowledge engineers use PROTÉGÉ to create knowledge-entry tools for new application areas, the syntactic structure of the generated visual languages is similar to that of HTN, although the details of each language are necessarily different. Figure 10, for example, shows a graphical

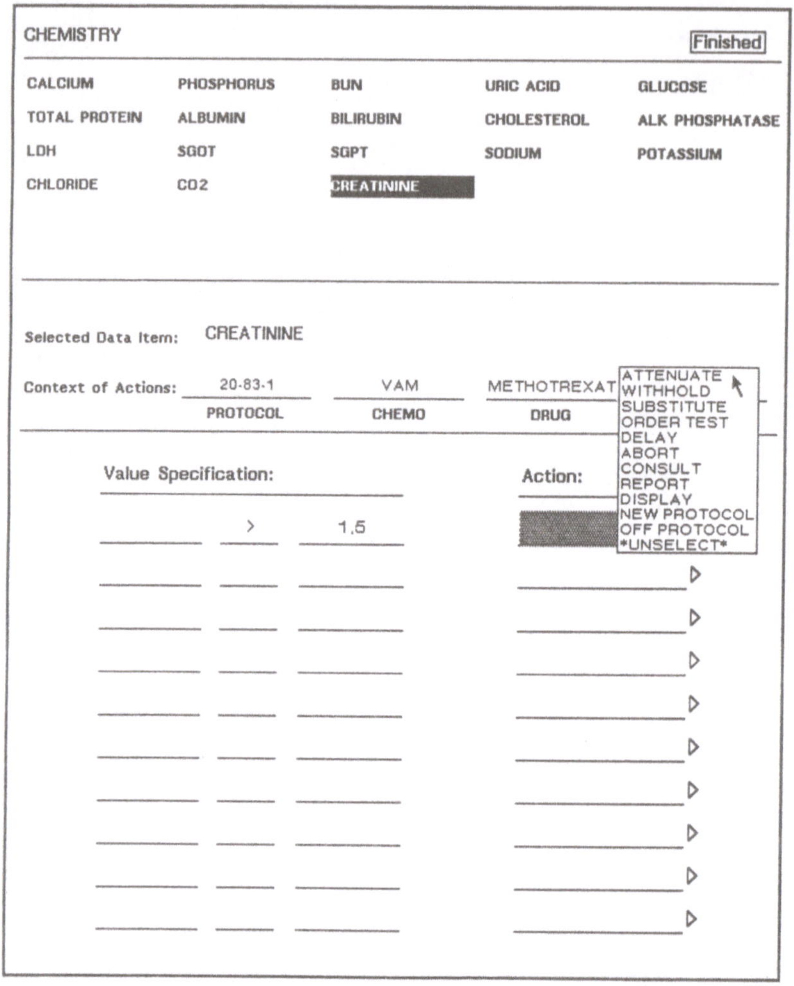

FIGURE 10. p-OPAL form for entering actions to take that are predicated on laboratory test results. The actions shown in the pop-up menu are relevant for the cancer-therapy domain. Here, the user is about to designate an action to take if a patient's serum creatinine level rises to more than 1.5 mg/dl. Compare this form with the HTN form in Figure 9.

form from p-OPAL, the knowledge editor created for entry of protocols for cancer therapy.[7] Although the layout of the p-OPAL form in Figure 10 is analogous to that of the HTN form in Figure 9, the p-OPAL form necessarily deals with a dissimilar set of input conditions, contexts, and actions. Just as the forms in HTN are specialized for entry of knowledge about drug therapy for hypertension, the forms in p-OPAL are specialized for entry of knowledge about cancer-treatment protocols. The two application domains, however, are related in that both comprise tasks that can be solved using the method of skeletal-plan refinement—the only kinds of domain tasks that knowledge engineers can model using PROTÉGÉ.

5.2. Iconic Knowledge Entry

All visual languages generated by PROTÉGÉ include a facility to create iconic flowcharts for describing the procedural aspects of individual planning tasks. This flowchart language is based on the iconic portion of OPAL[18] and includes visual methods for denoting sequential operations, concurrency, branching, iteration, and exceptional conditions. Whereas the individual domain-specific operations that users can specify within a flowchart are derived expressly from the domain model entered into PROTÉGÉ, the mechanisms used to represent flow of control from one such operation to the next are built into the language and consequently do not vary with the application area.

Figure 11 shows the specifications for administering an experimental

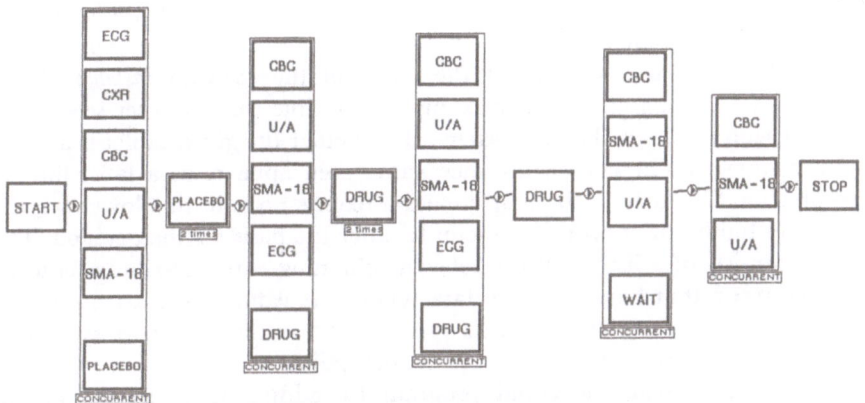

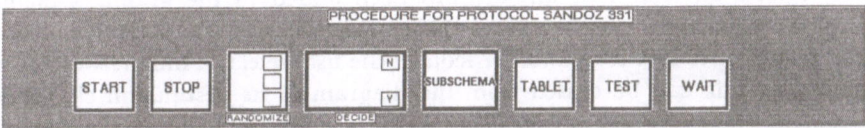

FIGURE 11. HTN environment for describing the procedures associated with specific hypertension PROTOCOLS. The flowchart designates a precise sequence of TABLETS to be administered (both experimental *drugs* and *placebos*) concurrent with a number of scheduled laboratory tests. (The abbreviations ECG, CXR, CBC, U/A, and SMA-18 stand for electrocardiogram, chest X-ray examination, complete blood count, urinalysis, and sequential multianalysis of 18 blood-chemistry tests, respectively.)

protocol for hypertension therapy as entered into HTN. The user has created the flow diagram within a large region on the workstation screen that initially was blank. Beneath this region is a palette of *reference* icons that correspond to some of the basic elements of the flowchart language. These icons include basic control operators such as START (begin a procedure), STOP (terminate a procedure), and DECIDE (binary branch). A RANDOMIZE icon allows the user to indicate changes in control flow that are arbitrary—a common situation in medical research protocols, in which patients may give their consent to be assigned at random to one of several alternative treatment plans in an effort to determine which therapy might be preferable. The SUBSCHEMA icon provides the capability to create "graphical subroutines," thus adding a form of procedural abstraction to the visual language. The remaining icons in the palette (TABLET, TEST, and WAIT) correspond to the classes of planning entities that compose hypertension PROTOCOLs, described by the knowledge engineer using PROTÉGÉ (see Figure 5).

When the user selects one of the reference icons with the mouse, a copy of that icon appears in the main graph region. The user then can position the new icon anywhere in the region by moving the mouse. If the user adds a domain-dependent icon such as TABLET or TEST, a pop-up menu appears from which the user can select the name of the relevant *instance* of the particular planning entity. (For example, any time that the user selects the TABLET icon in Figure 11, the system asks whether the given tablet is a DRUG or a PLACEBO.) The chosen instance name then appears as a label for the graph icon. Similarly, if the user creates a DECIDE node in the flowchart, the program builds an appropriate menu to enter the basis for the decision. The menu consists of a list of all the relevant planning-entity attributes entered into PROTÉGÉ that have Boolean data types. The value of the attribute that the user selects from the menu is used by the resultant expert system to determine the flow of control at the branch point.

The user creates a visual program by adding icons to the graph, positioning them appropriately, and drawing links between them. When the user selects an icon that already has been added to the graph, a menu appears, allowing the user to move the icon elsewhere, to erase the icon from the graph, or to link it to another icon. If the user selects a link between two icons, the link can be erased from the diagram or its destination changed. Selecting the graph region itself brings up a menu that allows the user to designate iterative or concurrent processes by drawing boxes around groups of icons with the mouse. The result is a what-you-see-is-what-you-get environment that allows application specialists to create detailed flowcharts rapidly.

The flowchart created with HTN shown in Figure 11 describes a typical experimental protocol for hypertension therapy in which physicians first administer a placebo tablet for three visits, while monitoring the patients' baseline blood pressure. The physicians then prescribe an active antihypertensive drug for several visits, then withhold all medication and observe the patients for any withdrawal effects. Concurrent with this procedure, a number of laboratory investigations are performed at designated intervals. HTN transparently converts the visual specification into an augmented transition network that is stored within the expert system's knowledge base.

Components of the iconic language for protocols in HTN are similar to those of the iconic language for protocols in p-OPAL (Figure 12). Although the p-OPAL visual environment includes the standard control-flow icons (START, STOP, RANDOMIZE, DECIDE, and SUBSCHEMA), the domain-specific icons in p-OPAL reflect the model of *cancer therapy* that the knowledge engineer entered into PROTÉGÉ. The p-OPAL flowchart language in Figure 12 deals with the notions of stratification steps (recording designated patient attributes that may later prove to be of prognostic value), chemotherapies (drug combinations), and X-ray therapies (XRT). The protocol that has been

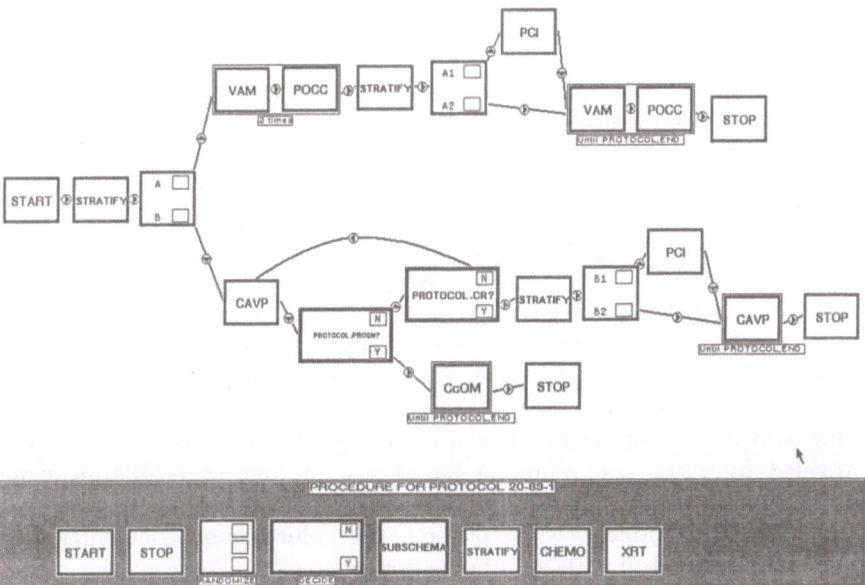

FIGURE 12. p-OPAL environment for describing procedures associated with specific oncology PROTOCOLS. The procedure for a lung-cancer protocol randomly assigns patients either to receive two alternating chemotherapies (VAM and POCC) or to receive a single chemotherapy called CAVP. Patients who have a complete response to either form of treatment (as indicated by the value of the attribute PROTOCOL.CR) may be randomly assigned to receive prophylactic cranial irradiation (PCI). Compare this flowchart with that of the HTN protocol in Figure 11.

entered in Figure 12 determines treatment for a kind of lung cancer and indicates a procedure that tests a complex standard therapy against a more simple, experimental drug regimen.

By filling in the blanks of the various graphical forms and by drawing appropriate flowcharts, application specialists can use visual environments such as those in HTN and p-OPAL to produce large knowledge bases without reliance on knowledge engineers. The users never need to consider how their entries might be converted to production rules and other knowledge-base structures. The necessary translation is done without the user's awareness. Instead, application specialists directly manipulate domain-specific icons and forms, concentrating on familiar, intuitive concepts. Nonprogrammers can use the visual languages created with PROTÉGÉ to produce expert-system knowledge bases rapidly, and relatively painlessly. The visual language in PROTÉGÉ itself assists knowledge engineers in the development of such custom-tailored knowledge-entry languages in the first place.

6. Discussion

As the use of expert-systems technology has moved from research laboratories to commercial settings, knowledge engineers have constructed systems of enormous scope and complexity. It is no longer exceptional for knowledge bases to contain hundreds or even thousands of production rules and other data structures. Implementing and maintaining any software system of such size is a formidable problem. The expected difficulties are particularly acute for knowledge engineers, however, because expert systems embody domain-specific problem-solving behaviors that rarely can be intuitive to people who are not themselves experts in the application area. As a result, many researchers have sought to develop languages for knowledge acquisition and knowledge-base maintenance that can be used by application specialists *directly*. Although success in attaining this goal using text-based approaches has been meager,[27] the abstractive power provided by visual programming has shown promise in facilitating communication between humans and computers.

OPAL, for example, was one of the first graphical knowledge-entry tools that could be used directly by application experts.[17] The program, which combines a forms-based entry mechanism[19] with an iconic flowchart language,[18] served as an exemplar for the custom-tailored tools that knowledge engineers can now develop using PROTÉGÉ. In 1986, system builders used OPAL to enter over 36 cancer-therapy plans into the ONCOCIN knowledge base. (Knowledge engineers formerly had required several weeks or months to encode each therapy plan using traditional techniques.) As with the knowledge-editing tools created with PROTÉGÉ, the ability to visualize knowledge bases in terms of domain-specific graphical metaphors provided application experts with powerful abstractions that had not been available previously.

PROTÉGÉ, unlike OPAL and the tools that PROTÉGÉ generates, is intended for use by computer scientists. PROTÉGÉ's graphical forms are designed not to insulate users from unfamiliar concepts but rather to provide knowledge engineers with a structure that simplifies entering and browsing through an intricate set of specifications. The relationships among concepts are emphasized, both by the grouping of associated blanks on the same form and by the logical connections that the user follows from one form to the next. PROTÉGÉ consequently gives its users many of the advantages of hypertext but imposes a rigid structure that provides guidance capabilities that are impossible in free-form hypermedia. For example, all attributes of an entity in the application domain are necessarily displayed together (see Figure 6). There thus can be no ambiguity regarding which attributes are part of the knowledge engineer's evolving model and what roles those attributes may play in problem solving.

The graphical knowledge-entry languages described in this chapter permit users to express only very specialized concepts. These languages are not designed for general programming. Like other visual languages for knowledge acquisition that have been developed as demonstration projects,[28, 29] and like those that are now becoming available commercially,[13, 14] PROTÉGÉ constrains what a knowledge engineer can say about the world. The task-specific languages that PROTÉGÉ generates (for example, p-OPAL and HTN) further limit the concepts that a user can express to particular kinds of applications. None of these knowledge-acquisition languages, however, is designed to provide a general-purpose programming environment. Indeed, in the traditional construction of expert systems, comprehensive *textual* languages such as LISP have been widely supplanted by the more specialized languages of expert-system shells.[1] The complexity of the real-world tasks that knowledge-based systems attempt to emulate and the complexity of the task models that developers consequently must construct to perform those emulations favor the use of more specialized, high-level languages.

Unlike most expert-system shells, however, PROTÉGÉ adopts a language that is intended not only for a particular knowledge-representation formalism (the hierarchies of frames and attached rules assumed by ONCOCIN[20]), but also for a particular method of problem solving (skeletal-plan refinement). Accordingly, PROTÉGÉ's language demands that the user clarify how each application-specific concept that is entered relates to the presupposed problem-solving method. It is not sufficient, for example, for a knowledge engineer to stipulate that users may enter certain data into the target expert system; the engineer also must declare how those data might influence the skeletal plans that the expert system will generate. The PROTÉGÉ language forces the user to elucidate how the entered knowledge is applied during an expert-system consultation, making the resultant knowledge bases more transparent and more maintainable.[7, 21] Although researchers have created several knowledge-acquisition languages that similarly highlight the roles in which domain knowledge is used during problem solving,[8] PROTÉGÉ is the first tool to incorporate such a language having a predominantly visual syntax.

The custom-tailored languages that PROTÉGÉ generates presuppose not only a particular knowledge-representation formalism (ONCOCIN's hierarchy of frames and attached production rules) and a particular problem-solving method (skeletal-plan refinement), but also a particular application domain (namely, whatever classes of application tasks were described by the knowledge engineers who used PROTÉGÉ to create the languages in the first place). The PROTÉGÉ-generated languages thus incorporate strong application-dependent semantic assumptions that simplify the entry of complex specifications by users who typically have never before "written" computer programs. The languages' specialized semantics, coupled with their precise, visual syntax, make tools such as P-OPAL and HTN well suited for the creation of large knowledge bases in appropriate application areas.

Developers of visual languages have suggested that graphical representations are useful in aiding computer-naïve users in the independent development of applications software.[16] Clearly, the proliferation of commercial spreadsheet systems testifies to the power of graphical metaphors. *General-purpose* visual languages, however, have not yet been widely disseminated; the predictions made several years ago that visual languages would largely eliminate the need for traditional applications programmers[30] have not been borne out. Critics of graphical programming (such as Brooks[11]) maintain that software is inherently difficult to visualize and that the various dimensions of computer programs (control flow, variable scoping, data structures, and so on) are impossible to communicate in an integrated fashion in finite space on a two-dimensional display screen. The argument is that computer graphics, no matter how abstract, cannot harmonize these different views. Visual languages, however, are enormously powerful when there is only one dominant perspective required for programming—as is the case when a person creates a spreadsheet, for example.

In PROTÉGÉ, the view that knowledge engineers and application specialists take of the knowledge being entered is singularly shaped by the model of skeletal planning built into the system's graphical forms. With each visual language that PROTÉGÉ generates, the user's view of the knowledge is further shaped by the model of the application area entered into PROTÉGÉ.

Knowledge-base development, both with PROTÉGÉ and with the custom-tailored tools that PROTÉGÉ produces, is thus qualitatively different from standard programming. With these graphical tools, system builders do not need to integrate the notions of data and control flow to assemble models of some nascent system's behavior; rather, they work from the top down, within the unified framework provided by PROTÉGÉ's model of skeletal planning. PROTÉGÉ users start with a predefined model of problem solving (that of skeletal-plan refinement), specialize that model for a set of application tasks (in creating tools such as P-OPAL and HTN), then ask domain experts to refine those task models further to produce usable knowledge bases. The guidance offered by this approach, however, restricts the classes of expert systems that knowledge engineers can create to those for which skeletal-plan refinement is an appropriate problem-solving method.

Despite the semantic structure provided by the skeletal-planning method and the potential for visualization afforded by PROTÉGÉ's graphical forms, the difficult modeling problems that plague knowledge acquisition do not completely disappear with the methodology presented in this chapter; there still is a bottleneck. PROTÉGÉ, however, facilitates the modeling process by making explicit and readily examinable the assumptions underlying a knowledge engineer's characterization of an application area. PROTÉGÉ then uses the knowledge engineer's model to generate a special-purpose language—one with semantic primitives that are sufficiently abstract to ease the translation of an application specialist's mental models of particular domain tasks into sets of concrete specifications. In the development of expert systems, visual languages tailored to specific application tasks are a means for coping with the complexity associated with the construction of large knowledge bases.

Acknowledgments

This work was funded by grants LM-07033 and LM-04420 from the National Library of Medicine. Computing facilities were provided by the SUMEX-AIM resource under NIH grant RR-0075 and through equipment gifts from Xerox Corporation and Corning Medical. Dave Combs developed much of the system software required by PROTÉGÉ. Samson Tu and Cliff Wulfman developed the domain-independent version of ONCOCIN with which PROTÉGÉ operates. Peter Rudd helped me to develop the HTN knowledge-acquisition tool for hypertension protocols. Ted Shortliffe, Bruce Buchanan, and Larry Fagan participated in many valuable discussions. Dave Combs and Lyn Dupré provided comments on a previous draft of this chapter.

References

1. W. B. Gevarter, The nature and evaluation of commercial expert system building tools, *Computer* **20**, 24–41 (1987).
2. S. Spang (Ed.), The new AI pioneers: The knowledge merchants, *Spang Robinson Report on AI* **3**, 1–8 (July 1987).
3. R. Davis, Applications of meta level knowledge to the construction, maintenance, and use of large knowledge bases, Ph.D. dissertation, Stanford University, Stanford, California, Report STAN-CS-76-564, 1976.
4. B. G. Buchanan, D. Barstow, R. Bechtal, J. Bennett, W. Clancey, C. Kulikowski, T. Mitchell, and D. A. Waterman, Constructing an expert system, pp. 127–167, in *Building Expert Systems*, F. Hayes-Roth, D. A. Waterman, and D. B. Lenat (Eds.), Addison-Wesley, Reading, Massachusetts, 1983.
5. S. Tuhrim, J. A. Reggia, and M. Floor, Expert system development: Letting the domain specialist directly author knowledge bases, pp. 37–56, in *Expert Systems: The User Interface*, J. Hendler (Ed.), Ablex, Norwood, New Jersey, 1988.
6. J. H. Boose, A knowledge acquisition program for expert systems based on personal construct psychology, *Int. J. Man–Machine Stud.* **23**, 495–525 (1985).
7. M. A. Musen, *Automated Generation of Model-Based Knowledge-Acquisition Tools*, London, Pitman, 1989.
8. S. Marcus (Ed.), *Automating Knowledge Acquisition for Expert Systems*, Kluwer, Boston, 1988.
9. M. A. Musen, Conceptual models of interactive knowledge-acquisition tools, *Knowledge Acquisition* **1**, 73–88 (1989).
10. B. G. Buchanan and E. H. Shortliffe, *Rule-Based Expert Systems: The MYCIN Experiments of the Stanford Heuristic Programming Project*, Addison-Wesley, Reading, Massachusetts, 1984.
11. F. P. Brooks, No silver bullet: Essense and accidents of software engineering, *Computer* **20**, 10–19 (1987).
12. P. E. Johnson, What kind of expert should a system be? *J. Med. Phil.* **8**, 77–97 (1983).
13. M. Stelzner and M. D. Williams, The evolution of interface requirements for expert systems, pp. 285–306, in *Expert Systems: The User Interface*, J. Hendler (Ed.), Ablex, Norwood, New Jersey, 1988.
14. A. T. Rappaport and B. R. Gaines, Integration of acquisition and performance, pp. 25-1–25-20, in *Proceedings of the Third Knowledge Acquisition for Knowledge-Based Systems Workshop*, J. H. Boose and B. R. Gaines (Eds.), SRDG Publications, Department of Computer Science, University of Calgary, Calgary, Alberta, Canada.
15. B. Sheil, Power tools for programmers, *Datamation* **29**(2), 131–144 (1983).
16. B. A. Myers, The State of the Art in Visual Programming and Program Visualization, Computer Science Department, Carnegie Mellon University, Pittsburgh, Pennsylvania, Technical Report CMU-CS-88-114, February, 1988.
17. M. A. Musen, L. M. Fagan, D. M. Combs, and E. H. Shortliffe, Use of a domain model to drive an interactive knowledge-editing tool, *Int. J. Man–Machine Stud.* **26**, 105–121 (1987).
18. M. A. Musen, L. M. Fagan, and E. H. Shortliffe, Graphical specification of procedural knowledge for an expert system, pp. 15–35 in *Expert Systems: The User Interface*, J. Hendler (Ed.), Ablex, Norwood, New Jersey, 1988.
19. M. A. Musen, D. M. Combs, J. D. Walton, E. H. Shortliffe, and L. M. Fagan, OPAL: Toward the computer-aided design of oncology advice systems, pp. 166–180 in *Selected Topics in Medical Artificial Intelligence*, P. L. Miller (Ed.), Springer-Verlag, New York, 1988.
20. S. W. Tu, M. G. Kahn, M. A. Musen, J. C. Ferguson, E. H. Shortliffe, and L. M. Fagan, Episodic skeletal-plan refinement based on temporal data, *Communications of the Association for Computing Machinery* **32**, 1439–1455 (1989).
21. J. McDermott, Preliminary steps toward a taxonomy of problem-solving methods, pp. 225–256 in *Automating Knowledge Acquisition for Expert Systems*, S. Marcus (Ed.), Kluwer, Boston, 1988.
22. B. Chandrasekaran, Generic tasks in knowledge-based reasoning: High-level building blocks for expert system design, *IEEE Expert* **1**, 23–30 (1986).

23. P. E. FRIEDLAND AND Y. IWASAKI, The concept and implementation of skeletal plans, *J. Automated Reasoning* **1**, 161–208 (1985).
24. W. J. CLANCEY, Heuristic classification, *Artificial Intelligence* **27**, 289–350 (1985).
25. J. S. BENNETT, ROGET: A knowledge-based system for acquiring the conceptual structure of a diagnostic expert system, *J. Automated Reasoning* **1**, 49–74 (1985).
26. D. M. COMBS, ODIE: A System for Design and Management of Form-Based Interfaces, Medical Computer Science Group, Knowledge Systems Laboratory, Stanford University, Stanford, California, Technical Report 225, September, 1988.
27. C. M. KITTO, Progress in automated knowledge acquisition tools: How close are we to replacing the knowledge engineer?, pp. 14-1–14-13 in *Proceedings of the Third Knowledge Acquisition for Knowledge-Based Systems Workshop*, J. H. Boose and B. R. Gaines (Eds.), SRDG Publications, Department of Computer Science, University of Calgary, Calgary, Alberta, Canada.
28. M. J. FREILING AND J. H. ALEXANDER, Diagrams and grammars: Tools for mass producing expert systems, pp. 537–543 in *The First Conference on Artificial Intelligence Applications*, IEEE Computer Society Press, New York, 1984.
29. D. E. MAHLING AND W. B. CROFT, Knowledge acquisition for planners, pp. 18-1–18-18 in *Proceedings of the Third Knowledge Acquisition for Knowledge-Based Systems Workshop*, J. H. Boose and B. R. Gaines (Eds.), SRDG Publications, Department of Computer Science, University of Calgary, Calgary, Alberta, Canada.
30. A. MACDONALD, Visual programming, *Datamation* **28**(11), 132–140 (1982).

III

VISUAL PROGRAMMING

One major thrust of visual languages is their use in program design and development. Kazuo Matsumura and Shuichi Tayama discuss some of the underlying principles that enter into the development of a programming language, including semantic, syntactic, and pragmatic factors, and policies governing the use of various visual characteristics. They then describe some experiments with a visual interface design method, 50SM, based on these principles. An iconic programming environment, HI-VISUAL, proposed by Aulikki Hirakawa, M. Tanaka, and T. Ichikawa provides fruitful facilities for the development of large icon programs which include user action guidance, top-down/bottom-up program development, and integration of existing (sub)systems. A system implementation is also presented. Finally, Dexter Kozen *et al.* present a visual language without a lexical syntax, ALEX, used in the context of high-level parallel programming.

5

VISUAL MAN–MACHINE INTERFACE FOR PROGRAM DESIGN AND PRODUCTION

Kazuo Matsumura and Shuichi Tayama

1. Introduction

Along with the development of new computer input/output devices and with the diversification in computer users (both laymen and experts, beginners and skilled technicians, and so on), there is a growing demand for highly functional man–machine interfaces. And this interface is required to closely resemble the communication between man and man. To realize this, the machine may be made to possess man's common knowledge, making implicit communication possible. Or the conversational expressing power between man and machine must be greatly reinforced. Visual interface is intended to be highly instrumental in adopting this latter approach.

The visual man–machine interface is playing a major role in increasing the productivity achieved by various computer users. One prominent example of the use of such man–machine interface is in icons and multiple windows. This interface does not simply assist in direct visual understanding, but also brings about other psychological benefits, such as facilitating studying and adding interest.

In the program design and production field, computer-aided design (CAD) is being intensively experimented with. Visual interfaces are also

KAZUO MATSUMURA • Systems & Software Engineering Laboratory, Toshiba Corporation, Kawasaki 210, Japan.   SHUICHI TAYAMA • Design Center, Toshiba Corporation, Tokyo 105, Japan.
© 1986 IEEE. Reprinted from the 1986 Computer Society Workshop on Visual Languages, June 25–27, 1986, Dallas, Texas, pp. 71–80.

receiving attention here, for the reasons stated above. This report discusses the concept of introducing such a man–machine interface for program design and production.

The following two aspects are involved in the introduction of a visual interface for program design:

1. Why are visual interfaces needed?
2. Which visual interface category is the most elegant, easy to understand, and manipulate?

The main reasons why visual interfaces are better are as follows. Computer programs have to handle various abstract concepts, such as the kinds of elements that constitute the program (procedures, data, modules, decisions, etc.), the properties of each element (size, etc.), the interrelation between elements (control flow, data flow, hierarchical structure, etc.), and so on. By making these elements more concrete and distinct, the final program becomes easier to understand and easier to communicate with. Several visual aspects are also included, such as type identification, size, flow direction, and so on.

For these reasons, various diagrams are used, such as flow charts, N–S charts, Petri nets, data flow graphs, structure charts, state transition diagrams, SADT diagrams, and so on. Various tools have been suggested for a program design that includes preparation of these various diagrams also. In these tools, the visual interface is intended to substitute for a conventional user interface, which employed textual commands, with an interface which is closer to our daily routine activities (such as pushing a switch, moving things, and so on). In other words, the operation target actually becomes visible, while the operation itself also becomes a visible image.

In this way, the visual interface is advancing in the program design field, both in expressing the design and in operating the design tools. Most of the papers published in the past on visual interfaces discussed the use of graphic descriptions and dealt mainly with tool functions and advantages thereof. Today, however, as visual interfaces are becoming common in computers, a discussion on which visual interface category is better is required, considering the fundamental theory and citing concrete examples. This was discussed in Refs. 1 and 2, which both deal with icons' understandability.

This chapter describes results of an investigation on how to make a visual interface effective, studying it with regard to the three aspects of design expression, tool operation (including coordination), and icon system. This chapter is expected to clarify the trend toward the introduction of visual interfaces by citing practical examples.

.This chapter is based on the following assumptions:

1. Design method merits/demerits will not be discussed. Section 2 briefly describes design method characteristics, and subsequent sections focus mainly on the reasons for introducing visual interfaces to support the design method.
2. Design expression is to be achieved by using tools.
3. An ideal computer and workstation are used that have all operating facilities at the required level. However, the display will employ the existing high-resolution (1280 × 1024 pixel) color display.

2. Design Method and Tools (Presumptions)

An outline of the design method and its tools is presented here, as a prelude to the discussion on visual interface introduction given in Section 3 and thereafter.

2.1. Characteristics of Design Method

The module design method which we have developed is called 50SM (50-step/module method). The fundamental concepts for this 50SM are as follows:

1. *Fifty-step restriction on the module.* In coding, modules as the program construction units, including process modules or data modules, shall be restricted to within 50 steps. This makes the program consistent and easy to understand at a glance, simplifies the logic, and improves program quality.
2. *Three module categories.* Module design is a method of expressing a program, using a combination of three module categories, called process, data, and package modules. Process modules contain subroutines, functions, procedural macros, etc. Data modules contain variables, constants, files, interface data for external I/O devices, etc. The third category, the package module, realizes the concept of data abstraction and library (such as a graphic-processing library, etc.) and is expressed as a set of process and data modules.
3. *Module components reuse.* Programs should be produced using a combination of module components whose quality is guaranteed.

Design description method TFF (Technical description Formula for Fifty-step/module design) has been prepared as a basis for concretely realizing all the above concepts. TFF features are as follows:

1. *Form sheets for module specifications.* Standard form sheets have been prepared for drawing out design specifications of modules and

module relation diagrams. External specifications prescribe the external behavior of a module and its effectiveness; internal specifications
prescribe the control structure and/or data structure for the module.
2. *Easily understandable design diagram.* Internal specifications are given in
the form of a design diagram, as shown in Figure 5 (details are discussed later, together with the diagram). Each box shows a process
or data and can be described in further detail using three different
hierarchical structures: sequential, repetitive, and branching, which
are symbolized by ⊐⊏ , ⧗ , and Ⅰ , respectively. When read in the
vertical direction, the relevant level can be understood. Each module
is expressed with one sheet. Its spreading to other lower modules is
expressed by ⊂⊃.

2.2. Supporting Tools Functions

We are developing a set of computer tools to support design method
5OSM. An outline of its main functions is given in the following.

1. Editor to edit form sheets.
   - Displays and edits multiple sheets concurrently.
   - Inputs and displays written Japanese.
   - Generates a module relation diagram automatically.
2. Design review support for form sheets.
   - Traces along the program control path and prepares test specifica-
     tions using path branching conditions.
   - Predicts the review end using the traced path coverage.
3. Coding while viewing the design diagrams on form sheets.
4. Operation simulation on design diagrams, at the time of the execution test.
5. Reusable module components retrieval at the time of design, and so
   on.

All these functions are centered on the design diagrams written on form
sheets and are intended to permit coding and testing while watching the
other related design diagrams, using multiple windows.

3. Visual Interface Basic Scheme

As mentioned in Section 1, it is hard to train someone, even a skilled
computer technician, in the operation of many diverse hardware and
software categories. Under these circumstances, the question of how the

visual image should be basically used to enable simple and natural communication is examined below.

3.1. Concept

To introduce visual interface in program design, three factors—semantic, syntactic, and pragmatic—which constitute the basis for visual communication[3] are defined as follows.

1. *Semantic:* The visual image meaning should be easily understood.
   - The programmer must understand the visual image meaning.
   - The visual image should be easy to remember.
   - It should not be inconsistent with established image categories.
   - It must not include images with unrelated meanings.
2. *Syntactic:* Each visual image must be consistently related to others.
   - Visual elements must permit grouping for individual applications or specific meanings and must not be inconsistent. The visual elements referred to here include shape, size, color, density and portrayed quality, combinations, action, overall performance, and so on.
   - Each visual image should be comprehensible in relation to other visual images.
   - The most important image must appear prominently.
   - The visual images flow must conform with the work flow.
3. *Pragmatic:* The visual image must be suitable to the user and his or her practice.
   - The visual image must match the user's background (nationality and experience field).
   - It must be visible from anywhere within its usage range.
   - It must not be deformed when enlarged or reduced.
   - It must not interrupt the work in progress.
   - It must not be tiring to watch.

3.2. Policy

Another major goal for the visual interface lies in improving work results without deteriorating work efficiency. For this, it is important to set the levels for ordinary textual commands and visual interface, as shown in Figure 1.

In 50SM, as mentioned in Section 2, a large number of tools will be used. Therefore, the level is set using the target shown in Figure 1 (shaded portion). In other words, the main operation is carried out using visual

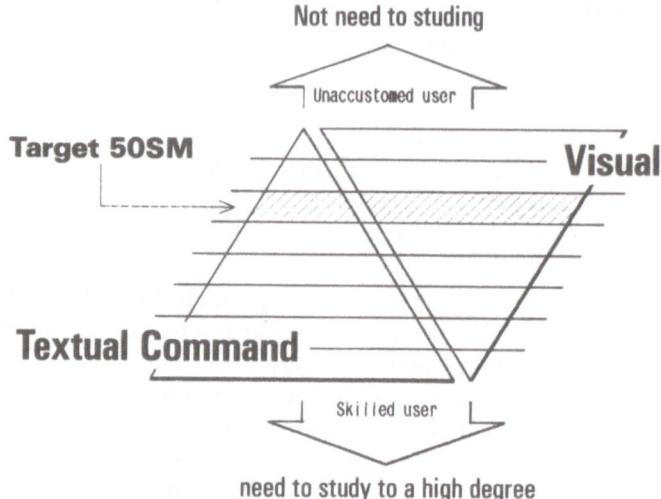

FIGURE 1. Level setting for textual command and visual factors.

interface, so that the programmer can comprehend it in a short time, while only some of the textual commands (or menus) remain.

The following presents the policy for each visual element.

1. Shape
   - Since tools support programming, a familiar image related to programming and computer (that is, the shape which comes to mind from its name and meaning) is utilized efficiently (Figure 2).
   - Simple shapes, such as a circle, a triangle, and a rectangle, are emphasized. Various concepts are expressed using different combinations of these shapes.
   - Typefaces (fonts) are selected to suit usage and the needed degree of emphasis and are retained consistently throughout the tools (Figure 3).

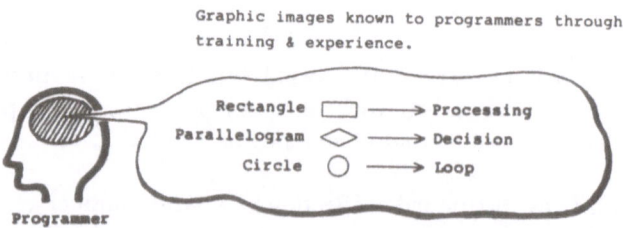

FIGURE 2. Use of graphic images known to programmer.

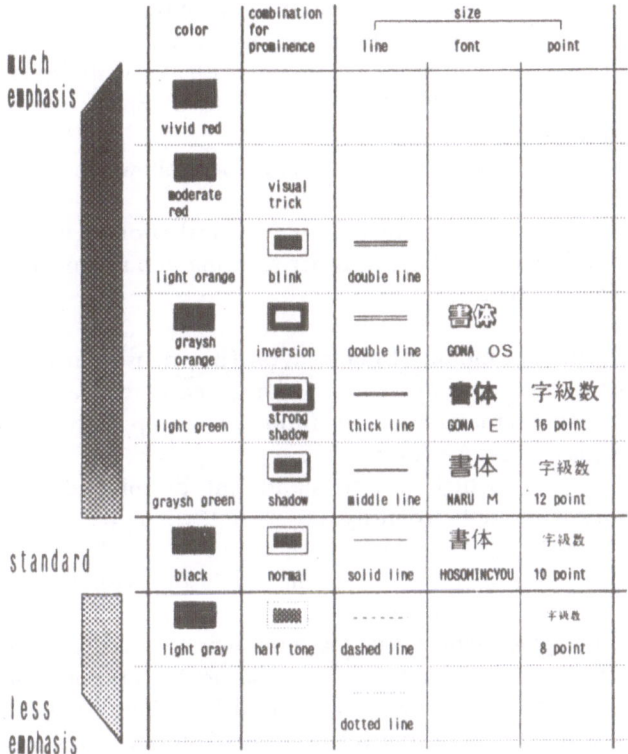

FIGURE 3. Emphatic order for visual elements.

2. Size

- Line thickness, size and kinds of characters, window size, and their interrelation are taken into account from the standpoint of human engineering, psychology, and visual design sense.
- A display window size is emphasized that can be read at once, as far as possible.
- Menus, icons, windows, and other items whose display is to be inverted are provided with thicker characters and outlines in order to make them appear prominently when inverted.

3. Color

- Dull gray tint is used as the main color, with bright gray at prominent points, to permit long hours of work.
- Characters which the user can edit are displayed in dark blue, while others are displayed in black for the purpose of easy identification.

- White backing is used in order to make the colors notable, and the colors are set in an emphatic order, as shown in Figure 3. The eight colors in Figure 3, coupled with the white background and dark blue color for characters, are used consistently.

4. Combinations
   - As a rule, the degree of prominence follows the order shown in Figure 3.
   - In display, items which have identical prominence are restricted to a maximum of 10, in order to bring about consistency and easy identification.

5. Density
   - Optimum amount of information (box density, maximum character count, and other restrictions), easy to grasp as seen from human engineering considerations, is set up in the limited areas of display, windows, and so on.
   - The parts which are to stand out prominently are shown in noticeably higher density.

6. Action
   - Operation is made rhythmic by using visual tricks (such as pop-up, blink, rubber band, and animation, etc.).
   - If the place where user's attention is focused (usually the cursor position) and the place where the next operation is to take place are far apart, they are emphasized by using visual tricks.
   - If a time lag exists between issuing of an operator's instruction and its execution, visual tricks are used to make the user feel at ease.

7. Performance
   - This is a tool which even unaccustomed users can use in a pleasant way, over long periods, employing operating techniques such as windows, icons, and pop-ups.
   - Windows, pop-ups, and boxes are shaded to create emphasis and stereoscopic image, so that they look like existing things.

4. Design Expression Visualization

Our concrete plan to make design expression visual is given below.

4.1. Module Classification

Figure 4 shows the symbols for process, data, and package module categories. In programs, rectangles and circles are generally used to express the functions, processes, data, system, status, and so on. Therefore, symbols

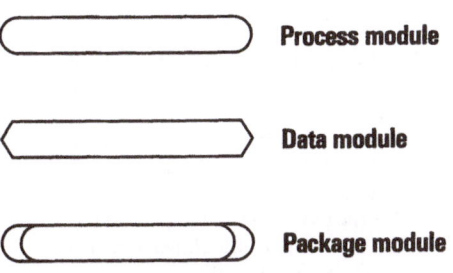

FIGURE 4. Symbols for different modules.

resembling them are used to express new module concepts possessing a component image. A concrete "hard" image is given to a data module, while the image for a package module is associated to a set of modules. Adequate horizontal space is provided inside the symbols in order to enter a 10-character module name. Names are difficult to manipulate and comprehend if they are too short or too long.

4.2. Table Form for External Specification

An example of external specification is given in the upper sheet (window) of Figure 8. Module category and name appear prominently in large size at the top left position. Descriptive text is mainly used in external specification entries. The entries are "title," "outline," "exception processing," "belong to package name," "usage format," "usage restrictions," and "reference document ID." The entries are arranged in an easily comprehensible order in table format, since they are not strongly interrelated in any specific way.

4.3. Design Diagram for Internal Specification

Items required to design diagrams are taken up as assessment items, as listed in Table 1. We came out with as many as four different proposals, from which one was selected after being assessed by both visual design experts and program experts. Figure 5 shows the final refined version.

The description for each meaningful process set or data set is enclosed within a box □. The most natural order of arranging these boxes for easily understanding them is from top to bottom along the process flow. Another important point is to clearly define their levels in order to simplify their hierarchical design/understanding. These two directions, that is, the vertical direction depicting the story and the lateral direction indicating detail entry level, are shown in Figure 5. A certain level can therefore be understood by following the range indicated by the straight line |.

TABLE 1

Design Diagram Assessment Items

Programming aspects:
    1. Easy-to-understand program flow?
    2. Simple level identification?
    3. Easy to read?
    4. One form sheet can display 20 boxes
       (which will be translated into about
       50 steps of coding)?
    5. Each symbol meaning easy to remember?

Visual design aspects:
    6. Design well rounded off?
    7. Design not old-fashioned?
    8. Diagram impression exists?
    9. Is information volume per unit area
       appropriate?
    10. Do vital parts immediately catch the
        user's eye?

Sequential, repetitive, and branching structures for process control (or data) are assigned symbols ⊟, ♟, and ♦, respectively. A rectangle depicts a straight line image, a circle depicts a loop image, and a triangle depicts a select-and-branch image. In programming, the branching structure is conspicuously different from the other two structures. Since this is an important point, it is emphasized with a deep colored (or solid) triangle.

The box is wide enough to accommodate 15 Japanese characters. More than half the descriptions per box for actual design documents are found to contain less than 15 characters. Another reason for selecting this size is that two adjacent diagrams, projecting the detail level of depth 5, are adequate, presuming the size of Japanese characters to be the smallest (8 point).

The "entry" symbol and "exit" symbol are designed in the same way as "label," because they all represent a place. In addition, the symbols for "goto label," "exit from repetition," "module call," "data reference," etc., which are box modifying symbols, are arranged laterally at the side of the box (see Figure 5).

4.4. Module Relation Diagram

As a rule, the format of the module relation diagram is identical to that for the design diagram (see Figure 6). Each module is assigned one line for displaying the module name as well as the module title. In this way, the

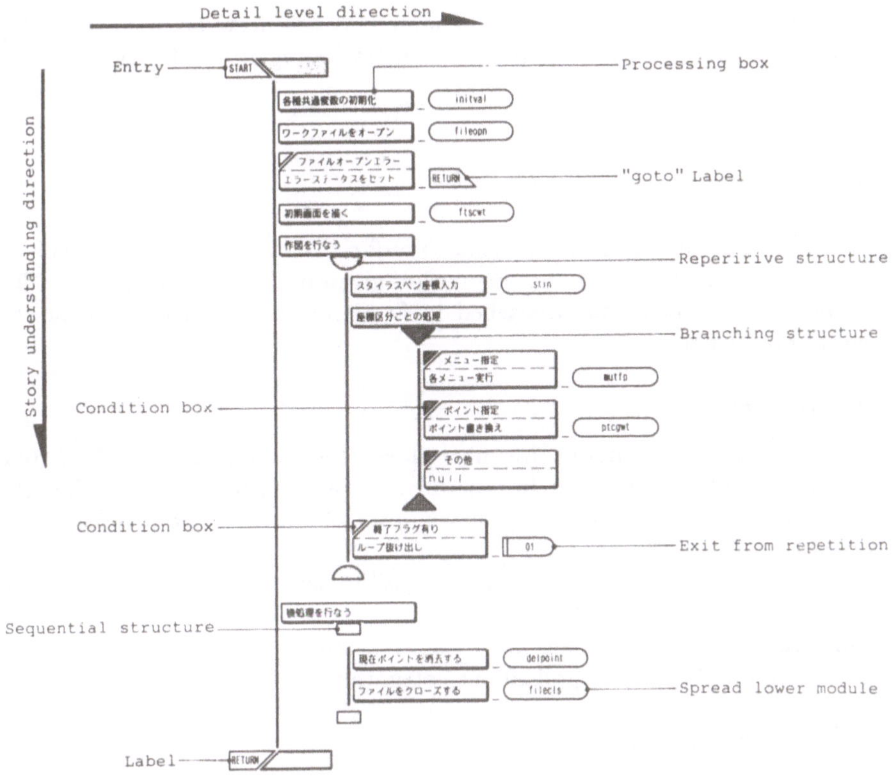

Detail level direction

Entry ——— START ——————————————— Processing box

各種共通変数の初期化 — initval

ワークファイルをオープン — fileopn

ファイルオープンエラー
エラーステータスをセット RETURN ———— "goto" Label

初期画面を描く — ftscwt

作図を行なう ——————————— Reperirive structure

スタイラスペン座標入力 — stin

座標区分ごとの処理 ——————— Branching structure

メニュー指定
各メニュー実行 — mutfo

Condition box

ポイント指定
ポイント書き換え — ptcgwt

その他
null

Condition box

終了フラグ有り
ループ抜け出し 01 ———— Exit from repetition

Sequential structure —— 後処理を行なう

現在ポイントを消去する — delpoint

ファイルをクローズする — filecls ———— Spread lower module

Label ——— RETURN

Story understanding direction

FIGURE 5. Example of design diagram.

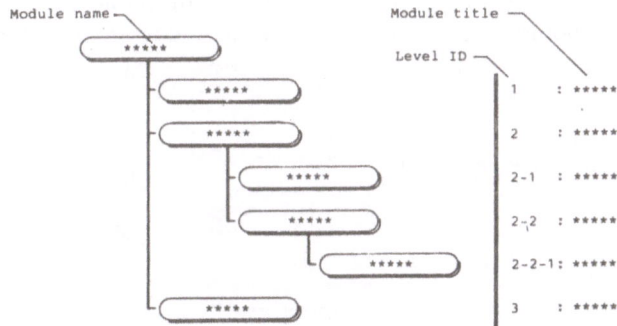

Module name ———— *****

Module title ————

Level ID ————

*****

1 : *****

*****

2 : *****

*****

2-1 : *****

*****

2-2 : *****

*****

2-2-1: *****

*****

3 : *****

FIGURE 6. Module relation diagram.

area on the right side of the module name may be effectively used to display other information regarding the module (including level ID and management data, etc.).

5. Visual Interface for Tool Operation

This section discusses the visual interface as used to operate a tool, in a way that matches the design expression given in the previous section. The visual interface principle, described in Section 3, has been applied for the entire object here.

5.1. Window Frame

The multiple window title field shows the kind of displayed module (Figure 7). The window to be operated on is indicated by changing the color (or tone for a monochrome window) of the window (title bar and frame).

The design is made as simple as possible, and a basic shape is used so as not to affect the visibility of data contained in the windows. Light gray, dull green, and dull orange are used as window frame colors, permitting easy division of specific applications categories.

5.2. Window and Sheet

As a rule, all sheet contents are displayed in the window. Therefore, the sheet appears enlarged/reduced in proportion to the window size. (However, a special command can be used to partially display or scroll through the sheet.) One reason for this proportional size is that image comprehension of the design diagram occurs prior to character reading, especially in the internal specification. Another reason is the assumption that the internal specification should not be very large in size, due to the 50-step/module restriction.

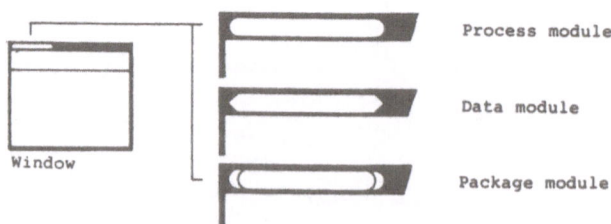

FIGURE 7. Title field in window.

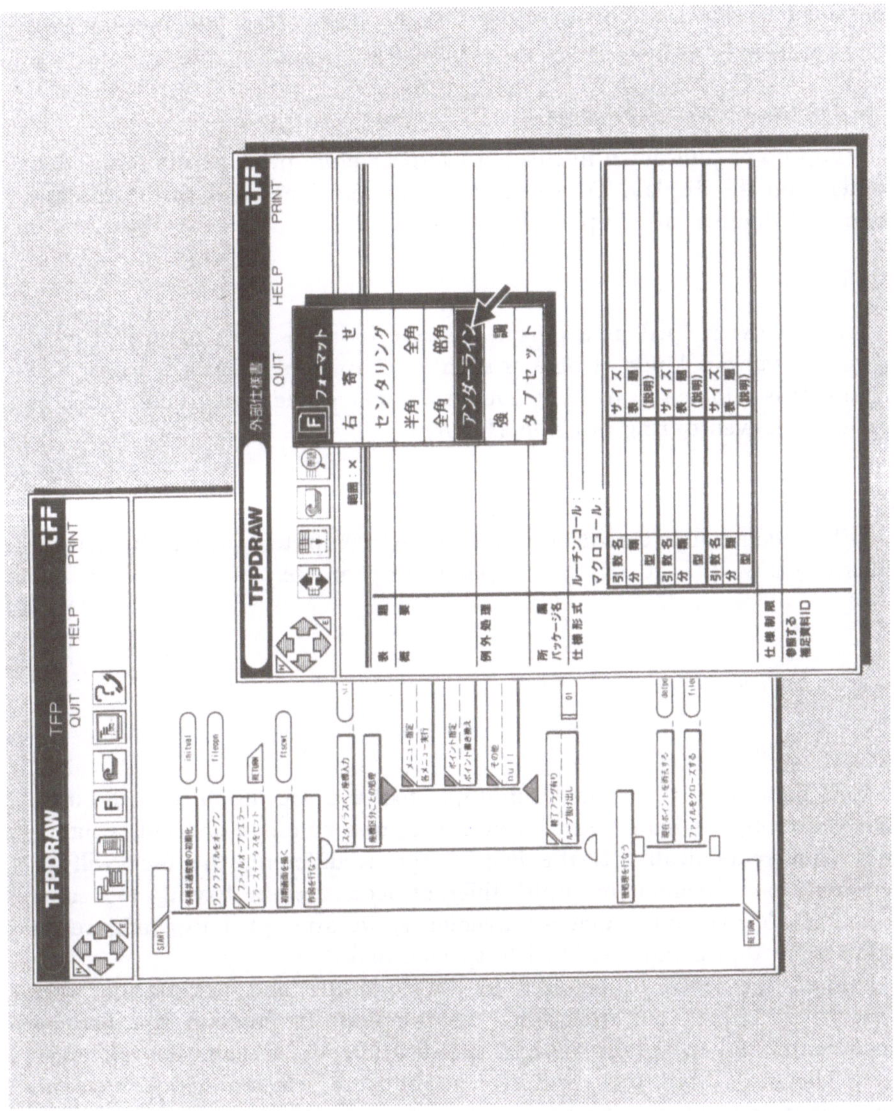

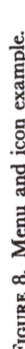

FIGURE 8. Menu and icon example.

5.3. Menu Bar and Icon

As a rule, up to 10 icons can be displayed in the menu bar. If more than 10 detail menus are involved, menus that are less frequently used are contained in one icon. By selecting this menu, relevant pull-down menus (text expression) can be called (see Figure 8).

5.4. Pop-Up or Pull-Down Menu

Pop-up or pull-down menus must appear more prominently than other contents on the display. To accomplish this, the same color as the window color and shadows are employed (Figure 8).

5.5. Cursor

An arrow is used as a cursor, because it is the most natural way to point out various kinds of objects such as characters, windows, icons, and menus. It is dull red to make it noticeable against the background (such as a window), even during fast shift (Figure 8).

5.6. Point for Characters (Pointing Symbol)

The rectangular cursor usually found on computers (inside character is inversed) is used, as it only has to point out characters.

6. Icon Systemization

6.1. Icon System

As mentioned in Section 2, multiple tool sets are supplied to the user. Between tools, the icons must be shown using a common concept semantically and syntactically. If the icon design is different, the user will be required to remember multiple different icon designs having the same meaning. To overcome such inconvenience, we attempted to configure an icon system that is not restricted to specific tools.

First, the terms to be used in the computer and workstation were systemized. Expressions describing the functions in function specification documents and program design specification documents for all tools were checked. From this, primitive terms were selected which have no dependence on any specific applications. As a result, some groups of terms were formed, as shown in Table 2, taking into account the operation and object aspects.

Icons were prepared expressing the meaning of each of these terms.

TABLE 2
Term Systematization[a]

Operation terms grouping	Object terms grouping
Input/output	Character
Check	Data
Edit	Graph
Calculate	Medium
Manage	Device
Set	Resource
Move	Value
Control	Code
Send	System

[a] Only group names are indicated. For the terms included in each group, see the Appendix.

Maximum priority was given to semantics. Next, the images inside each group were made, taking into account their syntactic factors (in preparing icons, identical shape was used for interrelated terms). The term system was prepared first so as to prevent generation of identical expressions having different meanings in any one group. For details about the icon system, see the Appendix.

The icon system devised here is intended to constantly play the motif role. In other words, the icons to be used with actual tools will be refined in design to match the demanded display performance (resolution and color capacity) and the type and nature of applications. In either case, however, the refining will be done to match the existing circumstances, while inheriting the element which most forcefully expresses the meaning (usually the shape). Figure 9 shows an example of such design refinement which inherits the nature of its application. The image of " + " is seen inherited. Of course, if the motif is equipped with excellent semantics and syntactics, it becomes identical to the design-refined icon.

6.2. Icon System Evaluation

The following two experiments were conducted to evaluate the icon system semantics and syntactics.

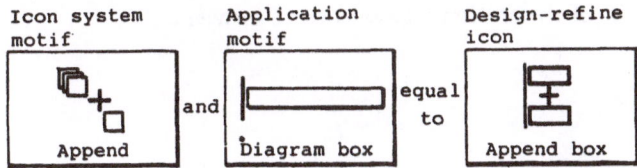

FIGURE 9. Example showing design refinement from icon system.

Subjects. The subjects were 27 students who had received programming training. Of these, 12 participated in experiment 1, and 15 participated in experiment 2.

Experiment 1 (Semantics Evaluation). Experiment 1 was conducted twice. In the first experiment, the students were given independent icons and asked to write down their meanings freely, after being told only that the icons are used in relation to computers and for program design. In the second experiment, the students were told the meaning of each icon, and the same experiment was conducted one week later with the same students. The icon system was evaluated using a total of 81 icons from levels 1 and 2. (For details on levels, see the Appendix.) To prevent the icon from being evaluated in a certain context, questions were asked at random after dividing the students into several groups.

Experiment 2 (Syntactics Evaluation). The students were shown in advance about 20 icons together with their meanings and were then presented (a large number of) other icons in the form of a question and were asked to write down the meanings they associated with the 20 icons shown.

The system was evaluated by using a total of 30 icons in levels 1 to 3. For icons whose meanings were shown in advance, ones with primitive shape and meaning were selected from the total. It was presumed that the students had already memorized them.

Results of Experiment 1. About 49.4% of the students gave correct answers in the first experiment; about 81.6% gave correct answers in the second experiment conducted one week later (Figure 10). This showed that simple study enabled the students to understand the meaning of the icons.

The experimental results are listed in Table 3. The results of the first experiment are marked with "|," and results of the second experiment results are marked with "○." Marks "|" and "○" set apart indicate icons whose meaning is easy to learn.

In Table 3, the answers are ranked semantically from A to D:

Rank A. In the first experiment, more than 70% of the students gave correct answers.

Rank B. In the second experiment, more than 70% of the students gave correct answers.

Rank C. In the second experiment, more than 30% and less than 70% of the students gave correct answers.

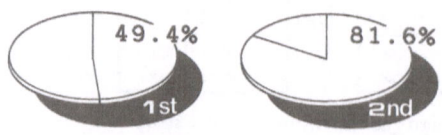

49.4%   81.6%
1st   2nd

FIGURE 10. Correct answers in experiment 1.

TABLE 3

Semantic Evaluation Result

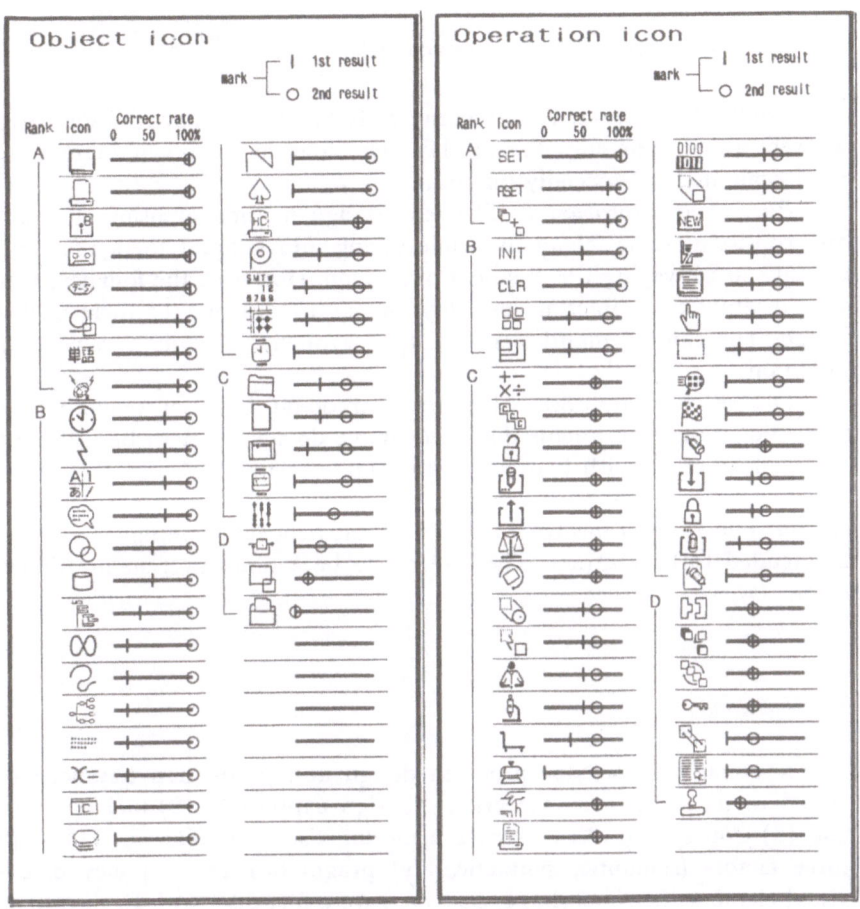

Rank D. In the second experiment, less than 30% of the students gave correct answers.

Remarks on Experiment 1. Object icons accounted for most of those evaluated as good semantically. Of these, icons symbolizing a concrete object are superior semantically while icons using an abstract motif are semantically inferior. In the preparation of icons, object ones are preferable because they are easier to comprehend.

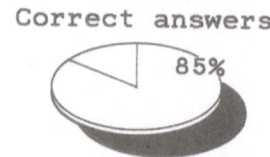

FIGURE 11. Correct answers in experiment 2.

Results of Experiment 2. As many as 85% of the students gave correct answers about syntactics (Figure 11). The four icons shown in Figure 12 were evaluated as especially inferior.

Remarks on Experiment 2. The icon design method of using systematic and consistent visual elements, while taking into account the syntactics, is effective in conveying the meaning of an icon. However, the four icons that were evaluated as inferior lost their semantics because of their uniform image. Therefore, semantics, rather than syntactics, should receive major attention.

Problems and Reflection. There is a trade-off between semantics and syntactics. The experiments discussed above do not seem to be sufficiently thorough to distinguish between and evaluate them.

A term system was used here as the starting point in creating the icon system. Therefore, it has been affected by the delicate meanings of term and has tended to be abstract. There seems to be a different systemization for icons.

7. Conclusion

A visual interface for program design and production has been discussed in terms of three aspects: (1) design expression, (2) tool operation, and (3) icon system. As a basic scheme for visual interface for (1) to (3), three factors (semantic, syntactic, and pragmatic) and a policy of even visual elements (such as shape, size, etc.) were first discussed. Each proposal for (1) and (2) was then given with clear reasons. For aspect (3), an icon (motif) system was proposed in order to uniformly use icons with a set of tools. Practical experiments revealed that this icon system has good semantics and syntactics, but also has some problems.

FIGURE 12. Worst icons.

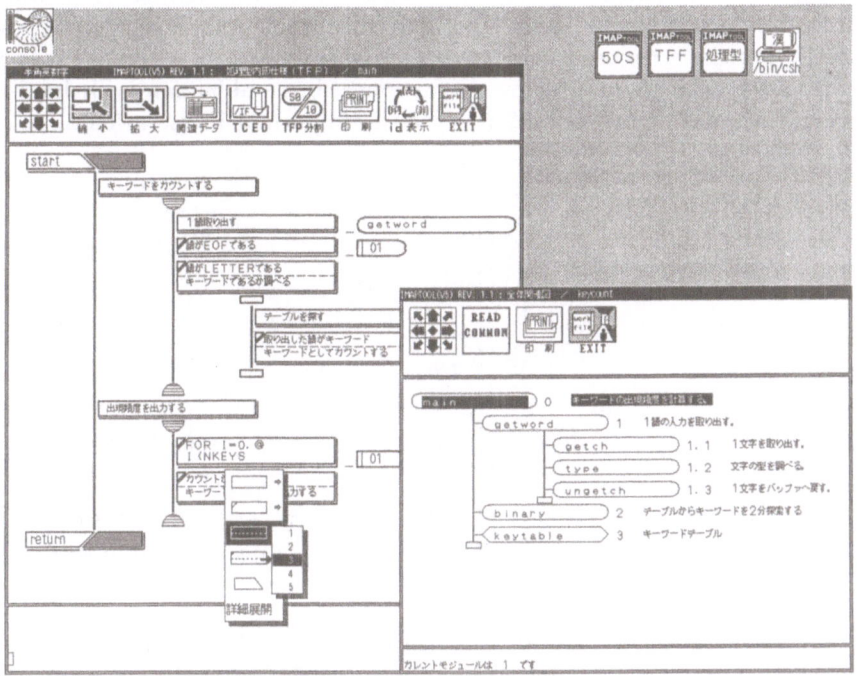

FIGURE 13. CRT display example.

Tools are developed for program design and production. Figure 13 shows a CRT display example of a tool. Ideal results, as stated in this paper, cannot be achieved due to current software and hardware restrictions. In the future, we intend to refine the tools, conforming to the visual interface submitted here.

We intend to refine the icon system, not only for the tools described, but also to make it entirely applicable to any software tools.

Appendix: Icon System Example

An icon system can be divided into two categories: operation icons (verb) and object icons (noun). For both of these, the terms used in program design and production, as well as in its support tools, are well defined as a three-level-system. The standard icon motif is also matched with the term system. Level-1 terms are top-level abstract terms, divided into nine categories for operation icons, and into nine categories for object icons. Level-2 terms are concrete terms that are included in level-1 terms. Level-3 terms show examples of expressing functions, in combination with level-2 terms (verb and noun). Level-2 is especially important in use as motif.

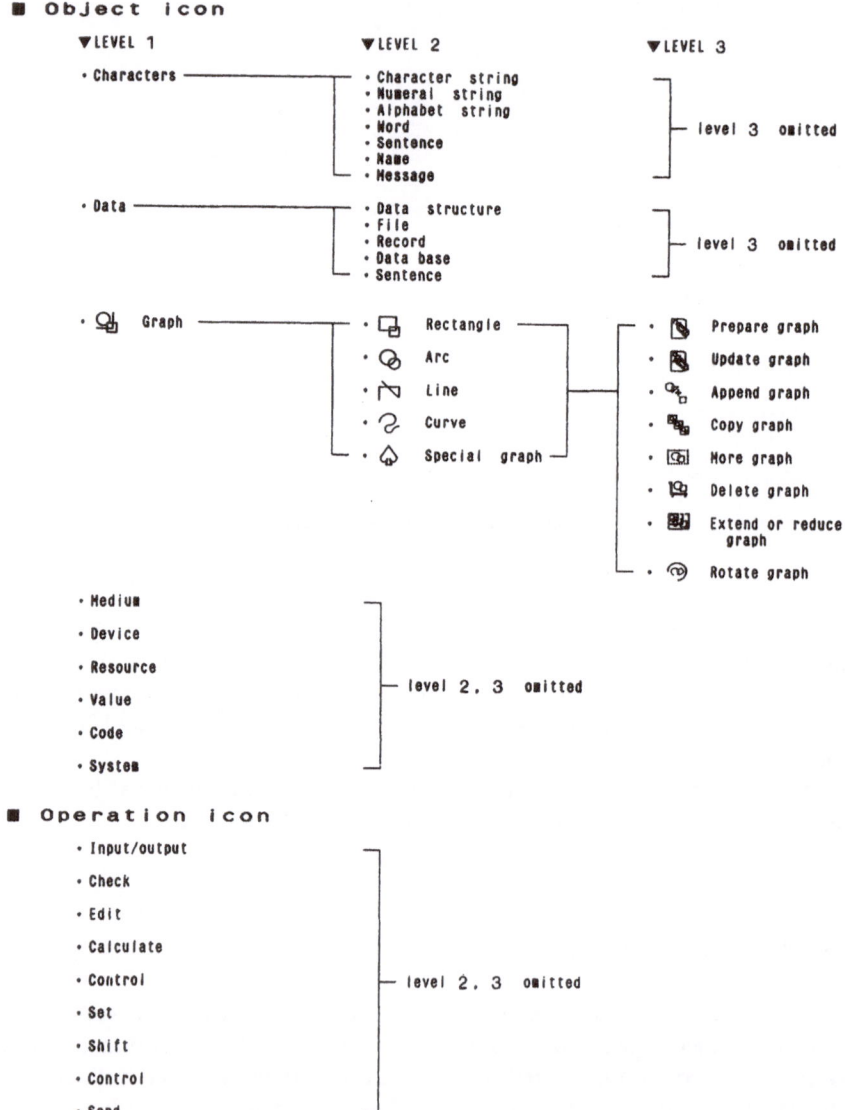

Acknowledgments

We are extremely grateful to Professors K. Hiramatsu and S. Moriya of Tokyo Denki University for their valuable advice concerning the assessment of the icon system, and for providing student subjects for the experiments. We also appreciate the cooperation of Mr. Igarashi of the Design Division, Toshiba Corp., and Murakoshi Aisaku Design Co. in deciding on the design diagram and the icon system. And we would be remiss not to mention the assistance of Mr. Takahashi and Mr. Ishikawa of the Systems & Software Engineering Laboratory, Toshiba Corp., in providing the original of a term system and other informative comments.

References

1. *The Seybold Report*, Vol. 10, No. 16, April 27, 1981.
2. G. ROHR, Understanding visual symbols, IEEE Computer Society Workshop on Visual Languages, December 1984, pp. 184–198.
3. Symbol Signs, prepared by the American Institute of Graphic Arts New York, and the U.S. Department of Transportation, 1975.

6

HI-VISUAL ICONIC PROGRAMMING ENVIRONMENT

M. Hirakawa, M. Tanaka, and T. Ichikawa

Abstract

We earlier proposed a visual programming language, HI-VISUAL. HI-VISUAL supports visual interaction in programming whereby objects such as data and functions are represented in terms of icons. Programming is carried out simply by arranging icons on the display screen.

In this paper, we extend HI-VISUAL as an environment for iconic programming by providing the following facilities: (1) navigation for program development and system operations, (2) interpretation mechanisms for icon programs and system operations, based on the object-oriented concept, (3) top-down and bottom-up development of programs, and (4) integration of existing (sub)systems.

The architecture of HI-VISUAL for programming, execution, and management of icon programs will also be presented.

1. Introduction

Even users specialized in a particular field of computer application may not be familiar with computers and will therefore be faced with difficulties in making programs because conventional programming languages have a text-based syntax, for which professional knowledge and experience in programming are required. The purpose of our study, then, is to develop a user-friendly programming environment which is easy to use for nonexpert

M. HIRAKAWA, M. TANAKA, and T. ICHIKAWA • Faculty of Engineering, Hiroshima University, Higashi-Hiroshima 724, Japan.

programmers and requires less experience in programming and systems operation.

One approach to attaining this is the utilization of visual information in programming.[1] The user makes a program through visual interaction with the system. This kind of interaction scheme can be broadly termed a "visual language." In visual languages, information to be visualized is (1) an object such as file, data, and program, (2) an algorithm of the program, or (3) a data structure.

Star[2] and Macintosh are examples of category 1 in which objects are visualized by means of icons. SDL/PAD[3] and state transition diagram language,[4] which visualize algorithms in the form of Problem Analysis Diagrams (PAD) and state transition diagrams, respectively, are examples of category 2. The systems in category 3 visualize data structure by means of forms or graphics. QBE[5] and form languages[6,7] are examples.

There are also systems which work with combinations of categories 1, 2, and 3. Pict,[8] Tinkertoy,[9] and construction game kits (pinball games, for example) support both 1 and 2. An example of systems which support 1 and 3 is ISIS-V.[10] PECAN[11] and VISE[12] are examples of systems supporting both 2 and 3.

In the visual programming environment HI-VISUAL we present here, object, algorithm, and data structure are visualized by means of the icon, data flow graph, and spatial placement of icons, respectively.

HI-VISUAL, first proposed as a language supporting visual interaction in programming,[13] is extended in this chapter as an environment for iconic programming by providing the following facilities: (1) navigation for program development and system operations, (2) interpretation mechanisms for icon programs and system operations, based on the object-oriented concept, (3) top-down and bottom-up development of programs, and (4) integration of existing (sub)systems.

HI-VISUAL's architecture for programming, execution, and management of icon programs will also be presented.

In Section 2, a formal definition of the icon is given. Programming and system facilities in HI-VISUAL are described in Sections 3 and 4, respectively. Implementational issues of HI-VISUAL are given in Sections 5, 6, and 7. In Section 5, an organization of the system is described. Interpretation mechanisms for icon programs and system operations are presented in Sections 6 and 7, respectively.

2. Icon Definition

Icons represent the objects to be managed in the system, such as files, data, and programs. In HI-VISUAL, an icon consists of two parts: *internal* and *external.* The *internal* part gives the meaning of the object the icon represents; the *external* part is a visualization of the meaning and is displayed on the display screen.

The *internal* part consists of three attributes: *substance, concept,* and *type. Substance* represents the functional description or value of an object. *Concept* gives the conceptual name of an icon. It is utilized for navigation of iconic programming and classification/retrieval of icons. *Type* represents the type of an icon and is classified into the following seven types, as shown in Figure 1.

  a. DATA: An icon which represents data, such as characters, numbers, and images.
  b. DATA CLASS: An icon which represents the class of data. Data class is similar to the class in the object-oriented concept and manages not only a data type but also functions applicable to data items which belong to the data type. Data classes are managed hierarchically according to their semantics; then functions are inherited along the data class hierarchy.
  c. PANEL: An icon which represents a display space for the management of a set of icons. Panel is similar to the directory of a conventional file system. A window and a menu are regarded as the panel. A panel can contain icons which represent panels, and thus panels form the hierarchy of panels.

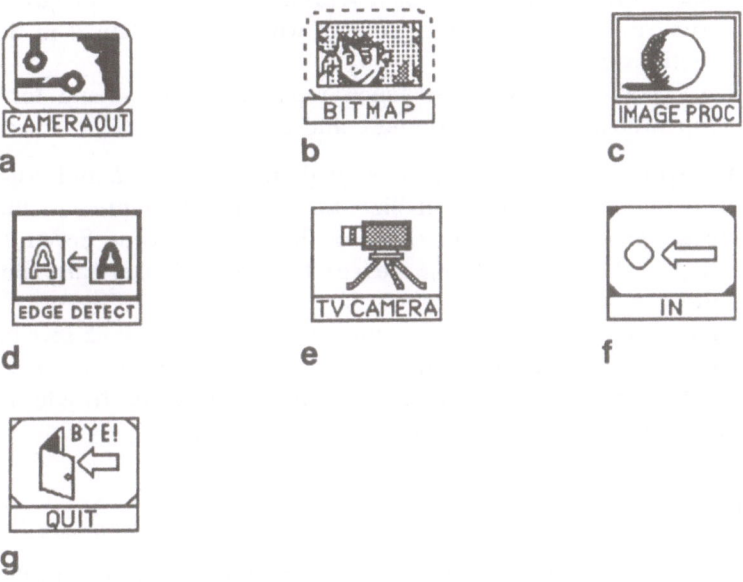

FIGURE 1. Icon types.

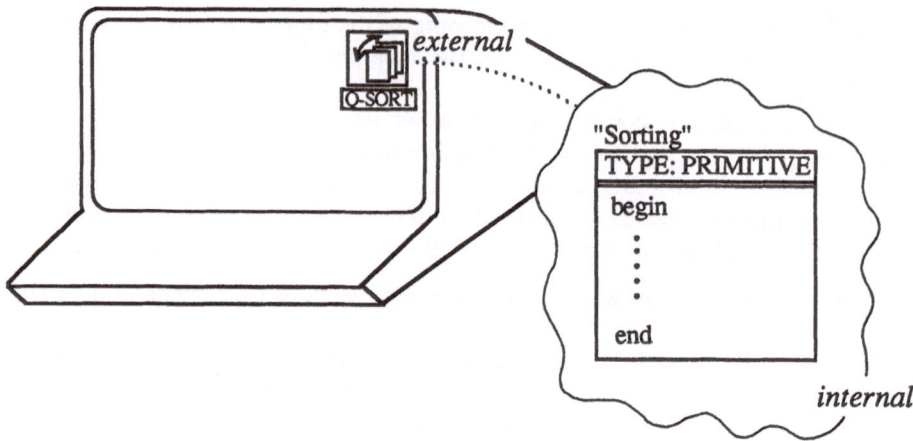

FIGURE 2. An example of *internal* and *external* parts of an icon.

d. PROGRAM: An icon which represents an icon program specified by the user.

e. PRIMITIVE: An icon which represents a basic program which is prepared by the system designer as a built-in function. Both program icons and primitive icons will hereafter be referred to as function icons.

f. CONTROL: An icon which represents the control of flow of data such as loop and switch, both of which are explained in Section 3 with examples.

g. COMMAND: An icon which represents a command for system operations, such as run, undo, and exit.

The *external* part consists of three attributes: *image, label,* and *shape. Image* represents the image which symbolizes an object. *Label* represents the name of an icon. *Shape* represents the shape of the frame of icons. Seven different shapes are defined depending on the icon type, and these are also illustrated in Figure 1.

Figure 2 shows an example of the icon in which a quick sort program is represented. The program code located between begin and end is the *substance.* "Sorting" is the *concept,* and the *type* is primitive. In addition, 🎏 is the *image,* Q-SORT is the *label,* and □ is the *shape.*

3. Programming Facilities

HI-VISUAL provides interactive, icon-based programming facilities. In this section, we explain how programming is carried out in HI-VISUAL.

3.1. Iconic Programming

HI-VISUAL supports multi-windows on the display. Figure 3 shows the display organization. A window on which an icon program is specified is called an iconic programming window. The iconic programming window is composed of the following two areas:

1. Programming Area: An area for creating an icon program.
2. Stack Area: An area for displaying program icons which are being edited in the programming area.

In addition to the iconic programming window, the system also displays an icon menu window and a pop-up command menu window.

Programming is carried out in HI-VISUAL as follows.

First, the user selects an icon from the icon menu by using a pointing device such as a mouse and locates it at a suitable place in the programming area. If the icon is a function icon, its output is presented to the user. At this time, when the icon is executable, the system activates it immediately to

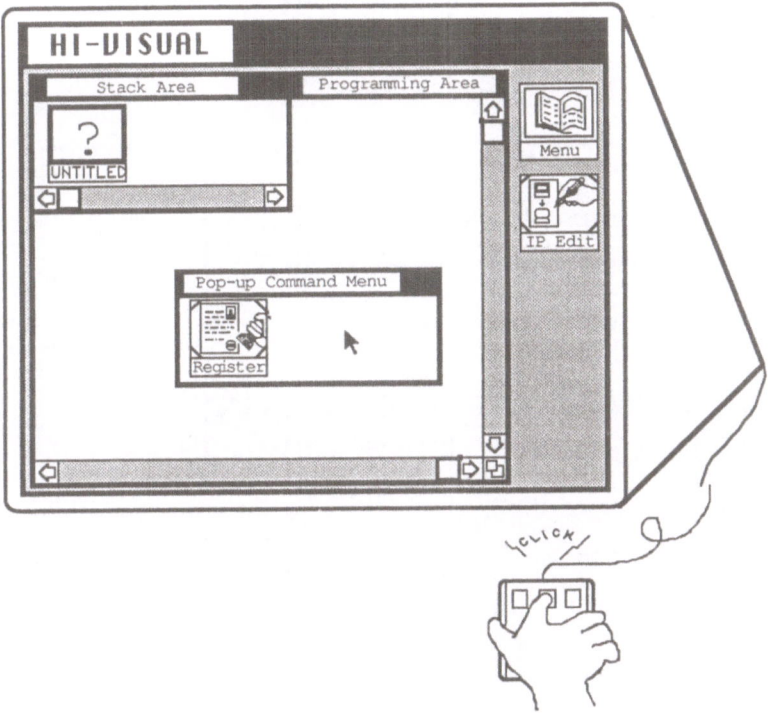

FIGURE 3. Display organization.

execute the associated function and displays the miniaturized representation of the resultant data. On the other hand, if the function icon is not executable, the system displays a data class of the resultant data. Here, the term "executable" means either (1) no input data of the icon is needed or (2) all input data have already been provided.

Next, the user selects and places another icon on the screen and specifies connections between icons to form the necessary flow of data. The system executes the icon and displays the resultant data on the screen in the way described above.

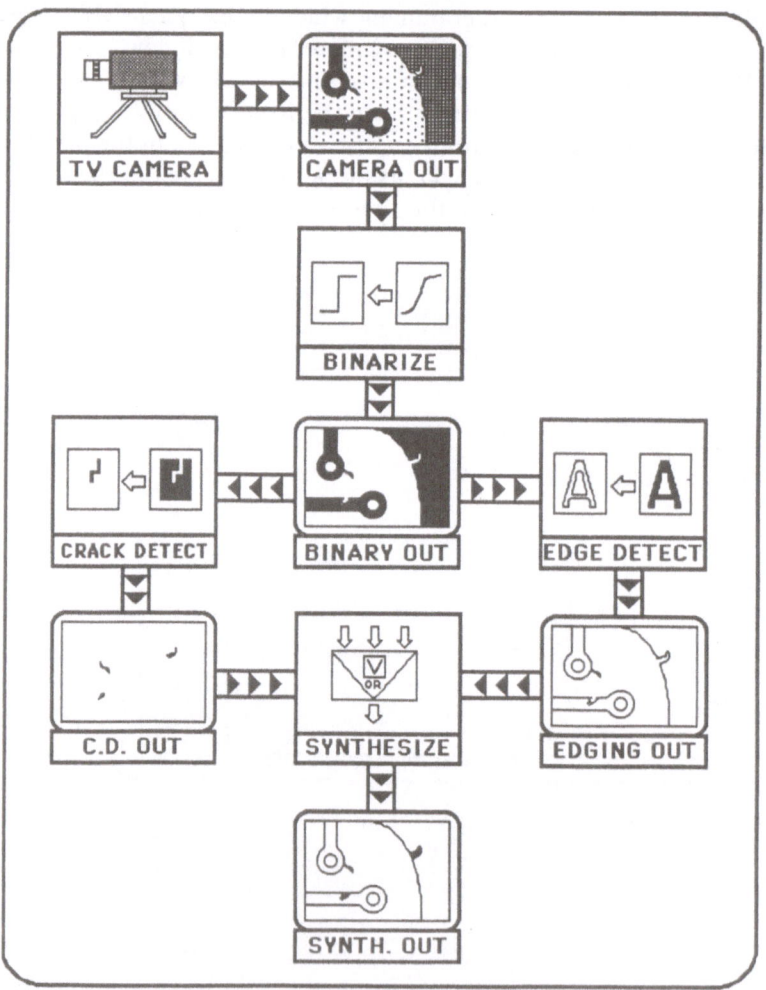

FIGURE 4. An example of an icon program.

The procedures described above are repeated until the program development is completed. The user can make a program by confirming the program behavior interactively at every step of program development. If the result does not meet the user's intention, the user can replace the icons previously specified with others.

Figure 4 shows an example of the icon program, an image processing routine for the detection of cracks in an input image. The function specified by this program is as follows. First, the image which is taken from the TV camera is binarized by the application of the BINARIZE icon. The binary image is then applied to both CRACK DETECT and EDGE DETECT icons. Finally, both of the resultant data (C.D. OUT icon and EDGING OUT icon) are applied to the SYNTHESIZE icon, which performs the logical OR operation. SYNTH.OUT is the final result obtained on completion of the program execution.

HI-VISUAL also provides two types of control icons: a loop icon for specifying the iteration of procedures and a switch icon for specifying the change of the flow of data. Loop icons are either counter loop or conditional loop.

In a counter loop, the number of iterations is specified by using a data icon. Figure 5 shows an example of a counter loop in which the value of the fifth power of 2 is calculated. The process specified in the square is repeated until the number of iterations reaches the iteration condition. Two input data (initially, both set to 2) are multiplied by each other. The intermediate result and the data from an input are brought back to the inputs. When this process is repeated four times, the program outputs the final result (value of 32), as shown in the figure.

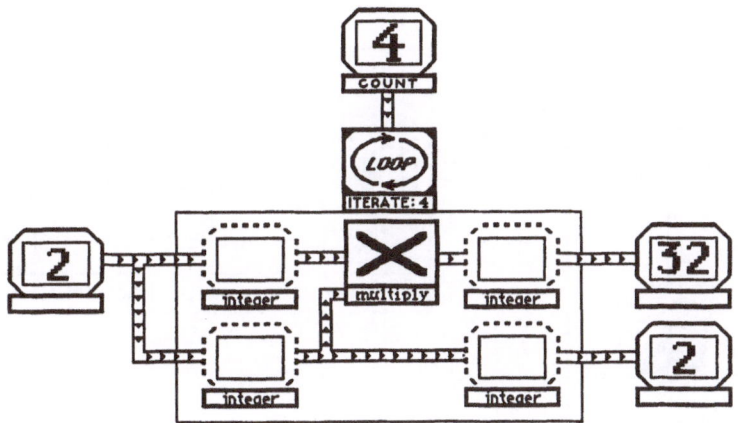

FIGURE 5. An example of a loop icon (counter loop).

Figure 6 shows an example of a conditional loop for neutralizing a sample liquid. In this example, the sample is assumed to be an alkaline liquid. The comparison condition is specified by icons as shown in the figure. Acid is gradually added to the sample until it becomes neutral.

Figure 7 shows an example of switch icons. As for conditional loop icons, the conditional part is specified by icons. If the comparison condition in the switch icon is true (the sample is alkaline), input data to the switch icon are transferred to the icon connected to the $\sqrt{}$-side of the switch. Otherwise (the sample is acid), input data are transferred to the icon connected to the ×-side of the switch.

In an iconic programming system, since an icon program is specified by the arrangement of existing icons, the applicability of the system basically depends on the set of primitive icons provided. If the primitive icons for image processing are available, programs for new image processing applica-

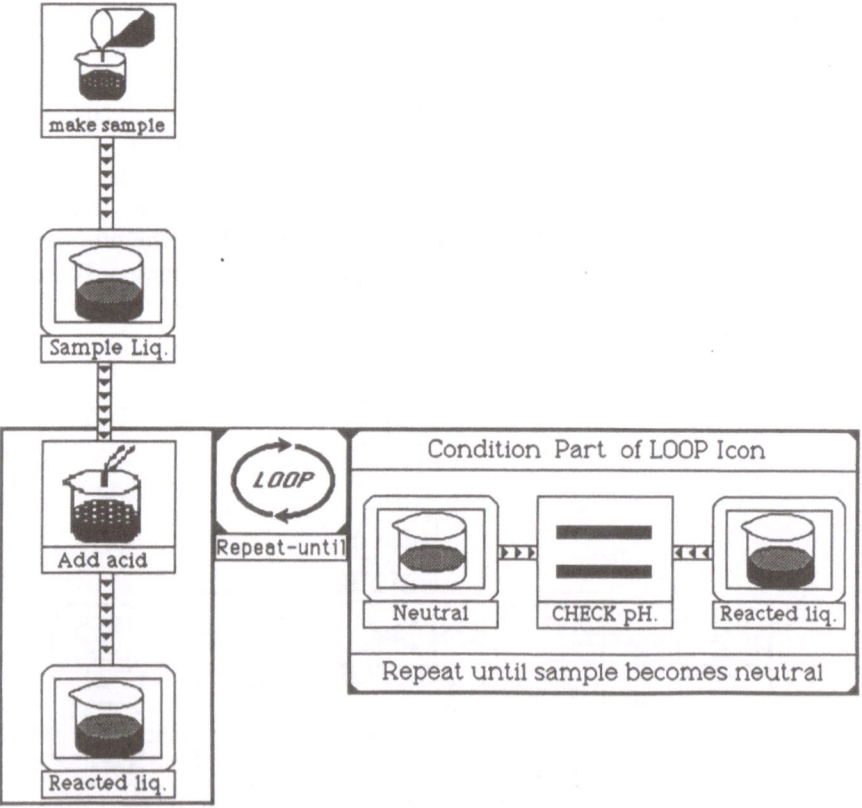

FIGURE 6. An example of a loop icon (conditional loop).

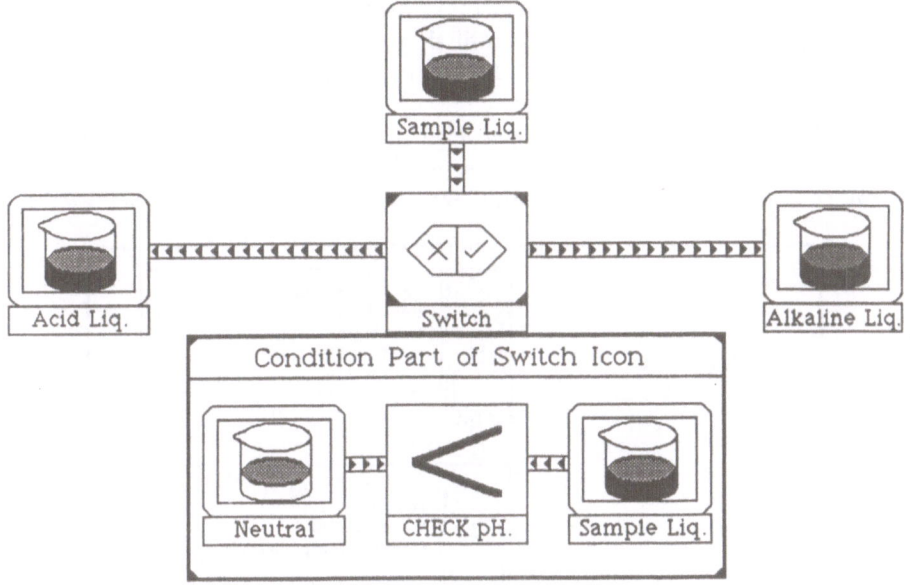

FIGURE 7. An example of a switch icon.

tions can be developed by the system. If the primitive icons for office information processing are available, programs for execution of higher-level office
procedures can be developed by the system. In HI-VISUAL, a tool for defining
primitive icons is provided. Details of the tool will be explained in Section 5.

3.2. Bottom-Up and Top-Down Development

Interactive programming capability is applied to HI-VISUAL as we
described in the previous subsection. Programs are specified through the
help of a demonstration showing an example of the execution. This
"programming-by-example" scheme[14] is effective especially when the
system is applied to an environment where tasks are not well defined in
advance of the program development. The program which is created by the
user can be defined as a new (program) icon at a higher level of program
abstraction and used to create a new program. However, since interpretation and execution of icons are carried out repeatedly during the process of
program development, the user is hindered by the fact that (1) execution
speed decreases and (2) precise specifications of the program have to have
been completed before implementation of the program starts. These
problems seem to be serious when the size of a program is fairly large.

Capability of program development based on the top-down approach is provided as a countermeasure to these problems. Details of the program modules can be left unspecified until they become clear in the lower level of module hierarchy. Figure 8 shows an example of top-down program development.

The user first makes an upper-level program by defining input/output parameters (data classes) of program icons in a lower level and specifying connections between them. In this example, DATA1 results from PRG1,

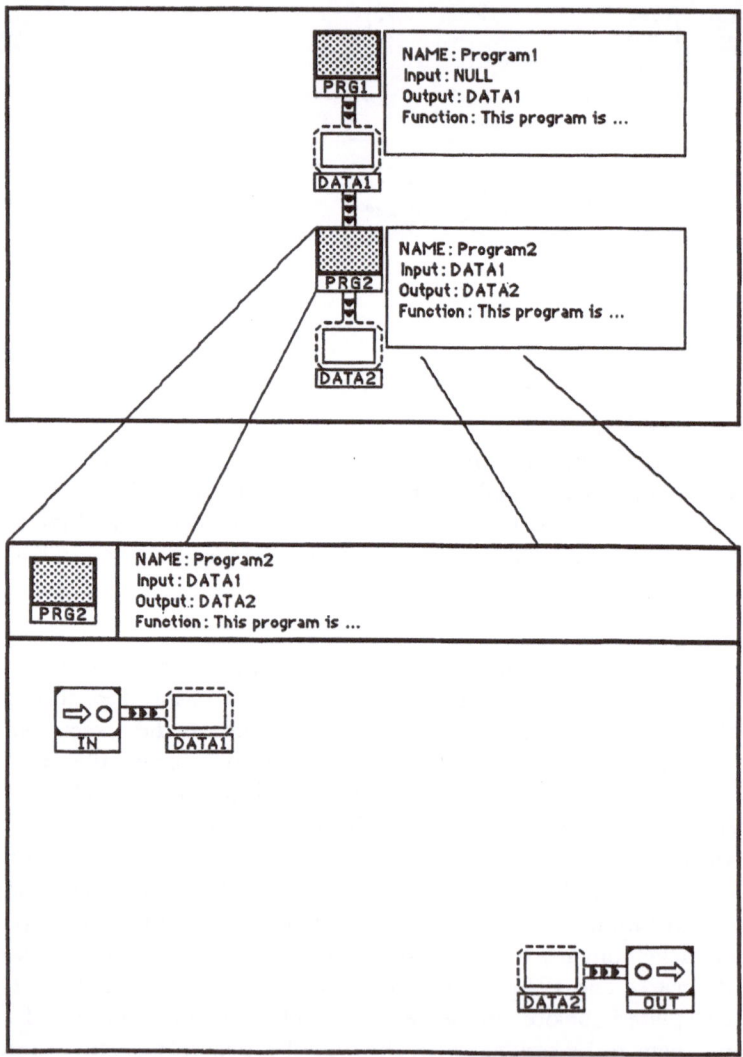

FIGURE 8. An example of top-down programming.

and DATA2 results from PRG2 with DATA1 as its input. Here it is noted that DATA1 and DATA2 are both data class icons, since input values have not been provided at this time. Small windows appear beside the program icons for the specification of program modules.

Next, when the user clicks a program icon, a new window appears in which details of the program in a lower level are specified. The program icon which is going to be edited is displayed at the upper-left corner of the window. Details of the program are specified in the program area, in which input and output parameters (data classes) are presented to the user so that the consistency is kept on data classes of upper- and lower-level programs.

4. System Facilities

HI-VISUAL provides two types of navigation facilities. One is for iconic programming, and the other for system operations.

In programming navigation, the system displays a list of all candidate icons that can be used at each step in programming. The user can make a program interactively by asking the system which icons can be used. For this purpose, an icon-based browser is provided in the system.

When a particular data icon or data class icon is specified, the browser displays the following information: (1) the specified icon itself, (2) candidate primitive/program icons which can be connected to the specified data or data class, (3) superclass and subclasses of the specified data class, (4) class values of the specified data class, and (5) class methods of the specified data class.

The user selects an icon displayed in the browser and continues the programming. If the expected icon is not found, the user selects a superclass icon in the superclass field and then browses through the class hierarchy until he gets the expected function icon.

Navigation for system operation helps the user know (1) the system reaction in response to the user's action, such as pressing a mouse button and moving the cursor and (2) the system commands which can be used depending on the cursor position. Furthermore, the system accepts the combination of (1) and (2). Interpretation mechanisms of the navigation will be described in Section 7.

HI-VISUAL also provides capability to integrate existing (sub)systems. In HI-VISUAL, a (sub)system is represented as an application icon which is one of the command icons. The application icon is defined syntactically as the combination of a window on which the (sub)system runs and a command menu containing commands which the (sub)system accepts. The *substance* of an application icon is the executable routine of the corresponding (sub)system.

Input/output of the (sub)system is directed to the window on which the (sub)system runs, and the user interface of the (sub)system is changed to an icon-based interface. An advantage of the system integration in HI-VISUAL, therefore, is that it provides a unified user interface for the different (sub)systems. HI-VISUAL is expanded to a larger system by getting existing (sub)systems as application icons.

The precise mechanism of system integration will be described in Section 7.

5. System Organization

A prototype system of HI-VISUAL is implemented on a workstation. An organization of the system is shown in Figure 9. The system consists of five components: Kernel, Inference Engine (IE), Icon Execution Manager (IEM), Icon System Manager (ISM), and Icon Tools (IT).

1. *Kernel:* Kernel supports system primitives, such as process control, device handling, display and window management, and database management.

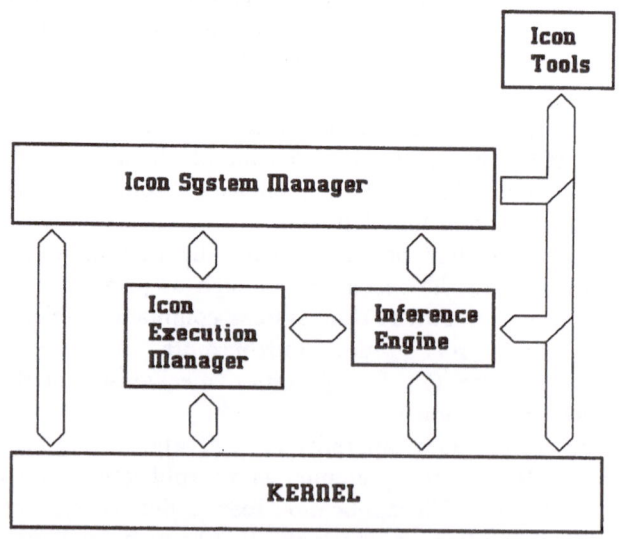

FIGURE 9. System organization.

2. *Inference Engine (IE):* IE supports the following four facilities in connection with the database management system in Kernel:

   a. *Interpretation of user's action:* The way the user's action is interpreted may vary according to the situation. In the system, interpretation of user's action varies depending on the current state and the history of states.

   b. *Classification/management of icons:* Icons are classified and managed according to both *types* and *concepts*. This makes it possible, for example, for the system to retrieve icons effectively.

   c. *Reply to a help request:* IE works to offer adequate help messages in response to the user level in cooperation with Help System in IT (as described below). The user level is changed by the user himself or by the system dynamically according to the frequency of errors, the nature of the errors, etc.

   d. *Navigation of the user's action:* IE supports navigation in programming and manipulation of the system. For example, it navigates the selection of an icon to be applied and informs the user of system reaction in response to the user's action.

3. *Icon Execution Manager (IEM):* IEM manages the interpretation and the execution of icons. When an icon placed on the programming area is executable, IEM requests the process controller in Kernel to generate processes for the execution of the icon.

4. *Icon System Manager (ISM):* ISM plays the central role in the system and supervises the other four components. The facilities in ISM are the management of icons currently displayed on the screen, interpretation of the user's action in cooperation with IE, and invocation of the components to carry out the user's request.

5. *Icon Tools (IT):* IT provides useful tools for iconic programming and manipulation of the system. There are six tools as described below.

   a. *Icon Image Editor (IIE):* IIE is a graphic editor for creating icon images.

   b. *Primitive Binder (PB):* PB is used when the system designer defines the primitive icons. Figure 10 shows the process of primitive icon definition. The existing application source code program written in a conventional programming language is attached to the communication source code program, and the combined code is compiled into an object code program. PB binds an icon image created by using IIE to the object code program. After that, the system designer defines a data class to which the primitive icon belongs.

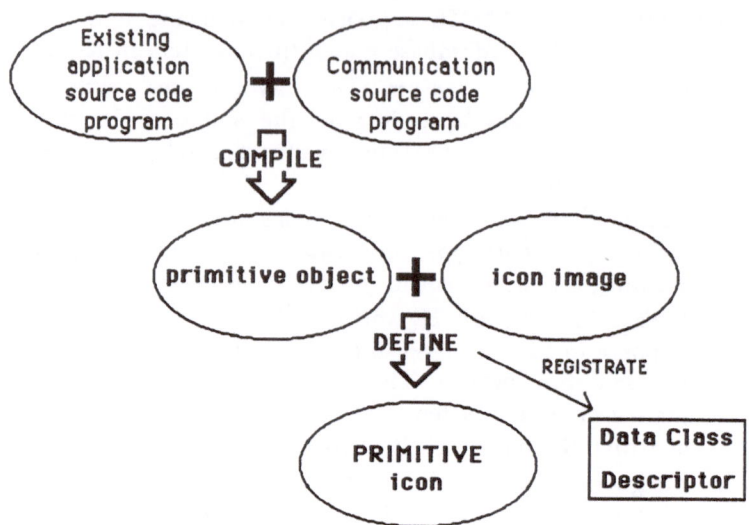

FIGURE 10. Definition of primitive icons by using PB.

c. *Browser (BR):* BR is an icon-based browser which helps the user retrieve icons, as described in Section 4.

d. *Help System (HS):* HS works in cooperation with IE to offer adequate help messages to the user, according to the state of the system and the user's experience level.

e. *User Interface Designer (UID):* UID is provided so as to allow the user to define a user-oriented interface. Specifically, UID is a tool for specifying rules which are used in IE. For example, functions which are assigned to each button of the mouse could be changed by replacing each rule corresponding to the action with another rule.

f. *Application Binder (AB):* AB is used when the system designer defines an application icon associated with an application window on which a (sub)system runs. Figure 11 shows the process by which the (sub)system is integrated. AB binds an icon image created by using IIE to a sending routine of a command sequence which is applicable to the (sub)system and defines them as a command icon. After all the commands are defined as command icons, they are bound to an application panel and defined as an application window. Lastly, AB binds both the application window and the existing application object code program to an icon image created by using IIE and defines them as an application icon.

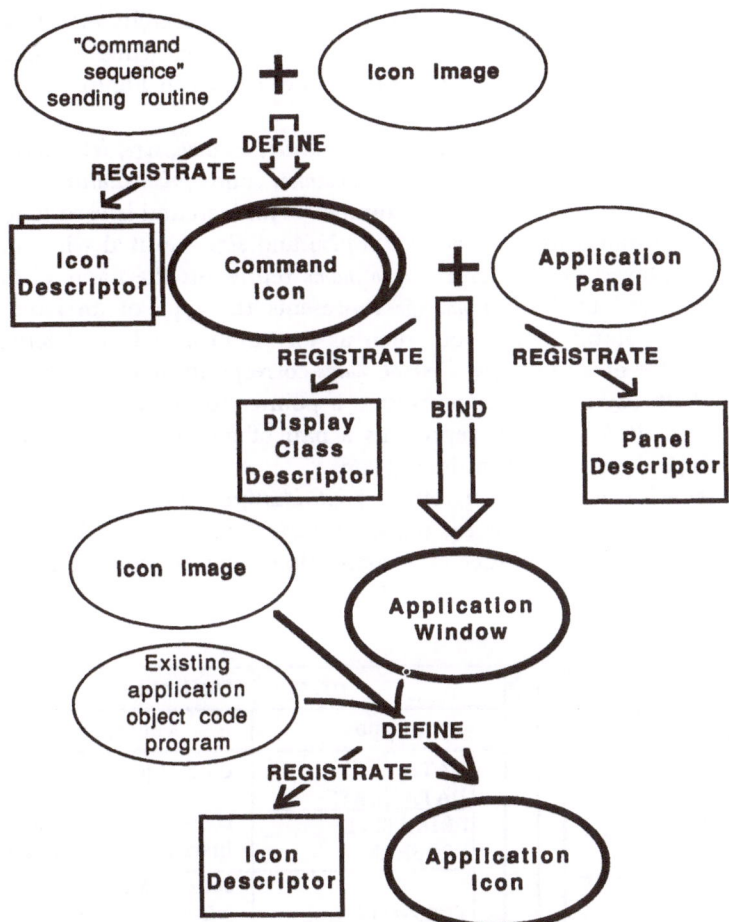

FIGURE 11. Integration of applications by using AB.

6. Execution of Icon Programs

6.1. Descriptors

In HI-VISUAL, icons and icon programs are managed by the descriptors. The following five descriptors are provided: icon descriptor (ID), joint descriptor (JD), line descriptor (LD), data class descriptor (DD), and panel descriptor (PD). ID manages the information of the icons themselves. Specifically, it manages the *internal* and *external* parts of the icon. JD manages the information of the connection between icons in the icon programs. LD manages the lines between icons. DD manages the hierarchy of data classes. PD manages the information of a display area in which icons are displayed. The formats of ID, JD, DD, PD, and LD are shown in Figures 12, 13, 14, 15, and 16, respectively.

ID consists of nine attributes: *icon_identifier, location, size, icon_name, icon_type, status, concept_name, help_message_pointer*, and *private_attribute_pointer. Icon_identifier* represents the unique number of an icon and is used to identify the icon with others in the system. *Location* and *size* are used when an icon image is displayed on the screen. *Icon_name* represents the name of an icon and is displayed as *label. Icon_type* represents the type of an icon. *Status* represents the status of an icon, such as lock/unlock of icon deletion and visible/invisible of icon image. *Concept_name* corresponds to *concept* in the *internal* part. *Help_message_pointer* represents a pointer to the help message of an icon. *Private_attribute_pointer* represents a pair of pointers to the icon image and the type-dependent icon description.

JD consists of seven attributes: *joint_identifier, private_attribute_pointer, icon_type, input_data_class, sender, output_data_class*, and *receiver. Joint_identifier* represents the unique number of a connection between icons. The last four attributes are used for data passing. Data is sent from an icon pointed to by

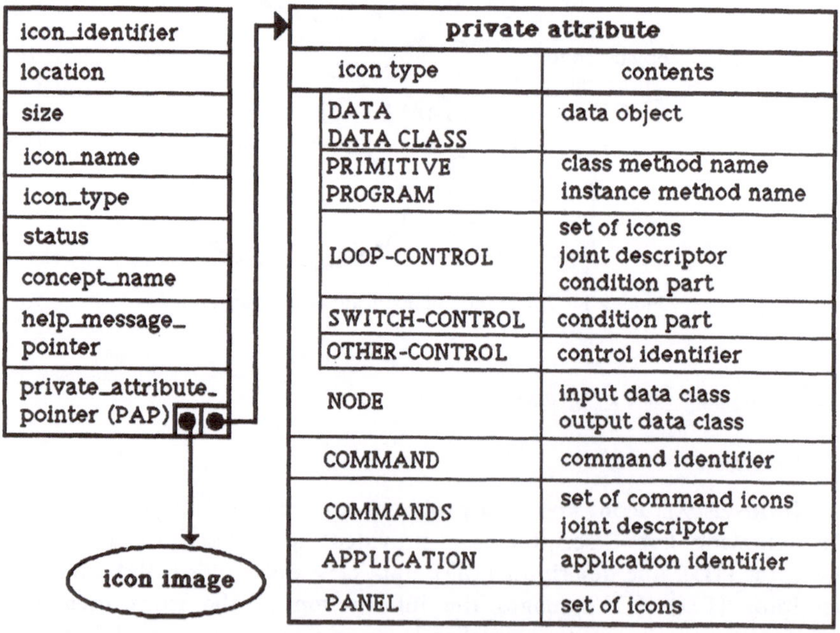

FIGURE 12. Icon descriptor (ID).

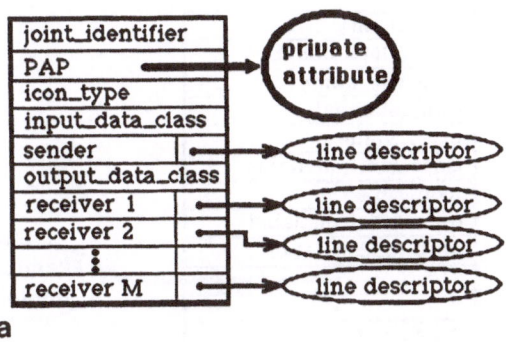

a

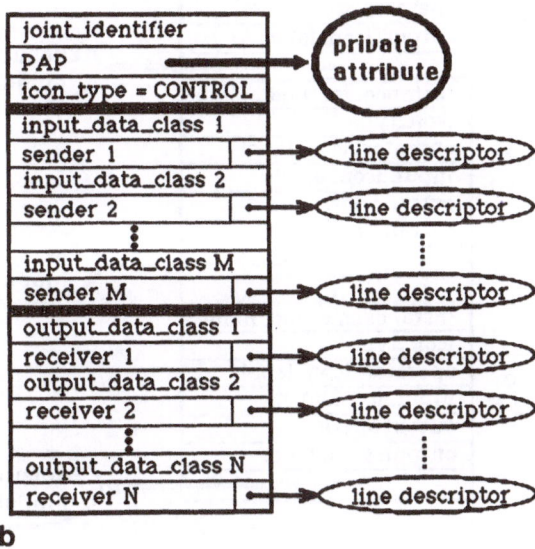

b

FIGURE 13. Joint descriptor (JD): (a) in the case of DATA, DATA CLASS, PROGRAM, and PRIMITIVE CLASS icons; (b) in the case of CONTROL icon.

sender field and sent to an icon pointed to by *receiver* field. *Input_data_class* and *output_data_class* represent data classes of these input and output icons.

DD consists of seven attributes: *class_name*, *superclass_name*, *subclass_name*, *data_element*, *class_value*, *class_method*, and *instance_method*. *Data_element* represents a set of data classes which are elements of a lower-level data class when the data type of the data class is record type. *Class_value* represents a set of values which can be commonly accessed by all methods in the data class. *Class_method* represents functions which are applicable to the class of

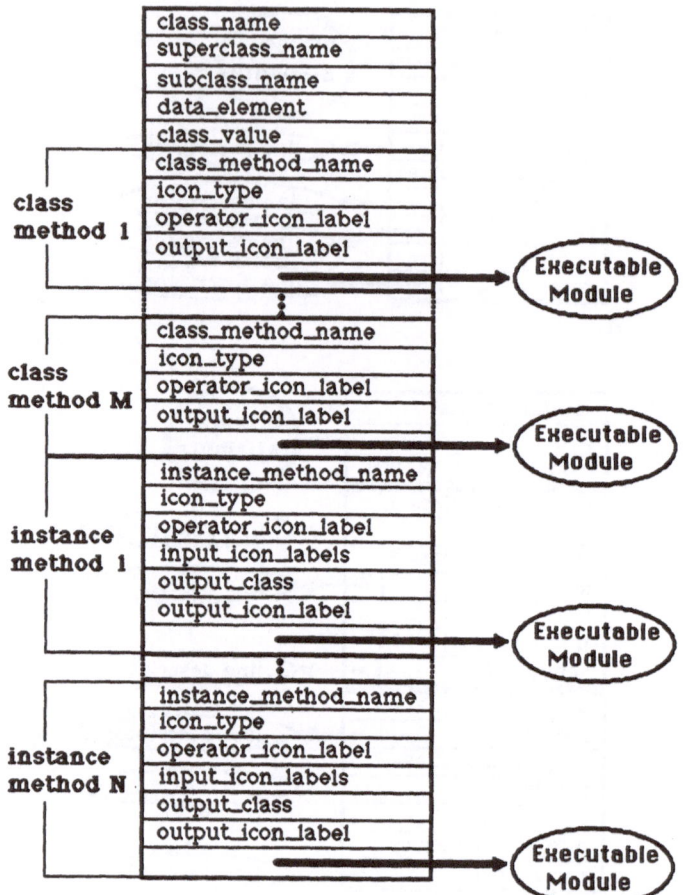

FIGURE 14. Data class descriptor (DD).

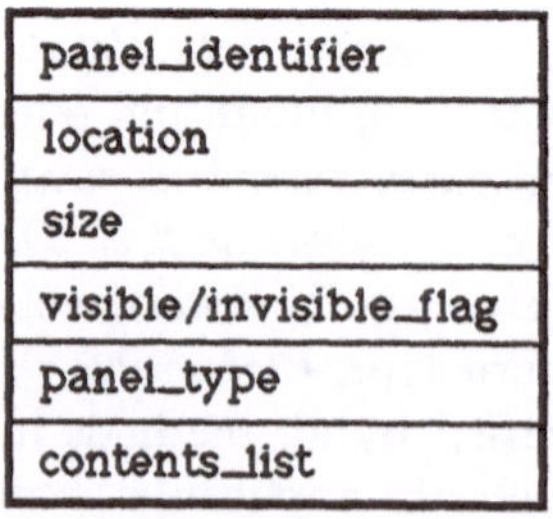

panel_identifier
location
size
visible/invisible_flag
panel_type
contents_list

FIGURE 15. Panel descriptor (PD).

| line_identifier |
| start_node |
| internal_node |
| $\vdots$ |
| end_node |

FIGURE 16. Line descriptor (LD).

data, such as creation (instantiation) of the data. *Instance_method* represents functions which are applicable to each item of data belonging to the data class.

PD consists of six attributes: *panel_identifier, location, size, visible/invisible_flag, panel_type,* and *contents_list. Visible/invisible_flag* determines whether or not the panel is displayed. If a panel is in invisible state, icons in the panel are also made invisible. *Panel_type* represents a type of panel such as paging

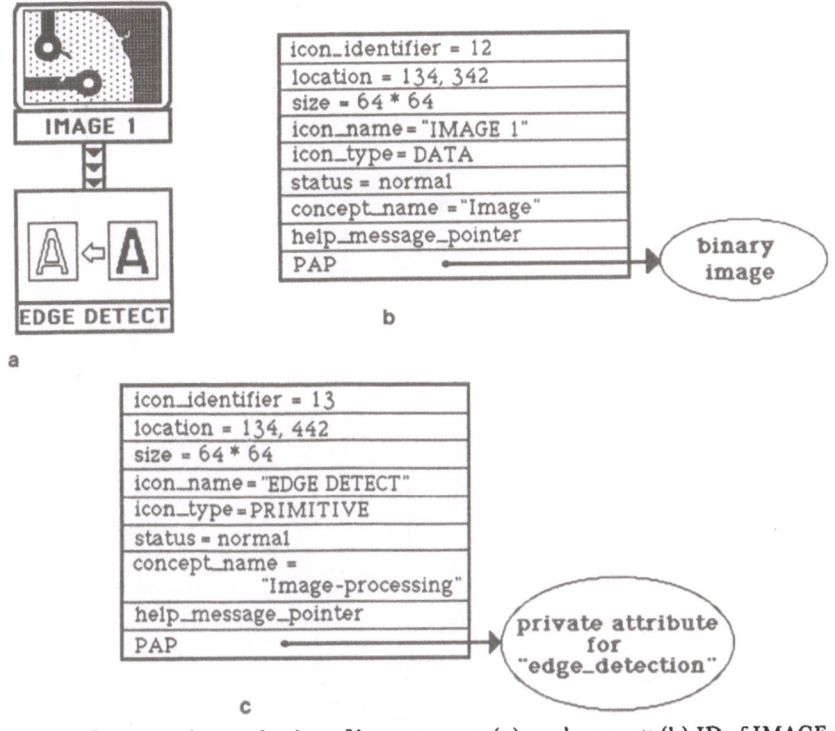

FIGURE 17. Interpretation mechanism of icon program: (a) user's request; (b) ID of IMAGE 1; (c) ID of EDGE DETECT; (d) DD of image, gray image, and binary image; (e) result of execution; (f) ID of resultant data (EDGING OUT); (g) joint descriptor.

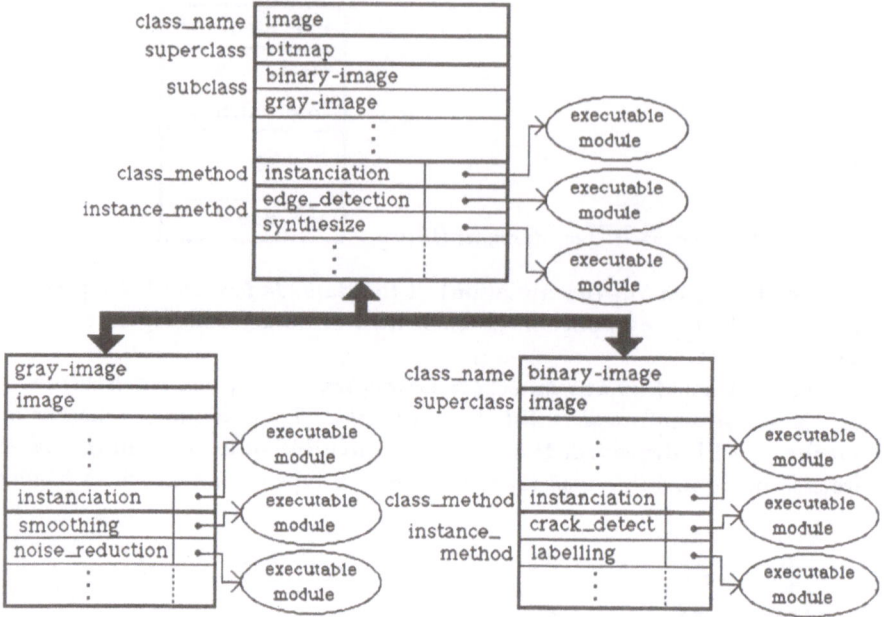

d

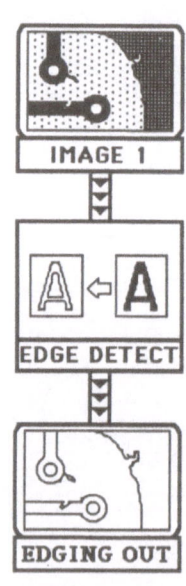

e

FIGURE 17. (*Continued*)

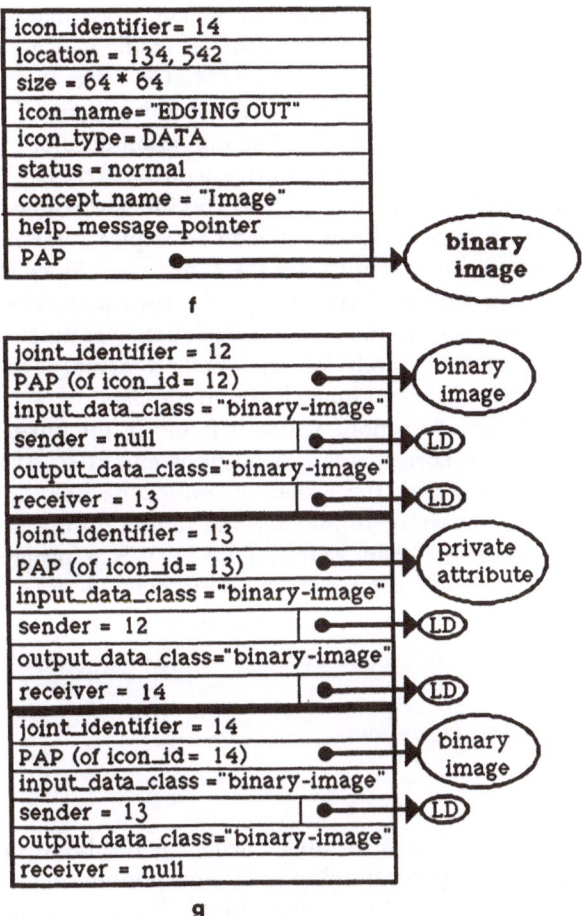

FIGURE 17. (*Continued*)

panel, sliding panel, and scrolling panel. *Contents_list* represents icons and lines which are contained in the panel.

LD consists of four attributes: *line_identifier*, *start_node*, *internal_node*, and *end_node*. *Line_identifier* represents the proper number of the line. *Start_node* represents the start point of the line. *Internal_node* represents the intermediate node of the line. *End_node* represents the end point of the line.

6.2. Execution Mechanism

In this section, we will explain how the execution of icon programs is carried out by means of descriptors. Figure 17 shows an example which will be used for the explanation. Assume that image, gray-image, and binary-image data classes have been defined as shown in the figure.

First, when the user places an icon (IMAGE 1) in the programming area, an icon descriptor corresponding to the icon is generated in the system. Since the icon is the data icon, no further operation occurs.

Next, when the user places a primitive icon (EDGE DETECT) which has a method named "edge_detection" and specifies the connection between these two icons, the system generates an icon descriptor corresponding to the primitive icon and a joint descriptor for the connection. Since the input data class of the primitive icon is binary-image, the system searches the binary-image data class for the method "edge_detection." Failure of the search causes invocation of the search for the method again. The class to be searched is a superclass of the binary-image data class.

The method "edge_detection" which is found in the image data class is then activated and the corresponding routine is executed. After the execution of the icon is completed, the system generates the icon descriptor, joint descriptor, and line descriptor to manage the resultant data as a new icon.

On the other hand, when EDGE DETECT is a program icon, the execution of the icon is carried out in the same manner as explained above after the icon is decomposed to a combination of primitive icons.

7. Execution of System Operations

7.1. Display Object

A *display_object* consists of an object which is displayed on the screen, such as a window, icon, programming area, and pop-up menu, and a set of operations which are applicable to the object. A *display_class* represents a group of similar *display_objects*. Like data classes, *display_classes* form a hierarchy, and operations in the *display_class* are inherited along the hierarchy.

Display_objects are icons, panels, or lines and are managed by IDs, PDs, or LDs, respectively. The *display_class* is managed by a display class descriptor (DCD).

The format of DCDs is shown in Figure 18. A DCD consists of four attributes: *display_class_name*, *superclass_name*, *subclass_name*, and *method*. *Method* represents the methods which are applicable to the *display_class* and consists of two fields: *command_selector* and *pointer_to_executable_routine*. *Command_selector* is the method name. *Pointer_to_executable_routine* represents an executive routine of system command such as run, delete, and move or a routine for sending a command sequence to an application (sub)system.

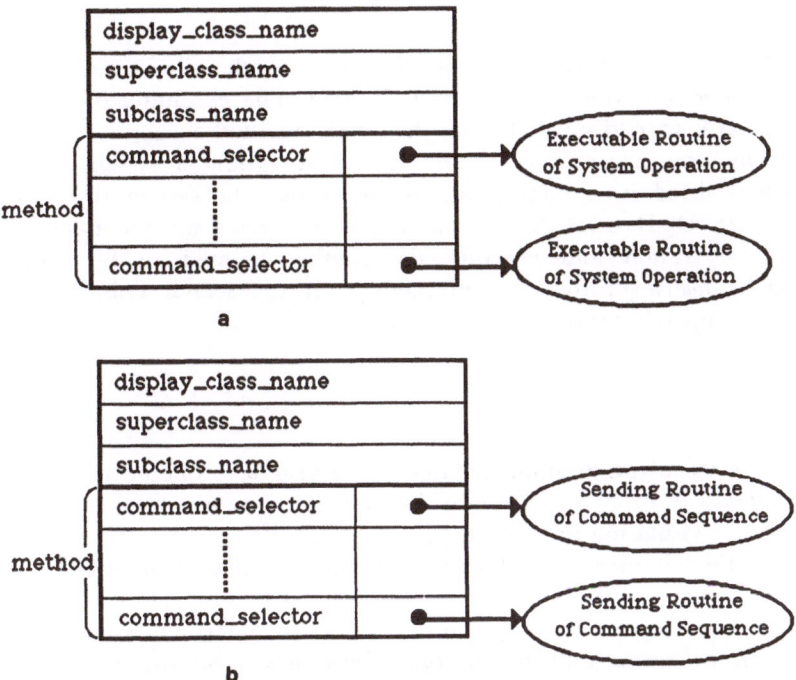

FIGURE 18. Display class descriptor (DCD): (a) DCD for system operation; (b) DCD for application command.

In addition, the system can navigate the user's action by showing the system commands in the pop-up command menu which can be applied to a currently selected *display_object*. The implementation of this facility is simply done by using DCDs. The system displays command icons which correspond to the methods in DCDs of both the class to which the *display_object* belongs and its superclass.

Furthermore, as mentioned in Section 4, HI-VISUAL provides the facility to expand the system by the integration of existing application (sub)systems. An application (sub)system is an instance of *display_class* and consists of a window on which the application (sub)system runs and a list of commands which are applicable to the (sub)system. A list of commands is specified in the *method* of DCD corresponding to the *display_class*. Commands of the (sub)system are displayed as command icons, and the user specifies what he wants to be run by pointing to command icons.

An application (sub)system is managed as a subclass of Application Panel class. Invocation of the (sub)system is carried out by pointing to the application icon which corresponds to the (sub)system.

7.2. Interpretation Mechanism

Every system operation in the system is considered as a message to the *display_object* on which the cursor is located. The execution of the system operation is carried out following the object-oriented concept.

The user selects a command icon representing a system operation, which is listed in a pop-up command menu. The system then searches *methods* in DCD corresponding to the *display_object* for the name of the system operation and executes the routine pointed to by *pointer_to_executable_routine* of the selected method. If the search fails, the system searches superclasses of the *display_class*.

8. Conclusion

The visual programming language HI-VISUAL, proposed earlier by us, was designed to allow the user to make programs effectively with the support of visual information in programming.[13]

In this chapter, we extended HI-VISUAL as an environment for iconic programming by providing the following facilities: (1) navigation for program development and system operations, (2) interpretation mechanisms for icon programs and system operations, based on the object-oriented concept, (3) top-down and bottom-up development of programs, and (4) integration of existing (sub)systems.

The architecture of HI-VISUAL for programming, execution, and management of icon programs was also presented. Icon programs and every system operation in the system are managed through six descriptors: icon descriptors, joint descriptors, line descriptors, data class descriptors, panel descriptors, and display class descriptors. The execution of icon programs and system operations are carried out following the object-oriented concept. It is noted that HI-VISUAL can be expanded to a larger system by defining the existing (sub)system as an application icon which is one of the command icons and provides a unified user interface for the different (sub)systems.

A prototype system is implemented by using C language on VAX 11/750 in connection with VAXstation 100 under the VMS operating system.

Acknowledgments

We are grateful to the former graduate students of the Information Systems Laboratory, Hiroshima University, S. Iwata, I. Yoshimoto, and N. Monden for their contributions to the development of HI-VISUAL.

References

1. S. K. CHANG, T. ICHIKAWA, and P. A. LIGOMENIDES (Eds.), *Visual Languages*, Plenum Press, New York, 1986.
2. D. C. SMITH, C. IRBY, R. KIMBALL, and E. HARSELM, The Star user interface: an overview, Proceedings of the AFIPS Conference, No. 51 (NCC '82), June 1982, pp. 515–528.
3. H. MAEZAWA, M. KOBAYASHI, K. SAITO, and Y. FUTAMURA, Interactive system for structured program production, Proceedings of the IEEE Conference on Software Engineering, March 1984, pp. 162–171.
4. R. J. K. JACOB, A state transition diagram language for visual programming, *IEEE Comput.* **18**(8), 51–59 (1985).
5. M. M. ZLOOF, QBE/OBE: a language for office and business automation, *IEEE Comput.* **14**(5), 13–22 (1981).
6. N. C. SHU, FORMAL: a forms-oriented visual directed application development system, *IEEE Comput.* **18**(8), 38–49 (1985).
7. S. B. YAO, A. R. HEVNER, Z. SHI, and D. LUO, FORMANAGER: an office forms management system, *ACM Trans. Office Information Syst.* **2**(3), 235–262 (1984).
8. E. P. GLINERT and S. L. TANIMOTO, Pict: an interactive graphical programming environment, *IEEE Comput.* **17**(11), 7–25 (1984).
9. M. EDEL, The Tinkertoy graphical programming environment, Proceedings of IEEE COMPSAC '86, October 1986, pp. 466–471.
10. J. W. DAVISON and S. B. ZDONIK, A visual interface for a database with version management, *ACM Trans. Office Information Syst.* **4**(3), 226–256 (1986).
11. S. P. REISS, PECAN: program development systems that support multiple views, *IEEE Trans. Software Engineering* **SE-11**(3), 276–285 (1985).
12. A. K. ARORA, D. K. CHAN, J. C. FERRANS, and R. GORDON, An overview of the VISE visual software development environment, Proceedings of IEEE COMPSAC '85, October 1985, pp. 464–471.
13. N. MONDEN, I. YOSHIMOTO, M. HIRAKAWA, M. TANAKA, and T. ICHIKAWA, HI-VISUAL: a language supporting visual interaction in programming, Proceedings of the IEEE Workshop on Visual Languages, December 1984, pp. 199–205.
14. R. V. RUBIN, Language constructs for programming by example, Proceedings of the ACM–SIGOIS Conference on Office Information Systems, October 1986, pp. 92–103.

7

ALEX—AN ALEXICAL PROGRAMMING LANGUAGE

Dexter Kozen, Tim Teitelbaum, Wilfred Chen, John Field, William Pugh, and Brad Vander Zanden

1. Introduction

ALEX is an experimental graphical language for high-level parallel programming. Data structures are represented graphically on the screen and manipulated in much the same way that an algorithm would be described to a colleague on the blackboard. Extensive use is made of high-resolution color graphics and the mouse.

ALEX is not a programming language is the conventional sense, because *there is no syntax* in the traditional lexical sense.* The programmer creates an internal program representation directly and interactively. A display manager maintains a window into the internal program, providing a customized view of a selected portion of the program structure. Shape, color, and other visual cues are used extensively and may be modified to taste. Powerful primitives are provided for creating and revising the program and for customizing the display. Especially important are primitives to suppress undesired information.

---

* This rather controversial idea is due to Snyder[1]; we coin the term *alexical.* Just as functional programming aspires to "liberate programming from the von Neumann style,"[2] alexical programming aspires to liberate programming from an obsolete style of communication that harks back to the days of teletypes and card punches.

DEXTER KOZEN, TIM TEITELBAUM, WILFRED CHEN, JOHN FIELD, WILLIAM PUGH, and BRAD VANDER ZANDEN • Computer Science Department, Cornell University, Ithaca, New York 14853.

It is tempting to think of the graphics appearing on the screen as the language ALEX. However, the interactive or conversational language that is used to associate functions with their inputs and outputs, position functions and data objects on the screen, and perform the myriad other tasks associated with specifying a program is every bit as much a part of ALEX, and a serious design consideration. In this respect, ALEX is more accurately described as a programming environment.

Building a production-quality compiler is a secondary goal of our project; our primary interest is in exploring various alexical ways of expressing algorithmic ideas. For this reason, we have resisted the temptation to create a general-purpose language but have instead restricted our attention to a particular application domain, namely, numerical matrix algorithms. These algorithms tend to use simple data structures and exhibit a high degree of inherent parallelism of a certain type well suited to our approach. At present, the only data structures ALEX supports are multidimensional arrays of integers, reals, and complex numbers, but very powerful primitives are provided within this limited domain. We believe that the ideas and techniques we are developing will apply more generally.

In Section 2, we review some related work. In Section 3, we describe the principal features of the ALEX user interface. In Section 4, we discuss implementation considerations. The description of the internal representation of programs and compilation issues will be the subject of a forthcoming paper.

2. Related Work

Previous graphical languages have concentrated on representing the control flow, data flow, or topology of a program. For example, PECAN provides features such as flowcharts and Nassi–Schneiderman diagrams that give pictorial representations of control flow.[3] ALEX differs from these languages in that they emphasize the graphical representation of control flow, whereas ALEX emphasizes the graphical representation of data objects. Apart from hardware design tools, we are aware of no other graphical language with this emphasis; this is corroborated by a recent article in *Computer*.[4]

In general, parallel languages in current use require the programmer either to specify parallelism at the processor level, explicitly specifying message routing, or to use sequential structures that a parallelizing compiler then attempts to remove. Data flow languages such as VAL and ID define control flow in terms of data dependencies.[5, 6] These languages exploit fine-grain parallelism at a low level and are lexical and not graphical.[7] The Program Visualization (PV) system attempts to specify the overall structure of a program graphically.[8] Languages like OCCAM and parallel Fortran address the physical processors explicitly. POKER[1] embodies the idea of alexical syntax but is intended primarily for low-level parallel programming and circuit design. ALEX differs from these approaches in that it allows the programmer to express the natural parallelism of a parallel algorithm at a high level, independent of the number or names of processors.

3. Principal Features of ALEX

ALEX is a functional language.[2] Of conventional languages, it is closest to FP or a data flow language with recursion. ALEX allows the graphical representation of two types of objects: *data objects* and *functions*.

3.1. Data Objects

ALEX's data objects are integer, real, or complex scalars and multidimensional arrays of scalars. They are represented on the screen by rectangles of various sizes, shapes, and colors. A data object should not be thought of as a block of storage locations but rather a conceptual organization of data as it is flowing through the program.

Data objects may be created anew by menu selection or copied from an already existing data object. If a data object is copied, then a data dependency is automatically established between the old and the new data object. Data dependencies are represented by *color matching* (see Section 3.4 below). Colors may be selectively suppressed to reduce visual complexity and then later redisplayed if desired.

The *type* of a data object is either specified through menu selection or inherited from a related data object. Limited polymorphism is permitted, but polymorphic types must be instantiated before compilation. Dimensions of arrays are available as data.

Data objects may have selected subobjects, which appear as smaller rectangles superimposed on the original data object. For example, one or more rows or columns may be selected from a matrix. Selection of subobjects is discussed below in Section 3.5.

3.2. Temporal Arrays

A dimension of an array may be regarded as either *spatial* or *temporal*. In general, a temporal dimension is one in which there are data dependencies among the elements, and a spatial dimension is one in which there are no such dependencies. Although the distinction is conceptually useful, ALEX does not formally distinguish between them; all data manipulation operations apply equally to both.

An array with a temporal dimension is called a *temporal array*. Temporal arrays are most useful in accumulating the partial results of loops, with each entry in the array representing the output of one iteration of the loop. Each iteration of a loop can make use of the results of prior iterations by accessing the appropriate entries of the temporal array. This representation of loops, in conjunction with the selection of a "typical" array element as described in Section 3.5 below, gives a convenient way of specifying a loop by describing a single (typical) iteration. This mirrors very closely the way we think about and describe loops informally. Although we are usually only interested in the data produced by the last iteration of the loop, occasionally the output is the entire temporal array. Such examples distinguish temporal arrays from ordinary **for** loops.

3.3. Functions

A *program* or *function* is a tree-like hierarchical structure. There is a library of primitive system-defined functions, and compound functions may be built by the user from data objects and previously defined functions. Each function has an associated set of typed inputs and outputs, which are data objects.

Functions may appear on the screen in *expanded* or *contracted* form. While a function is being programmed, it is displayed in expanded form and takes up the entire screen. Programming is performed by creating or copying data objects and functions, positioning them on the screen, and establishing data dependencies between them. Once programmed, a function can be contracted to a small box containing an icon created by the user. It can then be saved in a library for later use, copied, etc.

In addition to the standard numeric functions, system-defined functions are provided for conditional evaluation, sorting, merging, and selection and permutation. Functions can be polymorphic in the sense that their types need not be completely specified; but all types must be instantiated before compilation.

There are no *global* objects. All data used inside a function must be passed to it as an input parameter or created. This is consistent with the philosophy of functional programming.[2]

3.4. Representing Data Dependencies

Data dependencies within a function are represented by *color matching*, or coloring the source and destination data object the same color. An example of color matching is shown in the Appendix. Many other graphical data flow languages use lines or arrows, which we have avoided for two reasons: in complicated programs, lines quickly begin to look like spaghetti on the screen; and lines require sophisticated routing algorithms in the display manager.

Colors are local to the function; they can be reused outside the function or in a subfunction to indicate a different dependency. A data object receives its color when it is created, either inheriting it from the parent object from which it was copied or receiving a unique color if it was created anew.

Because of the scoping of colors, a data dependency that crosses a function boundary cannot be indicated by color matching. It is instead indicated by relative position, as follows. When a function is displayed in expanded form, the inputs are so designated by attaching them to the ceiling, and the outputs are so designated by attaching them to the floor. When the function is contracted, the inputs appear as tiny lobes along the top of the function box *in the same order as in the expanded form*, and similarly for the outputs. The dependencies between the formal (inside) and actual (outside) parameters are indicated by relative position along the floor or ceiling.

3.5. Manipulation of Objects

ALEX has powerful primitives for moving and reshaping data objects and selecting subobjects. We feel that the primitives for selecting subobjects are quite novel and interesting. For example, one commonly wants to select the first or last element of an array or row of a matrix. To select the first row of a matrix, one first creates a floating row of the matrix, which can be carried by the cursor up and down the length of the matrix but may not leave it. Slamming the row up against the top of the matrix twice in quick succession causes the row to stick to the top of the matrix and become the first row. This will also work for the $(i + 1)$st row, if the ith is already selected; one just slams the floating row up against the already selected row. One can also select a row of a matrix whose index is designated by a computed arithmetic expression.

It is also possible to sweep out an interval between two selected elements or the top or bottom of an array and select a "typical" element in that interval. This is used with a spatial dimension to specify parallelism, as described below in Section 3.6. It is used with a temporal dimension to specify a **for** loop, as follows. A temporal array is created of length $n + 1$, where n is the desired number of iterations. The first element is selected and an initial value inserted. Then a typical element (say the ith) is selected from the interval $1...n$, some operation performed on it (the value of i is available in this computation), and the result inserted in the temporal array at the position following the typically selected element. This computation is replicated automatically and invisibly for all i in the interval $1...n$. The final result is then extracted from the last element of the temporal array.

Input and output parameters, as mentioned in Section 3.4, are so designated by attaching them to the ceiling and floor, respectively, of the function box. That a particular data objects is to be an input is indicated by slamming it twice in quick succession against the ceiling, at which point it sticks. Similarly, two arrays of length n can be coalesced into a $2 \times n$ matrix or an array of length $2n$ by slamming them together.

3.6. Parallelism

ALEX is well suited to the tightly coupled, synchronous, single-instruction–multiple-data parallelism that occurs frequently in scientific and numerical computations. When a "typical" element, row, or column from an array is selected, then any operation subsequently performed on that typically selected element will be replicated automatically and invisibly across the entire array. This corresponds to the "apply-to-all" functional form in functional programming. The matrix multiplication example in the Appendix embodies these features: the programmer selects a typical row of the first matrix and a typical column of the second, chooses scalar multiplication and vector addition function boxes from the program library and applies them to those two vectors, and finally inserts the resulting scalar into the appropriately selected element of the output array.

3.7. Filtering Information

It is difficult enough poring over a printed listing of a sequential program, flipping through several pages of **then** clause to find the **else**, and so on. The complexity is further compounded in the presence of parallelism. Some programming environments support elision (...), but it is usually considered an extra nicety to be incorporated into a pretty-printing algorithm, and certainly not a first-class part of the language.

We consider the suppression of unwanted information utterly essential in large-scale parallel programming. ALEX provides primitives for suppression of color and encapsulation. In the latter, a family of subfunctions and data objects can be collected into a new function. Inputs and outputs are created automatically to account for existing data dependencies crossing the boundary of the new function.

3.8. Other Features

The language incorporates primitives for restructuring flow of data, for redimensioning arrays, for splitting arrays according to Boolean conditions, for shifting, rotating, permuting, and transposing arrays, and for customizing the-display. These features will be described in more detail in a later paper.

There are also means for moving about the program tree, for saving and retrieving functions from libraries, and other housekeeping operations; these are not particular to ALEX and need not be described in this chapter.

4. Implementation

We have implemented a prototype of the user interface. It is written in Common Lisp using the X window system and runs on Sun workstations. The examples in the Appendix are actual screen images produced by the prototype.

Appendix:

Figures 1–8 show how matrix–matrix multiplication would be programmed in ALEX. These figures are actual screen images produced by our monochrome prototype. Unfortunately, the medium prevents adequate illustration of the dynamics of program creation, which is an important aspect of the language.

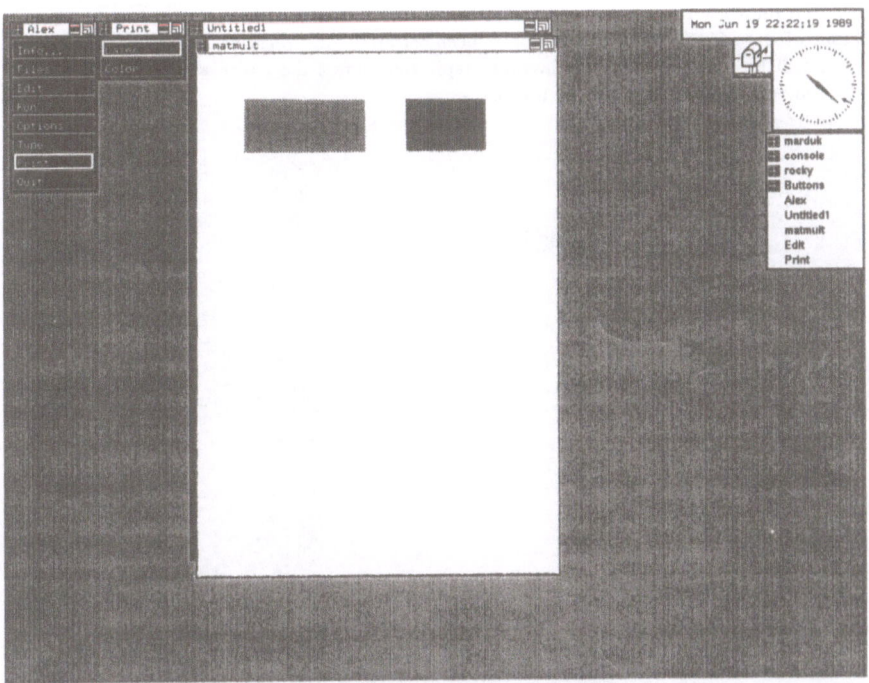

FIGURE 1. Two input matrices are created.

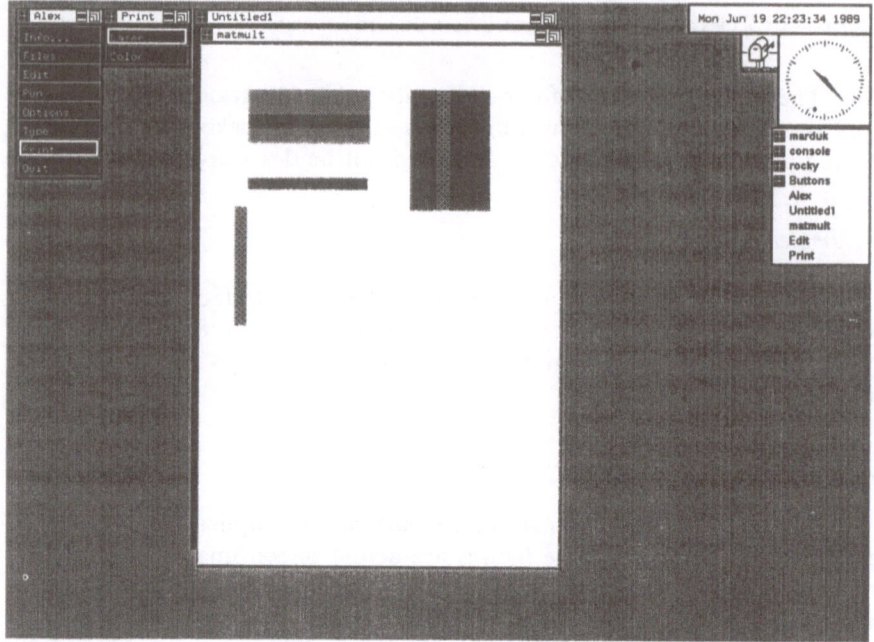

FIGURE 2. The vertical dimension of the second matrix has been constrained to equal the horizontal dimension of the first. A typical row of the first matrix (say, the ith) and a typical column of the second (say, the jth) have been selected. Any operations performed on these vectors will be automatically and invisibly replicated across the entire array. The data from these two vectors have been copied down.

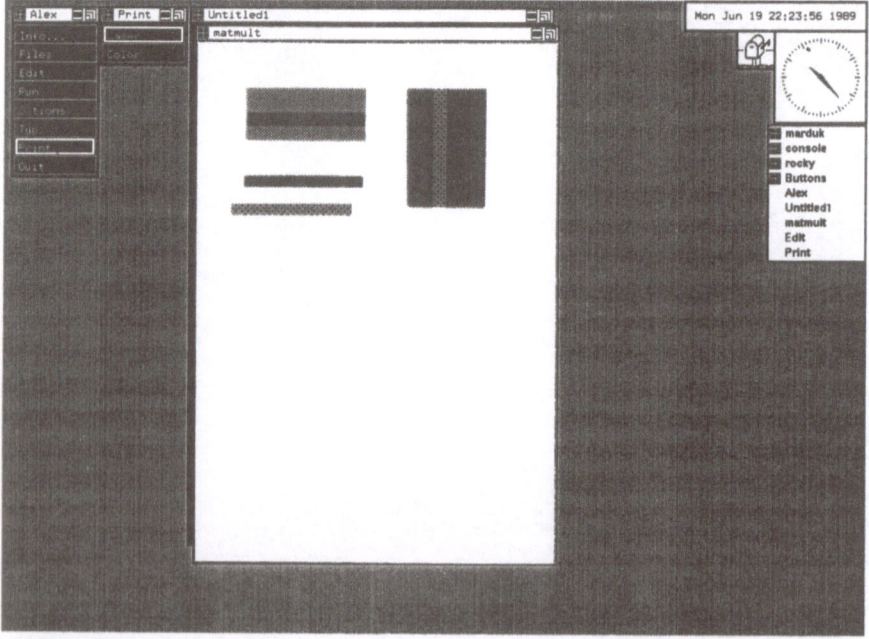

FIGURE 3. The second vector has been transposed and the two vectors juxtaposed. They will be coalesced into a $2 \times n$ matrix.

FIGURE 4. We wish to compute the dot product of the two vectors. A typical column (say, the kth) of the $2 \times n$ matrix is selected. This is a vector of length 2.

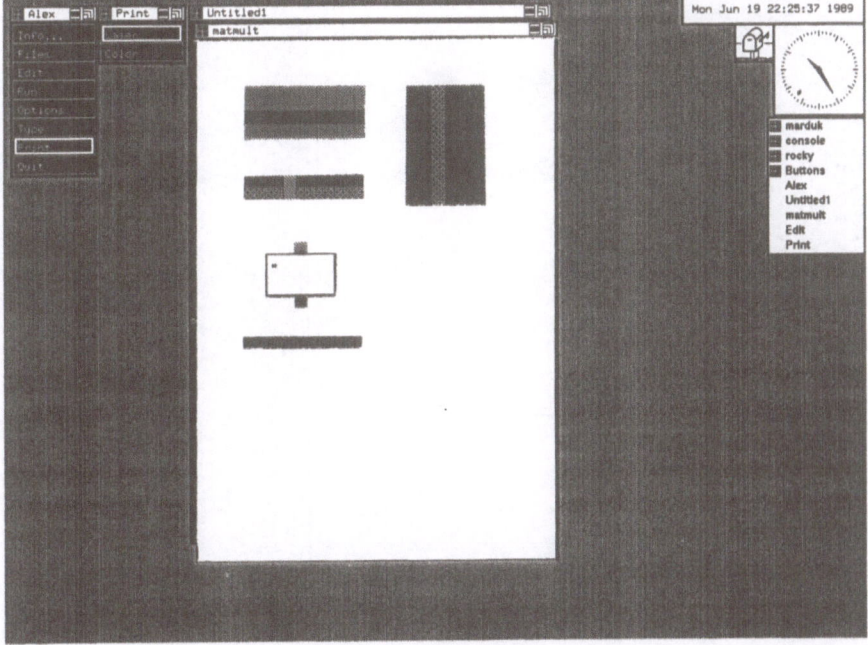

FIGURE 5. The two elements of the vector selected in Figure 4 are multiplied using a function obtained from the library. The output is inserted into the kth element of a $1 \times n$ vector. This vector was created by copying one of the vectors selected in Figure 2 *without* a data dependency.

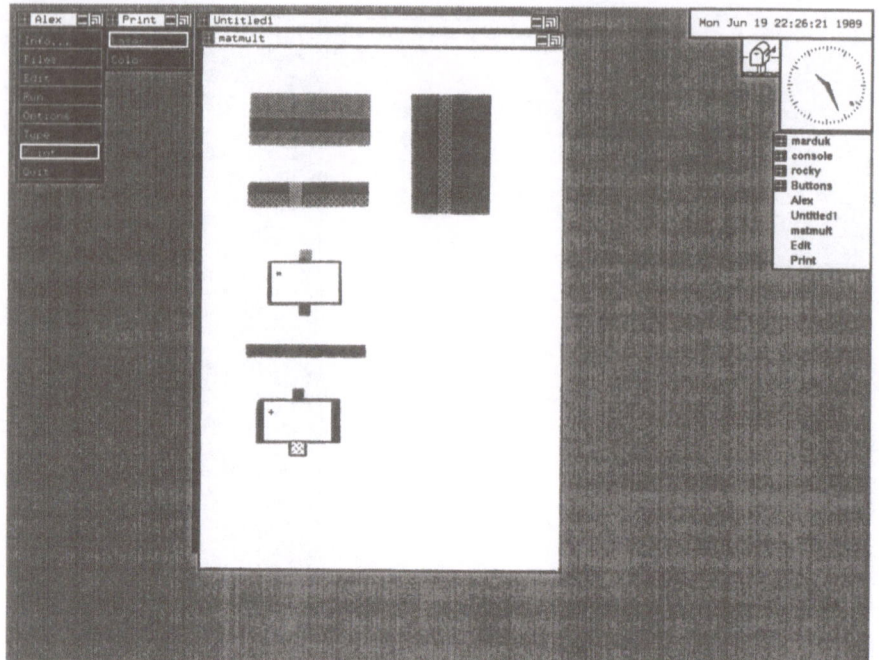

FIGURE 6. The sum of the elements of the $1 \times n$ vector is computed using a function obtained from the library.

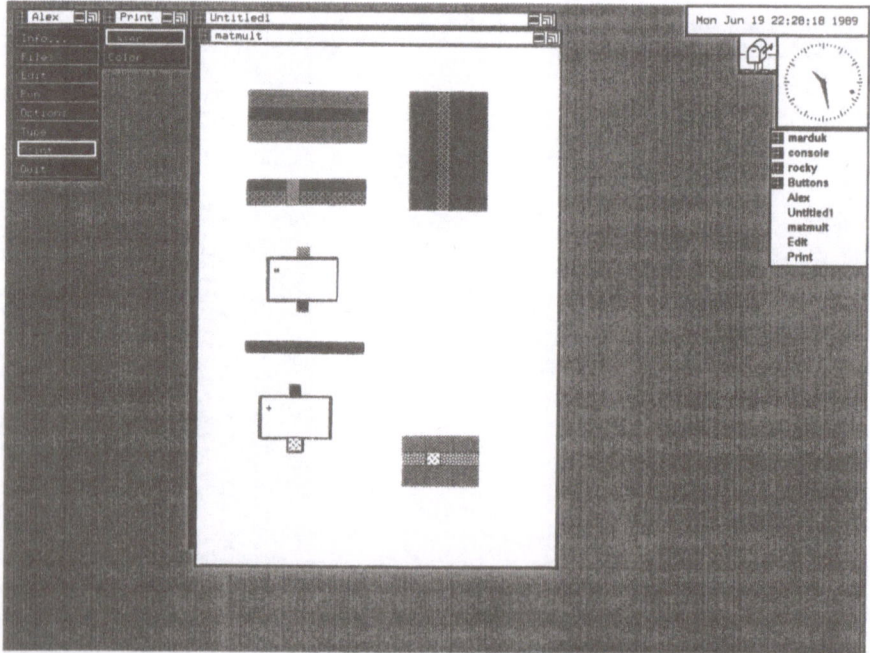

FIGURE 7. The resulting scalar is inserted into the (i, j)th element of an output matrix. The dimensions of the matrix have been specified by copying data from the edges of the input matrices in Figure 1. The indices i and j are also available from the selected row and column of the input matrices.

FIGURE 8. The box has been contracted and can now be saved, copied, and so on. The two lobes on the top are the two input matrices, and the lobe on the bottom is the output matrix.

Acknowledgments

We thank Larry Carter, Jens Dill, Bruce Esrig, Jeanne Ferrante, David Loshin, Alex Nicolau, Prakash Panangaden, Frank Schmuck, and Larry Snyder for valuable discussions. We thank Greg Bradler, Mark Lee, Mark Rowland, Greg Travis, Oscar Waddell, and Jim Wen for their assistance in the implementation of ALEX.

This work was supported by NSF grant DCR-8602663 to D. Kozen and NSF grant DCR-8514862 to T. Teitelbaum.

References

1. L. SNYDER, Parallel programming and the POKER programming environment, *Computer* **17**(7), 27–36 (1984).
2. J. BACKUS, Can programming be liberated from the von Neumann style? A functional style and its algebra of programs, *Commun. ACM* **21**(8), (1978).

3. S. P. Reiss, Graphical program development with PECAN program development systems, Proceedings of the ACM Sigsoft-Sigplan Software Engineering Symposium on Practical Software Development Environments, April 1984, pp. 30–41.
4. G. Raeder, A survey of current graphical programming techniques, *Computer* **18**(8), 11–25 (1985).
5. K. P. Gostelow and R. E. Thomas, A view of dataflow, pp. 1079–1086 in *Proceedings of the 1979 National Computer Conference*, New York, June 1979, AFIPs Conference Proceedings, Vol. 48, AFIPS Press, Arlington, Virginia, 1979.
6. J. R. McGraw, The VAL language: description and analysis, *TOPLAS* **4**(1), 44–82 (1982).
7. J. B. Dennis, Dataflow computation, pp. 346–398 in *Control Flow and Data Flow: Concepts of Distributed Programming*, M. Broy (Ed.), Springer-Verlag, Berlin, 1985.
8. G. P. Brown, R. T. Carling, C. F. Herot, D. A. Kramlick, and P. Souza, Program visualization: graphical support for software development, *Computer* **18**(8), 27–35 (1985).

IV

ALGORITHM ANIMATION

Closely related to the subject of visual programming is the idea of using visual animations to show the operation of algorithms. Robert Duisberg discusses how such animation can be used in the analysis of algorithms, illustrating this by use of the Smalltalk-based system, Animus, in the animation of a selection sorting algorithm. In the second chapter in this section, Esa Helttula, Aulikki Hyrskykari, and Kari-Jouko Räihä critique several animation systems before presenting their own Pascal-based system, ALADDIN.

8

VISUAL PROGRAMMING OF PROGRAM VISUALIZATIONS

A GESTURAL INTERFACE FOR ANIMATING ALGORITHMS

ROBERT DUISBERG

1. Introduction

Program animation has a growing role to play in software engineering. After all, "an algorithm must be seen to be believed, and the best way to learn what an algorithm is all about is to try it."[1] The perceptual endowments of people are strongly optimized for real-time image processing, and the medium of interactive graphics is simply a broader channel than, say, text by which to communicate information about the internal state of a complex dynamic process. As computer technology matures, it is becoming possible, and therefore increasingly important, for new systems to accommodate their users' idiosyncrasies, as opposed to the traditional situation which required users to assimilate all the peculiarities of the system. In this respect, animation can be seen as an integral part of a software design and development environment, with particular utility for debugging, process monitoring, and documentation.

In order for such potential to be realized, however, an animation system must meet certain requirements. First, the system must be "easy" to use. This requirement stems from the experience that direct programming of

ROBERT DUISBERG • Computer Research Laboratory, Tektronix, Inc., Beaverton, Oregon 97077. Present affiliation: School of Music, University of Washington, Seattle, Washington 98191. This paper also appears as CRL Technical Report #87-20.

animations is a very arduous task, even for an experienced programmer in an environment such as Smalltalk* which offers high-level support for graphics.[2] In such a directly coded animation, some 80% of the total body of code is devoted to driving the graphics, with the remainder running the underlying algorithm. Such a situation is clearly unacceptable for purposes of debugging, for example, in which the user might like to build a quick "throw away" animation, to see some detail of passing interest. Such considerations have led us to investigate so-called "novice programming environments" in which the system is able to compile detailed graphics code based on the users, manipulation of high-level icons[3] and, as described in this chapter, animation by gestural example.

Another requirement for an algorithm animation system is a clean separation between the graphics code and the algorithmic code. Conceptually, the algorithm is an object under test, and the animation is a probe to monitor its behavior. The presentation should show the algorithmic code unaltered, or with only indications (e.g., font changes) of where "probes" have been inserted. But the actual coding of the animation should be transparent to the user, with the system handling as many of the details as possible.

Addressing these requirements has led to this research toward an environment in which it is possible for a user to construct an animated algorithm by drawing objects, demonstrating motions of the objects in the drawing, and indicating points in the algorithm where such motions should be triggered, *without ever having to write a line of graphics code.* After providing some background, we will describe in this chapter, chiefly through a detailed account of a sample animation, the procedure that a user would follow in creating an animation in our system. The system described here, while operational, is considered to be experimental work in progress, which nonetheless demonstrates the potential of exciting new means for programming animations. In the final section of the chapter, we will indicate directions of further research, especially how these new facilities may be integrated into more powerful and more general environments.

2. Related Algorithm Animation Techniques

A number of techniques have been used to animate programs in a variety of systems. The BALSA system at Brown University,[4] for which an impressive library of animated courseware was created to teach an algo-

---

* i.e. "Smalltalk-80" which is a registered trademark of the Xerox Corp.

rithms course, relies upon interlineal insertions of procedure calls, known as *InterestingEvents*, into the code being animated. This is consistent with the essentially hand-crafted character of the BALSA animations and does not present a problem for the course-ware environment, in which the users (students) will be expected to interact in prescribed ways and will not want to alter animations fundamentally, or to build new ones. However, this approach is inconvenient in a software engineering environment, for the reasons outlined above.

The use of "Active Values" is an animation technique that is found, for example, in the LOOPS system,[5] whereby actions may be specified to occur upon access to particular variables. Aspects of this technique have been implemented in our system, but, thus far, the principal "action" that occurs upon access to a "bugged" variable is simply to give access to the part of the picture representing the variable. The actual movements in the picture are keyed to the message selectors (i.e., operators) in the program under test, in a manner similar to the use of TriggerConstraints in the Animus system.[3]

Animus was built on top of ThingLab,[6] a constraint-based simulation system built in Smalltalk, with the extension consisting of the implementation of constraints involving time. TemporalConstraints allowed the user to specify in a declarative way how an animation is to evolve, either by writing the differential equations of motion of parts of physical simulations or by declaring that certain events in the underlying program should trigger the occurrence of some complex sequence of graphical responses. Toward the same end, the present system allows the user to demonstrate by gesture a sequence of graphical actions and then specify what program event should trigger this response by pointing at the desired selector in the program.

3. An Overview of the Present System

A guiding concept in the implementation of the system described here is that there exist two parallel domains in an animation. First is the domain of the program, represented as text, parse trees, or compiled code, and second is the domain of the graphics, including both the static structure of the pictures and their dynamics. The existence of these two separate domains implies the need for three sets of editing facilities: one for editing the program, another for constructing the static and dynamic graphics, and a third for describing and editing the *relationships between* the two domains. The elements of these three facilities are provided in the window shown in Figure 1.

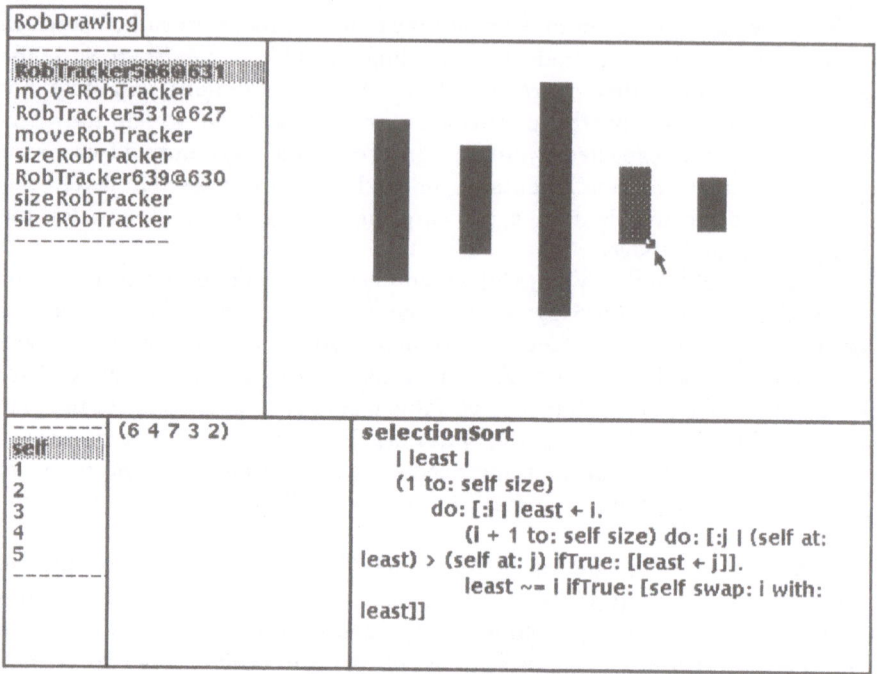

FIGURE 1. A program animation environment.

Program editing is well understood, but environments for editing dynamic graphics are an area of active research. The dynamic graphics editor used here was developed by Ward Cunningham in collaboration with this author and is described in greater detail in Ref. 7. Our emphasis in developing our editor was to experiment with capturing the dynamics of the user's gestures. Thus, the "drawing" facility is deliberately limited to the placing and shaping of black rectangles. However, every gesture the user makes, in moving or shaping a picture element, is sampled and recorded and listed in the "history pane" (the upper left pane in the figures), from where it can be recalled, replayed, undone, named, edited, grouped with other gestures, bound to different figures in the drawing, acted upon by other gestures, and so forth. The key idea to enable the direct manipulation of dynamic temporal features is the "spatialization" of time. Thus, in Figure 2, a gesture may be displayed (in the upper right pane) as a trail of points, and its endpoints may be dragged about to shape it or attach it to other figures. A classic paradigm for the spatialization of time is music notation,

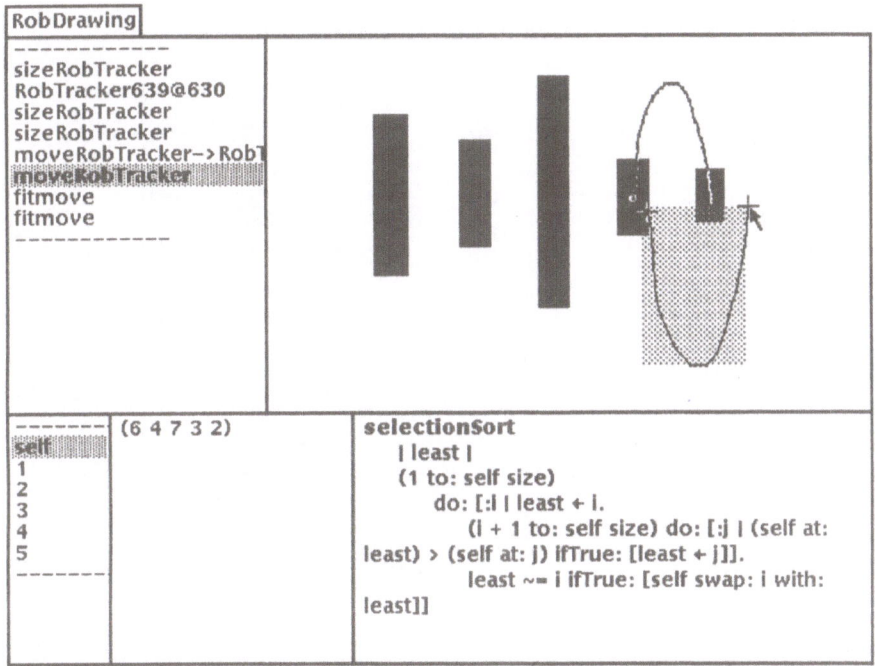

FIGURE 2. Two gestures being bound to data.

in which time is mapped onto horizontal position. This has led to experimentation with the notion of "scoring" of gestures, especially groups of gestures, as shown in Figure 3. Pursuing the metaphor, here the "staff" may be an indication of the object to which a gesture applies, while the "pitch" or vertical position might be bound to color or to position along some axis. We are currently exploring the utility of such devices.

The focus of this chapter is the third facility, by which such gestures may be specified to occur in response to changes in the program state, as detailed in the next section. Again the interface is gestural, consisting essentially of the acts of selecting a gesture, group of gestures, or figure in the drawing, and then indicating, in another pane of the window, the variable, selector, or element in the data structure that the graphical entity is to represent. From these indications, a table of such relationships is constructed. Then the program may be recompiled, taking the relationships into account, including appropriate graphics code at the proper points.

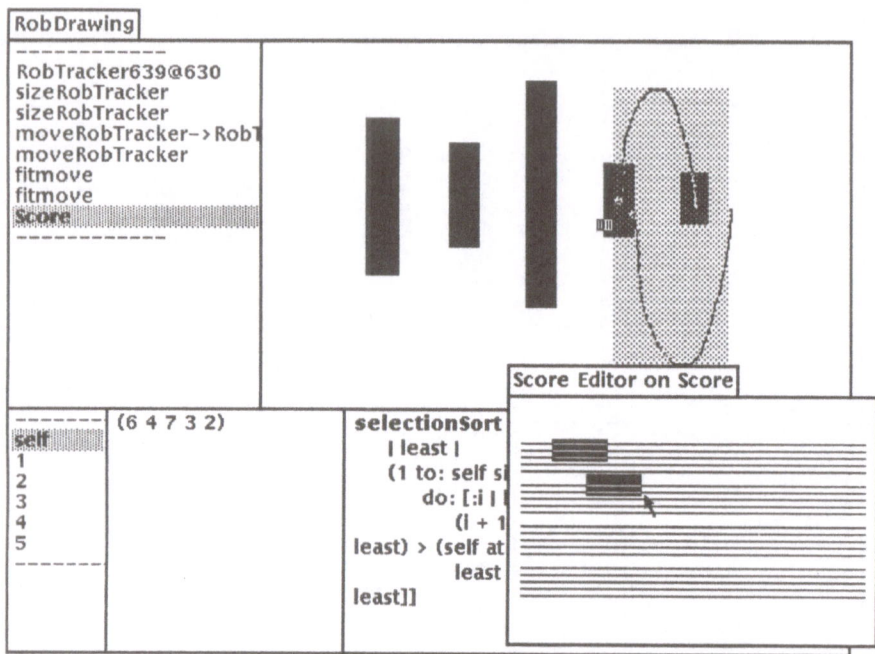

FIGURE 3. Elements of a score adjusted so that their relative onsets are shifted in time.

4. Building an Animation

The style of interaction achieved in our system is perhaps best demonstrated by describing the constructing of an animation of a simple example. Suppose that we wished to watch the behavior of a selection sorting algorithm on a particular array of data, a typical testbed for algorithm animation. Presumably, in a Smalltalk environment, class Array must implement a method for a protocol such as "selectionSort." Execution of the line

$$\#(6 \quad 4 \quad 7 \quad 3 \quad 2)\,\text{animate:}\ \#\text{selectionSort}$$

will open a window with panes showing the data structure (the literal array receiving the message) which will execute the algorithm and a view onto the code of that algorithm, along with a pane in which to draw a picture and demonstrate the motions that the animation is to execute. Figure 1 shows such a window in which we have drawn five vertical bars to indicate the elements of the array to be sorted. The pane in the upper left is a transcript of the history of all the gestures used to construct the picture shown in the upper right.

In studying sorting algorithms, it is natural to wish to see the order in which elements are swapped, so the swaps should be shown in the picture when they occur in the program. To accomplish this, we would first demonstrate a gesture to cause an element to "hop" to the side, as shown in Figure 2. Such a "hop" gesture can be used as one half of a "swap" gesture, when made to act on appropriate elements of the picture.

Selecting this new gesture in the history list causes it to be shown as part of the picture, so that we may in turn manipulate it, performing gestures upon gestures, meta-gestures if you will. Thus, the gesture may be selected, duplicated, and made "bindable" by pointing with the mouse and making a couple of menu selections. The endpoints of the bindable gesture appear with binding handles on them, shown as cross hairs. To do the connecting, these handles may be selected with the mouse and dragged over to and dropped onto one of the bars representing array elements, stretching the gesture in the process. When the binding handle is released onto a bar, the bar flashes to confirm that the gesture has been bound to it as its origin or destination. The duplicate of the gesture, which becomes the other half of the swap, would be bound so that it leads in the opposite direction to that of the first gesture.

These two gestures may be grouped together into a unit (a score), since the two parts of the action are to occur simultaneously in response to a single program event. This score can be editing as shown in Figure 3 so that the relative timing and duration of the two gestures can be modified by directly manipulating the bars representing their durations in the score window.

The crucial step at this point is to be able to express when in the execution of the program the score is to be "played." Here, of course, the score should play when the message "swap:with:" is received by the array. This connection between the gesture and the program is established by first selecting the score in the picture pane and then choosing the menu item "identify." The user then sees a flashing "rubber-band" line and may select a string of text in the code pane at the bottom of the window. Upon completion of the selection, the line blinks to indicate confirmation, and the font for the selected token is changed to italics, as shown in Figure 4.

Note that although the user may have selected the text "swap:" alone, the system recognizes that this is just a part of the compound selector "swap:with:" and therefore highlights and italicizes the remaining portion of the selector. This is possible since the code window maintains a parse tree of the inspected code, so that the act of selection returns not just text, but a pointer to the appropriate parse node, in this case the one for the complete

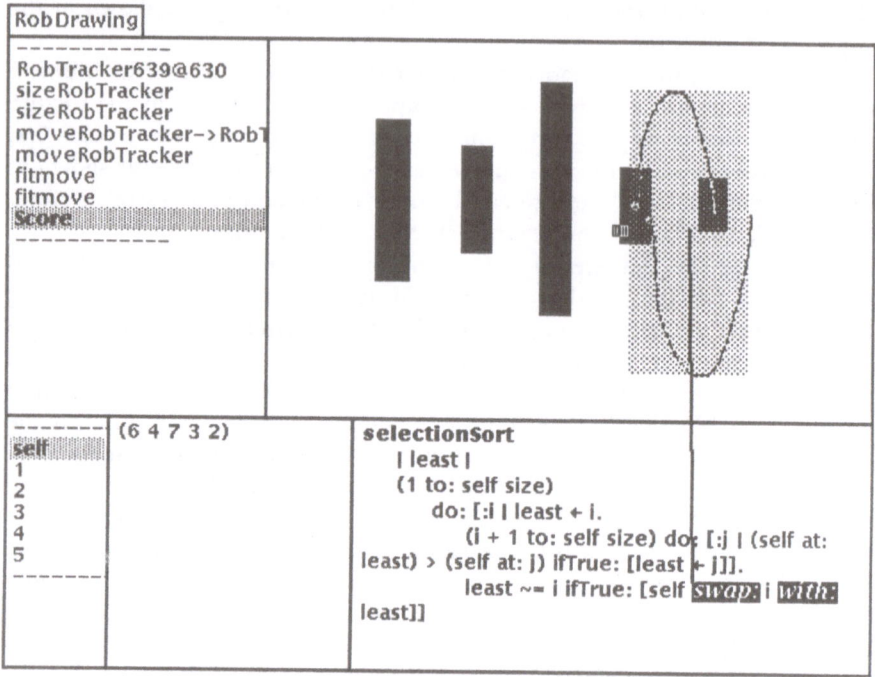

FIGURE 4. Identifying a gesture with a message in the program.

"swap:with:" selector. In addition, the system generates an instance of class Association relating the animation gesture and the parse node for the selected token and enters the Association into a RelationsDictionary.

The information contained in the RelationsDictionary is the essential element used to drive the animation when the user makes the menu selection "run" in order to perform the sort routine upon the given array. Before the program is run, it is first recompiled using the relations. In this recompilation stage, messages whose selectors are found to have animation actions associated with them are expanded into compound messages which first perform the animated action and then send the original message itself. At first glance, this may seem quite involved, tantamount to implementing a special-purpose compiler for the task. But in an object-oriented style, with the functionality distributed among a number of classes, the problem is dramatically simplified. Indeed, the capability can be provided by adding a single protocol to a number of the classes used by the Smalltalk compiler itself. The Smalltalk compiler scans a source method as a string and constructs a graph of parse tree nodes as an intermediate representation of the method.

These nodes are instances of VariableNode, BlockNode, AssignmentNode, and so on, all subclasses of ParseNode. Each of these classes is provided with a method to respond to the message "reinterpretWith: relations." In most cases the receiver simply returns itself. But a MessageNode first checks its selector to see if it is among the relations and, if so, constructs a new compound message node (i.e., a BlockNode) which will perform the animations specified as well as the original message.

Now an important issue here is that the gestures must be dynamically rebound at run time to different graphical objects, depending upon the parameters passed to the "bugged" message. That is, if we were to run the animation as we have constructed it thus far, each time a swap occurs in the program, the gestures we have demonstrated will occur, but they will be replayed verbatim. Clearly, we intended instead to have given an exemplar swap gesture, which was meant to be generalized as a swap between any two indexed elements of a group. We must therefore have the means to express that the arguments of the "swap:with:" message are to be interpreted as indices into an array, and we need to have access to the corresponding

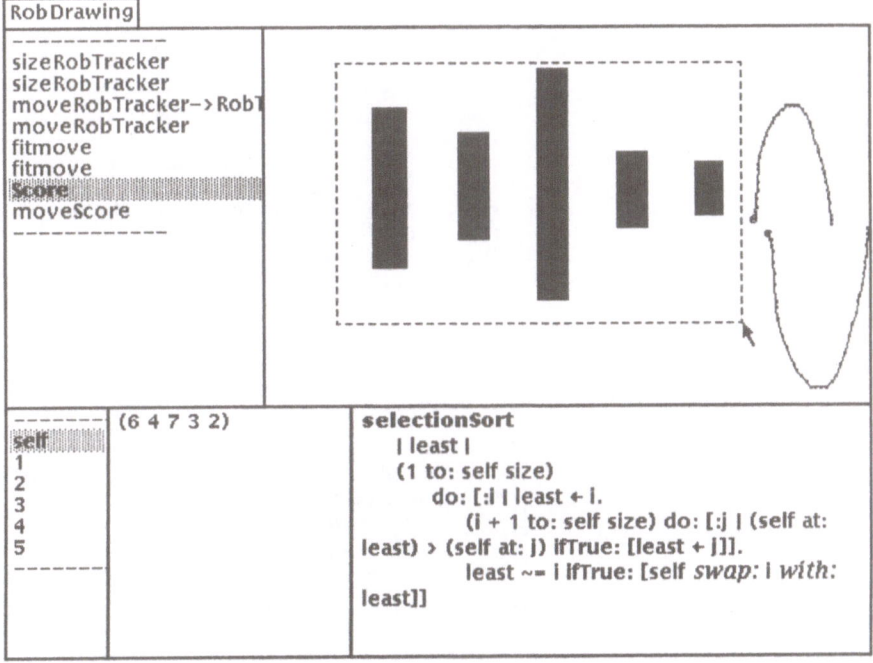

FIGURE 5. Group selecting the elements of the array.

elements of a graphical group, so that the gestures can be rebound to the appropriate bars at run time.

   This is accomplished in the following fashion. We need, naturally, to declare the bars representing the elements of our array to be a group representing the array as a whole. So we make a "group selection," as shown in Figure 5, and then choose "group" in the menu to declare that all the elements selected should be combined into one object. Now the group appears with a handle which is an instance of class "Indexor," appearing on the left side of the group selection box. By clicking the mouse on the indexor handle, we are again invited (by the flashing rubber-band line) to draw a relation between an index into the group and a token in the program. Thus, we can identify the parameters "least" and "i" to refer, in the graphics, to indexed elements of the group pictured, as shown in Figure 6. Now, upon choosing "run" from the menu, the gestures are successively bound to appropriate bars and the swapping appears as the program executes, as in Figure 7.

   If, in addition, we wished to animate the comparisons before the swaps, we could in a similar fashion probe the access messages "self at: least" and

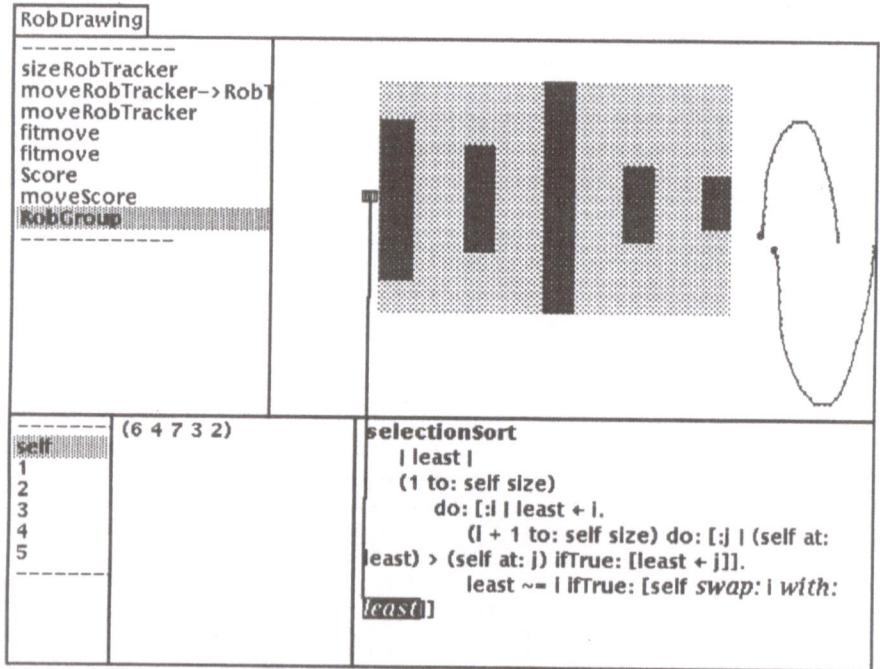

FIGURE 6. Identifying parameters to be indices into the array.

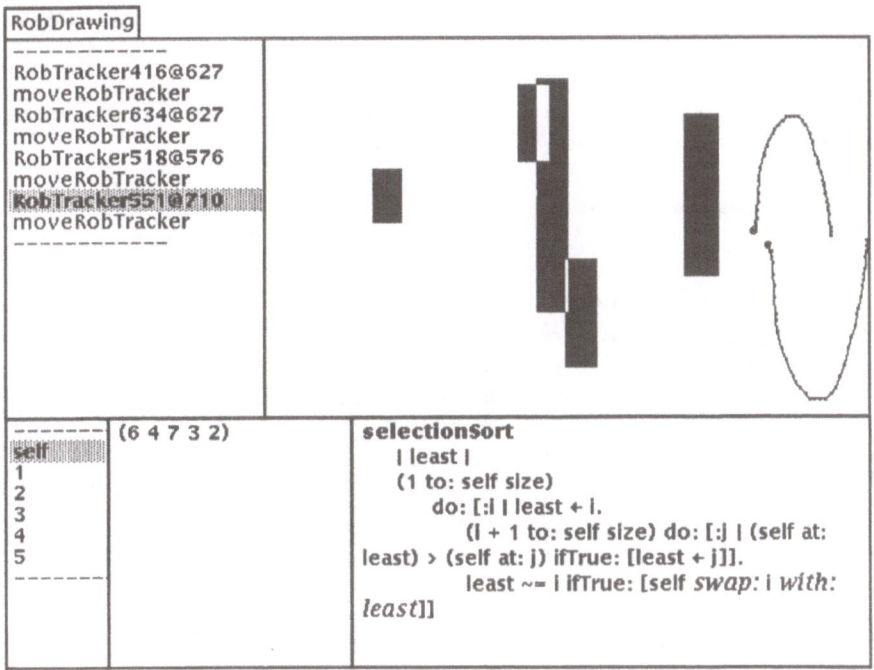

FIGURE 7. The elements of the array swapping positions.

"self at: j." A convenient gesture for showing this access before the comparison is to make the bar briefly grow and shrink. This gesture is then identified with both instances of the selector "at:," as before. Again, the arguments must be identified as indices into the array. When the sort is run, the compared elements will be highlighted sequentially.

Alternatively, if we want the two bars to be highlighted simultaneously in the comparison, we could form a pair of gestures into a score, as we did in the complex gesture for swapping, and identify this score as being triggered on the selector " <." Notice now that the receiver and argument to this binary selector are no longer indices but the values themselves. In order to gain access to the appropriate part of the picture then, the bars should be identified with the particular values they represent. This is done either by selecting one of the bars, and the menu item "identify," and attaching the end of the rubber-band line to one of the elements shown in the inspector on the data structure in the bottom-left pane or, more simply, by identifying the group of elements in the picture with the array itself, which then, by default, identifies the respective elements. In recompilation now, the gestures are rebound to the bars associated with the values looked up in the relations dictionary.

It is instructive to show the transformation the code undergoes in the process of recompilation. In this last example, the actual code generated, with probes set on "<" and "swap:with:" is as follows:

selectionSortAnimated
```
|least|
(1 to: self size) do: [:i | least ← i.
    (i + 1 to: self size) do: [:j |
        [ ( #aLiteralScore rebindGestures:
            ( #literalRelationskeysAtValues:
                        (Array with: (self at: least)
                                with: (self at: j)))) play.
            (self at: least) > (self at: j)] value
                            ifTrue: [least ← j]].
    least˜ = i ifTrue: [[( #aLiteralswap rebindGestures:
        (Array with: ( #aLiteralarray dynamicAt: i)
            with: ( #aLiteralarray dynamicAt: least))) play.
self swap: i with: least] value]]
```

Clearly, this code is more involved and obscure than the original seen in the code view of the window. The material added by the system is shown above in italics. Fortunately, the user need never see such code; it is generated by the system and is not readily accessed, except by interrupting and opening a debugger during execution of the animation. The changes consist in that the bugged messages such as "swap:with:" have been replaced by a block (enclosed in square brackets). The first statement in the block sends the message "play" to the swap score which first has its gestures bound to the appropriate elements of the array. A block is executed upon receiving the message "value," and the value returned is the value of the last statement. Since the last statement is the original statement to have been executed, the value of the block is the same as the unanimated statement, in case the value was to be used for side effect.

5. Further Directions

As mentioned earlier, the system described is experimental, deliberately limited in generality, but sufficient to demonstrate a promising mode of interaction. One of its limitations is that it allows instrumentation of programs at only one level in the calling stack. As in the example, one could only identify animations to occur in response to messages in the procedure appearing in the lower-right code view. In object-oriented environments, the calling stack is typically deep, making this an unrealistic limitation. A more recent extension allows indications to be made into code viewed in any arbitrary browser, though this raises some scoping issues that have yet to be resolved.

In addition, recognizing the power in constraint systems for building and running structured and dynamic graphics, we are integrating the gestural interface for describing animations as a front end to a constraint-based animation system. Animus and ThingLab, with their libraries of predefined graphical objects with well-constrained behavior, would be a great help in providing the user with a set of standard data-structure visualizations, enabling a user to construct a program animation quickly. Also, instead of this system's ability to draw an unspecified relation between objects, the constraint systems will allow the declaration of a wide range of constraint relationships between graphics and code or data, greatly increasing the generality and semantic richness of this style of interaction.

References

1. D. KNUTH, *The Art of Computer Programming*, Vol. 1, Addison-Wesley, Reading, Massachusetts, 1973.
2. R. L. LONDON AND R. A. DUISBERG, Animating programs using Smalltalk, *IEEE Comput.* **18**(8), 61–71 (1985).
3. R. DUISBERG, Constraint-based animation: the implementation of temporal constraints in the Animus system, Ph.D. thesis, University of Washington, Seattle, 1986. Published as U. W. Computer Science Department Technical Report No. 86-09-01.
4. M. H. BROWN AND R. SEDGEWICK, A system for algorithm animation, *Comput. Graphics* **18**(3), 177–186 (1984).
5. M. STEFIK, D. G. BOBROW, S. MITTAL, AND L. CONWAY, Knowledge programming in LOOPS: report on an experimental course, *AI Magazine* **4**(3), 3–13 (1983).
6. A. BORNING, The programming language aspects of ThingLab, a constraint-oriented simulation laboratory, *TOPLAS* **3**(4), 353–387 (1981).
7. W. CUNNINGHAM, Captured Gestures as Animation Primitives, Technical Report 87-18, Computer Research Laboratory, Tektronix, Inc., December 1986.

9

PRINCIPLES OF
ALADDIN AND OTHER ALGORITHM ANIMATION SYSTEMS*

Esa Helttula, Aulikki Hyrskykari, and Kari-Jouko Räihä

Abstract

Animation is a useful tool in teaching and developing algorithms. The idea of animating algorithm executions was suggested in the sixties, but the technology for producing real-time animations with reasonable cost matured in the early eighties. Since then several animation systems have been developed. The most influential of these systems are surveyed in this paper. A closer look will be taken at the animation system ALADDIN which is being developed in the University of Tampere.

1. Introduction

Computer programs have traditionally been linear, one-dimensional objects. The few systems that have made use of a two-dimensional notation for describing the program, such as the database query language Query-By-Example[1] or the famous VisiCalc[2] with its numerous successors, have been instant successes.

The development of graphical workstations has increased the

* This work was supported by the Academy of Finland.

ESA HELTTULA, AULIKKI HYRSKYKARI, and KARI-JOUKO RÄIHÄ • Department of Computer Science, University of Tampere, SF-33101, Tampere, Finland.

possibilities of using graphics in program development. A graphical, two-dimensional representation is natural especially in data flow programs, which the programmer intuitively understands as two-dimensional objects. Research is under way also for finding suitable two-dimensional representations for traditional programs written in sequential languages.[3,4]

All the above systems deal with visual programming: the description of a program using graphical, two-dimensional notations. However, graphics has also another role in programming environments: it can be used to illustrate the properties of traditional programs. This is usually called program visualization. Surveys that clarify these terms can be found in Refs. 3, 5, and 6.

Furthermore, there are two aspects of program visualization: the visualization of code and the visualization of data. Techniques for the former are well known. They range from primitive tracing systems where program lines are highlighted to complete, comprehensive programming environments, of which PECAN[7] is perhaps the utmost example.

In this report we deal with the other side of program visualization: the visualization of data. The term algorithm animation is often used in this context. Briefly, the idea is that the system produces a series of pictures that illustrate the execution of the program. The pictures should help in improving the viewer's intuition of how the program works. It has even been suggested that by watching a good animation, the viewer feels rather than sees the execution of the algorithm.

A research project dealing with visualization of data was launched in 1986 in the University of Tampere. The project is developing a system (called ALADDIN*) for generating animations of algorithms. The system will be used both in teaching old algorithms and in developing and analyzing new algorithms. The purpose of this report is to serve as an introduction to the project and to describe the main ideas on which ALADDIN is based. A more detailed description of the use and implementation of ALADDIN is given in Ref. 8.

2. Related Work

The first algorithm animations were films. One of the earliest was a film for animating linked lists.[9] A famous film that illustrates the behavior of sorting algorithms was produced in Toronto by Baecker.[10,11] It can well be considered to be the main stimulus for the research in the animation of

---

* ALADDIN is an acronym for *al*gorithm *a*nimation *d*esign and *d*escription using *in*teraction.

algorithms. However, producing films is slow and expensive, and research soon concentrated on computerized animation.

In this section we will cover the existing animation systems. The emphasis is on describing the strong points of each system. A more extensive survey can be found in Ref. 12.

2.1. BALSA-I and BALSA-II

The best-known animation system is BALSA, developed at Brown University by Marc Brown and Robert Sedgewick. BALSA may be considered as a pioneer algorithm animation system that stirred general interest in algorithm animation. Many of the ideas introduced in BALSA have later been used in other systems.

There are two versions of the system. BALSA-I[13, 14] is implemented on the Apollo and Sun workstations, while Marc Brown's second version of the system, BALSA-II,[12, 15, 16] is implemented on the Macintosh. The basic structure of the systems is the same, though there is some difference in terminology and in implementational issues between them. The most notable difference between the systems is in the user interface, due to the strong influence of Macintosh on BALSA-II.

There is a wide collection of very impressive example animations built up for both of the BALSA versions. BALSA is also the only algorithm animation system with which quite a lot of experience in real use has been acquired. Both versions have been used for several years in teaching programming and data structures. Animations created with BALSA have also been used in teaching other subjects such as physics and even neurology.

The most attractive feature of BALSA is its flexible and versatile environment for running the animations. The animation may consist of several views, each of which illustrates the execution of the algorithm from a different point of view. Figure 1 shows the run-time environment of BALSA-II with two running algorithms, each of which is illustrated with two views. The user can choose which views he or she wants to see during the animation and control the locations and sizes of the view windows. The user can zoom the view in a window, stop the animation, and bring a new view into a window or scroll the view in the window. In BALSA-I, even the reverse execution of some simple animations is possible. The user may also change the values of the parameters associated with either of the algorithms, the input values or the graphical appearance of the view. The available options depend always on the programmer of the animation; a parameter can be reached only if the programmer implements the code for it.

Scripting has proved to be a nice facility in BALSA. Scripting means a possibility to record the graphical events occurring during the animation of

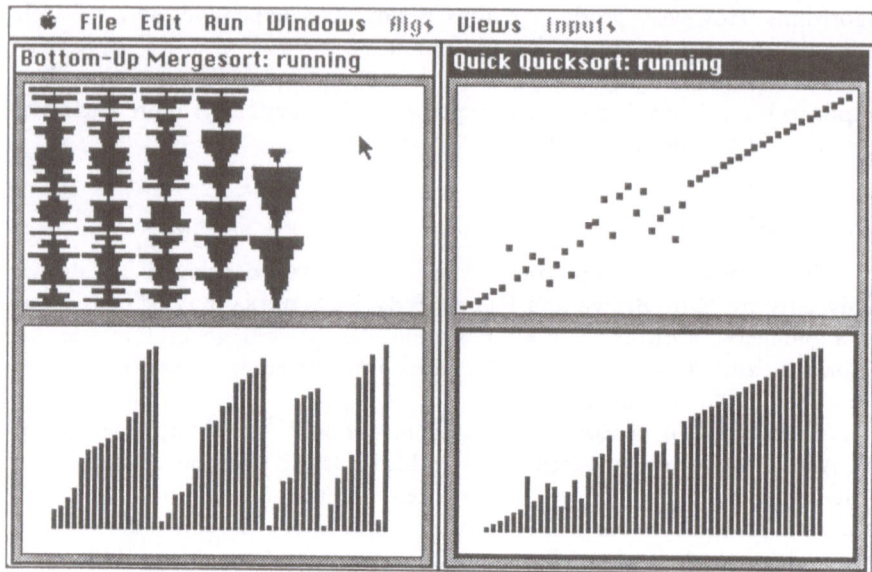

FIGURE 1. Animating two sorting algorithms with BALSA-II.

an algorithm. It can be used in building more complex demonstrations. Another advantage achieved by scripting is the possibility to build "algorithm races," that is, to give the user an illusion of several simultaneously running programs (as in Figure 1).

Implementing an animation for an algorithm is based on the notion of interesting events. The programmer locates in the algorithm the points that are of interest from the animation point of view. The interesting events may be either input or output events. With input events, the algorithm gets the inputs it needs, and with output events, the algorithm sends a message to the views to update themselves. The interesting events are written as procedure calls, which the programmer adds to the algorithm in the places where he or she wants something to happen during the animation.

The programmer also has to provide the code that is executed when the input or output event is encountered, that is, the code for the input generators and the view managers. The input generators are procedures that pass the input values to the algorithm. This way the programmer can provide the user of the animation with several ways of generating the input. The essential idea in implementing the view managers is to divide the task between modelers, which maintain the data needed in drawing the display, and renderers, which actually take care of the drawing. Thus, several different views may be built using the information of one modeler.

BALSA assists the programmer in these tasks by providing templates which help in producing the needed code segments. For example, when implementing a view, the programmer has to give only the code which is specific for the view. The programmer does not have to worry about general stuff such as managing the windows or passing control to the view modeler or renderer while the animation is running. The implementation of BALSA-II gives the impression that the interfaces for input generators and view managers are more carefully defined than they were in BALSA-I. This gives the programmer better possibilities to reuse previously implemented old views and input generators, thus simplifying his or her work remarkably.

2.2. Movie and Stills

Jon Bentley and Brian Kernighan have devised a set of tools for UNIX that enable the animation of programs.[17] First, the animator augments a program with print statements that produce a script file. The script file can then be fed to either the movie program or the stills program. The movie program produces a movie, and the stills program produces pictures that can be included in troff documents.

The script file contains commands that the movie and stills programs understand. Some available commands are text, line, and circle for outputting text and geometric objects, view for setting the current view, and click for marking interesting events. Pieces of text, geometric objects, and views can be labeled to make it easy to erase them later. Parameters are used to choose the size and justification of text, thickness of lines, and hollowness of circles. The use of a script file makes the system language independent, as it does not matter what program produced the script file in the first place. A script file can also be written by hand.

The movie program takes as input a script file and produces a movie on a Teletype 5620 terminal or a Sun workstation. The user has a set of commands to play the movie forward or backward at various speeds or to step through certain interesting events one by one. The movie can consist of different views, and the user can change their location.

The stills program is implemented as a preprocessor for the pic drawing language, which feeds the troff document formatter. With stills, it is rather easy to insert snapshots of an animation into a document.

Processing the script files before feeding the movie and stills programs introduces many possibilities. Making movies or pictures of algorithm races can be done simply by merging the script files produced by those algorithms. The synchronization of the race is accomplished by basing the merge on the number of certain interesting events in the script files.

The set of graphical primitives is small, which limits the quality of movies and pictures produced by the system. The main objective, on the other hand, has been to make the system simple to use.

2.3. Animus and Related Systems

Robert Duisberg has been involved with several animation systems. The first,[18] which he built together with Ralph London from Tektronix, is really not a special-purpose animation system at all. Rather, it exploits the Smalltalk programming paradigm for producing the animations. For instance, when two elements of an array are swapped in a sorting algorithm, an exchange message is sent to an object that corresponds to an array element. In addition to a method for actually carrying out the swap in the array, the object could also contain a method for visualizing the change in the graphical display. Thus, animation could essentially be achieved by "piggybacking" it on the algorithm code.

This sounds tempting, but in practice there are difficulties. If the program is not composed of suitable messages, extra messages might have to be added for the purposes of animation. Another problem is that the resulting animation may not be realistic: if several views are used in the animation, the views are updated sequentially, not simultaneously as the viewer would expect. These are some of the reasons that prompted the development of a complete algorithm animation system, called Animus.[19,20]

Animus is based on ThingLab,[21,22] a system for object management. It removes the problems with sequential view updates by controlling event handling itself. More interestingly, constraints can be used for specifying some of the visual effects. For instance, a constraint might say that the distance of two nodes (in a graph animation) must remain unchanged. Then moving one of the nodes would automatically trigger an event that moves the other one.

Recent research has concentrated on a gestural specification of the animation steps.[23] To visualize the swapping of two elements in an array, the user would drag the icon of an element from the old position to the new one. The system tracks the mouse movements and constructs a log of events that can be further edited and manipulated textually.

2.4. Other Animation Systems

A project at Computer Corporation of America[24] produced a prototype system that has been used in the animation of a few typical data structure algorithms. The funding of the project has been discontinued.

An interesting application of animation is in studying parallel algorithms. This area has recently attracted considerable attention.[25,26,27]

This research might eventually lead to special-purpose animation systems. The emphasis in this area is in visualizing the communications, not the computation.

3. Design Principles of ALADDIN

ALADDIN is being implemented on the Macintosh computer. The editor is written in Lightspeed Pascal, and it can be used to generate animations of Modula-2 programs (Modula-2 is the language used in the introductory programming courses at the University of Tampere). ALADDIN is intended to be primarily a tool for teaching data structures and algorithms, but it should also find use in the research of algorithms.

The main motivation for building ALADDIN has been the desire to make the creation of new animations easy, without sacrificing the quality of the result. Existing systems offer two solutions for creating new visualizations of objects:

1. Existing visualizations are collected into a library, from which they can be used as such or mimicked to create a slightly different animated object.
2. If the animator wants to create a completely different visualization, he has to resort to graphics programming (possibly using a specialized language, as in `movie/stills`).

Our goal has been to give the user complete freedom in designing the visualizations without forcing him to prepare complicated graphics programs. Therefore, ALADDIN consists of an animation editor and an animation execution environment. The editor can be used as a fairly standard Macintosh text editor when writing the Modula-2 code for the algorithm. It has also facilities for graphically specifying the animation.

The animation is described by interleaving the graphical specification with the program text. The specification is composed of three kinds of components, each of which has counterparts in conventional programming. The user can insert graphical types, graphical variables, and animation statements into the program code. A new algorithm can be animated in a couple of hours. The idea is illustrated with an example in the next section.

Interleaving the specification of the animation with the program code has been criticized in the papers cited above, on the grounds that it makes a flexible handling of different views difficult during algorithm execution. However, in our system each view is displayed in a different window, and thus the appropriate collection of views can be easily selected by closing the uninteresting windows. Moreover, animation steps are associated with conditions (Boolean expressions); thus, the collection of views that are maintained can easily be chosen by setting some Boolean variables.

We have tried to minimize the amount of Modula-2 code that must be added to the program for the purposes of animation. The control variables discussed above (called "ghost variables" in Ref. 12) are one case where a small addition to the original code seems useful and tolerable. Another situation arises when the animated program does not contain a control structure that is needed for animation. For instance, to illustrate the parts of a visualization, it might sometimes be useful to highlight the essential objects (and perhaps assign initial values to their components) one by one before starting the execution. This might require adding a Modula-2 loop to the program, since the animation statements do not contain iteration.

While we are striving for a general-purpose system, we also intend to assist the user by providing utilities that can be used in specific areas. One such case occurs in the animation of graph algorithms, where an automatic routine for computing the layout of the nodes in the graph will be provided. Otherwise, the location of each object would have to be determined in the specification of the animation, either as coordinates or by the use of features of the graphical editor.

At the moment, we are building a basic version and have put some topics aside for further research. For instance, if the amount of data is large, it is difficult to fit enough on the screen. How should one focus on the correct part of the data, and how could the focus be smoothly switched from one place to another? At present, we do not intend to provide the possibility of algorithm races. While such races are illustrative, the timings in them are extremely hard to get right, so that the result of the race is fair to all participating algorithms. Finally, script writing tools will be designed carefully and added to the system later.

4. A Brief Example

In this section we briefly show what kind of animations we are aiming at and give a couple of illustrative examples of the steps needed for specifying the animation. For interested readers, a more detailed description of the design process of an animation can be found in Ref. 8.

It is difficult to describe dynamic views statistically. Two snapshots (Figures 2 and 3) are used below to give a flavor of how Dijkstra's shortest-paths algorithm could be animated. The algorithm is assumed to be known and is not described here. The graph used consists of five nodes, and the costs between nodes can be seen in the pictures. The pictures also show that node 1 is the starting node (it has a wider contour than the others).

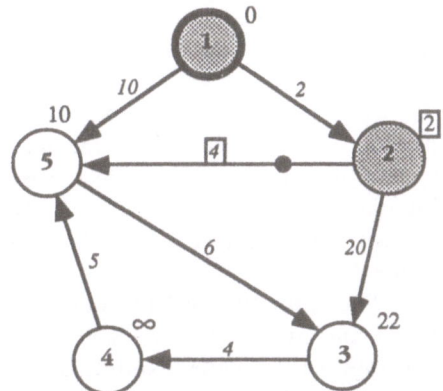

FIGURE 2. Computing the cost of a path.

In Figure 2, nodes 1 and 2 are shaded to show the fact that the shortest paths for them have already been found. The length of the path handles node 2; it updates the distances of the nodes directly accessible from node 2. The new distance of node 5 will then be lower, only 6 instead of 10. The recomputation is illustrated with a rolling ball along the cheaper path and with frames around the costs that are used in computing the new cost of the path from node 1 to 5. When the ball reaches node 5, the old distance will blink a couple of times before being replaced by the new one.

The snapshot in Figure 3 indicates the process of choosing the node to be handled after node 2. The distances from node 1 of all unhandled nodes are examined, and the node with the shortest distance is chosen. In the snapshot, the distances of nodes 3 and 4 are being compared, which is why they are highlighted by inverting the distances. The smaller of the two will then be compared to the distance of node 5.

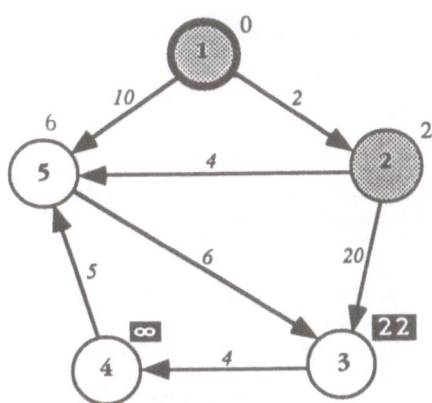

FIGURE 3. Choosing the next node after node 2.

Finally, when the execution of the algorithm is completed, all nodes will be shaded, and the distance from node 1 will be shown beside each node.

How is the above animation produced using ALADDIN? First, the user must open (or write) the code for the algorithm with the editor of our system. The overall design of the editor complies with the Macintosh user interface guidelines. The editor has a built-in drawing facility for designing various object types, which can be composed of any number of basic elements.

The animation of Dijkstra's algorithm has two types of objects, namely, nodes and arcs. Figure 4 illustrates the design of an object type for nodes. The object type (called NodeImage) has three elements. The master element is the circle that denotes the node. The other elements are text elements for the label and the cost. Each basic element has a number of attributes that can be specified in the object type definition and later changed with an animation statement.

All parts of the specification are shown as small iconic boxes within the program code. The box contains a miniature of the picture designed using the editor, together with the name of the object type. It is natural to place the boxes for object type definitions among the type definitions in the animated program. After the user has designed the types, he or she must

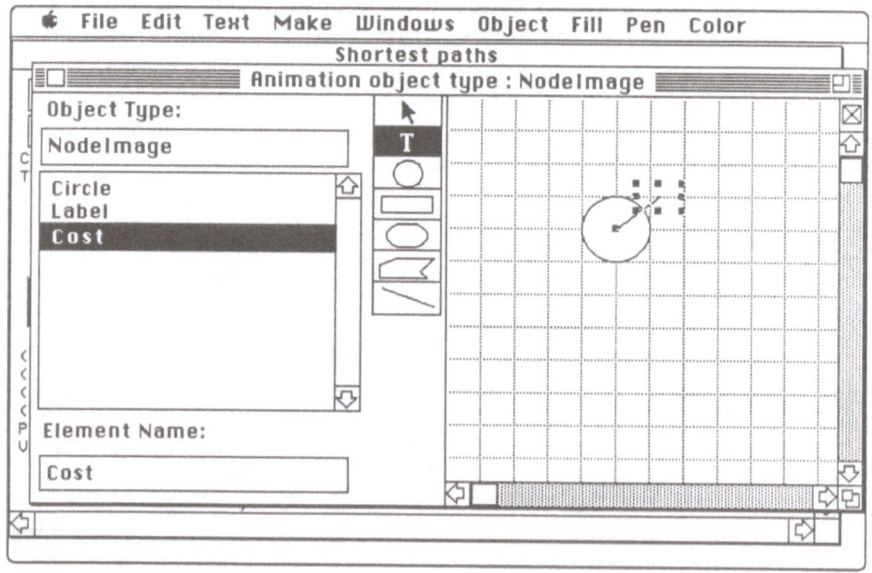

FIGURE 4. Designing an object type NodeImage.

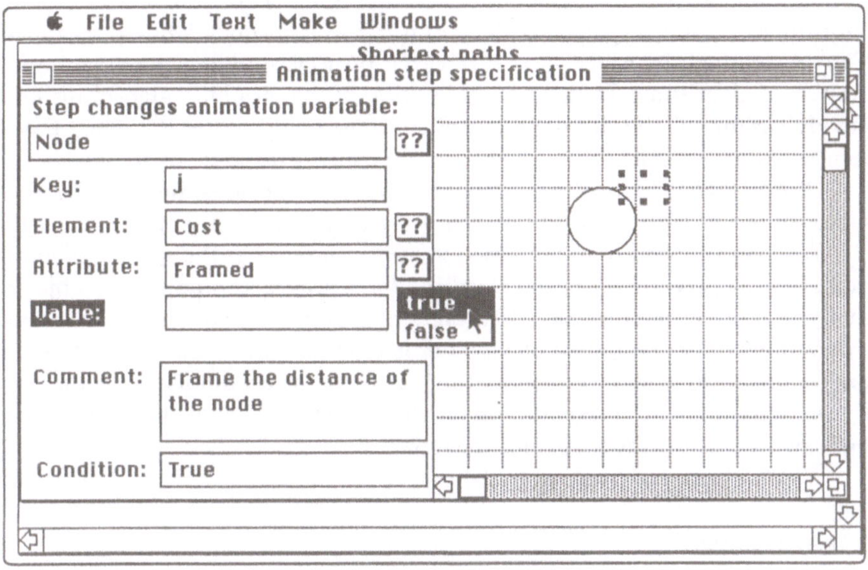

FIGURE 5. Specifying an animation step.

declare graphical variables using those types. In this case, the user declares a set whose elements are of type NodeImage and another set for arcs.

In addition to types and variables, the user must specify the animation statements. Animation statements can be used to create new graphical objects in a given window, to change the appearance of an object in an animation step, and to produce various effects.

The animation objects are created with a key (or many keys) that can later be used to access the objects again. The actual animation is composed of many steps, each of which can be specified graphically as in Figure 5.

The iconic box that represents an animation step in the program shows the picture of the object type being manipulated in the step, along with a comment describing the step. Hopefully, this makes it easy to get a general idea of the animation process from the program text, without disturbing too much the actual reading of the code. It is also possible to hide all the iconic boxes, if the user only wants to work with the original program code.

5. Concluding Remarks

We began the project by building up experience on how to write animations. Our first animations include an animation of AVL trees on the

Apollo using BALSA[6] and an animation of some new disjoint set union algorithms[28] using Lightspeed Pascal on the Macintosh.[29] The prototypes of the system will be tested in real research projects studying the design and analysis of algorithms. In fact, the animation of the set union algorithms has already prompted the development of some new algorithms.[29] They have been evaluated empirically and shown to outperform previous methods.

Graph layout algorithms are a spin-off research area inspired by the implementation of ALADDIN. Some results are presented in Refs. 30 and 31.

We believe that an animation system that integrates the specification of animation steps with a graphical editor for drawing the animated objects finally makes the undeniable advantages of animation available to a casual programmer. The main goal of ALADDIN is to enable the production of high-quality animations in a very short time. Experience accumulated in the use of ALADDIN will be used to guide the development of the prototype implementation toward reaching this goal.

Acknowledgments

Thanks to Marc Brown, Erkki Mäkinen, and Heikki Mannila for useful discussions. This work was supported by the Academy of Finland.

References

1. M. M. ZLOOF, QBE/OBE: A language for office and business automation, *IEEE Comput.* **14**(5), 13–22 (1981).
2. D. H. BEIL, *The VisiCalc Book* (Atari, Apple, and IBM editions), Reston Publishing Co., Reston, Virginia, 1983.
3. G. RAEDER, A survey of current graphical programming techniques, *IEEE Comput.* **18**(8), 11–25 (1985).
4. S.-K. CHANG, Visual languages: a tutorial and survey, *IEEE Software* **4**(1), 29–39 (1987).
5. B. A. MYERS, Visual programming, programming by example, and program visualization: A taxonomy, Proceedings of the CHI '86 Conference on Human Factors in Computer Systems, April 1986, pp. 59–66.
6. A. HYRSKYKARI, Visualization of Program Executions (in Finnish), Report B-1987-4, Department of Computer Science, University of Tampere, February 1987.
7. S. P. REISS, PECAN: Program development systems that support multiple views, *IEEE Trans. Software Engineering* **SE-11**(3), 276–285 (1985).
8. E. HELTTULA, A. HYRSKYKARI, and K.-J. RÄIHÄ, Graphical specification of algorithm animations with ALADDIN. Proceedings of HICSS22, Hawaï, January 1989, IEEE Computer Society Press, pp. 892–901.
9. K. C. KNOWLTON, L6: Bell Telephone Laboratories Low-Level Linked List Language, Black and white sound films, Bell Laboratories, Murray Hill, New Jersey, 1966.
10. R. M. BAECKER, Two systems which produce animated representations of the execution of computer programs, *SIGCSE Bull.* **7**(1), 158–167 (1975).
11. R. M. BAECKER, Sorting Out Sorting, film, Dynamic Graphics Project, Computer Systems Research Institute, University of Toronto, 1981.

12. M. H. Brown, Algorithm animation, Ph.D. thesis, Brown University, Providence, Rhode Island, 1987. Also published in the *Distinguished Dissertations* series by MIT Press, Cambridge, Massachusetts, 1988.
13. M. H. Brown and R. Sedgewick, A system for algorithm animation, *Comput. Graphics* **18**(3), 177–185 (1984).
14. M. H. Brown and R. Sedgewick, Techniques for algorithm animation, *IEEE Software* **2**(1), 28–39 (1985).
15. M. H. Brown, Exploring algorithms using BALSA-II, *Computer* **21**(5), 14–36 (1988).
16. M. H. Brown, Perspectives on algorithm animation, Proceedings of the CHI '88 Conference on Human Factors in Computer Systems, May 1988, pp. 33–38.
17. J. Bentley and B. Kernighan, A System for Algorithm Animation: Tutorial and User Manual, Computing Science Technical Report No. 132, AT & T Bell Laboratories, Murray Hill, New Jersey, January 1987.
18. R. L. London and R. A. Duisberg, Animating programs using Smalltalk, *IEEE Comput.* **18**(8), 61–71 (1985).
19. R. A. Duisberg, Animated graphical interfaces using temporal constraints, Proceedings of the CHI '86 Conference on Human Factors in Computer Systems, April 1986, pp. 131–136.
20. R. A. Duisberg, Animation using temporal constraints: An overview of the Animus system, *Human Comput. Interaction* **3**(1), 275–307 (1987–88).
21. A. Borning, The programming language aspects of ThingLab, a constraint-oriented simulation laboratory, *ACM Trans. Programming Languages Systems* **3**(4), 353–387 (1981).
22. A. Borning and R. Duisberg, Constraint-based tools for building user interfaces, *ACM Trans. Graphics* **5**(4), 345–374 (1986).
23. R. A. Duisberg, Visual programming of program visualizations. A gestural interface for animating algorithms, Proceedings of the 1987 Workshop on Visual Languages, Linköping, August 1987, pp. 55–66.
24. G. P. Brown, R. T. Carling, C. F. Herot, D. A. Kramlich, and P. Souza, Program visualization: Graphical support for software development, *IEEE Comput.* **18**(8), 27–35 (1985).
25. U. Solin, Parallel Algorithm Animation, Report A50, Reports on Computer Science & Mathematics, Abo Akademi, Finland, July 1986.
26. J. M. Stone, Visualizing Concurrent Processes, IBM Research Report RC12973, July 1987.
27. M. Zimmermann, F. Perrenoud, and A. Schiper, Understanding concurrent programming through program animation, *SIGCSE Bull.* **20**(1), 27–31 (1988).
28. H. Mannila and E. Ukkonen, The set union problem with backtracking, in *Proceedings of the Thirteenth International Colloquium on Automata, Languages, and Programming (ICALP 86)*, Springer-Verlag, New York, 1986, pp. 236–243.
29. E. Helttula, Analysis and animation of set union algorithms (in Finnish), M.Sc. thesis, Department of Computer Science, University of Tampere, Tampere, Finland, January 1988.
30. E. Mäkinen, On circular layouts, *Int. J. Comput. Math.* **24**, 29–37 (1988).
31. H. Sirtola, Graph layout algorithms (in Finnish), M.Sc. thesis, Department of Computer Science, University of Tampere, Tampere, Finland, May 1988.

V

SIMULATION ANIMATION

Animation is useful not only for studying the behavior of algorithms, but also for simulating the operation of more general systems. Dave Bridgeland describes Simulacrum, developed for the simulation of relatively mechanical systems, illustrating its use in the simulation of elevator control systems. Charles E. Hughes and J. Michael Moshell approach animated simulation from the viewpoint of spreadsheets. Combining these ideas with object-oriented programming, they produce an interesting system, Action Graphics, for describing and animating a simulation. In the final chapter in this section, Timothy C. Lethbridge and Colin Ware take a more fine-grained look at the subject of animation, discussing the use of behavior functions to produce apparently purposeful behavior of graphic objects.

10

SIMULACRUM: A SYSTEM BEHAVIOR EXAMPLE EDITOR

Dave Bridgeland

1. A Medium for Software System Examples

Our mission at the Software Technology Program at MCC is to significantly improve the quality and productivity of large complex software design. One approach to achieving this goal is to record the rationale and process of early project decisions.[1] A complex web of issues, problems, decisions, requirements, rationale, and alternative behaviors—the "issue base"—is built as a software project develops. This issue base can later be explored by newcomers to a project or old-timers who have forgotten why some decision was made. Furthermore, changes in requirements might be propagated and understood in terms of their effects on design decisions.

To understand what sorts of objects belong in the issue base, we examined the activity of upstream software development—what do designers do to understand a new problem and to begin to structure solutions to that problem? One common activity in upstream development is the creation of examples of system behavior. Adelson and Soloway[2] and Kant and Newell[3] both found empirical evidence of software designers testing partial models of behavior using specific examples. In their studies, a designer would build or augment a partial model of desired behavior, imagine a realistic situation, and mentally simulate his model against the imagined example. Often this would reveal unstated requirements or problems with the imagined system.

To better understand the nature of upstream design activities, we performed our own empirical study of individual designers solving the lift

DAVE BRIDGELAND • Artificial Intelligence Laboratory, Microelectronics and Computer Technology Corporation, Austin, Texas 78701. This chapter was completed while the author was on the staff of the Software Technology Program at MCC.

problem.[4] Each subject attempted to specify the behavior of an elevator control system to meet certain requirements. In this study we found many examples of subjects building examples of elevator behavior. Typically, a subject would sketch a configuration of floors, elevators at various positions, and passengers at various places making requests for transportation. The subject would then reason about how this lift system might behave and change through time.

Examples seemed to play several roles in upstream design:

- Examples elicit issues in the individual creating the example. (For example: "In this situation, the elevators all race to pick up passenger Joe. *Issue*: What should we do about race conditions?")
- Examples cause unstated requirements to be realized. (For example: "If this processor fails in this situation, the whole elevator system crashes, leaving people stranded everywhere. *Requirement*: It's very important for there to be no single point of failure.")
- Examples lead to refinements of solution behavior. (For example: "Joe leaves the elevator, so there are no more requests either from within the elevator or from a floor. Which direction should the elevator travel now? *Solution*: There should be a third direction, STANDING-STILL, meaning the elevator is traveling neither up nor down.")
- Examples reveal the problems with some solution already proposed. (For example: "A continual stream of people at the second floor going down can prevent any elevator from servicing requests on higher floors. *Problem*: This proposed solution violates stated requirements about guarantee of service.")

Many of the lift study subjects attempted to sketch the behavioral examples as they explored them. However, paper proved to be a rather poor medium for these sketches. It is hard to diagram the way a configuration of lifts and people might change through time. Hence, often the examples were not recorded at all. Any potential value as a record of decisions made in the upstream was lost forever.

Some kind of drawing tool which could naturally handle changes through time was needed. This tool should allow designers to sketch an example system behavior, edit it, save it to disk, and communicate the sketch to other designers. Furthermore, such a tool should not force a designer to attend to many details which detract from the nature of the design task.

2. Domain Independence

In an attempt to build a useful example editing tool, I initially built a simple domain-independent example editor. Using this editor, one could draw lines, boxes, arrows, and other graphic and textual objects in a standard graphics editing manner. The user could sketch the state of an elevator system (for example) and sequence such states to show an example of elevator behavior through time. This system, Simulacrum-1,* was a kind of animation system, but very different from existing commercial animation systems. Commercial systems allow a graphics professional to spend three months developing a polished 15-second television commercial. This system was built to allow an occasional user to spend 10 minutes developing a 10-frame animated sketch.

My use of the word "animation" in this paper is nonstandard. Using Simulacrum, a user could develop, edit, and save time-based sketches of behavior. A time-based sequence of sketches represented a sequence of states of a system at discrete time intervals. Once such a sequence was created, a user could browse through it, stepping through the system states. However, the sequence could not be "played" like a movie, with machine interpolation transforming the discrete changes in state into an illusion of continuity. This functionality may be interesting, but it does not seem central to the understanding of system behavior. Therefore, an "animation"—in this paper—means only a sequence of states in time.

There were several problems with Simulacrum-1. The sketch editor was domain-independent, so the objects manipulated by the editor were generic graphic things, such as lines, boxes, and lines of text. To make one conceptual change to a sketch, a user often had to perform many graphic operations. The translation from the conceptual level to the graphic level was both time-consuming and distracting.

Furthermore, the resulting animations often lacked conceptual integrity. A given conceptual relationship (for example, the notion that a user was bound for a given floor) could be drawn in many different ways, and was.

Finally, the relationship between the graphics and the intended semantics was not always clear to the browsers of animations created by others. There was no way to determine what a given state sketch meant, except to query the person who had drawn it.

---

* "Simulacrum" is an English word meaning "an insubstantial form or semblance of something."[5] Thus, it is highly appropriate for the first operational notions of the behavior of a system.

3. A Generic Animation Editor and A Custom Lift Editor

Simulacrum-2 was built to correct the deficiencies of Simulacrum-1. In particular, the semantics of objects in the lift problem—elevators, floors, passengers, etc.—were isolated and encoded, and direct manipulation[6] presentations of those objects and their relationships was custom-designed.* Thus, the editing is constrained and simplified; the user can create only plausible elevator system states. For example, the user can move a passenger to a floor or within a lift, but not on top of a lift, or between two floors. Because the semantics are explicitly encoded and have unique visual presentations, conceptual integrity is maintained. Finally, a user can explore the relation between the graphics and the system semantics by manipulating the graphics to see plausible alternate states of the system.

For example, Figure 1 shows a *snapshot*, a state of an elevator system. There are five floors of a building, three lifts, and two people. The lifts are sliders which can be moved to various levels. People can be created, moved to within lifts or on floors, or destroyed. Both lifts and floors have buttons which can be toggled to indicate that some elevator request has been made but not yet satisfied.

Simulacrum-2 attempts to be a WYSIATI system—what you see is all there is. All of the important objects and relationships are visually presented.

A generic animated object editor was built around the lift-specific presentations, so sequences of system states could be shown and edited. A Simulacrum-2 user arranges system snapshots into *clips*, linear sequences of behavior. Figure 2 shows a short clip of elevator behavior. At the top of the screen is a *map* of the clip. It shows which snapshots are *detailed* in the *comic strip* below. In Figure 2, all but the last snapshot are detailed. The Simulacrum-2 user can interactively browse through a clip by detailing any or all snapshots.

The relation between the individual snapshots in a clip is the *follows* relation, meaning that the right snapshot follows the left in time. This does not imply "immediately follows"; if state B follows state A, there could be many distinct system states not pictured between A and B.

The example behavior shown in Figure 2 is an individual, Joe, on the second floor calling for an upbound elevator. All three lifts are idle, so they race to fill the request. Several of the subjects in the lift study were concer-

---

* This is cheating of course. Building a direct manipulation graphics interface for this domain was time-consuming and required some expertise. It is certainly not something that a software designer wants to do on his or her way to writing a specification of an elevator control system. In a later section, I will explain how one might be able to automate some of this process.

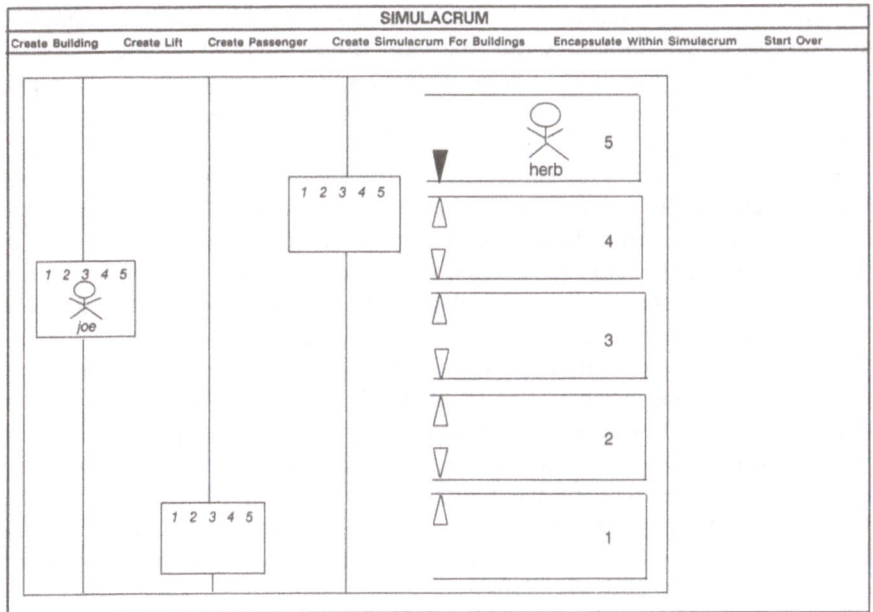

FIGURE 1. An elevator system snapshot.

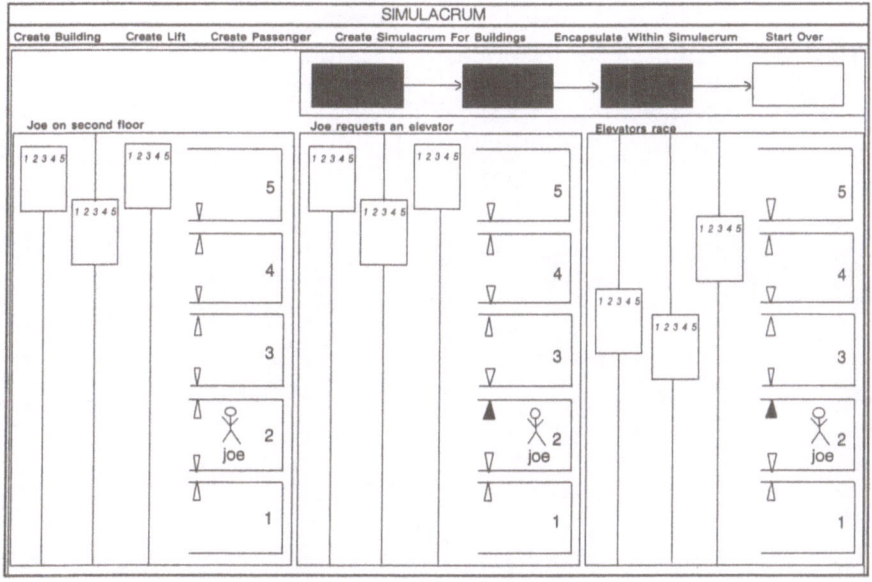

FIGURE 2. An elevator system clip.

ned with this "race condition" behavior and treated it as an "unexample," an example of behavior they did not want their system to exhibit.

It is often convenient to represent divergent behavior in an example, either because the desired system behavior is nondeterministic or because the environment in which the system exists is considered to be nondeterministic. A *scene*, a tree of snapshots, is used to represent such a situation. Figure 3 shows the example of Figure 2 augmented with another possible behavior. In this case, only one elevator picks up Joe. Note that only two of the snapshots in the clip are detailed in the comic strip. Any number of the snapshots in the map can be detailed, as Simulacrum-2 sizes the detailed snapshots to fit the space available.

To better understand the uses and limitations of detailing examples of behavior, I applied Simulacrum to itself. Thus, potential new behavior for Simulacrum could be explored through examples. This was possible because all the graphic presentations and mouse handling are built on top of a resizable software layer, so the nesting of Simulacrum within Simulacrum was rather straightforward. Furthermore, Simulacrum-2 itself is largely WYSIATI, semantically representing and visually presenting most of its important objects and relationships. Note that Simulacrum-2 does not visually present or semantically represent the Simulacrum-2 user. Hence,

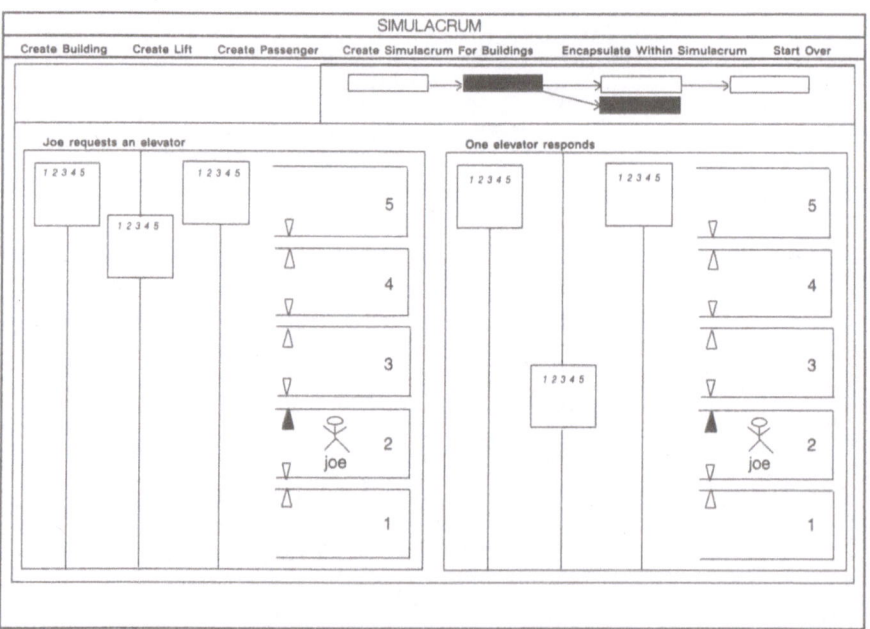

FIGURE 3. Another clip from a scene.

examples of proposed Simulacrum behavior are not as transparent as examples of elevator behavior. For example, if I want to show Joe the elevator passenger pressing buttons and riding lifts, I have a pictorial presentation of Joe doing those things. But if I want to show Mel the Simulacrum user manipulating elevator presentations in various ways, I can only show the various states of Simulacrum and indicate in the textual comments what Mel is doing to bring about these states. Of course, the presentation of Simulacrum-2 could be extended to show the actions of the user.

Figure 4 shows an example of a simple Simulacrum-2 behavior, the ability to *extend* a snapshot, to create an identical copy of some snapshot to follow that snapshot. On the top half of the figure is an outer (Simulacrum) snapshot. This Simulacrum snapshot is composed of two inner (lift) snapshots, a simple elevator situation which is about to be extended. The bottom outer snapshot shows the Simulacrum state after it has been extended but before any further editing.

Extension is also used to create representations of divergent behavior, as Figure 5 shows. Here the first inner snapshot is extended. The bottom outer snapshot shows the situation after the extension and some subsequent editing.

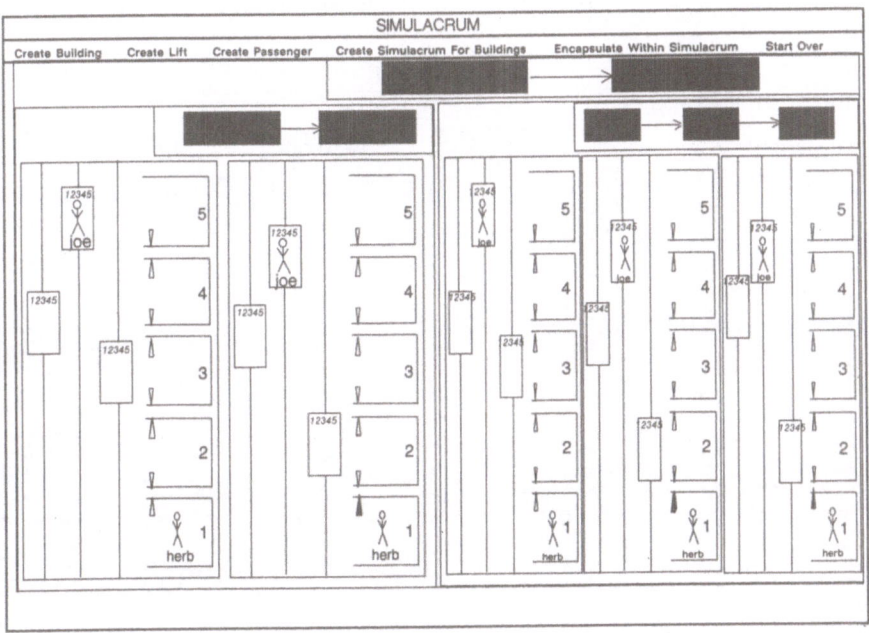

FIGURE 4. The Simulacrum behavior extension.

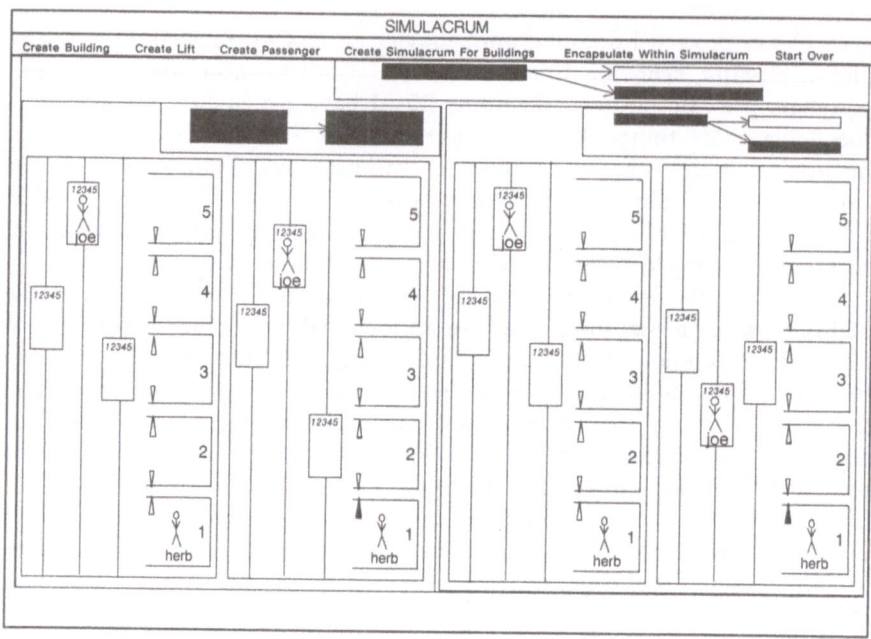

FIGURE 5. Another view of extension.

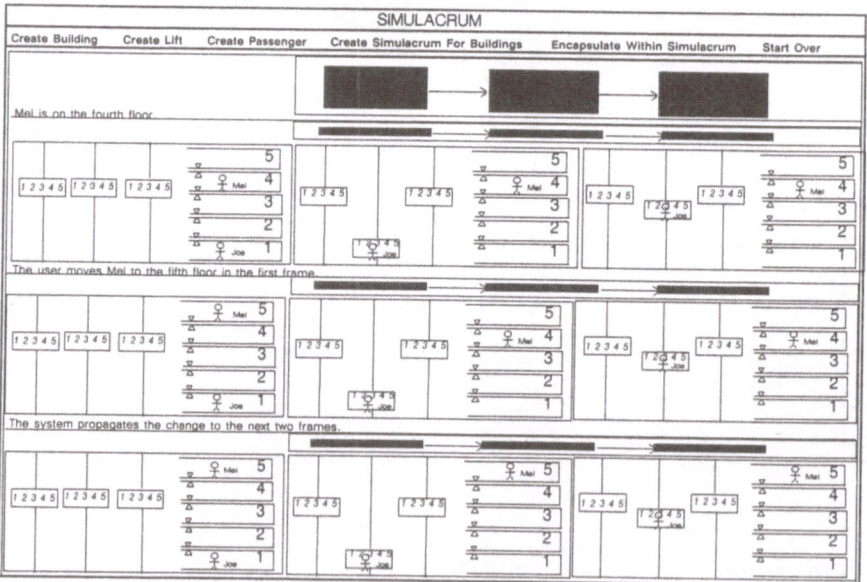

FIGURE 6. Extrapolation.

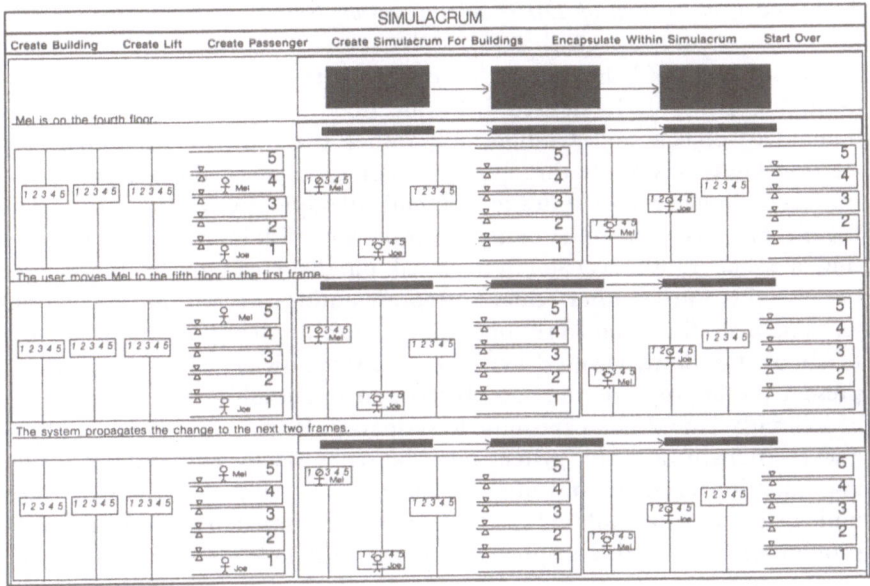

FIGURE 7. More complex extrapolation.

Note that Figures 4 and 5 detail different snapshots from the same (outer) map. They are examples of different facets of the extension operation, so they are collected together, as divergent behavior from a single snapshot. A Simulacrum user could understand extension by browsing through this single scene.

Extrapolation and interpolation are more complex behaviors not yet supported by Simulacrum-2. However, we can explore the meaning of these behaviors without actually implementing them. A Simulacrum user could edit some snapshot and extrapolate the changes to all snapshots which follow. Figure 6 shows an example of a Simulacrum user changing the floor location of Mel, a lift user, and having that change propagated to subsequent snapshots. Note that the semantics of extrapolation is, in general, domain specific. In Figure 7, a similar extrapolation is made which causes an elevator to be requested at floor 2, not at floor 1, and for the elevator to subsequently stop at floor 2 rather than floor 1. Although the desired behavior may not yet be completely understood, examples of that behavior can be created and recorded for future reference and communication.

4. Visual Construction of Direct Manipulation Editors

Some kinds of behavior are more difficult to represent as Simulacrum-2 examples, particularly desired behavior that implies an extension of the domain of objects and relationships, rather than just an arrangement of existing kinds of objects through time. For example, a Simulacrum-2 user can save Simulacrum-2 states to disk and subsequently rebuild a state from the file. However, examples of more complicated disk interaction (e.g., reverting a scene to the version last stored on disk) cannot be represented, because there are neither semantic representations nor visual presentations for the disk files and disk operations. Before giving examples of disk behavior, the Simulacrum-2 user needs to semantically model and visually present the appropriate domain objects and relationships.

Simulacrum-2 is an incomplete system: in its present form, the objects and relations in a target system must be semantically modeled, and direct manipulation presentations of those objects and relations must be custom-built before any examples of behavior can be recorded. This is an expensive proposition, even with a state-of-the-art user interface management system,* and is certainly not something that a software designer wants to do on his or her way to understanding the behavior of some target system.

There are two problems here. Simulacrum needs some way of allowing the user to easily specify object types and relationships. For example, at any time a LIFT has a set of buttons, a LOCATION (perhaps a real number indicating its position against the height of the building), and a set of PASSENGERS. Although the LOCATION and the set of contained PASSENGERS can change, the set of BUTTONS cannot. This kind of specification could probably be entered and edited through a standard knowledge representation language frame editor.

The harder problem is visually tying the objects and relationships to interactive graphics. For example, the Simulacrum user must specify how to draw a LIFT given its LOCATION, where to draw the lift's BUTTONS and PASSENGERS, how to draw a BUTTON, and so on. Furthermore, the Simulacrum user must specify the way that the location and contained passengers are to be edited by a user. Conceivably, the user could start with a SLIDER cliche (from a library of graphical cliches), graphically edit it to look like a lift, and connect the height of the SLIDER to the real number

---

* Simulacrum-2 is built on Symbolics's Genera 7 User Interface Management System.[7] This system allows a user interface to be built at a higher level of abstraction and, in particular, allows typed interactive graphical presentations to be created without the need to write mouse-handling code. With the UIMS, the marginal cost of adding a new kind of object to Simulacrum-2 is reduced to the code required to draw the object in object-specific coordinates.

in the LOCATION of the LIFT. Then the positions and sizes of the BUTTONS and the PASSENGERS could be described visually with constraints.[8]

Montalvo recommends a completely different approach to building interactive presentations of a given semantics. She suggests[9] that the cognitively correct presentation of something is a kind of knowledge and should be represented in a knowledge representation language. She suggests that graphics could be created declaratively, through the use of perceptual properties like *above* and *squiggliness*. If practical, an interface building system based on such high-level constructs would be even more appropriate for designers quickly constructing graphical interfaces to system objects and relationships.

In short, Simulacrum needs a mechanism of some sort to allow the user to visually construct a direct manipulation interface to an arbitrary set of objects and relationships. Such an interface editor, a kind of second-generation user interface management system, could (of course) be useful in many domains.

5. Summary

Creating examples of system behavior is one way system designers analyze, understand, and describe proposed behavior. These examples should be recorded as part of the web of upstream decisions and rationale.

To explore the recording and editing of examples, I built Simulacrum-2, an example editor and arranger, and applied it to itself. Although useful to understand what is required for a generic example editor, Simulacrum-2 is incomplete in that adding new domain-specific objects and relationships requires both time and expertise. A second-generation user interface management system would alleviate these problems. Built on top of such a UIMS, Simulacrum could play a role in the capture of rationale and process in upstream software design.

References

1. J. CONKLIN AND D. BRIDGELAND, Beyond macro-iteration: an organic model of system design, in Proceedings of the 3rd International Software Process Workshop, pp. 57–63. IEEE Computer Society, 1986.
2. B. ADELSON AND E. SOLOWAY, The role of domain experience in software design, *IEEE Trans. Software Engineering* **SE-11**, 1351–1360 (1985).
3. E. KANT AND A. NEWELL, Problem solving techniques for the design of algorithms, *Information Processing and Management* **20**(12), 97–118 (1984).

4. R. GUINDON, H. KRASNER, AND B. CURTIS, A Model of Cognitive Processes in Software Design: An Analysis of Breakdown in Early Design Activities by Individuals, Microelectronics and Computer Technology Corporation Technical Report (1987).
5. *Webster's New Collegiate Dictionary*, G. & C. Merriam Company, Springfield, Massachusetts, 1981.
6. B. SCHNEIDERMAN, Direct manipulation: a step beyond programming languages, *IEEE Comput.* **16**(8), 57–80 (1983).
7. SYMBOLICS, INC., *Programming the User Interface*, Symbolics, Cambridge, Massachusetts, 1986.
8. A. BORNING, ThingLab—A Constraint-Oriented Simulation Laboratory, Xerox Palo Alto Research Center Technical Report SSl-79-3, July, 1979.
9. F. MONTALVO, Diagram understanding: associating symbolic descriptions with images, 1986 IEEE Computer Society Workshop on Visual Languages, 1986, pp. 4–11.

11

ACTION GRAPHICS
A SPREADSHEET-BASED LANGUAGE FOR ANIMATED SIMULATION

Charles E. Hughes
and J. Michael Moshell

1. A Personal Journey from Textual to Visual

In his book *Mindstorms*,[1] Seymour Papert describes a vision of how computers can create "micro worlds" in which the innate beauty of mathematics, physics, and other sciences are revealed to children. Many of us who are interested in helping children develop their problem-solving skills share his vision.

This introductory section describes four of our early efforts to produce problem-solving environments, or micro-world generators, for children. This progression of systems shows how our ideas about visual programming evolved from textual sequential programming, with visual displays, to entirely new programming paradigms.

1.1. Computer Power

In 1979, we started our first major effort to develop a visual programming environment, designed specifically to help children become better problem solvers. With the support of a grant from the National Science Foundation,[2] we assembled a group of high school teachers, graduate students, computer science faculty, an artist, and an educational psychologist. Our intent was to create a programming environment that was appropriate for junior high and high school students.

CHARLES E. HUGHES and J. MICHAEL MOSHELL • Computer Science Department, University of Central Florida, Orlando, Florida 32816.

Several events occurred in 1979 that made our immediate goals attainable. The Apple II had just become available. Its support of color graphics could be used to capture the attention of students and to make the experience of interacting with a computer enjoyable even for a nontechnical audience. Its Pascal system provided a reasonable (by 1979 microcomputer standards) programming platform on which to produce new software.

Working in small teams, we created an interpretive environment for Pascal, an animation library, a music library, a full-screen program editor, hundreds of example programs, and a one-semester high school curriculum. Our supporting material included a teachers' manual, a student text, and a set of enrichment activities for the more ambitious students.[3]

The Pascal programming environment we had created was a precursor to today's sophisticated programming visualization systems. The program editor was fully integrated with the interpreter. A single keystroke was sufficient to start interpretation of the program being edited. This program could then be scrolled at a variable rate, including one source statement at a time. As a line of source entered the text window on the lower part of the screen, the statement was interpreted and its graphical effects were observed in the upper part of the screen. In general, students wrote programs that produced animation, using the integrated graphics and music procedures.

One of the more interesting projects, done by students in a small rural Tennessee school, produced an animation of *Romeo and Juliet*, with frogs and pigs as actors. This was an encouraging example of a carry-over from the programming course into a nontechnical academic subject.

1.2. Visible Pascal

Our early experiences with Computer Power were so encouraging that we created a new, much improved version of our software. This new system, called Visible Pascal,[4] is intended to be used in the home.

Visible Pascal shares common features with other program visualization systems, such as MacPascal,[5] Alice,[6] and BALSA-II.[7] Where it differs most markedly is in its focus on cognitive as well as physical separation of program display and program output. Not only are program dynamics and output displayed in different windows (a common feature of the visualizing interpreters listed above), but we also supply a totally graphical output medium with $2\frac{1}{2}$-dimension animation capability. This means that there is maximal cognitive separation between what a program *is* and what it *does*.

Despite our technological successes with Visible Pascal, experience showed us that this type of visual programming environment does not seem to result in the desired transfer of problem-solving skills into other areas of learning. All textual programming languages, including Pascal, are inherently complex to the point that it takes young students an entire course just to master the technical skills of programming.

The cognitive separation of the processes of program creation and program execution is extremely difficult to deal with, even when text is used for one and graphics for the other. Computer programming of this sort does not appear to foster portable problem-solving skills. None of this diminishes the value of learning to program in languages like Pascal. It is just that our lofty goals of improving general problem-solving skills are apparently unattainable in this manner.

1.3. Picture Programming

Early in our analysis of Visible Pascal's effectiveness, we recognized its unsuitability for young children. Clearly, they should not have to deal with a textual programming language. To meet their needs, we designed and implemented a text-free programming environment called Picture Programming.[8]

The thoughts that led us to create Picture Programming are expressed beautifully by Alan Kay:

> As children we discovered that clay can be shaped into any form simply by shoving both hands into the stuff. Most of us have learned no such thing about the computer. Its material seems as detached from human experience as a radioactive ingot being manipulated remotely with buttons, tongs and a television monitor.
> What kind of emotional contact can one make with this new stuff if the physical access seems so remote?[9]

We wished to create an environment where the objects and their manipulations were familiar to children; one in which punctuation and obscure semantics were not a barrier to learning. In Picture Programming, the programmer plays the role of a movie director. The director (programmer) creates animated sequences by instructing actors to perform tasks in some prescribed order. In this system, programs are composed entirely of graphical icons that represent visible actions, actors, and control commands.

Picture Programming splits the display screen into three windows—a script area, a movie area, and a menu area. The movie area is in the middle of the screen and is the largest of the three. It displays the animation produced by the actions that make up a program. At any time, the picture frame in this area corresponds to the current point of execution of the program. The script at the top of the screen displays a portion of the program that has been created. The menu area at the bottom displays icons for actors and actions that can be inserted into the program script.

The icons that are used to select actors are

and those icons used for actions are

The actor icons represent those in the Adventure troupe, one of five built-in troupes. Each icon is selected by a corresponding keystroke or a mouse select. Here, pressing the key labeled "3" or clicking on the third actor icon adds the icon for a Wizard to the script window. The effect of selecting an actor is to make that actor visible and to make it carry out any actions we may request until a new actor is chosen.

The action icons represent directions to which actors can respond. The four footprints, labeled "6" to "9," are used to tell actors to walk left, right, up, or down, respectively. If we press a "7" several times, the wizard walks over several paces to the right. We can then flip him upside down by adding the icon associated with the "4" key. We can turn him right side up by pressing "4" a second time.

In addition to these menus, there is a ghost actor and a music menu. When the "ghost" of an actor is selected, the actor becomes invisible. While invisible, an actor can still take directions, but the visual effects of these actions are not seen. A ghost is often used when "staging" an actor, prior to its introduction into a story. When the music icon is selected, a new menu of note icons opens up. Inclusion of note icons in a story provides sound effects and primitive music.

Figure 1 shows icons for a picture program that causes a Minotaur and a Gorgon to roll across the screen, while fighting. The two actors are made to interact by alternately selecting one and then the other. There is no parallel simultaneous action. The |: and :| icons group actions that are to be repeated a fixed number of times, eight in this example.

As a script is created, the corresponding animation is produced immediately, one frame at a time. Whenever the cursor is backspaced over a script icon, the semantics of that icon are undone. Thus, backspacing over a "walk right" icon causes the actor to walk left. Forward cursor movement reexecutes icons as the cursor passes over them. A completed script, or even a partial one, can be executed at full speed, or slowly. It can even be run

FIGURE 1. Dueling demons.

backwards! There are no syntax or semantic errors, except that the script might not produce the desired story.

Picture Programming is clearly a visual programming language, not just a visible environment for a textual language. It removes the problems of learning a complex lexicon. It breaks down the barrier between creation and seeing the effects of creation.

As an environment in which children can be creative, Picture Programming is a success. However, while it focuses on several important aspects of problem solving, those of planning, prototyping, and incrementally altering a solution, it has no capability to deal with problems involving number or symbol manipulation.

1.4. Geomeasure

After developing visual environments that were biased toward classical programming, we spent some time reassessing our approach. We looked carefully at our own rapidly changing habits. Whereas in the past we would write programs to solve repetitive problems, we now used spreadsheets as much as possible. In 1985, we set out to see how well spreadsheets could serve the problem-solving needs of junior high and high school students. To do so, we built two prototypes, one called Geomeasure[10] and the other called Formula Vision.[11]

Geomeasure (abbreviated Geo) is a system that combines a symbolic spreadsheet, a graphical sketching system, and a lesson script interpreter to create an environment that is appropriate for teaching problem-solving skills in a geometric domain. This spreadsheet differs from most others in that each of its cells is symbolically named, rather than being referred to by a coordinate system.

Geo delivers the utility of a spreadsheet, the greatest single achievement in microcomputer-based problem-solving software, in a form that is appropriate for use by students. With a spreadsheet, they are able to experiment with many approaches, and study many instances of each approach, without having to laboriously carry out repetitive calculations.

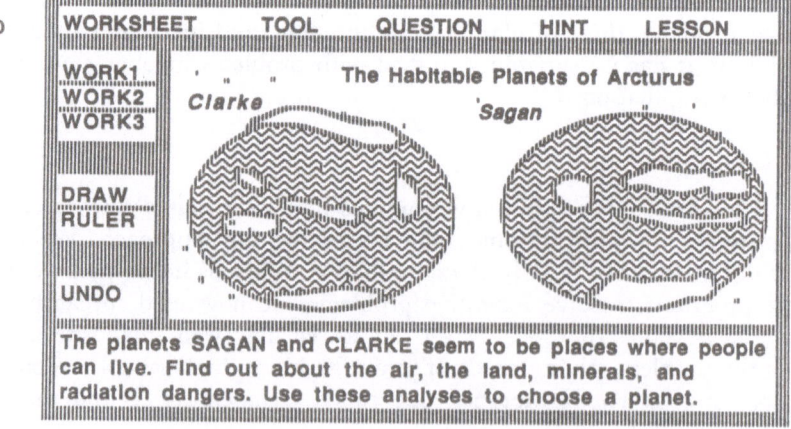

Figure 2. Colonizing a distant solar system.

c

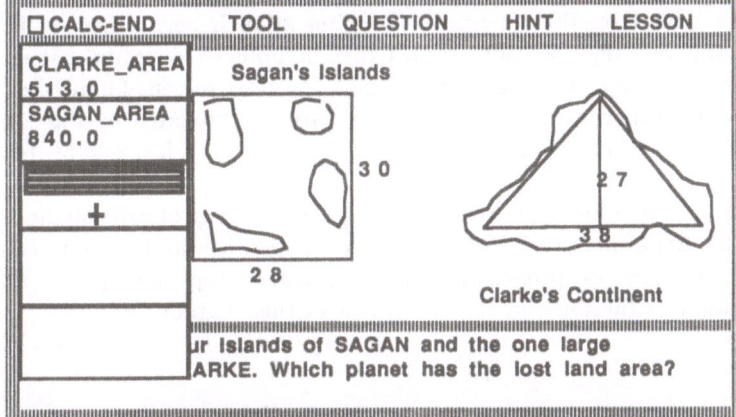

WORKSHEET   TOOL   QUESTION   HINT   LESSON

WORK1
WORK2
WORK3

DRAW
RULER

UNDO

Sagan's Islands

3 0

2 8

Clarke's Continent

2 7

3 8

Here are the four islands of SAGAN and the one large
continent of CLARKE. Which planet has the lost land area?

d

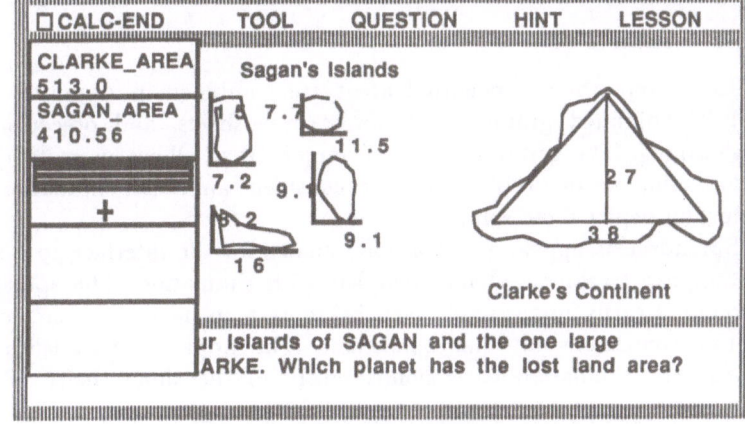

☐ CALC-END   TOOL   QUESTION   HINT   LESSON

CLARKE_AREA
513.0

SAGAN_AREA
840.0

+

Sagan's Islands

3 0

2 8

Clarke's Continent

2 7

3 8

ur islands of SAGAN and the one large
ARKE. Which planet has the lost land area?

e

☐ CALC-END   TOOL   QUESTION   HINT   LESSON

CLARKE_AREA
513.0

SAGAN_AREA
410.56

+

Sagan's Islands

5   7.7

11.5

7.2   9.

9.1

2

1 6

Clarke's Continent

2 7

3 8

ur islands of SAGAN and the one large
ARKE. Which planet has the lost land area?

FIGURE 2 (Continued)

To see how Geo works, consider the problem posed and solved in the sequence of screens in Figure 2. In this exercise, students are made part of an exploration team that is to colonize a distant solar system. Their first task is to choose an appropriate planet to explore, between two candidates. One of the bases for their decision is the size of the land masses on the planets. This is a challenging problem since the bodies of land come in irregular shapes, for which there is no obvious way to calculate an exact area.

Figure 2a–c displays the problem, as it is presented to the students. The rest of the figure traces the attempts of a group of students to verify their hypothesis that Clarke's single continent has a greater land mass than all of the islands of Sagan, combined.

Looking at Figure 2d, we see that the students have drawn a triangle inside Clarke's continent and have enclosed all of Sagan's islands within a single rectangle. They are estimating a lower bound on Clarke's area and an upper bound on that of Sagan. Looking at their spreadsheet cells, we see that this first try does not support their hypothesis since the triangle's area is less than that of the large rectangle. The next screen, Figure 2e, shows a successful experiment in which Sagan's area is estimated by the sum of the areas of a set of rectangles, each of which surrounds just one of the islands.

The system described here, Geomeasure, and Formula Vision (a variant that adds unit management) are useful problem-solving environments. Experimenting with them has helped us to envision a radically different way to program, using the spreadsheet metaphor. This new paradigm is the topic of the remainder of this chapter.

2. Action Graphics in Action

2.1. An Overview

Ideas from three conceptual areas are combined in Action Graphics (AG):[12] animated graphics, free-form spreadsheets, and object-oriented programming. The result is an environment that allows users to quickly develop solutions to problems and to construct animated simulations that graphically depict these solutions.

Spreadsheets appear to be a good choice for the interface to a system that supports problem solving, coupled with simulation. The spreadsheet paradigm is easily understood, even by those who have no desire to learn about a computer's internal operations. The apparent parallelism of a spreadsheet's evaluation corresponds nicely to the simultaneity of many real-world processes.

In AG, a named collection of graphical objects, together with a set of spreadsheet cells, is called a *scenario*. Scenarios provide both the computational and the graphical parts of a problem's solution. In most scenarios developed within AG, the cells are used to compute values and to control animation of the graphical objects. This combination of cell values and animation provides a mixed-media quantitative/qualitative output that is usually much more informative than a single-medium output.

Cells. As in all spreadsheets, each cell in AG has a value and a formula to compute its value. A cell accepts as input the values of other cells, applies a formula to those values, and produces its own value. The value produced may in turn be input to other cells.

Unlike the cells in most other spreadsheets, AG's cells do not occupy a position in a rectangular array. Instead of being bound together by position, they are bound by name. If cell A needs to use the value of another cell in its formula, the input cell's name appears in an input line of cell A. The input line also contains a parameter, which is a local variable name that will be bound to the value of the input cell. Name associations may be formed explicitly, by typing in the cell's name, or implicitly, by drawing a connecting arc from the input cell's name field to the receiving cell's input line.

In our current prototype, we allow cell formulas to be arbitrary Lisp s-expressions. This use of Lisp would not be desirable for a system that we planned to distribute to others. It is, however, convenient for testing the concepts we are introducing in AG.

Cells are created using a cell editor that is an integral part of the AG system. This editor allows cells to be added, removed, and altered. It includes an emacs style editor for entering formulas and other textual fields of a cell.

Figures. AG figures are objects that are created using an integrated graphics editor. This graphics editor is fairly standard, having features that are similar to MacDraw[13] and a host of other object-oriented graphical editors.

Figures can be made to move using animation functions that the user codes into the formulas of cells. These functions cause, as a side effect, the animation of figures. Figures may be told to move along paths (a path is a special type of figure), to move in arbitrary directions, to rotate, to change color, to become invisible, and so on.

User Interface. The AG user interface screen is shown in Figure 3. It is divided into two parts, the animation (figure) area and the spreadsheet (cell) area. In the animation area, the user creates and edits figures. In the spreadsheet area, the user creates and edits cells.

AG input is primarily mouse oriented. Both the cell and figure editors are controlled with mouse-selectable icons and pull-down menus. The keyboard is used to create the text part of figures and to enter the textual

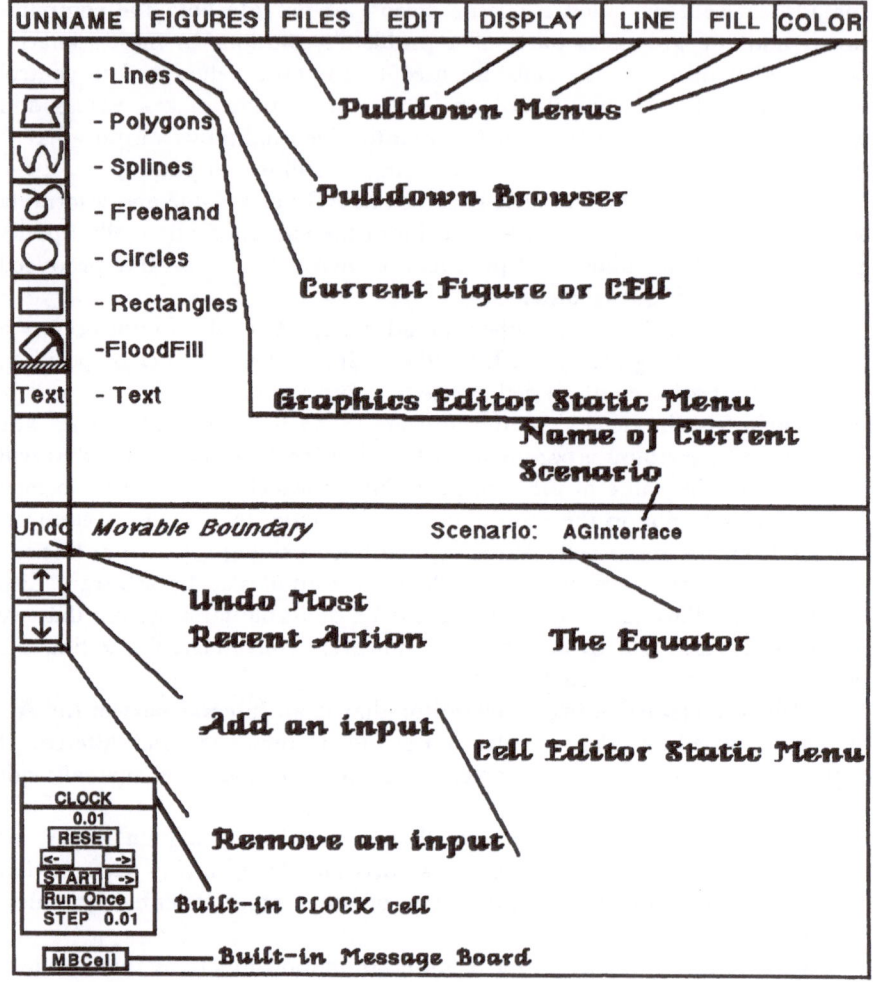

| UNNAME | FIGURES | FILES | EDIT | DISPLAY | LINE | FILL | COLOR |

- Lines
- Polygons
- Splines
- Freehand
- Circles
- Rectangles
-FloodFill
- Text

Pulldown Menus

Pulldown Browser

Current Figure or CELL

Graphics Editor Static Menu

Name of Current Scenario

Undo   *Movable Boundary*   Scenario: AGInterface

Undo Most Recent Action   *The Equator*

Add an input   *Cell Editor Static Menu*

Remove an input

CLOCK
0.01
RESET
<-   ->
START ->
Run Once
STEP 0.01   *Built-in CLOCK cell*

MBCell ———— *Built-in Message Board*

FIGURE 3. The Action Graphics user interface.

contents of cells. Execution of a scenario is controlled with the mouse and special buttons on the CLOCK cell. The RESET button returns cells to their initial values. The START button initiates execution of a scenario by causing the evaluator to begin incrementing the clock value.

2.2. A Problem-Solving Scenario

As our first example of a user interaction with AG, we consider the following problem. A construction crew wants to build a bridge to Manatee

TABLE 1
Cost of Bridge Spans

Span length (m)	Cost
5	$70
10	$160
15	$260
20	$360
25	$470
30	$590
35	$710
40	$830
45	$960
50	$1090

Island, about 200 meters from the shore of Mango Lake. A bridge is made of *piers* and *spans*. The Mango Lake Zoning Council requires that all the spans in a bridge be the same length and that if the bridge is too long, then the excess part must be on the island (that is, the mainland part of the bridge is anchored at the shore of the lake.)

Our crew is given a price list for the cost of parts necessary to build the bridge. Each pier costs $100. Spans can be purchased in lengths that are multiples of 5 meters, ranging from 5 to 50 meters long (see Table 1). Longer spans reduce the number of piers, but the cost per linear meter increases as the spans become longer. The problem to be solved is "How much will the cheapest bridge to Manatee Island cost?"

In presenting this to a group of students, we first tell them about the existence of a class of objects in AG called *BRIDGE*s. Animated bridges can be built, and taken away, by including a cell called "BridgeCell" in a scenario. BridgeCell looks like

BridgeCell	
(buildBridge (self) (Position? Start) length spans)	
length	SpanLength
spans	NbrSpans

The two inputs to BridgeCell are the length of each span and the number of such spans to be placed in the current bridge. There is also a requirement that the user create a figure called "start" and place this figure where the bridge is to start (the leftmost span position.)

The function (formula) associated with this cell is a call to the AG-provided Lisp routine "build-Bridge." This routine has four arguments.

The first is the previous bridge structure, which will be destroyed before building the new one. The description of this structure is the "value" of BridgeCell and can be directly referred to by the Lisp function "(self)." The second argument is the starting position for the leftmost span. The third argument is the length of each span, and the fourth is the number of spans to be used.

As a first attempt, our problem solvers might develop the scenario seen in Figure 4. The *Graphics Workarea* contains four figures: the Mainland,

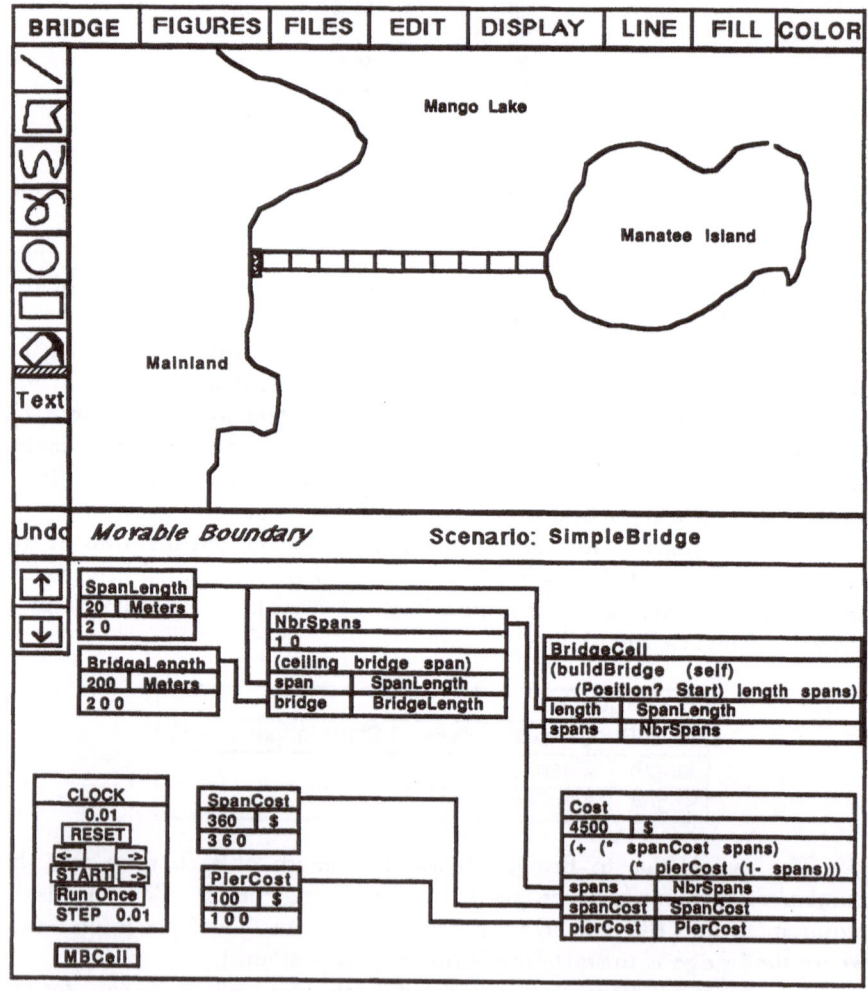

FIGURE 4. A first experiment at bridge building.

Manatee Island, Mango Lake, and the desired Start point for the bridge. The coordinate position of any figure can be found by using the function Position?; for example, (Position? Start) returns the list (Start-x, Start-y). The coordinate position for any graphical object is the x, y position where the user started to draw the object. In the case of "Start," this is its upper left corner. Other figures might be started at some presumed center of gravity, for example, in the center of a wheel that we wish to spin.

The *Cell Workarea* contains seven cells, in addition to the system-defined cells CLOCK and MBCell. The cells SpanLength, BridgeLength, SpanCost, and PierCost have simple values defined by numerical constants. The number of spans (the NbrSpans cell) is computed by taking the ceiling of the quotient of the BridgeLength and the SpanLength. The cost (the Cost cell) is computed by adding the sums of the costs of all spans and all bridges. The building of the bridge (the BridgeCell cell) depends on the length and number of spans. The bindings of the input parameters for NbrSpans, Cost, and BridgeCell are shown by both arcs and names in Figure 4.

As data is entered in the SpanLength, BridgeLength, SpanCost, and PierCost cells, the values and side effects associated with NbrSpans, Cost, and BridgeCell become obsolete. As is common with spreadsheets, AG can operate in an automatic or a manual update mode. If the automatic mode is chosen, then the change is propagated without any user request to do so. AG's manual update mechanism is a bit more flexible than those of other spreadsheets. A user can request propagation of all changes or of just the change to a single, selected cell.

Whenever an update needs to be carried out, AG must analyze the current topology of the spreadsheet, using data flow analysis algorithms in order to determine a precedence list for cell evaluations.[14, 15] This operation is usually trivial since AG remembers its previous analysis and uses it if no links between cells have changed.

A common way for a user to evaluate an AG spreadsheet is to use the RESET button on the clock. Each cell is then reset to its initial value (a user-established value that defaults to 0 for the CLOCK and to NIL for all other cells.) Next, cells that do not depend on any other cells (root cells, including the CLOCK) are evaluated. Finally, each cell that is directly affected by any cell whose value has changed is reevaluated. This last stage of evaluation continues, in the data-flow-analysis-based order, until the spreadsheet "settles down."

In our example, the cells are ordered [(SpanLength, BridgeLength, SpanCost, PierCost, CLOCK), NbrSpans, (Cost, BridgeCell)]. The first set of five cells could actually be done in parallel, if we were running on a multiprocessor machine. The evaluation of the NbrSpans cell must await the SpanLength and BridgeLength cell evaluations. The Cost and BridgeCell evaluations can occur in parallel, once the other cells have received values. The BridgeCell is evaluated for its graphical side effects. The bridge seen in Figure 4 is produced in this way.

This solution can be used by our students to experiment with various span lengths and span costs. They can even change the length of the bridge, creating one that stops in the middle of the lake, or perhaps overshoots the island. With a careful analysis, they can solve the original problem, observing the fact that the cheapest bridge is built using 25-meter spans.

AG visually shows its user how information flows through the cell network. This is done by changing the color of a cell while it is being evaluated.

2.3. Expressing Data Graphically

The above scenario makes no use of the CLOCK. A second scenario, appearing in Figure 5, uses the CLOCK cell to automate trying the different span sizes. Here, the cells BridgeLength, SpanLength, and SpanCost have been changed, and a new figure CostGraph has been added.

The BridgeLength is no longer a guessed value. We have placed a figure called Finish at the island's shoreline. Now the bridge's length can be computed as the distance between the "start" and "finish."

The cost of each bridge span is computed directly from the CostGraph figure. In this case, the graph, CostGraph, is drawn so that it represents a function that grows at a slightly faster than linear rate. All AG graphs are considered to have a range from 0.0 to 1.0 in both the x and y axes. Looking at this graph, we see that the y-value for $x = 1.0$ is actually plotted at a point that is above the highest point on the y-axis. This will give us a y-value that is, in fact, greater than 1.0.

AG implements graph-reading functions so that users can gain a better qualitative feel of problems, without needing to be concerned with precise values. The function (Graph-y? CostGraph x) returns the value y, where (x, y) is a point on the curve associated with CostGraph. Invoking the function Graph-y? also has the side effect of placing hash marks along the x and y axes. These marks reflect the chosen value of x and the corresponding y-value from the graph. When a scenario is run, the movement of these marks provides a strong visual realization of the function being computed by a graph.

The specific curve plotted here includes the x, y pairs shown in Table 2. A comparison of Tables 1 and 2 shows that they differ only in scale. The values in column 1 of Table 1 are 50 times those in Table 2. The values in column 2 of Table 1 are 1000 times those in Table 2. Looking at the new SpānCost cell, we see that it provides such scaling, so that it produces values

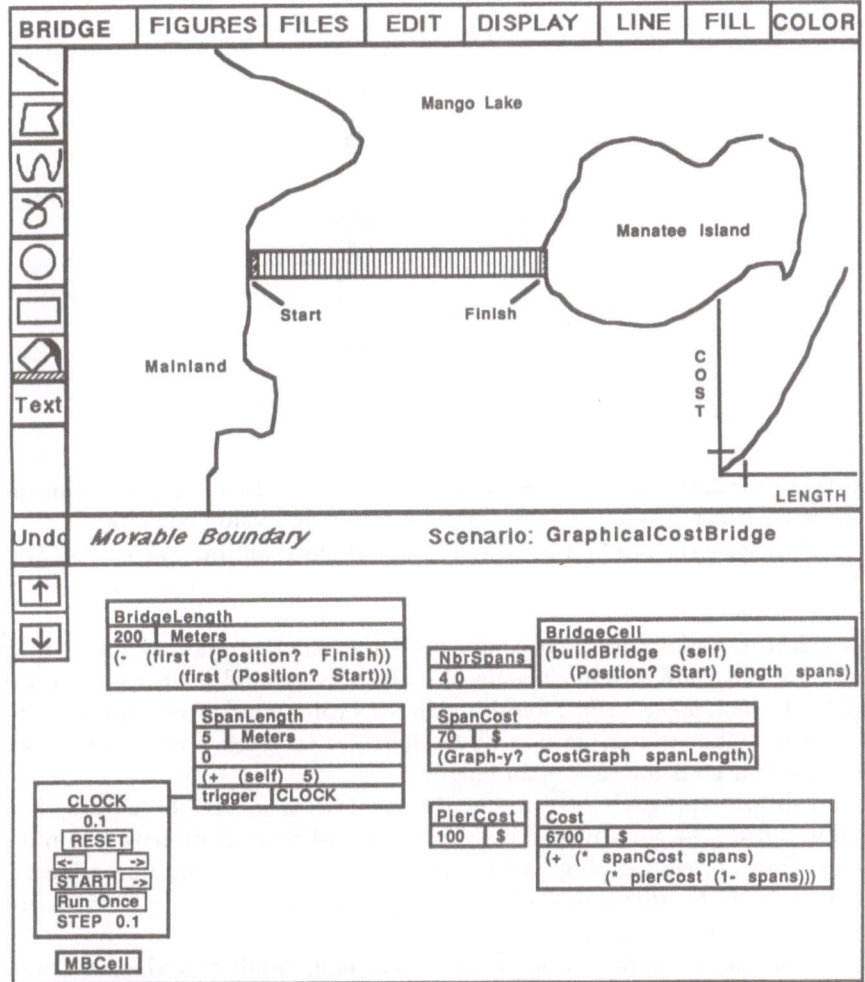

FIGURE 5. Automating the search for a solution to the bridge problem.

that precisely match our original table, whenever it gets the span lengths provided in the first table. Values for other span lengths can also be computed by this cell.

In our new approach, the SpanLength is calculated iteratively from its prior value. Briefly, the SpanLength value is initialized to 0, but immediately changed to 5 during the first evaluation. The simple formula (+ (self) 5) is a Lisp expression that evaluates to five more than the value returned by the function "self." In AG, (self) is always the value of the

TABLE 2
Values from Cost Graph

x-Value	y-Value
0.1	0.07
0.2	0.16
0.3	0.26
0.4	0.36
0.5	0.47
0.6	0.59
0.7	0.71
0.8	0.83
0.9	0.96
1.0	1.09

current cell. Since the SpanLength cell is connected to an output arc of the CLOCK, it is reevaluated each time the CLOCK's value changes.

This scenario can be run by selecting the clock button labeled START. "Starting" a scenario cycles the clock through its successive values, propagating each change of the CLOCK's value throughout the rest of the spreadsheet. This process continues until the STOP button is selected, or until the CLOCK's value reaches 1.0. In this example, we have set the CLOCK increment to 0.1, resulting in 10 evaluations of our spreadsheet. A student who transcribes very fast might get to observe and write down the different costs for each span length.

Another approach to running the scenario is to use the clock's right arrow button, →, to advance the clock, and all dependent cells, one more cycle. This "single-stepping" mode allows a student the time to more carefully observe the effects of each span length and the interplay between the cells that solve this problem.

Still another approach is to select the SpanLength cell, via the mouse, and then use the EVAL CELL operation (found in the DISPLAY menu.) This reevaluates SpanLength and any cells that are "downstream" from it.

The bridge building problem could actually be approached using a mathematical formula for computing span costs. The values from Table 1 and the corresponding graph used in the previous two solutions can be computed by the following cell:

SpanCost	
(* 10 (round (expt length 1.2)))	
length	SpanLength

Expt is a Lisp function that computes the value of its first argument raised to the power of its second argument. The span cost is computed from the span length based on a formula that relates the cost to 10 times the length to the power 1.2. We would not expect our students to devise this formula from the table or graph. Rather, we might give them such a formula in the hopes of leading them to gain a better understanding of exponential growth rates.

2.4. Levels of Abstraction

In Figure 5, several of the cells appear in very compact forms. In particular, the input list and the formula associated with NbrSpans are not displayed. AG allows cell components to be completely exposed, partially exposed, or completely hidden, except that the name field is always visible. Future versions of AG will even allow the name to be replaced by a small, descriptive icon.

In general, AG offers a user or lesson designer a large number of abstraction levels. Data can be explicitly numerical or can be graphically presented. Spreadsheet cells can appear in detailed forms, or they can be collapsed and even grouped into named collections called "composite cells." Dependencies between cells can be graphically or mnemonically displayed, or they can be completely hidden. In the next section, we will even see how the intended motion of an animated figure can be expressed graphically rather than procedurally.

2.5. A Simulation

Early attempts to implement large scenarios in AG revealed some basic limitations in the system that inhibited or prevented the construction of scenarios of the desired complexity. One of the most severe problems was the control of *discrete changes* in the essentially *continuous behavior* of the simulation objects.

The simple motion of objects such as balls, roller coasters, and elevator cars can be modeled using built-in AG animation functions and a small number of cells. These objects are easy to model because their behavior always follows a single pattern. Since the behavior pattern does not change, all of the cells that represent that object are involved each clock cycle in controlling the object's behavior.

We would like to simulate much more complex behavior with AG. The additional complexity can be placed into two categories: more complex patterns of behavior, and multiple behavior patterns for a single object. More complex behavior patterns can be modeled with additional functions, both built-in and user supplied, and more cells. Multiple patterns of behavior for a single object, however, introduce some entirely new problems.

AG supports multiple behavior patterns by providing two features, *composite cells* and *enabled/disabled cells*. A composite cell is a named collection of cells that appear and behave like a single cell to other parts of the spreadsheet. Cells, whether single or composite, can be disabled so that they do not take part in computation cycles. These cells can then be reenabled when their effects are again needed. A disabled cell is visually distinct from an enabled one since its border is formed using a dotted rather than a solid line.

A simple example of two distinct behaviors is the motion of a patrolling plane which is stationed on an aircraft carrier. This plane follows a regular patrol path, unless it is called back to the carrier.

Figure 6 displays our new scenario. There are seven figures: the aircraft carrier, the patrol plane, a pair of islands, some clouds, a textual version of the "Come Home" message, and a patrol path, represented by a line that loops from the carrier out over a search region.

The islands and clouds are included for visual effects. In our $2\frac{1}{2}$-dimensional world, figures that are "closer" to the viewer can block out parts of others that are farther away. The clouds are closer than the plane, which is closer than the islands. Thus, the visual effect is one of seeing the plane fly under clouds and over islands.

The initial state of the simulation is established by the cell called Init. Since this cell has no inputs, it is always executed whenever the scenario is "reset." The Lisp code in Init is used to enable the cell named Fly-Plane, disable Fly-Home, and turn off (make invisible) the ComeBack message.

The Fly-Plane cell describes the patrol characteristics of the plane by instructing the plane to move progressively along a path that starts and ends at the carrier. The pathway leads to the south of the carrier, then heads east under a white cloud. It then loops back toward the carrier, passing over two islands. The approach to the carrier brings the plane under a storm cloud and through a maneuver that aligns it for a proper landing.

The *path* moving operation is controlled by the Lisp procedure call

(FlyPath plane flight (self) time)

A path is a polygon (smoothed or unsmoothed), which is created as an ordinary figure. The starting point on the path is referred to as position 0, the ending as position 1, and all intermediate points are identified by numbers between 0 and 1.

The FlyPath routine expects four arguments. The first is a figure and the second is a path along which that figure is to fly. The final two

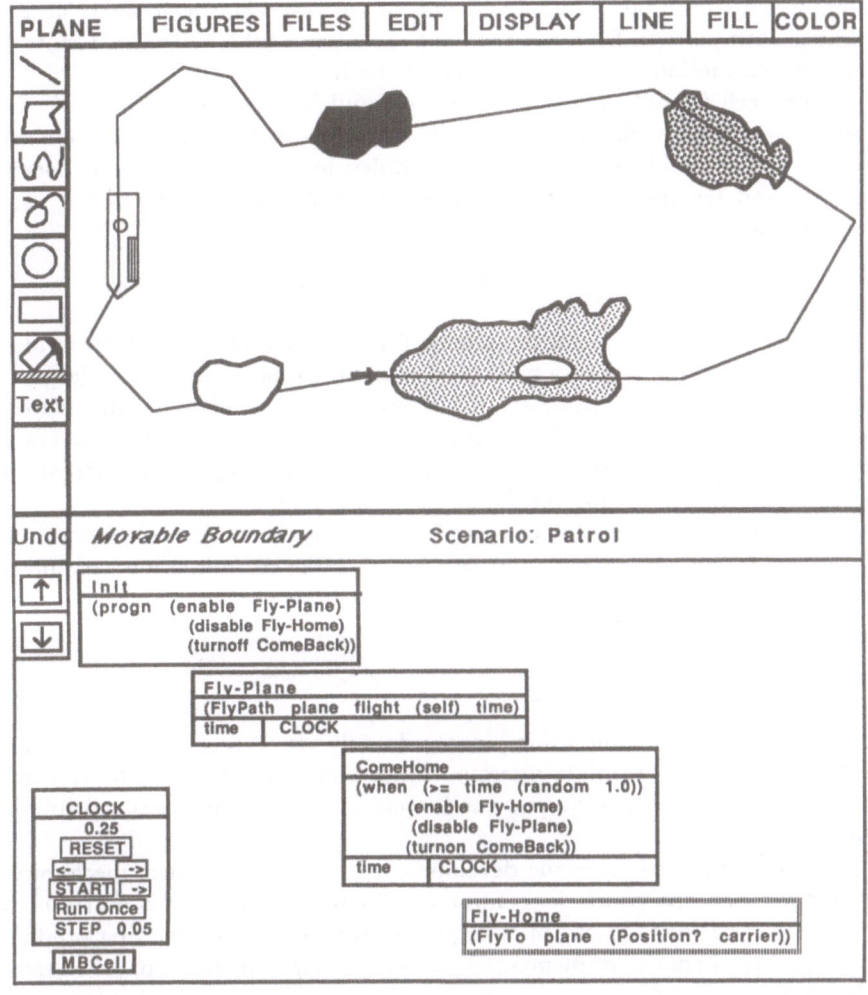

FIGURE 6. A simple simulation.

arguments indicate the start and end of the segment of the path along which the figure is to smoothly fly.

Our use of FlyPath specifies a start point of "(self)" and an end point of "time." The end point is easily explained. A simulation starts at the clock value 0 and ends at clock value 1. Since the local variable "time" is bound to the output of the cell CLOCK, it will receive values ranging from the path's starting position of 0 to its ending position of 1. The cryptic argument "(self)" takes advantage of the fact that the returned value of FlyPath is the ending path position. Thus, the value of the Fly-Plane cell starts as the ending path position from the previous execution of this cell. This results in the smooth motion of the plane along its path.

The cell ComeHome is intended to simulate a condition in which the carrier would immediately call back its patrol plane. In a full-scale scenario, this would probably be based on a complex test of factors such as enemy threats and weather conditions. In this example we have created a very simple test:

$$(> = time (random 1.0))$$

The Lisp (random 1.0) function call returns a randomly selected value between 0.0 and 1.0. As soon as the simulation time is at least as large as this randomly chosen number, the ComeHome cell changes the plane's behavior. This behavioral change is accomplished by disabling the Fly-Plane cell and enabling the Fly-Home cell. The textual message "Come Home" is also displayed, by turning on the figure called ComeBack.

The cell Fly-Home causes the plane to fly on a direct course from its current position back to the carrier. The FlyTo animation command accomplishes this.

2.6. The Space Weapons Scenario

Our previous simulation involved only two types of continuous behavior and a very simple discrete test for changing behavior. More complex behavior patterns require some formalism for designing and controlling the simulation.

This section describes the development of a discrete control mechanism which is superimposed on the continuous ("dataflow") behaviors represented by the spreadsheet. By way of example, we briefly describe the first production-quality scenario implemented in AG, a hypothetical space warfare situation.

At present, AG supports the use of Finite State Automata (FSA) models to describe complex interactions.[16] The FSA is used to control the selection of the correct continuous behavior pattern and the transitions from one pattern to the next. The FSA controller selects the set of cells (or composite cell) that correspond to and realize a particular behavior pattern. When the conditions that determine the object's current behavior pattern change, the FSA control changes states, disabling the current set of behavior cells and enabling the cells corresponding to the new behavior pattern.

The FSA control mechanism may be viewed as a design language, or a higher-level language, whereas the cell relationships represent the underlying low-level language. Composite cells play the role of subroutines within the low-level language.

The first large-scale scenario implemented in AG was the Space Weapons Scenario (SWS.) The "Constellation Vega" (CV), a Federation mother ship, is positioned motionless in deep space and is vulnerable to attack from Klingon penetrators. The Klingon penetrators, which have the code name "Buffalo," enter the CV's defensive zone and move directly toward the CV at a speed of 20 picoparsecs ("pikes") per minute. If a Buffalo reaches a point 400 pikes from the CV, it will attack the CV by firing a "King-Kong" missile.

The primary fighter type used by CV is the Tiger, which will patrol around the CV to a distance of 1000 pikes and attack any Buffalos that are detected. Tigers carry a search system for detecting Buffalos. This system has a range of 200 pikes, an azimuth range of 65 degrees to the left and right, and an elevation range of 5 degrees above and below the spacecraft's centerline.

Based on situation intelligence, the direction on the Klingon attack can be established to be within a 150-degree sector. Six radial patrol paths are defined within this sector, 25 degrees apart, extending out to 1000 pikes

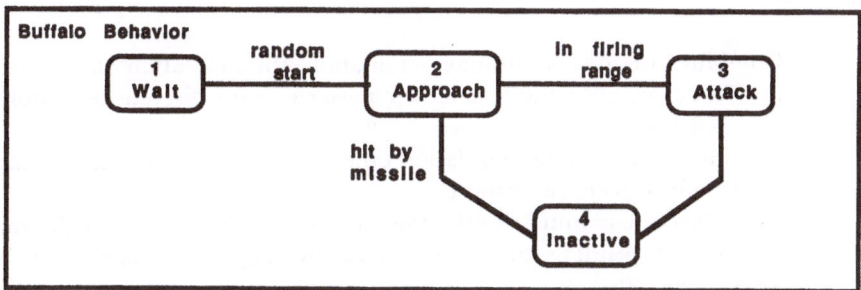

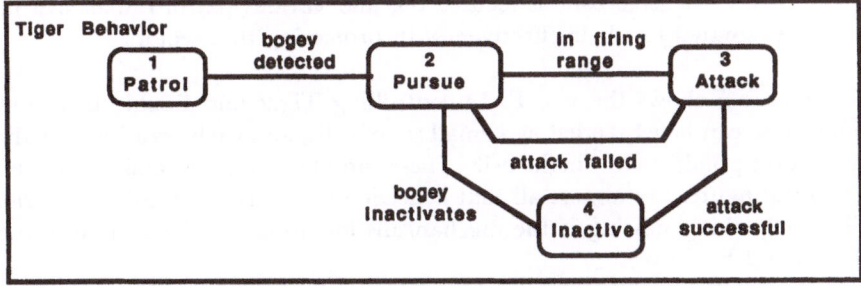

FIGURE 7. FSAs for the space weapons scenario.

from the CV. Each radial is patrolled by two Tigers, with the second Tiger starting on the radial when the first reaches the turnaround point. On the return leg, the Tiger makes a 360-degree turn to sweep the radial area with its search system.

When a Tiger detects an attacking Buffalo, it ceases patrolling its assigned radial and intercepts the Buffalo. It moves directly toward the Buffalo until it is within firing range (50 pikes) and then attacks. The Klingons may attack with as many as four groups of 16 simultaneously, with each group coming in at a random angle.

Preliminary analysis made it clear that the number of objects and object types in this scenario would overwhelm the capabilities of the PC-based implementation of AG. A subset of this specification was chosen for implementation. Tigers patrol a single radial; two Buffalos attack. They begin their attack at random times, at random points on a 25-degree arc centered on the CV, at a distance of 1050 pikes.

If a Buffalo is detected, the Tiger leaves the radial and pursues it. When it has closed to missile range, it attempts to destroy the Buffalo by repeatedly firing missiles until success or exhaustion of missiles. Each missile has a 65 % change of success.

Despite the simplifications, the key elements of the SWS were retained. They are:

- Combined discrete–continuous simulation; the simulation objects display multiple continuous behavior patterns, with discrete transitions between them.
- Simultaneity; multiple simulation objects are moving and interacting at any given scenario instant.
- Interobject communication; the Tigers communicate with the Buffalos by sending them "destroyed by Tiger" messages if their attack succeeds.
- Study of search pattern effectiveness; a single 25-degree sector of CV's defensive zone is focused on, and various patrol radials can be evaluated for their effectiveness in protecting that sector.

Figure 7 shows the two FSAs controlling Tiger and Buffalo behavior. Each state can be expanded as a small set of cells, and each transition condition corresponds to a single cell. These simple diagrams and associated graphical figures are almost all that is needed to describe the SWS scenario. (The only thing missing is the mechanisms for initiating the motion of the Tigers and Buffalos.)

Figure 8 shows how these pieces fit together to create the actual AG implementation. In studying this example, you should note the use of a

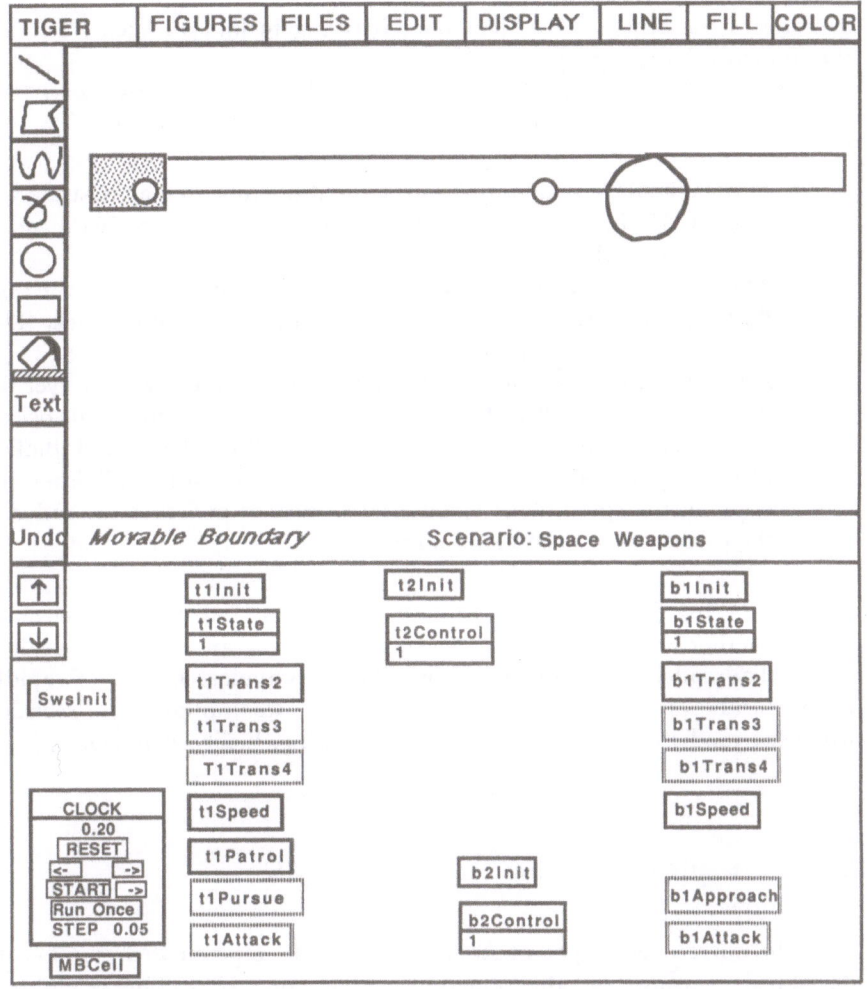

FIGURE 8. The space weapons scenario.

"message board," implemented through this MBCell. This allows messages to be broadcast to all cells that choose to read the board. Details of its operation and use are in Ref. 17.

We have implemented SWS in our PC-based Action Graphics environment, but there is as yet no automated tool for compiling FSA diagrams into the underlying spreadsheet. When such a tool is constructed, it will necessarily be an interactive "mixed initiative" tool, since the contents of the FSA cells and transitions are really natural-language "comments" about the *intentions* of the object. The Tiger pilot is trying to find an enemy aircraft; the Buffalo pilot is trying to destroy the CV.

Despite the simplifications imposed on SWS by the hardware and software substrate of AG, several worthwhile observations occurred.

- Buffalos achieve penetration to the point of launching against the CV around 10% of the time. This value is in accord with other (analytic) studies of similar scenarios.
- The scenario allows for two Tigers to acquire and pursue one Buffalo, allowing the other Buffalo to penetrate and attack. This naturally occurs in the simulation.
- A successful hit on a Buffalo may have already occurred, and yet the Buffalo may "get off a shot" at the CV before crashing. This occurs in the simulation because the cells controlling Tiger and Buffalo firing are not directly related (neither is "downstream" from the other in the spreadsheet evaluation sequence) and thus the order of their evaluation is nondeterministic.

This third feature was totally unanticipated and raised discussions about whether or not the underlying mechanism was an irrelevant accident or a valid model of the phenomenon. This is a typical benefit of rapidly reconfigurable interactive simulation: implicit assumptions are revealed when the model exhibits "emergent" or surprising, lifelike behavior.

3. The Use of Object-Oriented Programming in AG

The current prototype of Action Graphics is implemented in a locally developed version of the emerging Common Lisp Object System (CLOS).[18] The Central Florida Common Lisp Object System (CFCL)[19] provides an object-oriented extension to Gold Hill's *Golden Common Lisp* (Versions 1.01 and 286 Developer 2.2)[20] for the IBM PC, PC/AT, and compatibles.

Our goals for CFCL were to develop a simple implementation that maximizes power and flexibility, as well as source code clarity. Thus, CFCL lacks some of the special algorithms that make PCL, the Xerox Parc Portable Common Loops implementation, fast and efficient, but CFCL's code bulk is a fraction of PCL's.

The fundamental *objects* in CLOS and CFCL are classes, instances, methods, and generic functions.[21]

3.1. Classes and Instances

A *class* object determines the structure of a set of objects called its *instances*. Classes are defined in a way similar to the Common Lisp *defstruct* form—a class specifies that each instance has a certain set of named slots. A class can inherit slot information from one or more classes. A class that inherits from another class is said to be a *subclass* of that class. A class that inherits from more than one *superclass* uses *multiple-inheritance*. Classes are integrated into the Common Lisp type lattice, so that each class has a corresponding Common Lisp type. The special class *t* is a superclass of all classes except itself.

3.2. Methods and Generic Functions

In Lisp, we apply a function to an argument with the syntax

(myfunction arg1)

The same syntax is used in CLOS to apply a *method* (send a message) to an object:

(mymethod obj1)

The difference is that a function runs the same code regardless of the argument, while the code invoked by a method depends on the class or identity of an object. Like functions, methods can be defined on any number of arguments, but the method selected depends on the classes of *all* of the arguments. Methods can be defined for any Common Lisp type, as well as user-defined classes.

Any number of methods can be defined with the same name, as long as they are specialized for different classes of arguments. Since there can only be one Lisp function with a given name, the actual Lisp function that has the name of a method is called a *generic function*. The generic function is responsible for selecting the appropriate method to run based on the classes of the arguments. Generic functions are generated automatically when methods are defined. There is one generic function per unique method name, and a generic function can encompass a number of different methods sharing the same name.

3.3. Defining Classes

The *defclass* macro is used to define a new class. The defclass form takes either three or four arguments:

- a class name (required)
- a list of superclasses (required)
- a list of slots (required)
- a list of class options and values (optional)

Consider the following example:

```
(defclass CC (CELL GROUP)
    (nestingLevel                    ;how deeply nested
     pickedSubCell                   ;cell picked in this composite cell
     window                          ;area of screen used by this cell
     parent                          ;what CC is this embedded in?
     smallBasePoint                  ;base of miniature version of cell
     valueList                       ;parameter/argument pairs
     )
    (:accessor-prefix nil)
)
```

The new class is named "CC," short for composite cell. This class
inherits from its superclasses "CELL" and "GROUP." The slots specified
here, for example, parent, are specific to composite cells. In addition to these
CC specific fields, this class inherits all slots from the CELL and GROUP
classes. A careful look at the CELL class would reveal that it in turn inherits
all the capabilities and slots of the FIGURE class.

To see how this inheritance makes our implementation of AG easier,
consider the method Init for the class CC.

```
(defMethod Init ((obj CC))
    (call-next-method)
    (setf (textContents (functionField obj)) '("〈children〉"))
)
```

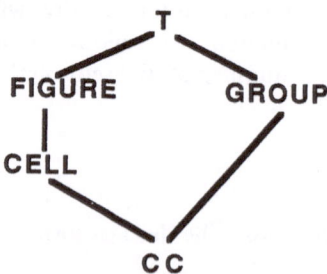

FIGURE 9. A portion of the AG class hierarchy.

The parameter specifications for this method say that it is specifically designed for use with objects in the class CC. There might be many other Init methods that have been defined, but this will be the one used if we apply the method (send the message) to a composite cell.

The first statement

(call-next-method)

invokes the Init method for the "closest" superclass of CC. Superclasses for CC are ordered CELL, GROUP, FIGURE, T. This ordering is based on the partial hierarchy described in Figure 9.

A search of the methods for CELL finds the method

```
(defMethod Init (obj CELL))
    (setf (nameField obj) (make-instance FIELD))
    ........., etc.
)
```

This will set all the fields that are initialized for cells, whether simple or composite. Once it completes, control is returned to the Init method for composite cells, where one of the initialized fields is changed to suit the specialized needs of a composite cell.

This inheritance feature, which is common to all object-oriented systems, greatly eased the task of implementing Action Graphics. As an example, it made it possible to implement the concept of composite cells in just two days, since we were able to reuse a large amount of debugged code that already supported ordinary cells, figures, and groups.

3.4. Classes and Behavior

There seems to be a natural match between the notions of classes, methods, and inheritance and the corresponding ideas of species, activities, and evolution that one finds in real-life objects. If we wish to add a class of vehicles called "tanks" to the Action Graphics library, we can browse for some existing class that has similar characteristics. We might, in fact, find two classes that can be combined, for example, "land vehicle" and "weapon launcher"[2] in order to evolve a new species called "tanks."

A simple example of this is found in our implementation of bridges.
Here, we defined a new class:

```
(defclass BRIDGE (FIGURE)
    ()
    (:accessor-prefix nil)
)
```

A bridge needs to be displayed, just like all graphical figures, but it has
additional activities (messages to which it responds.) Consider the three
methods, each named buildBridge, that are displayed below.

```
(defMethod buildBridge ((b 'nil) pos spanLength spans)
    (setf b (make-instance BRIDGE)
    (createBridge b pos spanLength spans) )

(defMethod buildBridge ((b BRIDGE) pos spanLength spans)
    (removeBridge b)
    (createBridge b pos spanLength spans)
)

(defMethod buildBridge ((b t) pos spanLength spans)
    nil      ;cannot build a bridge with this arg
)
```

The first two methods have almost the same purpose, to create and
display a bridge starting at position "pos," having "spans" sections, each of
length "spanLength." The parameter "b" is associated with the current version of this bridge. If no bridge yet exists, then b is *nil* and the first version
of the method is used. If a bridge already exists, the second or third version
could apply. The second is used, since it is more specific. Its effect is to
remove the old bridge before making a new one. The generic mechanism for
methods always selects the most specific version of buildBridge that is
available.

If we invoke the method buildBridge on any object, other than a bridge
or the value *nil*, the third method will apply, since all objects are in classes
that are subclasses of *t*, the universal class.

4. Constraints: An Alternative

The single-directional (functional) nature of the spreadsheet paradigm
is a fundamental source of the requirement for "programmer skills" that is

still found in Action Graphics. In Version 2, we are investigating the use of *symmetric constraints*[22–24] as an alternative mechanism for relating cells' values.

Constraint programming allows a user to express the behavioral properties of objects in terms of their relationships to each other and to events that might occur in a simulation. The exact procedural way that these constraints are maintained is handled by the constraint system, rather than by the user. In essence, a user expresses *intent*, and the system translates this intent into *action*.

As a brief introduction to how constraints might be used in AG style scenarios, let us once again consider the Bridge Building problem. Both the solutions we provided earlier in this chapter required the user to observe a large number of simulations before the optimum span length was determined. A constraint approach that automates this optimization appears in Figure 10.

This solution is based on the concept of *hierarchical constraints* introduced in Ref. 25. Here the first set of constraints (Level 1) are primary. We do not want the Start or Finish to move, since these are stationary markers at the Mainland and Island, respectively. We also require the use of an integral number of spans in the bridge. So long as we do not change these conditions, we will attempt to satisfy the Level 2 constraints.

Level1:
1) Start stay   /* Mainland and Island don't move */
2) Finish stay
3) nbrSpans is a positive integer

Level2:
4) Bridge.basePoint = Start.basePoint   /* Anchor Bridge at Mainland */
5) minLength = |Finish.basePoint − Start.basePoint|
6) spanLength*nbrSpans ⩾ minLength
7) pierCost = 100
8) spanCost = 10*(spanLength ↑ 1.2)
9) cost = nbrSpans*spanCost + (nbrSpans − 1)*pierCost

Level3:
10) cost = 0   /* Seek a cost that minimizes error for this constraint */

FIGURE 10. Constraints and the Manatee Project.

The second level of constraints is desirable, and Level 2 constraints are more important than constraints at all higher-numbered levels (3, 4, etc., if they exist.) Thus, we apply Level 2 constraints to solutions that satisfy all the Level 1 constraints. Our desire is to apply a finer sieve. We do not require a precise satisfaction of these constraints. We do, however, seek out solutions that are *best* (minimize the numeric errors) among the candidates from Level 1. This continues with Level 3 serving to refine the set of solutions from Level 2, and so on. The intent is to find a single, best solution, if possible.

In Figure 10, we have numbered all the constraints. This is not part of the constraint specification (no ordering exists within the constraints at a single level) but is used here to make our references clearer.

Constraint 4 specifies that the Bridge start at the edge of the Mainland. Constraint 5 requires that the Bridge length be at least the distance between the positions of the two figures called Start and Finish. This constraint can be satisfied in a number of ways. Three of the most obvious follow. First, we can keep Start and Finish where they are and change the minimum Bridge length to conform to their current distance apart. Second, we can keep Start where it is and move Finish so that its distance from Start matches the current value of minLength. Third, we can keep Finish where it is and move Start so that its distance from Finish matches the current value of minLength. Of these, only the first is acceptable since the other two would result in our denying the constraints at Level 1 in which the Start and Finish are not to be moved.

Constraint 6 relates the spanLength, the value of nbrSpans, and the Bridge length by dictating that the combined lengths of all spans must be at least as long as the desired bridge length. This means, for example, that a value of 20 for the spanLength and 200 for Bridge length forces nbrSpans to be at least 10.

Constraints 7 and 8 determine the cost of bridge components. Satisfying constraint 7 is trivial, but satisfying constraint 8 could be done by altering either the spanCost or spanLength. Constraint 9 relates the cost of the bridge to the number of spans and the costs of piers and spans. The pier cost cannot change, since it is anchored to a constant. The span cost is tied to the span length. Hence, this just gives us one more way to relate the three true variables Cost, spanLength, and nbrSpans.

Satisfying constraints 4 through 9 produces an infinite number of solutions for the values of the spanLength, nbrSpans, and Cost. Constraint 10 (the only Level 3 constraint) provides the finer sieve needed to get a single solution. This says that we wish to build the bridge for zero cost. But this cannot be done, since constraint 5 at Level 2 requires the bridge to be at least long enough to span the lake. Fortunately, we are not required to satisfy this Cost constraint exactly, but we must minimize the error associated with our solution. In effect then, constraint 10 seeks a minimum value for the cost.

At this early stage of design, it is clear that describing problems by means of constraints is at least as challenging as writing a program. However, there are ways of expressing constraints graphically[26, 27] or declaratively.[28] Moreover, constraints have the distinct advantage of describing the *problem* rather than the *solution*.

5. Future Directions

Presently, we are transporting Action Graphics from the PC/Lisp environment to a workstation/Smalltalk environment. We are exploring the use of symmetric constraints and looking for a consistent formalism that incorporates finite state control mechanisms (including Petri nets[29] and spreadsheets into a class hierarchy.

We are looking for new insights into the meaning of "method" and "message" in a context of continuously operating "behaviors" in systems with rich collections of both discrete and continuous actions. We have found tactical simulation to be a rich source of scenarios, stories, and unexpected insights into the design of software environments for modeling, simulation, and problem solving.

It is readily apparent that a system with Lisp expressions as cell functions is not really "user friendly." Unfortunately, constraints, in their current form, are also not easily expressed by novice problem solvers.

6. Acknowledgments

We owe a great debt to our dedicated students who produced prototypes for many parts of Action Graphics. Early versions of the AG system were implemented by Rod Rogers, Ron Conkling, and Shaun McCurdy. CFCL was developed by Rick Lewis and was first incorporated into AG by Lee Lacy. The concepts of using finite state and Petri net model controllers in AG were originally envisioned by Mikel Petty and Li Xin, respectively. The constraint approach to bridge building is based on a solution by Jennifer Burg. Clay Johnson has kept us honest and informed.

Support for this project has been provided by the National Science Foundation (Grant # SED-79-18991), the Naval Training Systems Center (NTSC), the Florida High Technology and Industry Council, and the Army's Project Management for Training Devices. Lieutenant Commander

David Blower of NTSC has collaborated with us throughout the duration of this project. The Space Weapons Scenario presented in this chapter was designed by him to investigate the feasibility of using AG for improving tactical skills.

References

1. S. Papert, *Mindstorms*, Basic Books, New York, 1980.
2. J. M. Moshell, C. E. Hughes, and R. M. Aiken, High School Microcomputer Science Education, National Science Foundation Grant SED79-18992, 1979.
3. J. M. Moshell, et al., *Computer Power: A First Course in Using the Computer*, McGraw-Hill, New York, 1982.
4. C. E. Hughes and J. M. Moshell, *Visible Pascal*, John Wiley and Sons, New York, 1985.
5. Think Technologies, MacPascal, Apple Computer, Inc., Cupertino, California, 1984.
6. Looking Glass Software, Ltd., Alice: The Personal Pascal, Software Channels, Inc., Kingswood, Texas, 1985.
7. M. H. Brown, Exploring algorithms using balsa-II, *Computer* **21**(5), 14–36 (1988).
8. C. E. Hughes, *IMAGINATION: Picture Programming*, John Wiley and Sons, New York, 1983.
9. A. Kay, Computer software, *Sci. Am.*, **1984** (September), 53–59.
10. C. E. Hughes and J. M. Moshell, Formula Vision, Gentleware Corp., Maitland, Florida, 1986; ISTE, Eugene, Oregon, 1989.
11. C. E. Hughes and J. M. Moshell, Graphical spreadsheet environments for problem solving, Proceeding of NCGA's Computer Graphics '87 Conference, Philadelphia, Pennsylvania, 1987, pp. 618–627.
12. J. M. Moshell, C. E. Hughes, L. W. Lacy, R. L. Lewis, and D. J. Blower, A spreadsheet-based visual language for freehand sketching of complex motions, Proceedings of the 1987 Workshop on Visual Languages, Linköping, Sweden, 1987, pp. 94–104.
13. Claris, MacDraw, Claris Corporation, Mountain View, California, 1988.
14. S. S. Muchnick and N. D. Jones, *Program Flow Analysis: Theory and Applications*, Prentice-Hall, Englewood Cliffs, New Jersey, 1981.
15. A. L. Davis and R. M. Keller, Data flow program graphs, *Computer* **15**(2), 26–41 (1982).
16. J. E. Hopcroft and J. D. Ullman, *Introduction to Automata Theory, Languages, and Computation*, Addison-Wesley, Reading, Massachusetts, 1979.
17. M. D. Petty, Tactical simulation in an object-oriented animated graphics environment, M.S.thesis, University of Central Florida, Orlando, Florida, April 1988.
18. D. G. Bobrow, K. Kabun, G. Kiczales, L. Masinter, M. Stefik, and F. Zdybel, CommonLoops: Merging Lisp and object-oriented programming, pp. 17–29 in *OOPSLA'86 Conference Proceedings*, Association for Computing Machinery, New York, 1986.
19. R. L. Lewis, J. M. Moshell, C. E. Hughes, and L. W. Lacy, CFCL—Central Florida Common Lisp Object System, Technical Report UCF-CS-87-06, University of Central Florida, Orlando, Florida, 1987.
20. Gold Hill Computers, Golden Common Lisp 286 Developer User's Guide, Version 2.2, Cambridge, Massachusetts, 1987.
21. B. Cox, *Object Oriented Programming*, Addison-Wesley, Reading, Massachusetts, 1986.
22. G. Sussman and G. Steele, CONSTRAINTS—A language for expressing almost-hierarchical descriptions, *Artificial Intelligence* **14**(1), 1–39 (1980).
23. A. Borning, The programming language aspects of ThingLab, a constraint-oriented simulation laboratory, *ACM Trans. Programming Languages Systems* **3**(4), 353–387 (1981).
24. W. Leler, *Constraint Programming Languages: Their Specification and Generation*, Addison-Wesley, Reading, Massachusetts, 1988.
25. A. Borning et al., Constraint hierarchies, pp. 48–60 in *OOPSLA'87 Conference Proceedings*, Association for Computing Machinery, New York, 1987.

26. A. BORNING, J. JAFFAR, S. MICHAYLOR, P. STUCKEY, AND R. YAP, Defining constraints graphically, pp. 137–143 in *Human Factors in Computing Systems, CHI '86 Conference Proceedings*, Association for Computing Machinery, 1986.

27. I. SUTHERLAND, Sketchpad: A man–machine graphical communication system, Proceedings of the Spring Joint Computer Conference, IFIPS, 1963, pp. 329–345.

28. N. HEINTZE, R. DUISBERG, B. FREEMAN-BENSEN, A. KRAMER, AND M. WODF, The CLP(R) Programmer's Manual, Monash University, Victoria, Australia, 1987.

29. J. L. PETERSON, *Petri Net Theory and the Modeling of Systems*, Prentice-Hall, Englewood Cliffs, New Jersey, 1981.

12

ANIMATION USING BEHAVIOR FUNCTIONS

Timothy C. Lethbridge
and Colin Ware

Abstract

This paper describes the use of behavior functions to create systems of graphic objects which appear to be behaving purposefully. These functions determine the motion of an object based on the status of the other objects in its environment. Several useful classes of behavior functions are described. Functions using just the positions of objects at the previous time interval can model pushing, pulling and tendency to maintain distance. When a second preceding time step is used, a wide array of behaviors can be obtained including avoidance, hitting, fish schooling and the playing of ball games.

1. Introduction

In effective animation, viewers receive the psychological impression of animacy when they are in fact seeing the simple movement of geometric shapes on a screen. We may perceive, for example, one object "shoving" another around, even though both shape and motion may be quite simple. In conventional animation, this perceived intentionality is achieved through the skill and intuition of the animator, who must achieve the behavior by specifying the position of the objects in a succession of time frames.

Computer-assisted animation is commonly done using systems which fill in the movement of objects between their locations at fixed points in time (key-frame animation[1]). Other systems are not so concerned with the

TIMOTHY C. LETHBRIDGE • Department of Computer Science, University of Ottawa, Ottawa, Ontario, Canada K1N 6N5.   COLIN WARE • School of Computer Science, University of New Brunswick, Fredericton, New Brunswick, Canada E3B 5A3.

ending points, but still move objects in defined paths based on various equations or constraints.[2]

The method of animation described here controls the movement of objects by feeding back the positions of objects at previous time steps into functions that determine what the objects do next. The essence of our approach is that we tell the objects how to behave rather than telling them where to be at specific times.

In order to make such animation easy to program, it is necessary to have suitable motion and interaction primitives which can control large segments of behavior with only a few simple parameters. Initially, one might doubt that simplicity could be achieved; however, the psychological literature indicates that perceived causality and animacy is surprisingly easy to obtain. A major work in this field was written by Michotte,[3] who defined the circumstances under which the interactions of objects evoke psychological impressions with such classifications as launching and entraining. Michotte, however, was severely constrained by the mechanical devices he used for experiments. With the aid of computer-generated graphics, the creation and investigation of such effects is far easier.

Marion, Fleischer, and Vickers identified several qualities considered important for human perception of animacy.[4] Perhaps the most essential component is intentionality; the actors must seem to be behaving in a purposeful, goal-directed manner. Marion *et al.* suggested that a necessary ingredient to achieve the perception of intentionality is a certain amount of randomness, in the sense of lack of repetition. This is necessary so that object motion does not appear to be too mechanical. They proposed achieving this element of "randomness" directly by introducing random elements into the system. However, from the mathematics of chaos, we know that for a system of reasonable complexity, the process of feeding outputs back into inputs results in sequences that tend not to repeat themselves even though they are totally deterministic. An objective of our work is to achieve perceived animacy without stochastic parameters. An advantage of avoiding true randomness is a more simple system.

Our goal has been to discover a rich and interesting set of behaviors that "seem to be" intentional, using simple functions. If such a set of behavior functions exists to be discovered, then the goal of "telling objects how to behave" can be a practical animation tool. As there is no obvious procedure for deriving such functions, our course of action largely involves trial and error. The research is facilitated by a program which allows the easy construction of as many different types of function as possible, together with a method for viewing the resulting animations in real time.

In what follows, first we describe the domain of deterministic behavior functions. We then give a description of the restricted class of behaviors we have studied thus far. We also present the simple language we used to describe this class of behavior functions. Finally, we present some preliminary results from our investigations.

2. Behavior Functions

In this discussion, we consider a graphical environment with n distinct objects. Several characteristics of each object are defined; of particular importance is the position vector, $\mathbf{p}_{it}$, of a given object i at time t.

We define a behavior function B_i as a function which determines the velocity vector (change in position) of an object over a discrete time interval. At time t, the behavior returned by function B_i is velocity $\mathbf{v}_{it}$. The new position of object i is calculated as

$$\mathbf{p}_{it} = \mathbf{p}_{it-1} + \mathbf{v}_{it} \tag{1}$$

The set of behavior functions we are concerned with are those for which the velocity of an object i at time t is a function of the positions of all the objects in the environment, including itself, at times $t-1, t-2,..., t-k$ for some finite number, k, of previous intervals. Thus,

$$\mathbf{v}_{it} = B_i \begin{bmatrix} \mathbf{p}_{1t-1}, \mathbf{p}_{1t-2}, \cdots, \mathbf{p}_{1t-k} \\ \mathbf{p}_{2t-1}, \mathbf{p}_{2t-2}, \cdots, \mathbf{p}_{2t-k} \\ \vdots \qquad \vdots \qquad \qquad \vdots \\ \mathbf{p}_{nt-1}, \mathbf{p}_{nt-2}, \cdots, \mathbf{p}_{nt-k} \end{bmatrix} \tag{2}$$

In the investigation reported here, we restrict ourselves to behavior functions where k is at most 2. In other words, the positions of objects at times $t-1$ and $t-2$ are the only variable inputs to the functions. From a practical point of view, these functions are the most interesting in that the overhead of storing the previous states of the system is minimized. To a large extent, we believe that the usefulness of our approach depends on the class of behaviors that can be captured in this way being rich and interesting.

3. Partial Response Functions

Every actor in an environment exists both as a stimulus, provoking the behaviors of the other objects, and as an actor, behaving in response to its environment. For conceptual simplicity, we find it necessary to define a set of "partial response functions," R_{ij}, which determine the partial response of each actor to each stimulus. We use the term partial response rather than behavior because the partial response is only a tendency to behave; partial responses to all stimuli must be combined at a higher level to determine behavior. We can express this set of partial response functions as a matrix in which each object appears twice, once as an actor a_i and once as a stimulus s_j.

$$
\begin{array}{c|cccc}
 & s_1 & s_2 & \cdots & s_n \\
\hline
a_1 & R_{11} & R_{12} & \cdots & R_{1n} \\
a_2 & R_{21} & R_{22} & \cdots & R_{2n} \\
\vdots & \vdots & \vdots & & \vdots \\
a_n & R_{n1} & R_{n2} & \cdots & R_{nn}
\end{array}
$$

The labels on the columns and rows of the matrix identify stimulus and actor objects, respectively. The elements of the rows are the partial responses of a given actor to each of the stimuli in its environment—the entire row represents the actor's behavior function. In practice, many elements of this matrix may be zero, meaning that an actor never responds to a given stimulus; where an entire row is zero, the object would be static and act as a stimulus to other objects only.

At a higher level, the organism must select among the various stimuli in its environment and decide which are to be responded to at a given instant. In principle, the function combining partial responses to form the complete behavior could be of arbitrary complexity. For the sake of simplicity, we sum the values returned by the partial response functions. Thus, the subset of functions that is the subject of our most intensive study considers the complete behavior as the sum of the independent responses, R_{ij}, to each object. The behavior function B_i in this subset can therefore be expressed as

$$
\mathbf{v}_{it} = \sum_{j=1}^{n} R_{ij}(\mathbf{p}_{it-1}, \mathbf{p}_{it-2}, \mathbf{p}_{jt-1}, \mathbf{p}_{jt-2}) \tag{3}
$$

where the objects i are the actors and the objects j are the stimuli.

Thus far, we have introduced a two-level hierarchy where a behavior function is made up of a number of partial response functions designating the response of an object to each other object in its environment. In fact, we find it necessary to subdivide even further so that partial responses are themselves composite functions consisting of "sub-responses."

The idea of a sub-response can easily be given by an example: Curiosity might cause an animal to approach an unknown object, and fear of the unknown might cause it to withdraw. Curiosity tends to dominate while the object is distant; fear tends to dominate with closer proximity. Very often, radically different behavioral forces exist at different distances, and together they make up the partial response of an actor to a stimulus. These components of partial responses are what we call sub-responses. Specifically, the partial response functions we have investigated are of the following form:

$$\mathbf{v}_{ijt} = \sum_{r=1}^{s} (M_{ijtr} + c_{ijr}) b_{ijr} \mathbf{D}_{ijtr} \tag{4}$$

Each of the expressions being summed is a sub-response, where the M are magnitudes and the $\mathbf{D}$ are direction unit vectors, all computed from $\mathbf{P}_{it-1}$, $\mathbf{P}_{it-2}$, $\mathbf{P}_{jt-1}$, $\mathbf{P}_{jt-2}$. Examples of these time-dependent magnitudes are fundamental ones such as Euclidean distance between nearest surfaces and velocity and the more complex such as time-to-reach and the ratio of distance to velocity. Examples of directions include towards, forwards, reflection, and orbital. The c and b are values that allow the fine tuning of the sub-response. We find in general that where some generic effect can be achieved by using different combinations of magnitudes and directions, a specific effect may be generated by appropriate values for c and b. The value b is composed of two parts—a response-distinguishing constant m_r and a weighting value u_r:

$$b_{ijr} = m_{ijr} u_{ijr} \tag{5}$$

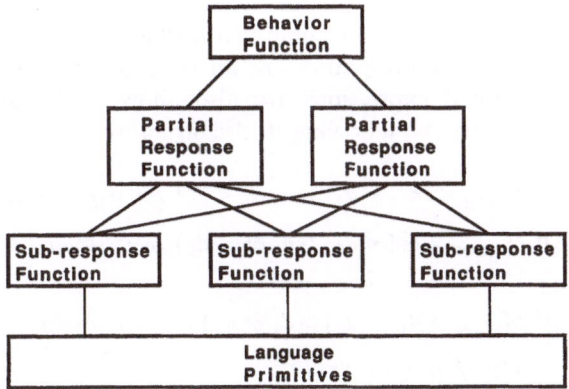

FIGURE 1. The hierarchy of functions used in behavior-function animation.

The u_{jr} of all sub-responses in a behavior function are guaranteed to sum to one; that is, for a behavior function B_i,

$$\sum_{j=1}^{n} \sum_{r=1}^{n} u_{ijr} = 1 \qquad (6)$$

Figure 1 illustrates the complete hierarchy of behavior, partial response, and sub-response functions.

4. The Animation Description Language

We use a simple nonprocedural language to describe the environment and behaviors. This may be called the "assembly language" of behavior function animation, since there is a logical correspondence between the statements and the behavior function equations. Only the most important elements of the language are described here. Full details of the language and its implementation can be found in the thesis by Lethbridge.[5]

A partial response is described by a series of one or more statements representing sub-responses. The general form for a sub-response is

$$\text{return}((M_{\text{symb}}\{+|-c\})\{*m\}\ D_{\text{symb}}\{\text{weight } w\})$$

with values in braces optional, and defaults being used for values not specified. M_{symb} and D_{symb} are symbolic names for the magnitude and direction time-dependent variables; c is the additive constant, m is the response-distinguishing part of b, and w is a weighting factor. We are not concerned with the w values summing to one—they are adjusted to u values by the interpretative program.

Several sub-responses can be combined into a list. The order in the list is not significant since sub-responses are all conceptually computed at the same time. Conditional expressions are also allowed; the general partial response is captured by the following if–else structure:

$$\{\text{if } M_{\text{range}} > d_1 | <d_2 | >d_1 \ \& \ <d_2\}\ \textit{sub-response-list}$$
$$\{\text{if } M_{\text{range}} > d_1 | <d_2 | >d_1 \ \& \ <d_2\}\ \textit{sub-response-list}$$
$$\vdots \qquad\qquad \vdots$$
$$\{\text{if } M_{\text{range}} > d_1 | <d_2 | >d_1 \ \& \ d_2\}\ \textit{sub-response-list}$$
$$\{\text{else } \textit{if–else-structure}\}$$

where M_{range} is the name of a time-dependent magnitude from the same set as M_{symb}, and the d values determine a range, possibly open-ended, in which M_{symb} must fall for the condition to be true. (Note that all else's encompass all subsequent rules.)

An example of a partial response might be:

```
if timetoreach < 0.5 return(velocity * 0.9 reflection weight
    100)
else
    return(velocity forwards weight 20)
    if distance < 100 return(velocity * 1.01 away)
    else
        if distance < 300 return(velocity * 1.01 towards)
```

In English sentences, this is saying if the actor object is about to collide with the stimulus, it is very important that it bounce off. Otherwise, if the distance is less than 100 units, the actor should be repelled from the stimulus. In the final case, if the distance is less than 300 units, the actor should be attracted. Visually, we see the actor mind its own business until the stimulus comes within range; then the actor starts to accelerate toward the stimulus. At a distance of 100 units, it begins to decelerate, and ultimately accelerates away again. If the actor is moving fast, however, we may see inadequate "braking," followed by a collision. On an ongoing basis, the tendency is for the actor to move alternately toward and away from the stimulus. The overall impression depends, though, on exactly what the stimulus is doing.

5. The Classification of Behavior Functions

One fundamental classification method is based on the maximum number of time steps involved in the calculations. Thus, we call a behavior function which determines behavior based only on the positions of objects in the environment at time $t-1$ to be a T1 behavior function. A behavior function which takes both $t-1$ and $t-2$ environments into account is a T2 behavior, and so on. As mentioned above, we have only investigated T1 and T2 behaviors.

From the observer's point of view, behaviors can be classified in order of increasing animacy. At the low end of the scale are the purely mechanical behaviors that are necessary so that objects obey fundamental physical laws. At the high end of the scale are behaviors that appear increasingly complex and purposeful. Note that those behaviors that "appear" to be increasingly complex need not be based on complex behavior functions. The appearance of "curiosity" is obtainable using functions which are relatively simple.

6. T1 Partial Responses

In T1 responses, behavior is based on the positions of objects at the previous $(t-1)$ time step. In general, T1 responses can model situations where one object gravitates toward a certain distance from another. More specifically, we have used them for clinging, pushing, pulling, chasing, attraction, escaping, and repulsion.

The only time-dependent variables available to T1 sub-responses are distance and interobject direction. We have experimented with several types of distance including Euclidean and inverse-square distance and have found that both of these produce perceptually similar behaviors. Therefore, we have generally restricted ourselves to functions based only on Euclidean distance. We have also investigated using distance between object centers versus distance between object perimeters. We find that distance from the object perimeter is the most useful and well worth the extra computational expense. To illustrate this, it is only by using the distance between perimeters that it is possible to model collision, bouncing, pushing, or pulling.

We construct T1 sub-responses using a single type of linear equation which has an additive parameter c and a multiplicative parameter m. These have the general form

```
if distance < d return(((distance - c) * m away)
```

The multiplicative parameter controls the responsiveness and speed of the actor. Both parameters used together control whether the actor is repelled from or attracted to the stimulus and in what ranges. The more interesting behaviors usually occur when several T1 sub-responses are operative at different distances. For example, a simple chasing and pursuing behavior is achievable if both objects react to each other with T1 responses.

One of the partial response functions might be the following:

```
if distance < 80 return(((distance - 80) * -0.15 away)
else
    if distance < 200 return(((distance - 80) * -0.083 away)
    else
        if distance < 500 return(((distance - 500) * 0.033 away)
```

This response would be decreasingly repulsive to 80 units of distance, increasingly attractive to 200 units, and then decreasingly attractive to 500 units. The overall visual effect depends on what the stimulus object is doing. In general, the actor gravitates to the 80-unit distance from its stimulus. If the other actor has a similar response function, but one for which its stable distance is less than 80 units, then this second actor (the stimulus to the first) becomes the pursuer; if its stable distance is greater than 80 units, then it is pursued. If one of the actors is perceived to be moving purposefully, it seems to push or pull the other actor at a distance, as if by a long rubber pole.

A useful T1 behavior can be obtained when the multiplicative parameter is near 1.0; if the partial response is

```
return(distance towards)
```

the resulting behavior appears as clinging, pushing, or pulling and has a very realistic feel about it, regardless of what the stimulus is doing. For example, if the actor is being pushed and the two meeting surfaces are not perpendicular to the direction of movement, the actor slides sideways, swings round to the rear of the stimulus, and ends up being pulled.

At this point, it is worth pointing out that many of the behaviors which are of interest, such as chasing and avoiding and pushing and pulling, inherently involve a relationship between more than one moving actor. Since the general T1 response is to gravitate to a given distance, it is easy to see why a purely T1 system of objects would tend to find an equilibrium situation and grind to a halt—there is nothing to stimulate the breaking of the equilibrium. Also, in the case of pure avoidance, it is easy to see how a T1 system would cause objects to diverge forever. Thus, while it is possible for useful elements of a system to be T1, the stability of the entire system requires T2 elements.

7. T2 Partial Responses

In T2 functions, behavior can be based on the positions of objects in the previous two time intervals. This opens up a wide variety of variables on which responses may be built, the most important being the velocity magnitude and the direction of movement.

7.1. Self-Oriented (Reflexive) Responses

Perhaps the most interesting and useful T2 responses are those where an object responds to its own previous velocity and direction of movement.

It has been found necessary to have at least some element of self-oriented response in every environment to prevent the system from coming to a halt. The simplest such partial response is

```
return(velocity forwards)
```

which has the effect of at least attempting to maintain the current movement (it could be overruled by more heavily weighted partial responses).

Self-oriented responses can be used to make an object have a characteristic velocity, to which it returns in the absence of other influences. This
characteristic, or homeostatic, velocity might be very slow in the case of, for
example, a grazing animal or relatively fast in the case of a hungry predator.
Self-oriented responses can also be used to do such things as limit the top
speed of an actor so that it is enabled to accelerate rapidly to some speed
while engaged in pursuit or avoidance but requires an increasingly powerful
stimulus to continue accelerating as it approaches its maximum speed.

An object with the following partial response tends to maintain a
velocity between 5 and 8 units per time interval unless strongly affected by
some other object:

```
if velocity < 1 return(velocity + 0.5 forwards)
else
    if velocity < 5 return(velocity * 1.2 forwards)
    else
        if velocity < 8 return(velocity forwards)
        else
            return(velocity * 0.8 forwards)
```

The first sub-response is necessary because if the velocity dropped to
zero, no amount of multiplication would cause acceleration.

7.2. Other T2 Responses

When self-oriented sub-responses are combined with T1 sub-responses,
the resulting partial response is a change in velocity as a function of
distance. (T1 responses alone control velocity directly.) Although similar
behaviors (chasing, pursuing, etc.) can be achieved as with T1 behaviors,
the appearance is somewhat different. The elements of delay and momen-
tum are the most prominent new features that can be made available with
appropriately designed responses. An actor, for example, might be slow to
start pursuing a stimulus. If the stimulus were to then suddenly change
direction, the actor might speed on, making a wide curve before it is
once again heading for its quarry. Another useful effect of the T1 and self-
oriented combination is the simulation of orbiting planets.

If time-to-reach is used in place of distance in some of the simpler
responses, they are modified in interesting ways. For example, a pursuer
may be able to get very close to a quarry before the quarry flees as long as
the pursuer is moving slowly. If the pursuer is moving rapidly toward the

quarry, the result would be different. Time-to-reach is distance divided by the change in interobject distance.

Another quantity, the ratio of distance to the stimulus' velocity, can be used in the simulation of "snapping up" and capture.

T2 behaviors can be based on magnitudes that are combinations of distance, velocity-of-self, velocity-of-stimulus, change-in-distance, and relative velocity. Each magnitude allows specific qualities to be added to the behavior, although some are much more useful than others. In addition to these new magnitudes, many new directions are available in which objects can move. One of the most useful of these is the reflection direction, which allows a simple physical bouncing partial response:

```
if timetoreach < 0.5 return(velocity reflection)
```

Another direction is the direction toward the path of movement of the stimulus—useful to give an animation an element of anticipatory action.

The essence of creating effective-looking animations is to combine simple sub-responses with differing qualities. The combined effect is not usually predictable, but is almost always interesting.

8. The Building of Complex Behavior Systems

Behaving systems can be put together in an infinite variety of ways.

Figure 2 illustrates an animated scene that evokes a particularly strong impression of animacy. The scene is composed of a collection of static objects that form the word "Pam" (for Perceived Animate Motion—the name of our software). There are four additional circles that form a caterpillar shape.

As we observe the scene, we see the caterpillar move around. It is very definitely "exploring." Sometimes it moves its head from side to side. At other times it moves in a definite direction for a while. Behavior at the "walls" or boundaries of the static objects varies. It may pull back or follow the outline. It is quite hesitant to "climb" onto the static objects, but occasionally does. The behavior of the caterpillar's own segments is also lifelike: there are rhythmic contractions from head to tail.

The animation can be left to run indefinitely. The caterpillar continues the same pattern of behavior but, in an observable time frame, never follows exactly the same path.

Five primary partial response functions govern the behavior. The directed arcs in Figure 2 indicate which stimulus–actor pairs use each partial response. The numbers on the arcs correspond to the descriptions below.

FIGURE 2. A frame from a simple sequence, showing partial responses as directed arcs.

1. The homeostasis function. This attempts to keep the head moving at about two units of velocity by compensating for deviations from that velocity.

```
if velocity < 2 return(velocity + 0.3 forwards weight 10)
if velocity > 2 return(velocity * 0.9 forwards)
```

2. The function that keeps the body segments together. If the segments fail to overlap by two units of distance, the rear segment is moved toward the one in front. At each time frame, this movement ripples back one segment, giving the rhythmic contractions.

```
if distance > -2 return(velocity + 1.0 towards)
```

3. The function that keeps the head away from the tail.

```
if changeindistance < 0 return(velocity + 0.1 away)
```

4. The function that causes the caterpillar to "explore" the objects. Within certain ranges, there is a weak attraction, and within other

ranges, there is a weak repulsion. The weakness of these effects allows them to be often dominated by partial response functions 1 and 3.

```
if distance < 5 return(velocity + 0.005 towards)
if distance > 5 & < 30 return(velocity + 0.001 away)
```

5. The function that prevents the caterpillar from passing through the outer walls.

```
if distance > -1 return(velocity reflection)
```

We have built many other quite complex behavior patterns. Examples include a humorous scene where eyes track erratically moving insects and an interactive hockey game.

The hockey example is interesting because it illustrates the fact that we can attach an object to a mouse and put it under human control (although overriding sub-responses prevent the human from driving the "player" through the wall). Objects such as the ball and the goalie react to the human-controlled player.

9. Behavior Function Problems and Solutions

Although new and interesting behaviors can easily be created by varying the response functions, it has been found somewhat difficult to create some behaviors, given a preconceived notion of what they should look like. This has been particularly the case when a more animate appearance is desired and when the interactions become more complex. Problems encountered when designing behavior functions can be grouped into two classes, those of a perceptual nature and those resulting purely from the mathematics of the system.

The primary perceptual problem is one of balancing, especially of velocity. Velocities must not be too slow or all appearance of animacy is lost. A too fast velocity, on the other hand, is hard to follow, especially since objects tend to move off screen edges. The screen-edge problem can be combated by "walls" objects, panning, zooming, or modular arithmetic causing a "wraparound" effect; however, these introduce their own problems.

Unnatural movements can also pose a perceptual problem. Their presence is usually due to a transition from one dominant response to another. However, sometimes movements which are physically unnatural, because they contain an abrupt change in velocity, can actually enhance the appearance of intentionality. It is as though the brain, unable to attribute a movement to a simple physical cause, attributes it instead to a deliberate action.

The mathematical class of problems tends to cause results that are totally unacceptable, but such problems are more easy to solve than perceptual problems. They occur when behavior functions are constructed with particular combinations of parameters.

Several situations are due to the fact that our animation technique is driven by feedback—there can be problems with both negative and positive feedback. Positive feedback has a tendency to be unstable. If it is uncontrolled, objects rapidly accelerate in some direction and disappear forever. Negative feedback causes damping down of motion—in its worst case, the animation stops completely. Both types of feedback are necessary to prevent uninteresting equilibrium, but careful choice of parameters and conditional operators is necessary to prevent extreme situations.

Another problem that frequently occurs is rapid oscillation of the actor. It is usually caused by partial responses that counteract each other in a slightly asymmetric manner or by one partial response that overcompensates for a given situation. A notable case is when the multiplicative parameter in a T1 response is greater than one.

Another mathematical problem is exact repetition of a sequence. The chances of this occurring rapidly decrease as the complexity of the system rises. A minuscule change in a parameter to one of the sub-responses is often all that is needed to prevent the repetition.

Discretisation can also pose a problem, manifesting itself in actions that continue when they should not. An example is objects that go through walls. This type of problem is most easily dealt with by altering thresholds or, for example, replacing distance by time-to-reach.

10. Discussion and Conclusions

The work we have done thus far has convinced us of the basic soundness of our approach. Using a few simple functions, we can display an animation in which apparently complex behavior is perceived. This is analogous to the natural universe, where a relatively small number of physical laws produces all the behavior we see in everyday life. The driving force in both cases is the concept of the chaotic system. The behavior produced by our technique is usually nonrepetitive and lacks the rigid mechanical quality that is characteristic of poor animation.

The following outlines some of our most important conclusions:

1. Programming with behavior functions can be computationally inexpensive. We have succeeded in producing real-time animations involv-

ing up to 10 objects with moderately complex behavior using an IRIS 2400 workstation equipped with a floating-point board.

2. It is natural to define functions for the interaction between pairs of objects in the system. These are "partial response functions" as opposed to "behavior functions" in that they must somehow be combined to generate a behavior. The behavior function itself is most easily conceptualized as some higher-level function which, for a given actor, combines its partial responses. We find simple summation of partial responses to be effective; however, we recognize that this type of behavior function has limitations.

3. Because, in the worst case, every objects reacts independently to every other object in the environment, calculating the state of an environment at a given time is fundamentally of order n^2, where n is the number of objects in the environment.

4. By taking only the state of the system at the previous two time steps, it is possible to model a number of behaviors that involve two moving actors. These include pushing and pulling, chasing and avoidance, attack, capture, ball dribbling, and orbiting.

5. An important class of behavior is that in which one object is permanently fixed (inanimate) and the other moves. Examples of this include bouncing off walls and obstacle avoidance. This kind of behavior is easy to construct and looks natural.

6. One of the most fundamental and essential classes of function is that in which an object has a tendency to respond to its own motions. This self-oriented behavior can be used to prevent objects or systems from going out of control or stopping altogether.

7. Most of the partial response functions that we have discovered have been found by chance or by means of a considerable amount of trial-and-error experimentation. We have not found it easy to deliberately design a function that causes an object to behave in a particularly way. However, once discovered, partial response functions tend to be robust in the sense that their parameters can be changed through a wide range of values with similar behavior still appearing. Thus, for example, "pushing" might be changed to "pushing hard" due to a change in parameter values. We conclude from this that for behavior functions to be a useful animation tool, it would be desirable for the animator to have a library of functions that generate standard behaviors; each of these functions should have well-designed parameters to control it.

8. One of the obvious limitations of the system we have implemented is that it is restricted to the motion of simple geometric objects: circles, rectangles, and convex symmetric objects made up of quarter-circles and rectangles. At present, we do not know whether the technique can be efficiently extended to more complex articulated objects.

References

1. N. MAGNENAT-THALMANN and D. THALMANN, *Computer Animation: Theory and Practice.* Springer-Verlag, Tokyo, 1985.
2. A. H. BORNING, The programming language aspects of ThingLab, a constraint-oriented simulation laboratory, *ACM Trans. Programming Languages Systems* **3**(4), 353–387 (1981).
3. A. MICHOTTE, *The Perception of Causality*, Methuen, New York, 1963.
4. A. MARION, K. FLEISCHER, and M. VICKERS, Towards expressive animation for interactive characters, Proceedings, Graphics Interface '84, pp. 17–20.
5. T. LETHBRIDGE, Perceived animate motion by simple deterministic rules of inter-object behavior, Master's thesis, University of New Brunswick, Fredericton, 1987.

VI

APPLICATIONS

The final section of the book presents the use of visual languages in a variety of application areas. The first chapter, by Enrico Barichella *et al.*, continues the theme of simulation, developed in the previous section, with an application in medical studies. Shi-Kuo Chang and Erland Jungert combine a classical idea, run-length encoding, with Chang's 2-D indexing of icons to develop a highly effective system for describing and manipulating spatial objects such as those found in geographic information systems. Donald B. Crouch and Robert R. Korfhage examine visual interfaces to aid the user of information retrieval systems. And the final chapter presents the ideas that Allen L. Ambler has been developing on the addition of new visual elements to the spreadsheet paradigm.

13

A VISUAL ENVIRONMENT FOR LIVER SIMULATION STUDIES

ENRICO BARICHELLA, MAURIZIO BERETTA,
NICOLA DIOGUARDI, PIERO MUSSIO,
MARCO PADULA,
MAURIZIO PIETROGRANDE,
and MARCO PROTTI

1. Introduction

The use of simulation tools is becoming more and more frequent in the everyday activity of the physician, at both researcher and practitioner levels.

Several problems arise in the medical interpretation and exploitation of the results obtained, because most computer-based simulation systems require a high level of competence in computer science for their control and proper use. Physicians, who are not computer professionals, are, on the other hand, responsible both for the interpretation of the results and for their application in medical practice.

This problem is one of the topics being dealt with by the GMSVP, Gruppo Medico Sistemistico di Via Pace, and this work is discussed here. Even if our goal is confined to the medical field, our proposed approach to dealing with this problem seems general enough to be suggested for adoption in other fields of application.[1, 2]

ENRICO BARICHELLA and MAURIZIO BERETTA • GMSVP—Gruppo Medico Sistemistico di Via Pace, Milan, Italy. NICOLA DIOGUARDI and MAURIZIO PIETROGRANDE • Institute of Internal Medicine, University of Milan, Milan, Italy. PIERO MUSSIO and MARCO PROTTI • Department of Physics, University of Milan, Milan, Italy. MARCO PADULA • CNR-SIAM, Milan, Italy.

The basic idea is to render computation more understandable and controllable by the user through a visual environment designed to fit in with the customary practice of the user, instead of imposing an environment that is more rational for the computer but foreign to the user's experience.[3, 4]

To this end, the metaphor of the instruments of the working environment familiar to the user is adopted. The tools that form the visual environment are designed so that the user can see the system as if it were an extension of his or her working environment; this means that the user's thinking habits and usual way of working must be respected, even though they may be improved. For example, the user is supplied with tools to check on the progress of the computation and to obtain the necessary insight into the system, which communicates with the user by extending his or her conventional specialist scientific or technical language.

In our case, the working environment taken into account is the physician's research laboratory. In this laboratory, graphic and pictorial aspects were very important even before the introduction of computerized tools, since physicians use icons, graphics, and sketches in normal conversation, both when communicating with each other and when documenting their work within the scientific community. A medical conversation is therefore itself a diagrammatic conversation, and this aspect must be maintained, thus ensuring the ability of the physician to communicate with the machine through diagrams, graphs, even qualitative ones, and sketches.[5, 6]

A second fundamental aspect is that these conversations must be recorded in logbooks, as happens in the laboratory, in such a way that the activity of an experiment or a cycle of experiments can be verified by others or summarized for publication. Both of these aspects are common in laboratories in many experimental fields. Our proposal is to meet these requirements by designing a visual environment named VISINT (*Vis*ual *Int*erface).

The tools of this environment are the computerized logbook (c-logbook) and the simulation programs.

In the c-logbooks, the physician carrying out the experiments keeps notes and documents on the different steps taken in his or her work, that is, the designing of tools, how he or she sets them up, the tests used to validate them, and collection of the results obtained from the experiments through use of the interactive simulating programs.

This proposal is the result of two cycles of experiments, during which two prototypes of the visual environment were tested by physicians' research simulation programs.

In this chapter, we focus our attention on one aspect of the design, the formal definition of physician–machine communication tools. To this end, the environment in which the computerized tools are to be used is described and the rules to be respected are deduced.

C-logbooks are therefore formally defined by the use of attributed conditional grammars, used here as generative devices.[7-9] This formalism was chosen because it describes, in a uniform and compact way, the bidimensional strings (the image that appears on the screen for the communication) and the sets of those strings that form the c-logbook. These c-logbooks are the basic tool that serves to enable the experiments in progress to be checked by the "computer-naive" physician. They are used to define the *in numero* laboratory, the created environment.

2. Liver Activity Studies

In a recent book, Dioguardi explained a systemic approach to the understanding and description of the human liver dynamic.[10] With this approach, it is possible to define with precision and describe as a unit both the physiological behavior and the functional failure of this organ. These ideas provided the impetus for studies by the GMSVP on liver physiology.

Studies and experiments on liver physiology are pursued along three different lines:[10] (a) *in vivo*, that is, studies and experiments on the liver in living organisms; (b) *in vitro*, that is, studies and experiments on liver cells maintained in a physiological solution outside the organism; and (c) *in numero*, that is, studies and experiment performed by hepatologists using computer programs simulating liver activity in the living organism.

These three kinds of experiments enable physicians to study the liver from different points of view and with different specific goals. The need is for a unique, unitary, and holistic interpretation of the three kinds of results. In other words, the same physician who designs and collects data by *in vivo* and *in vitro* studies has to be able to perform a coordinated experiment *in numero*. To this end, the computerized system with which the simulation experiment is performed must enable physicians to design and execute their *in numero* experiment in a way similar to that used for *in vivo* and *in vitro* experiments.

In their ordinary, noncomputerized activity, physicians are used to establishing their own scientific aims, to designing the consequent sequence of experiments, to designing and organizing their experimental setups, to designing each experiment, taking into account the devices and resources at their disposal in the laboratory, and, lastly, to performing the experiment. In all these activities, physicians keep track of their work, of their decisions, and of the explanations for their decisions in a logbook. Typically, they record their models and representations in the form of icons and sketches

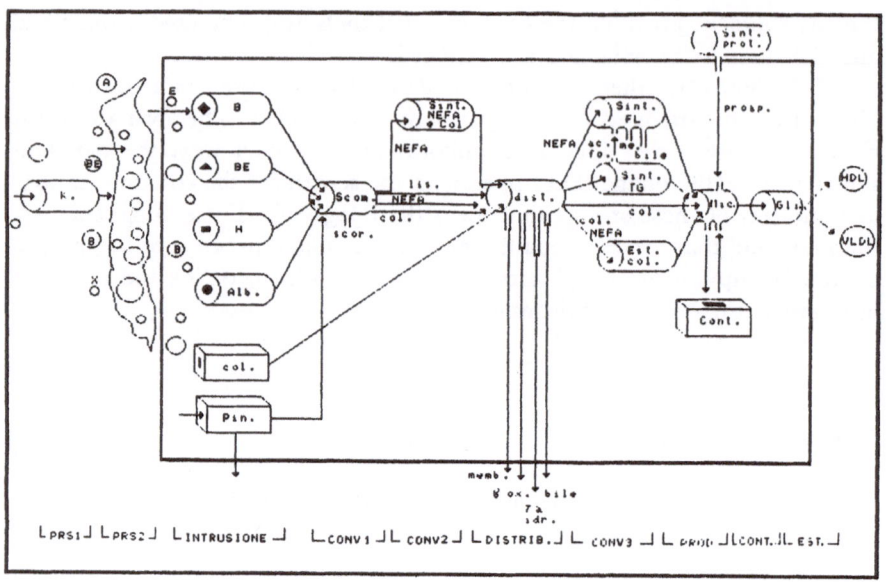

FIGURE 1. Model of the lipid solubilization experiment.

(Figure 1), their data in the form of graphs and tables (see Figure 2), and their explanations in the form of texts.

These messages convey implicit information only legible and understandable by those skilled in the field.[1] Note that, in the physician's language, the words "icon, text, and graph" have the same meaning as in common language.[11] So, for example, the word "icon" denotes a visual sign, synthesizing complex ideas and "sharing a visual likeness" with what it represents.[12-14] In the physician's language, therefore, icons by analogy, resemble the entities they refer to. Physicians also agree about how to react when the icon sign is recognized: that is, they define what influence the recognition will have on their behavior. This agreed reaction is here referred to as "interpretation" of the icon.[6, 15]

3. User's Requests

The simulation environment must enable physicians to perform their activities in a way familiar to them, so that they can understand and fully exploit the new experimental and conceptual tools of computer science. To this end, they need to be allowed to define their numerical laboratories in a way analogous to the design and organization of their experimental ones, that is, to define the kind of numerical tools they expect to use, the way these tools can be organized to simulate a specific subsystem, the kinds of results they expect to collect, and the way in which they want these results to be represented.

These activities have to be performed in accordance with the following "imperative": The hepatologist, who is not a computer scientist, has actively to understand and control (not just passively drive) the simulated *in numero* experiments.

In other words, the dynamic behavior of a program during its execution, which is usually hidden from view, must be made accessible to the physician, at least as regards the variables that are meaningful with respect to the simulated system.[16] Physicians have to be able to distinguish misleading results, due to numerical or implementation tricks, from meaningful ones, derived from their models, without having to be experts in the computer field.

Furthermore, physicians need to be allowed to define their specific *in numero* experiments, that is, to identify the tools with which they can simulate the specific systems they need to simulate, their interrelationships, and their interaction with the environment. Once the experiment has been defined, they need to define the simulation setup and, lastly, to execute the *in numero* experiment, establishing the specific initial state of the system under study and the specific environmental action to be taken on it, understanding the ongoing computation, and collecting data in a way which is sensible to them. Furthermore, they need to record the complete track of their simulation work so that their activities can be documented, communicated, and discussed at large. To meet these requirements, the system must (a) be friendly, that is, easy to use, easy to learn, easy to understand, and easy to remember, and (b) include nonambiguous diagnostics—that is, during interaction, the user is effectively helped in finding out and correcting possible errors with unambiguous messages.[17, 18] These tools enable users to come to a correct and safe conclusion of the job session without losing their work.[3, 17, 19]

After extensive use of a first prototype, it became clear that friendliness, as defined above, was not enough to guarantee the necessary control of the process by physicians. A new constraint, navigation control, was then discussed.[20, 21] Navigation control denotes the ability of the user to navigate properly through the simulation system. In other words, the user must be able to achieve the experimental strategy he or she has in mind by choosing, at the end of each transition, the proper one to trigger next within the set of those allowed.[22] Difficulties arise in pursuing this aim, especially when transitions are associated with iconic or verbal commands stored in structures efficient from the computer management point of view but not easily related to the semantics of the experiment by the user. To handle this problem, in the present proposal, the set of commands is partitioned into subsets, each one being associated with a specific kind of experimental activity.

Friendliness and navigation control are obviously necessary requirements but are not sufficient to guarantee the physician's understanding of the *in numero* experiment. The system is required to allow control of the computational process by the user. That is, physicians have to be able to understand the actual computational process (what is happening) during the execution of the program that realizes their models. To this end, they need to verify the intermediate and final computer results of the experiment, so that they can validate these results against their knowledge of the real system.[3]

Whenever possible, even algorithmic control should be provided. By algorithmic control, we mean that the user must be able to understand if the programs are the correct formal representation of the model proposed; the algorithm realized by the program must be expressed in a form such that users, other than those involved in the design, are able to verify its validity and its significance and understand the models of the system to be simulated from it.[3, 23] Algorithmic control will not be discussed here.

With regard to computational process control, two options were studied:

- the possibility for the user to be involved each time with the execution of the experiment, and not just with *a priori* planning of the inputs and of the events—that is, control of the computational process should be active, not passive;
- the possibility of obtaining a precise map of the ongoing simulation whenever required, of checking the state of every component subsystem involved in the simulation, and of changing it if required.

From these requirements, a number of design requirements and constraints are derived, and these will now be examined.

4. Toward Satisfaction of User's Requests

To meet these requirements, a visual interaction environment was envisaged.[4] This choice is made on the basis of the physician's habit of using icons and graphs in scientific communication, and therefore on the assumption that a familiar image might be more comprehensible and easily managed by a physician than the usual, purely text-based interaction.[16, 24]

An example of use of tools that enables the physician to handle data in a way easier for him or her and that provides better understanding of the system is to feed data in through a puck or a mouse that can be made to run over a system of Cartesian axes (Figure 2).

Thus, the physician specifies the input to the system, only taking into account the whole shape of the curves, which take on certain meanings within definite ranges, rather than the precision of a single number; the physician also avoids either manual operations, such as digitizing the numbers, or conceptual ones, such as numerical use of integrals and derivatives, which are possible sources of mistakes.

The proposed visual communication environment is based on the three elementary interaction entities that physicians use in their conventional environment: (a) icons, that is, visual signs that the user can immediately

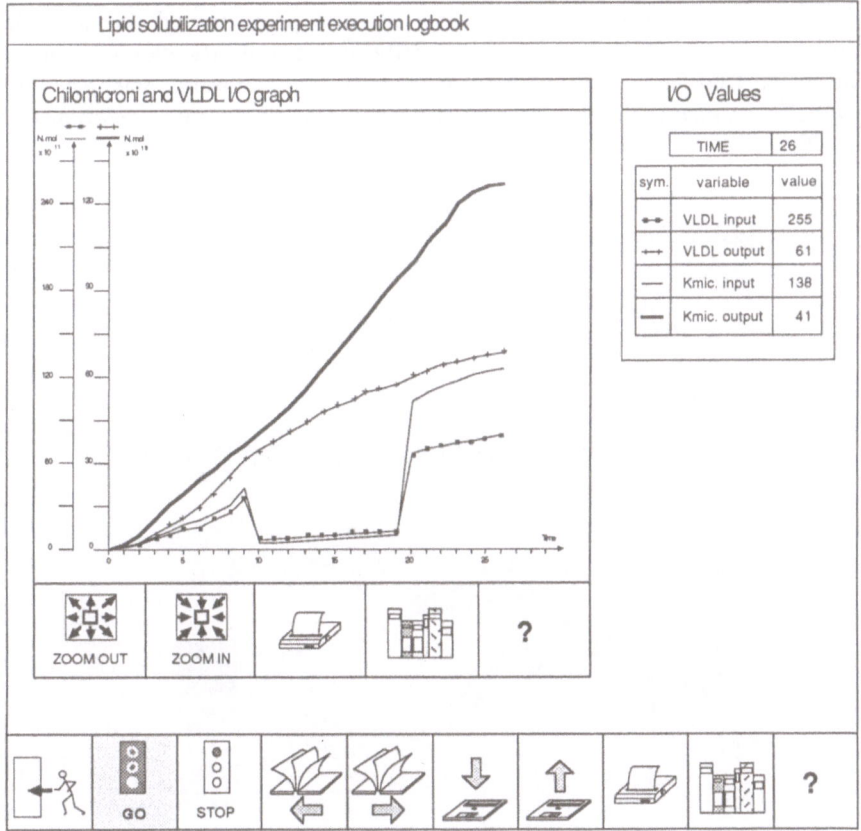

FIGURE 2. Lipid solubilization experiment execution logbook, the I/O page showing a graphical and an alphanumeric window.

recognize and interpret (Figure 3 is an example of an icon used in the first prototype of the system); (b) texts, which are here alphanumeric strings and tables, sometimes combined; and (c) graphs, which describe input to and output from the systems studied or the evolution of the systems' states. These graphs are curves represented on a system of Cartesian axes. In Figure 2, for example, input data about the two variables "chilomicroni" (Kmic) and VLDL are inserted by the hepatologist by drawing with a puck on a tablet, or with a mouse, the two curves (the thin curve and the one identified by the symbol ■), and the system replies with two new curves (the thick curve and the one identified by +) referring to output data.

Icons, texts, and graphs used in the interaction system refer to either the variables being manipulated or to the normal flow of the interaction. The use of these entities in the visual interaction environment requires that their definition and meaning be examined from several different points of view, so that the user's interpretation and the programmed one are adequately matched.[6, 25] Here we will briefly discuss only the case of icons, as the most frequent disputes that arise between computer scientists and physicians concern the meaning of the word *icon* or the interpretation of a specific icon.

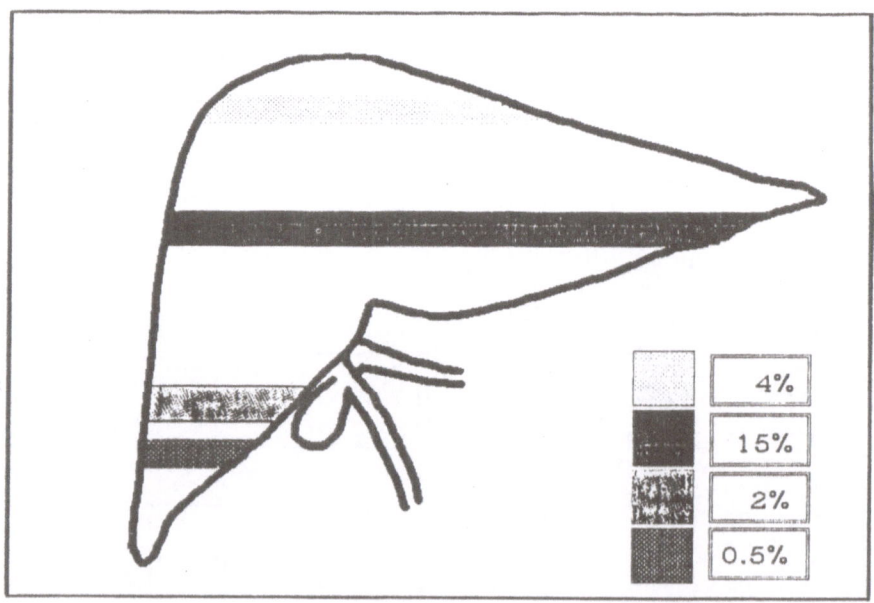

FIGURE 3. A liver icon used in the simulation system, showing the liver global activity.

5. Observations about Icon Use

In computer science, icons have been studied since computers began to be used for graphics, and, more recently, they have been used for the spatial management of data in database management systems (DBMS), for a general image-based man–machine communication, and in the management of help systems.[12, 14, 26, 27]

Tanimoto proposed the iconic/symbolic data-structure data type, or extended icon data type.[13]

This data type was recently extended to a generalized icon. Generalized icons are physical representation–logical representation pairs.[20, 21]

We prefer to denote by the word *icon* the graphical or pictorial entity interpreted by recognition of some structural invariant, this invariant resembling its meaning. Seen from this limited angle, icons constitute a special class of structure in which only the values of attributes may vary in the icon description.[28] As in every structure, icons are entities that can be expressed in two forms: external and internal to the system. Both external and internal forms may be oganized according to different criteria and for different purposes. An analogy can be made with numbers represented in different notations (e.g., positional versus Roman or hieroglyphic) and in different bases (e.g., decimal versus binary).

The external form of icons can be sensed, managed, and interpreted by a person and consists of a graphic representation on a suitable support (screen, paper, etc.).

The internal form can be interpreted and managed by a program. It consists of a data structure, that is, a structured collection of entities, together with the operations to be performed on that collection. The operations may be described by sets of rules.

A problem arises from this two-sided situation: how to make the user's interpretation fit the operations described by internal rules, so that no misleading interpretation of the computer's reaction to an icon will arise. This problem has been discussed elsewhere, but it is worthwhile to note that misunderstandings can arise even in person-to-person iconic communication.[6]

In the conventional experimental environment, an icon may be related to the activities or entities described. Different concepts may be related to the same icon; that is, the same icon may represent an activity, an entity, or both, depending on the context. This being the case, an observer recognizes the icon from the context, interprets it, and acts accordingly.

Note that there are often two levels of interpretation of an icon. At the first level, an entity is recognized, that is, a referent in the physical world is detected. At the second level, an activity is triggered by the recognition. For example, the icon in Figure 4a, once it is recognized as a book, triggers the activity "go to the next page."

In person–machine and machine–machine environments, an icon, once detected, may drive the computation into two different kinds of activity:

a. the execution of a task
b. the display of data that can be detected in a database or evaluated from a description of the icon

In the first case, the icon is a command icon; in the second, it is a data icon.

An icon is classified as "expert" whenever a knowledge base is exploited in the execution of one or more iconic activities related to it. In our experience, expert icons are mainly used in program–program communication.

Note that the knowledge bases used in the different steps are not unified. Each knowledge pocket is coded and managed independently and often reflects the points of view of different experts.

External or visual forms of expert icons are used whenever to control the computational process by a human being is needed.

Similar observations characterize the design of texts and graphs for physician–machine communication. This problem will not be discussed in greater depth here, because only the more general frame for this communication is addressed. Anyhow, these observations should be noted because they were at the base of some decisions we made on how to group different entities on the screen and on how to structure the general interaction system so that the user is able to gain a correct insight into the programmed interpretation of each entity and partial or misleading interpretation of the messages is avoided.

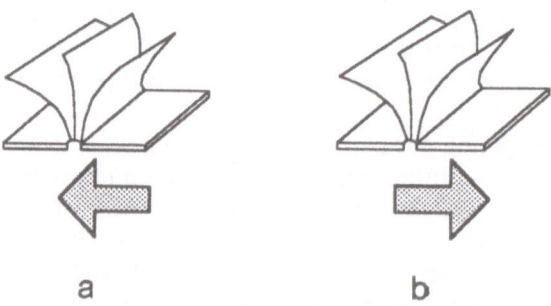

a   b

FIGURE 4. The change page icons: (a) go to next page; (b) go to previous page.

6. The Proposed Liver Simulation Laboratory

In the proposed visual environment, graphs and text are intended as units of information exchange expressed in a form suitable for person–person, person–machine, and machine–machine communication. We shall now focus our attention on person–machine communication, by specifying the tools for the creation of the visual environment as it appears to users.

The proposal is to record every transaction in the *in numero* laboratory in four computerized logbooks (c-logbooks), whose elements can be shown on the screen. There is a c-logbook for each of the physician's activities, namely, design of the laboratory, design of the experiment, and experiment execution, and one general c-logbook, which records how the laboratory was designed, implemented, and adapted itself and provides the access to the other c-logbooks.

A c-logbook (Lgb) is a collection of pages encased by a cover, which, in the formal description, is identified with the c-logbook itself. A page (Pg) is, in these terms, a white sheet, which can include a collection of non-overlapping windows, each window (Wnd) being a collection of nonoverlapping functional areas (FA). Similarly, FAs are even used to define the cover. FAs are memory areas in which icons, texts, and graphs can be written either by the physician or by the simulation program.

FAs simulate the areas in noncomputerized logbooks on which physicians write their notes or draw or paste figures, graphs, and data obtained from their instruments. FAs are classified on the basis of the kind of interaction they provide or of the type of information they bring. Thus, there are AFAs (alphanumeric functional areas), on which alphanumeric text can be written; GFAs (graphic functional areas), on which graphs are represented; and IFAs (iconic FAs) to display icons, which can be associated with several different kinds of data or activities. An IFA can be associated with a command. In this case, neither its external representation nor its meaning will be modified during use of the c-logbook. Whenever a command IFA is pointed to by the physician, the c-logbook reacts by executing the associated activity. An IFA may, on the other hand, be associated with data or even used to represent the simulated system, each of its functional activities being iconized as a box and the channels through which data are exchanged as arrows (Figure 5). Programs use this IFA to display the values of some state variables. Users modify them to change the state of the system being simulated.

Note that a similar kind of interaction, which enables the user to modify the situation being developed and the c-logbook to react accordingly, is also provided for by using AFAs and GFAs. This kind of interaction has no counterpart in the conventional noncomputerized logbook,

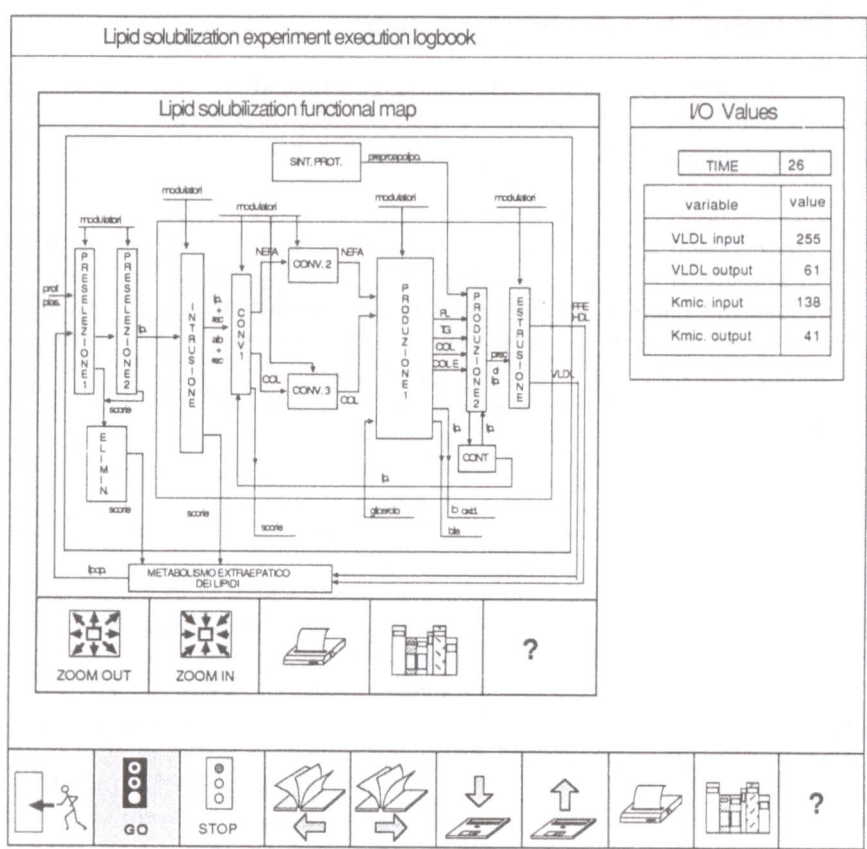

FIGURE 5. Lipid solubilization experiment execution logbook: the functional page showing functional model of an iconic window and an alphanumeric window.

which is only a passive tool for the physician. The problems and the possibilities stemming from it will not be considered here, nor will the problem of the definition of the form and meaning of the icons, which has been studied elsewhere.[6, 25] The present work deals only with the formal definition which makes controlled design of the *in numero* laboratory possible.

7. The Basic Tool: The C-Logbook

All the entities introduced in the previous section (FA, Wnd, Pg, Lgb) are spatially organized following, as far as possible, the editing rules used by physicians to organize and use their conventional logbooks.

With each of the four c-logbooks, and at any given moment, users have at their disposal the set of commands that are characteristic of the c-logbook and those that enable them to browse through a page, change the page, be helped by the system, and stop their activity. A c-logbook is identified by its cover, which has a title area (TA) of the AFA type on top, a set of pages (Pgs), and a command area (Lcs), in which the icons of the commands (Lca) available are displayed. Each page in the c-logbook has an optional title area, specifying its meaning, at the top and a blank sheet in which windows can be encased. Windows, in their turn, are composed of a title area and a functional area of interaction, called Aia or Iia or Gia, depending on its type (Alphanumeric, Iconic, or Graphic). Similarly, a window is called Awn, Gwn, or Iwn, after the type of its interaction area. When inter-

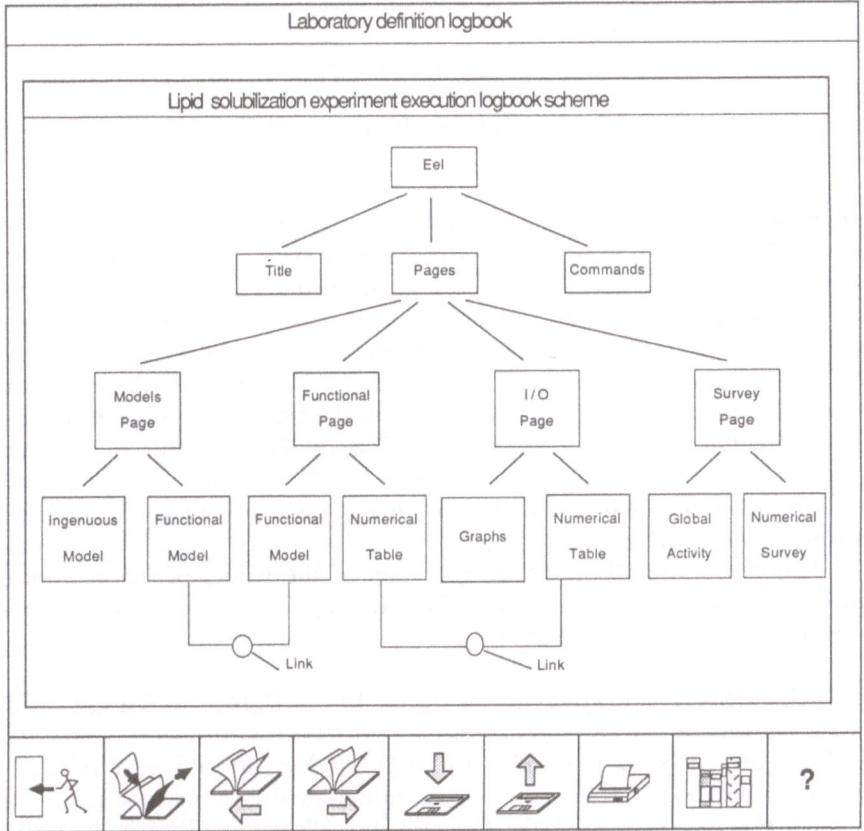

FIGURE 6. The laboratory definition logbook: a page showing a window representing the structure of the lipid solubilization experiment c-logbook.

action is required, a command area (Wcs) appears at the bottom of the window, in which the icons of the commands (Wca) available are displayed. In this way, each set of commands is clearly associated with the interactive experimental activity associated with the window. The screen, as a whole, appears as in Figure 6. These empirical rules have been translated into an attributed conditional grammar (acg), which is used to drive c-logbook design and implementation. An acg is a generative tool, used to derive a correct linear description of the *in numero* laboratory, the c-logbook, and the pages in the c-logbook. In this linear description, each entity is associated with a symbol and described by a set of geometrical and topological attributes, which determine the position in the c-logbook and the reciprocal relations of the entities. The value assumed by a specific instance of an attribute is called a "property of the hinted entity." Properties are used both to describe each entity to be used and to check the condition under which symbols are correctly derived.

A conditional attributed grammar is a 4-tuple $G = \langle T, Nt, P, S \rangle$, where T is the set of terminal-attributed symbols, Nt is the set of non-terminal-attributed symbols, P is a set of conditional attributed productions, and $S \in Nt$ is the start symbol.

For each $x_i \in T \cup Nt$, there exists a finite set of attributes $A(x_i)$, each attribute $\alpha \in A(x_i)$ having a set $D(\alpha)$ of finite possible values. Each production in P is divided into two parts: a conditional syntactic rule and a semantic one. Conditional rules make it possible to handle a situation in which the rewriting of a sequence of symbols may depend on the properties of their attributes. A conditional syntactic rule has the form $X \dashv Cs \mapsto Y$ where $X \in Nt$, $Y = y_1 y_2 \cdots y_m$, $s = s_1 s_2 \cdots s_k$ are strings over $T \cup Nt$. The left-hand part of the rule is called the antecedent, and the right-hand part, the consequent. C is the name of a predicate $C: s \rightarrow \{0, 1\}$. The syntactic rule is fired only if $Cs = 1$; that is, given a string on $T \cup Nt$ in which the antecedent appears, the antecedent is rewritten into the consequent only if the predicate is true.

Semantic rules allow the computation of the values of the attributes associated with symbols involved in the rewriting. The semantic rule is a set of expressions of the following form:

$$f : D_\psi(\alpha_{1\psi}) x \cdots x D_\psi(\alpha_{m\psi}) x \cdots x D_\omega(\delta_{1\omega}) x \cdots x D_\omega(\delta_{n\omega}) \rightarrow D_\xi(\gamma_{1\xi})$$

where $\psi, \omega \in \{X, y_1, \ldots, y_m\}$ and $\xi = X$; $\alpha_{i\psi} \in A(\psi)$, $\delta_{i\omega} \in A(\omega)$, $\gamma_{i\xi} \in A(\xi)$.

In this case, the set of terminal-attributed symbols T is $T = A \cup O \cup \{[\ , \ ]\}$. $A = \{$Aia, Gia, Iia, BS, Wca, Lca, TA$\}$ is the set of names of the entities forming a window, a page, or a c-logbook, while $O = \{\equiv, \|, \blacksquare, \bullet, \supseteq\}$ is a set of symbols denoting the reciprocal position of the two entities between which one symbol belonging to O is infixed. The specific meaning of each symbol can be derived by means of the semantic part of the rules in which it appears. $\{[\ ,\ ]\}$ are two symbols used to specify priority in the rewriting.

The set of non-terminal-attributed symbols is $\mathcal{N}t = \{$Lgb, Pg, Wnd, Awn, Gwn, Iwn, Pgs, Lcs, Wcs, Wns, Wss$\}$ and $S = $ Lgb.

Each symbol in $A \cup \mathcal{N}t$ denotes an areal entity on the screen. Each areal entity $\alpha \in A \cup \mathcal{N}t - \{Wns, Wss\}$ is formed by a set of pixels Shape(α), shaped as a rectangle. The areal entity α is described by its upper-left and lower-right pixel coordinates $x_1(\alpha)$, $y_1(\alpha)$ and $x_2(\alpha)$, $y_2(\alpha)$. These four numbers are organized into the vector "Tile: $\{x_1(\alpha), y_1(\alpha), x_2(\alpha), y_2(\alpha)\}$." Tile$(\alpha)$ and Shape(α) are the attributes of α.

Symbols Wns and Wss denote a set of n windows (with $1 \leqslant n \leqslant n_{max}$, where n_{max} is a number depending on the dimensions of the screen). Their shapes are no longer rectangular, and therefore their Shape(α) attribute is the union of the areal entities of the n windows, while Tiles(α) is the union of the positions of the n Tiles forming the windows. Tiles$(\alpha) = \{X_1(\alpha), Y_1(\alpha), X_2(\alpha), Y_2(\alpha)\}$, where $X_1(\alpha)$ is the set of upper-left pixel x-coordinates, $Y_1(\alpha)$ is the set of upper-left pixel y-coordinates, $X_2(\alpha)$ is the set of lower-right pixel x-coordinates, and $Y_2(\alpha)$ is the set of lower-right pixel y-coordinates.

In the set of attributed conditional rules P, Rule 1 defines the c-logbook, Rules 2 to 5 define c-logbook pages, Rules 6 to 14 define windows on pages, Rules 15 and 16 define window command areas, and Rules 17 and 18 define page command areas. For each rule, the syntactic part is shown, followed by the definition of the condition (if not previously stated) and by the associated semantic part, identified by a bullet. When a symbol appears more than once in a rule, subscripts are used to distinguish between the different occurrences.

1. Lgb $\rightarrowtail$ TA ON Pgs ON Lcs $\mapsto$ [TA $\equiv$ [Pgs] $\equiv$ [Lcs]], where α ON β means $x_1(\alpha) = x_1(\beta)$, $x_2(\alpha) = x_2(\beta)$, $y_2(\alpha) = y_1(\beta) + 1$; its associated semantic rule is:

 - Tile(Lgb) $\leftarrow \{x_1($TA$), y_1($TA$), x_2($Lcs$), y_2($Lcs$)\}$
 - Shape(Lgb) $\leftarrow$ Shape(TA) $\cup$ Shape(Pgs) $\cup$ Shape(Lcs)

2. Pgs $\rightarrow$ Pg

 - Tile(Pgs) $\leftarrow$ Tile(Pg); Shape(Pgs) $\leftarrow$ Shape(Pg)

3. Pgs$_1$ $\rightarrowtail$ Tile(Pgs$_2$) = Tile(Pg) $\mapsto$ Pgs$_2$ • Pg

 - Tile(Pgs$_1$) $\leftarrow$ Tile(Pg); Shape(Pgs$_1$) $\leftarrow$ Shape(Pg)

4. $Pg \dashv Wns$ IN $BS \mapsto [BS \supseteq Wns]$, where α IN β means:

$$Tile(\beta) = \{min\ X_1(\alpha) + a,\ max\ \Upsilon_1(\alpha) + b,\ max\ X_2(\alpha) + c,\ min\ \Upsilon_2(\alpha) + d\}$$

with $a, b, c, d \geqslant 0$; its associated semantic rule is:

- $Tile(Pg) \leftarrow Tile(BS);\ Shape(Pg) \leftarrow Shape(BS)$

5. $Pg \rightarrow BS$

- $Tile(Pg) \leftarrow Tile(BS);\ Shape(Pg) \leftarrow Shape(BS)$

6. $Wns \rightarrow Wnd$

- $Tiles(Wns) \leftarrow Tile(Wnd);\ Shape(Wns) \leftarrow Shape(Wnd)$

7. $Wns \dashv Wss$ NO–INTER $Wnd \mapsto [Wss \blacksquare Wnd]$, where α NO–INTER β means $Shape(\alpha) \cap Shape(\beta) = \varnothing$; its associated semantic rule is:

- $Tiles(Wns) \leftarrow \{X_1(Wss) \cup x_1(Wnd),\ \Upsilon_1(Wss) \cup y_1(Wnd),$ $X_2(Wss) \cup x_2(Wnd),\ \Upsilon_2(Wss) \cup y_2(Wnd)\}$
- $Shape(Wns) \leftarrow Shape(Wss) \cup Shape(Wnd)$

8. $Wss \rightarrow Wnd$

- $Tiles(Wss) \leftarrow Tile(Wnd);\ Shape(Wss) \leftarrow Shape(Wnd)$

9. $Wss_1 \dashv Wss_2$ NO–INTER $Wnd \mapsto Wss_2 \blacksquare Wnd$

- $Tiles(Wss_1) \leftarrow \{X_1(Wss_2) \cup x_1(Wnd),\ \Upsilon_1(Wss_2) \cup y_1(Wnd),$ $X_2(Wss_2) \cup x_2(Wnd),\ \Upsilon_2(Wss_2) \cup y_2(Wnd)\}$
- $Shape(Wss_1) \leftarrow Shape(Wss_2) \cup Shape(Wnd)$

In the following rules, index k is used to distinguish the type of windows and interaction areas with $k \in \{A, G, I\}$ (e.g., kwn denotes Awn or Gwn or Iwn), where A stands for alphanumeric, G for graphical, and I for iconic.

10–12. $Wnd \rightarrow Gwn\ |Awn|\ Iwn$

- $Tile(Wnd) \leftarrow Tile(kwn);\ Shape(Wnd) \leftarrow Shape(kwn)$

13. $kwn \dashv TA$ ON $kia \mapsto [TA \equiv kia]$

- $Tile(kwn) \leftarrow \{x_1(TA), y_1(TA), x_2(kia), y_2(kia)\}$
- $Shape(kwn) \leftarrow Shape(TA) \cup Shape(kia)$

14. $kwn \dashv TA$ ON kia ON $Wcs \mapsto [TA \equiv kia \equiv [Wcs]]$

- $Tile(kwn) \leftarrow \{x_1(TA), y_1(TA), x_2(Wcs), y_2(Wcs)\}$
- $Shape(kwn) \leftarrow Shape(TA) \cup Shape(kia) \cup Shape(Wcs)$

15. $Wcs \dashv Wca_1$ SIDE $Wca_2 \mapsto Wca_1 \parallel Wca_2$, where α SIDE β means $y_1(\alpha) = y_1(\beta)$, $y_2(\alpha) = y_2(\beta)$, $x_2(\alpha) = x_1(\beta) - 1$; its associated semantic rule is:

- Tile(Wcs) $\leftarrow \{x_1(Wca_1), y_1(Wca_1), x_2(Wca_2), y_2(Wca_2)\}$
- Shape(Wcs) $\leftarrow$ Shape(Wca_1) $\cup$ Shape(Wca_2)

16. $Wcs_1 \dashv Wcs_2$ SIDE $Wca \mapsto Wcs_2 \parallel Wca$

- Tile(Wcs_1) $\leftarrow \{x_1(Wcs_2), y_1(Wcs_2), x_2(Wca), y_2(Wca)\}$
- Shape(Wcs_1) $\leftarrow$ Shape(Wcs_2) $\cup$ Shape(Wca)

17. $Lcs \dashv Lca_1$ SIDE $Lca_2 \mapsto Lca_1 \parallel Lca_2$

- Tile(Lcs) $\leftarrow \{x_1(Lca_1), y_1(Lca_1), x_2(Lca_2), y_2(Lca_2)\}$
- Shape(Lcs) $\leftarrow$ Shape(Lca_1) $\cup$ Shape(Lca_2)

18. $Lcs_1 \dashv Lcs_2$ SIDE $Lca \mapsto Lcs_2 \parallel Lca$

- Tile(Lcs_1) $\leftarrow \{x_1(Lcs_2), y_1(Lcs_2), x_2(Lca), y_2(Lca)\}$
- Shape(Lcs_1) $\leftarrow$ Shape(Lcs_2) $\cup$ Shape(Lca)

8. A Definition of the C-Logbooks

As previously outlined, to enable the correct design and execution of each activity and the definition of the tools, a system based on the use of four c-logbooks is proposed. These c-logbooks are used to store the data of the activities performed in the different environments.

The first c-logbook, called general c-logbook (Glo), is for recording general data on the laboratory (i.e., c-logbooks available, active experiments, date and type of each activity developed) and makes possible the correct start of any activity required by using one of the other three c-logbooks.

The second c-logbook (Ldl) is used to store the *in numero* laboratory definition activity: that is, it makes possible the specification of the views necessary so that the physician can control the execution of the experiment, the computational tools available, and their mutual relationships in the experiment in progress. In terms of *in numero* experiments, this means specifying how many functional maps and points of view the physician wants to assume in order to control the experiment. Functional maps (Figure 5) represent, by graphical conventions, the subactivities, the fluxes, and the internal and external controls of the simulated system.[29]

With each tool and point of view is associated a window, in which suitable icons, graphs, and texts will be grouped. In specifying the laboratory structure, these windows have to be collected in pages. It is often useful for the physician to observe the experiment's evolution from the same point of view in different contexts. In this case, the same window appears on different pages, associated with other different data carriers. Figure 6 shows an Ldl documentation page. This page represents the structure of the lipid solubilization experiment c-logbook.[29]

The third c-logbook (Edl) is for storing the method used by the physician to design the individual experiment and each point of view previously specified. The physician, therefore, assigns a specific functional map to each window of the iconic type and specifies messages and variables to be shown in each window. The physician can specify whether variables are input ones (i.e., generated by the user) or output ones (generated by simulation programs). In addition, the physician establishes the scales on which variables are to be represented and specifies environment characteristics, that is, the mutual relationships of inputs.

The fourth c-logbook (Eel) collects these data related to the execution of the individual experiment. In this c-logbook, the different I/O forms are specified, and the dynamics of the experiment is recorded as previously described, using the c-logbook Edl.

9. The Lipid Solubilization Experiment C-Logbooks

The proposed conditional attributed grammar is used to define the c-logbooks which characterize every in numero experiment on the liver.

For example, the definition of the Eel logbook used in the lipid solubilization experiment is briefly commented on.[29] For the sake of conciseness, only the syntactic generation of an intermediate sentential form is shown. In any case, the generated sentential form is expressive for the physician because the nonterminal symbols appearing in it denote entities such as windows (Wnd) and c-logbook command set (Lcs) which are well defined and easily perceivable entities on the screen.

This generation can be described as follows:

$$
\begin{aligned}
&\text{Lgb} \Rightarrow [\text{TA} \equiv [\text{Pgs}] \equiv [\text{Lcs}]] \Rightarrow \\
&[\text{TA} \equiv [\text{Pgs} \cdot \text{Pg}] \equiv [\text{Lcs}]] \Rightarrow \\
&[\text{TA} \equiv [\text{Pgs} \cdot \text{Pg} \cdot \text{Pg}] \equiv [\text{Lcs}]] \Rightarrow \\
&[\text{TA} \equiv [\text{Pgs} \cdot \text{Pg} \cdot \text{Pg} \cdot \text{Pg}] \equiv [\text{Lcs}]] \Rightarrow \\
&[\text{TA} \equiv [\text{Pg} \cdot \text{Pg} \cdot \text{Pg} \cdot \text{Pg}] = [\text{Lcs}]] \Rightarrow \\
&[\text{TA} \equiv [[\text{BS} \supseteq \text{Wns}] \cdot [\text{BS} \supseteq \text{Wns}] \cdot [\text{BS} \supseteq \text{Wns}] \cdot \\
&\quad [\text{BS} \supseteq \text{Wns}]] \equiv [\text{Lcs}]] \Rightarrow \\
&[\text{TA} \equiv [[\text{BS} \supseteq [\text{Wss} \blacksquare \text{Wnd}]] \cdot [\text{BS} \supseteq [\text{Wss} \blacksquare \text{Wnd}]] \cdot \\
&\quad [\text{BS} \supseteq [\text{Wss} \blacksquare \text{Wnd}]] \cdot [\text{BS} \supseteq [\text{Wss} \blacksquare \text{Wnd}]]] \equiv [\text{Lcs}]] \Rightarrow \\
&[\text{TA} \equiv [[\text{BS} \supseteq [\text{Wnd} \blacksquare \text{Wnd}]] \cdot [\text{BS} \supseteq [\text{Wnd} \blacksquare \text{Wnd}]] \cdot \\
&\quad [\text{BS} \supseteq [\text{Wnd} \blacksquare \text{Wnd}]] \cdot [\text{BS} \supseteq [\text{Wnd} \blacksquare \text{Wnd}]]] \equiv [\text{Lcs}]]
\end{aligned}
$$

Note that the symbols "[ ]" never appear in an antecedent of a rule and, therefore, once generated, never change. They denote a whole entity, which is thereafter described by its component parts. The relationships between components are visually specified by symbols belonging to O; for example, in the second string "≡" denotes that the tile of the first entity is exactly on the tile of the second, having the same thickness, as is prescribed by the semantic part of the rules used.

In the documentation page of Ldl for this experiment, some subtrees assigned by the grammar to the Eel are shown. These subtrees show only information relevant for the physician: for example, in Figure 5, it was decided to show how pages have been defined and their titles and how many and what types of windows are on each page. The subtree shown corresponds to the string previously obtained. The complete formal definition obtained by the grammar makes possible implementation of a trap system which is used to help the physician in obtaining a correct definition of his or her tools.

Once the Eel is defined, an experiment must be specified by use of the Edl, and then the Eel specified can be used. Figure 2 shows the Lipid Solubilization Eel opened on a page with an I/O window and an alphanumeric resume window.

Two separate sets of commands are at the disposal of the physician. The first (Wcs) is linked to the I/O window management and enables the user to obtain a hard copy of the window, get information about it, fire the help, and zoom the window. These five activities are associated to window command areas (Wca).

The second command set (Lcs) is dedicated to the c-logbook management and makes it possible to end the experiment, stopping it while it is running, so that a physician can change environmental or state variables and restart, browse through the book, and so on.

Formally, the substring associated with the two nonoverlapping windows is thus

$$[TA \equiv GIA] \equiv [WCA \parallel\!\parallel WCA \parallel\!\parallel WCA \parallel\!\parallel WCA \parallel\!\parallel WCA]] \blacksquare [TA \equiv AIA]$$

The command set Lcs associated to the c-logbook can be formally defined in an analogous way to Wcs.

10. Conclusions

The purpose of the discussed visual environment[4] is to enable physicians who are "computer-naive" to define their own *in numero* experiments and to execute them without sacrificing a part of the physicians' skills in medicine. Furthermore, visual languages,[30] which are based on the icons, graphs, and sketches used by physicians in their usual communications, have to be exploited.

To this end, empirical observations about the working habits of physicians were analyzed and translated into a conditional attributed grammar. This device is used to specify c-logbooks used by physicians to execute and document the activities they perform in their *in numero* laboratories. The proposal has now to be validated by an extensive experimental use by physicians.

References

1. U. Cugini, F. Folini, and I. Vicini, A procedural system for the definition and storage of technical drawings in parametric form, Eurographics 88, Nice, September 1988.
2. A. Della Ventura, R. Schettini, and M. Zaniboni, Towards the automated interpretation of geological surveys, 1988 IEEE Workshop on Languages for Automation, Symbiotic and Intelligent Robotics, pp. 90–94, August 1988.
3. B. Garilli, A. Rampini, and P. Mussio, SAIA: a system for astronomical image analysis, in *Data Analysis in Astronomy*, pp. 257–261, V. Di Gesù, L. Scarsi, P. Crane, J. H. Friedman, S. Levialdi (Eds.), Plenum Press, New York, 1985.
4. N. C. Shu, Visual programming languages: a perspective and a dimensional analysis, pp. 11–34 in *Visual Languages*, S. K. Chang, T. Ichikawa, and P. A. Ligomenides (Eds.), Plenum Press, New York, 1986.
5. F. S. Montalvo, Diagrams understanding associating symbolic description with images, 1986 IEEE Workshop on Visual Languages, pp. 4–11.
6. P. Mussio, M. Padula, and M. Protti, Description based icon design, 1987 IEEE Workshop on Visual Languages, pp. 118–129.
7. K. S. Fu, A step toward unification of syntactic and statistical pattern recognition, *IEEE Trans. Pattern Anal. Mach. Intelligence* **PAMI-5**(2), 200–205 (1983).
8. P. Mussio, M. Protti, and M. Padula, Attributed conditional L-system. A tool for image description, 9th International Conference on Pattern Recognition, Rome, pp. 601–603, November 1988.
9. D. E. Knuth, Semantics of context-free languages, *J. Math. Syst. Theory* **2**, 127–145 (1986).
10. N. Dioguardi, *Il fegato: un sistema aperto*, Masson Italia, Milan, 1984.
11. U. Eco, *La struttura assente*, Bompiani, Milan, 1986.
12. W. H. Huggins and D. R. Entwisle, *Icon: An Annotated Bibliography*, The Johns Hopkins Press, Baltimore, 1974.
13. S. L. Tanimoto, An iconic/symbolic data structure scheme, in *Pattern Recognition and Artificial Intelligence*, pp. 452–471, C. H. Chen (Ed.), Academic Press, New York, 1976.
14. K. N. Lodding, Iconic interfacing, *IEEE Comput. Graph. Appl.* **3**(2), 11–20 (1983).
15. F. L. Varela, *Principles of Biological Autonomy*, GSR Amsterdam, North-Holland, 1979.
16. G. Raeder, A survey of current graphical programming techniques, *IEEE Comput.* **18**(8), 11–25 (1985).
17. L. Borman and L. Karr, Evaluating the friendliness of a timesharing system, *ACM SigSoc Bull.* **12**(7), 8–11 (1984).
18. D. A. Watermann and F. Hayes-Roth, An overview on pattern-Directed inference system, in *Pattern Directed Inference System*, D. A. Watermann and F. Hayes-Roth (Eds.), Academic Press pp. 3–22, New York, 1978.
19. H. Leggard, A. Singer, and J. Whiteside, *Lecture Notes in Computer Science*, No. 103, Springer-Verlag, Berlin, 1981.

20. S. K. CHANG, E. JUNGERT, S. LEVIALDI, G. TORTORA, AND T. ICHIKAWA, An image processing language with icon-assisted navigation, *IEEE Trans. Software Engineering* **SE-11**(8), 811–819 (1985).

21. S. K. CHANG, Image information system, *Proc. IEEE* **73**(4), 754–764 (1985).

22. O. CLARISSE AND S. K. CHANG, VICON: a visual icon manager, pp. 151–190 in *Visual Languages*, S. K. Chang, T. Ichikawa, and P. A. Ligomenides (Eds.), Plenum Press, New York, 151–190 (1986).

23. M. CONRAD, Staging of computer models in the life sciences, *Biosystem* **17**(2), 75–76 (1984).

24. Z. KULPA, Iconics: computer aided visual communication, pp. 280–281, in *Digital Image Analysis*, S. Levialdi (Ed.), Pitman, London (1984).

25. M. BERETTA, P. MUSSIO, AND M. PROTTI, Icons: interpretation and use, *1986 IEEE Workshop on Visual Languages*, pp. 149–158.

26. F. C. HEROT, Spatial management of data, *ACM Trans. Database Syst.* **5**(4), 493–514 (1980).

27. G. FISHER, A. LENIKE, AND T. SCHWAB, Knowledge-based help systems, *Proceedings on Human Factors in Computer Systems*, ACM, pp. 161–168 (1985).

28. D. MERELLI, P. MUSSIO, AND M. PADULA, An approach to the definition, description and extraction of structure in binary digital images, *Cvgip* **31**, 19–49 (1945).

29. N. DIOGUARDI, P. MUSSIO, M. PIETROGRANDE, A. CEFALO, M. ZUIN, AND M. T. RANDETTI, Model of the hepatic system producing and solubilizing lipids, *Atherosclerosis and Cardiovascular Diseases* **3**, 1039–1045 (1987).

30. S. K. CHANG, Visual Languages, a Tutorial and Survey, *IEEE Software* **4**(1), 23–39 (1987).

14

A SPATIAL KNOWLEDGE STRUCTURE FOR VISUAL INFORMATION SYSTEMS

Sнι-Kuo Chang and Erland Jungert

1. Introduction

In this chapter, a new approach for knowledge-based visual information system design based upon a spatial knowledge structure will be presented. In this spatial knowledge structure, the object-oriented data structure for image encoding is the run-length code (RLC).[1] The technique of symbolic projection[2] is used to generate descriptions of symbolic pictures. The technique of orthogonal relationships is then applied to identify basic spatial relations. With the use of this technique, objects with complex shapes can be segmented. Production rules can then be applied to derive more complex spatial relations from the symbolic projections.

Based upon this approach, a knowledge-based visual information system can be designed which supports spatial reasoning, iage information retrieval, and image visualization and manipulation.

Figure 1 shows the schematic diagram of a visual information system with the proposed spatial knowledge structure. The icon-oriented user interface utilizes the following modules to perform its function:

- *simple query processor:* retrieves objects based upon their names or coordinates

SHI-KUO CHANG • Department of Computer Science, University of Pittsburgh, Pittsburgh, Pennsylvania 15260. E. JUNGERT • Swedish Defense Research Establishment, S-581 11 Linköping, Sweden. Correspondence should be addressed to S. K. Chang.

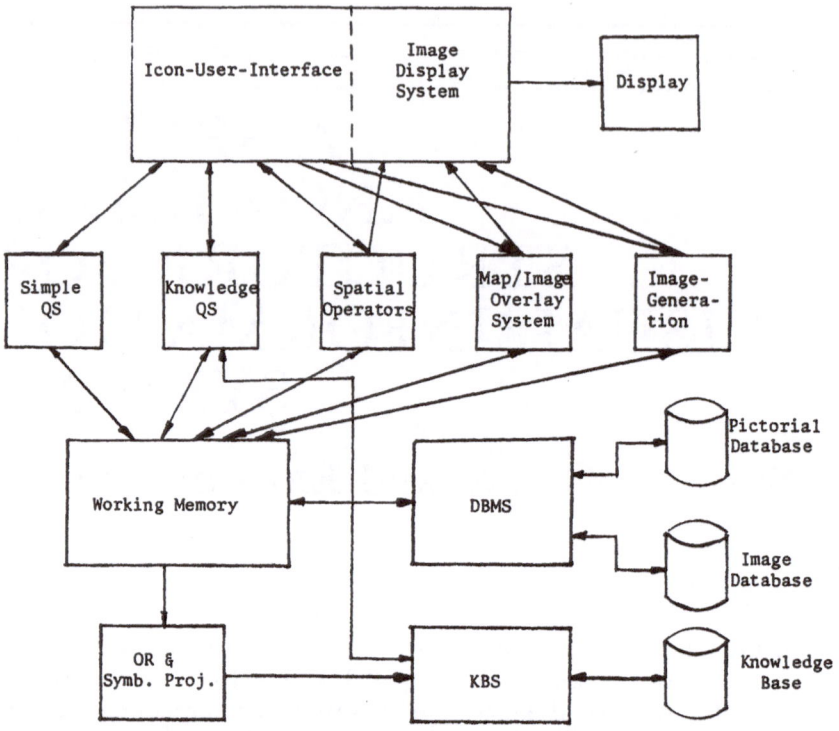

FIGURE 1. Schematic diagram of an image information system.

- *knowledge-based query processor:* processes complex queries involving spatial relations
- *spatial operators:* for creating new objects or testing certain spatial relations
- *image overlay system:* performs image display, window management, and image overlay
- *image generator:* converts RLC structures into images

Raw images are stored in an image database. The image attributes, the symbolic projections, and the RLC encoded images are stored in a spatial knowledge base managed by the DBMS (database management system). The production rules are stored in the knowledge base and managed by the KBS (knowledge-base management system). A working memory is used to keep all temporary data, such as newly created objects, extracted orthogonal relationships, derived spatial relations, and other kinds of application-dependent data.

The visual information system with the proposed knowledge structure is especially suitable for geographic information systems, but it will also be suitable for many other application areas.

2. Basic Data Structure Using Run-Length Codes

Run-length code has been used primarily for compacting image data. It can, however, also be used as a basic object-oriented data structure in visual information systems. The principle of the data structure is illustrated in Figure 2. In this example, map overlays are used. A map overlay is an image used for map production and contains normally just one single object type, for example, lakes or forests. Figure 2 shows that contrary to the general RLC, the information outside the objects is not saved. Only the object information or the object lines that belong to an object are saved. However, so far we cannot talk about objects, just about lines belonging to an object of some type. For each line we keep the coordinates of its start point, the length of the line, and the type of the object to which the line belongs. This structure is well adapted to a relational database. The relational scheme of the run-length-coded lines is

$$RLC - C(\underline{y, x,} \text{ length, type, nc})$$

where the identifying key is underlined.

To identify each single line, only the coordinates of the start point of each line are needed. As will be seen later, the order of the coordinates is

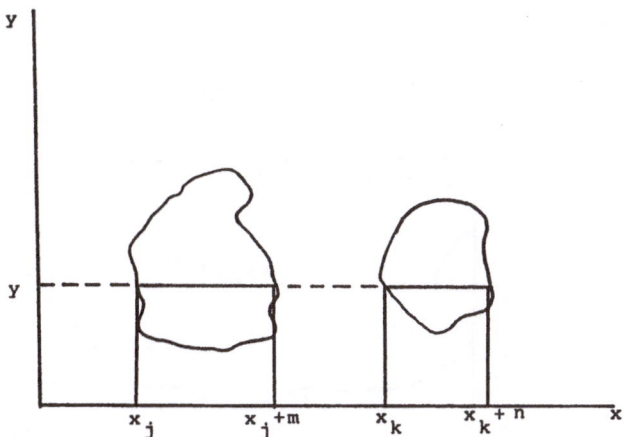

FIGURE 2. Run-length encoding of image data.

of importance. The attribute nc is used for identification of objects and will be discussed further below.

The RLC encoding is also valid for object types that are linear, for example, roads, or of point type, for example, landmarks. For these types, the lines are always one pixel long.

In an object-oriented system, all objects must be identified in a uniform way. This can be done either by using the name of the object or by using unique coordinates. Here both methods are used. Names are used because the users are more familiar with them, while the coordinates are used internally by the system.

In order to simplify retrieval of objects in the database, each object in the database will include coordinates that correspond to the minimum enclosing rectangle of the object. Figure 3 illustrates the correspondence between the obect and the rectangle.

The object relations corresponding to the description given above will include not only the given attributes but also application-dependent attributes, for example, the depth or pH value of a lake. However, such attributes will not be discussed further here. An object relation for closed object types will therefore look like

$$OBJ - CR(\textit{Name}, Yk, Xk, nc, Y1, X1, Y2, X2)$$

The relations for linear and point object types will be similar although there are no rectangles needed for the point object types.

The nc attribute is a unique integer attribute that corresponds to the name of the object. Since RLC relations always include the attribute, there is a logical link between each RLC line and the object in the object relation.

By using run-length-encoded data, a user can define an image (such as a map) which covers a certain area and display it. Furthermore, it is easy to display the data, compared to, for example, vector data, because the

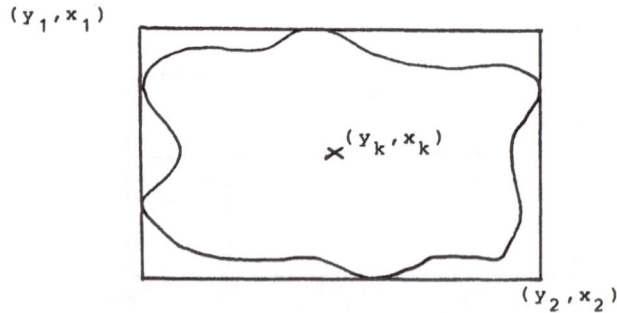

FIGURE 3. Minimum enclosing rectangle of an object and its key.

RLC-database

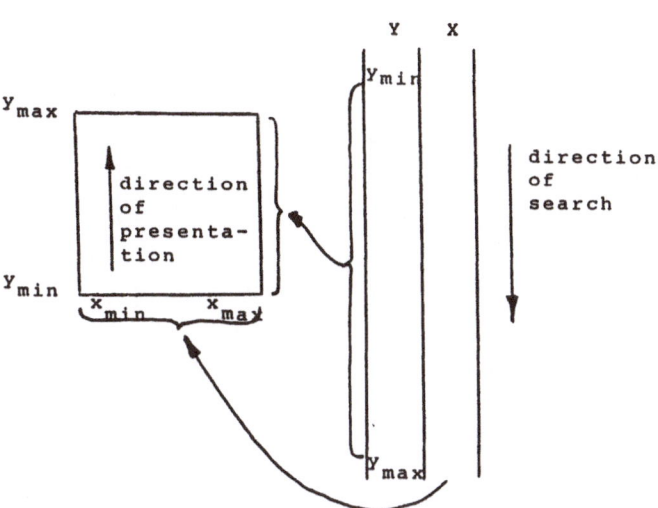

FIGURE 4. Sequential presentation of image data from RLC.

problem of cutting the image in order to make it fit into the display device is just a question of cutting horizontal run-length lines.

An important advantage in using the RLC data structure is that since the lines are first ordered with respect to their y-coordinates, all lines on a certain y-level can be accessed in sequence. Therefore, all lines within the interval $[y_{max}, y_{min}]$ can be read in sequence and the lines displayed in the same sequential order. Consequently, the process of displaying and reading image data is always done in sequence, and it does not have to be changed when handling the same relation. This process is illustrated in Figure 4.

The RLC structure has some additional advantages for map presentation. First, the method is scale independent for at least some scale intervals. Hence, it is fairly simple to implement zooming. Second, there is no need to implement any "fill" operations for the displaying of objects because filling will be performed automatically when interpreting RLC objects. Similarly, the holes inside an object will be generated automatically when the object is displayed.

3. Spatial Operators on RLC Objects

The creation of new objects from existing RLC objects can be done by set theoretic operations such as union, intersection, and exclusive or.

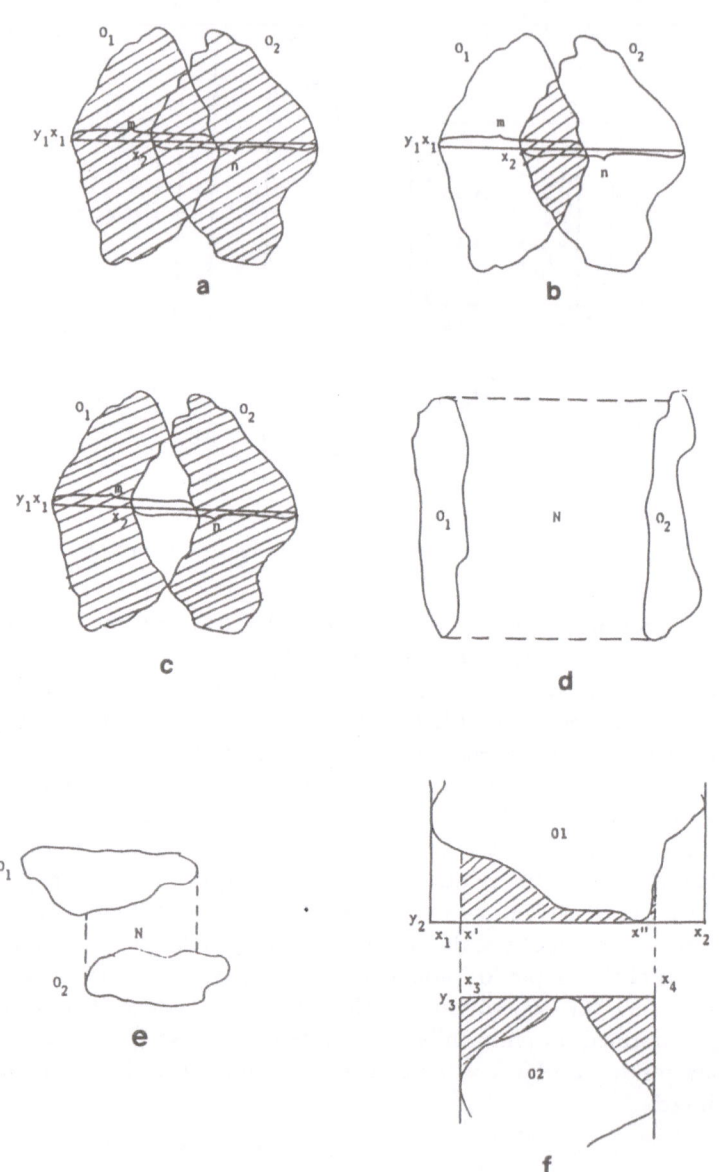

FIGURE 5. Spatial operators on RLC objects.

(a) *Union.* Suppose O_1 and O_2 are two overlapping objects of closed type (i.e., the boundary is a non-self-intersecting closed curve). As illustrated in Figure 5a, the union of these two closed objects, $O_1 \cup O_2$, can be constructed by combining the RLC for each specific y-value as follows:

$O_1: y, x_1, m$

$O_2: y, x_2, n$

$O_1 \cup O_2: y, x_1, m$ $(y_{1max} > y_{2max}$ and $y \leqslant y_{1max}$ and $y > y_{2max})$

y, x_2, n $(y_{2max} > y_{1max}$ and $y \leqslant y_{2max}$ and $y > y_{1max})$

$y, x_1, m: x_2, n$ $(x_1 + m < x_2)$

$y, x_1, x_2 + n - x_1$ $(x_1 + m \geqslant x_2)$

$y, x_2, x_1 + m - x_2$ $(x_2 + n \geqslant x_1)$

$y, x_2, n: x_1, m$ $(x_2 + n < x_1)$

y, x_1, m $(y_{1min} < y_{2min}$ and $y < y_{2min}$ and $y \geqslant y_{1min})$

y, x_2, n $(y_{2min} < y_{1min}$ and $y < y_{1min}$ and $y \geqslant y_{2min})$

(b) *Intersection.* Suppose O_1 and O_2 are two overlapping objects of closed type. As illustrated in Figure 5b, the intersection of these two closed objects, $O_1 \cap O_2$, can be constructed by intersecting the RLC for each specific y-value as follows:

$O_1: y, x_1, m$

$O_2: y, x_2, n$

$O_1 \cap O_2: y, x_2, x_1 + m - x_2$ $(x_1 + m \geqslant x_2)$

$y, x_1, x_2 + n - x_1$ $(x_2 + n \geqslant x_1)$

(c) *Exclusive Or.* As illustrated in Figure 5c, the exclusive or of two overlapping closed objects can be constructed as follows:

$O_1: y, x_1, m$

$O_2: y, x_2, n$

O_1 xor $O_2: y, x_1, m$ $(y_{1max} > y_{2max}$ and
     $y \leqslant y_{1max}$ and $y > y_{2max})$

y, x_2, n $(y_{2max} > y_{1max}$ and
     $y \leqslant y_{2max}$ and $y > y_{1max})$

$$y, x_1, x_2 - x_1 : x_2 + n - x_1 - m \quad (x_1 + m \geqslant x_2)$$

$$y, x_1, m : x_2, n \qquad\qquad\qquad (x_1 + m < x_2)$$

$$y, x_2, x_1 - x_2 : x_1 + m - x_2 - n \quad (x_2 + n \geqslant x_1)$$

$$y, x_2, n : x_1, m \qquad\qquad\qquad (x_2 + n < x_1)$$

$$y, x_1, m \qquad\qquad\qquad (y_{1\min} < y_{2\min} \text{ and}$$
$$y < y_{2\min} \text{ and } y \geqslant y_{1\min})$$

$$y, x_2, n \qquad\qquad\qquad (y_{2\min} < y_{1\min} \text{ and}$$
$$y < y_{1\min} \text{ and } y \geqslant y_{2\min})$$

The above-described operators can be used to create new objects from existing objects or to test the relationships among objects. For example, to decide whether an object O_1 is contained in another object O_2, it suffices to show that $O_1 \cup O_2 = O_2$ or, equivalently, $O_1 \cap O_2 = O_1$. Using this test, we can find the objects situated inside another closed object, for example, the islands inside a lake. The complement of an object O_1 contained in another object O_2 can be found by O_1 xor O_2. To decide whether a point object (or a linear object) O_1 is contained in another object O_2, we can check the RLC for each specific y-value as follows:

$$O_1 : y_1, x_1$$

$$O_2 : y, x_2, n$$

$$\text{Test: } x_2 \leqslant x_1 \leqslant x_2 + n \text{ and } y = y_1$$

(d) Horizontal Extension. Suppose O_1 and O_2 are two nonoverlapping closed objects. As illustrated in Figure 5d, the horizontal extension of O_1 and O_2 can be constructed as follows:

$$O_1 : y, x_1, m$$

$$O_2 : y, x_2, n$$

$$O_1 \sim O_2 : y, \min(x_1, x_2), [\max(x_1 + m, x_2 + n) - \min(x_1, x_2)]$$

In the above, $\min(x_1, x_2) = x_1$ if x_2 is undefined, and $\max(x_1, x_2) = x_1$ if x_2 is undefined.

(e) Vertical Extension. Similarly, we can define the vertical extension of two nonoverlapping closed objects O_1 and O_2, as illustrated in Figure 5e. To

facilitate computation, the vertical RLC for O_1 and O_2 should first be found. The vertical extension of O_1 and O_2 can be constructed as follows:

$$O_1: x, y_1, m$$

$$O_2: x, y_2, n$$

$$O_1 \mid O_2: x, \min(y_1, y_2), [\max(y_1 - m, y_2 + n) - \min(y_1, y_2)]$$

Figure 5f illustrates an alternative way to compute the vertical extension by first finding $x' = \max(x_1, x_3)$ and $x'' = \min(x_2, x_4)$, and then taking the union of the two shaded areas and the rectangle $(x', x''; y_2, y_3)$.

4. Symbolic Projections

We now describe the methodology of symbolic projections.[2] As an example, consider the picture shown in Figure 6. The 2-D string representation of the symbolic projections of the above picture f is

$$(u, v) = (a = d < a = b < c, a = a < b = c < d)$$

In the above, the symbol "$<$" denotes the left–right spatial relation in string u and the below–above spatial relation in string v. The symbol "$=$" denotes the spatial relation "at the same spatial location as" and usually can be omitted. Therefore, the 2-D string representation can be seen to be the *symbolic projection* of picture f along the x and y directions.

The 2-D string representation provides a simple approach to performing subpicture matching on 2-D strings. The *rank* of each symbol in a string u, which is defined to be one plus the number of "$<$" preceding this symbol in u, plays an important role in 2-D string matching. We denote the rank of symbol b by $r(b)$. The strings "$ad < b < c$" and "$a < c$" have ranks as shown in Table 1.

A substring where all symbols have the same rank is called a *local substring*.

A string u is *contained* in a string v if u is a subsequence of a permutation string of v.

FIGURE 6. A symbolic picture f.

TABLE 1

Ranks of Strings

v string: $a_1 d_1 < b_3 < c_3$
u string: $a_1 < c_2$

A string u is a *type-i 1-D subsequence* of string v if (a) u is contained in v, and (b) if $a_1 w_1 b_1$ is a substring of u, a_1 matches a_2 in v, and b_1 matches b_2 in v, then

Type 0: $r(b_2) - r(a_2) \geqslant r(b_1) - r(a_1)$ or $r(b_1) - r(a_1) = 0$

Type 1: $r(b_2) - r(a_2) \geqslant r(b_1) - r(a_1) > 0$ or $r(b_2) - r(a_2) = r(b_1) - r(a_1) = 0$

Type 2: $r(b_2) - r(a_2) = r(b_1) - r(a_1)$

Now we can define the notion of type-i ($i = 0, 1, 2$) 2-D subsequence as follows. Let (u, v) and (u', v') be the 2-D string representations of f and f', respectively. (u', v') is a *type-i 2-D subsequence* of (u, v) if (a) u' is a type-i 1-D subsequence of u, and (b) v' is a type-i 1-D subsequence of v. We say f' is a *type-i subpicture* of f.

In Figure 7, f_1, f_2, and f_3 are all type-0 subpictures of f; f_1 and f_2 are type-1 subpictures of f; only f_1 is a type-2 subpicture of f. The 2-D string representations are:

$$f \qquad (ad < b < c, a < bc < d)$$

$$f_1 \qquad (a < b, a < b)$$

$$f_2 \qquad (a < c, a < c)$$

$$f_3 \qquad (ab < c, a < bc)$$

Therefore, to determine whether a picture f' is a type-i subpicture of f, we need only determine whether (u', v') is a type-i 2-D subsequence of (u, v). The picture matching problem thus becomes a 2-D string matching problem. Efficient 2-D string matching algorithms have been developed[2] and applied to pictorial information retrieval problems.

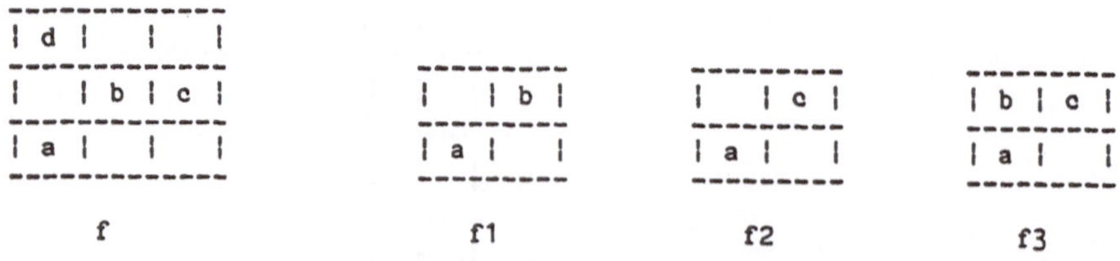

FIGURE 7. Picture matching examples.

5. Orthogonal Relations

Symbolic projections allow only two types of spatial relations left–right and below–above. To represent more complex spatial relations, we can first segment objects into components and then find all the left–right and below–above relations among the components. With spatial reasoning rules (to be described in Section 7), we can recombine these simple spatial relations into complex ones. These simple spatial relations are called *orthogonal relations*. In this section, we describe how to find orthogonal relations.

Since all run-length-encoded objects have the minimum enclosing rectangle available, three types of spatial relations between objects can be identified. These are for objects with:

- nonoverlapping rectangles
- partly overlapping rectangles
- completely overlapping rectangles

The case with nonoverlapping rectangles is trivial and will never cause any problems because the object relations are simple. The other two might sometimes cause problems, especially when one of the objects partly surrounds the other. Figure 8 demonstrates a problem of this type. The fundamental issue here is to find a method that easily describes the relations between the objects. The method is called orthogonal relations, because it deals with spatial relations that are orthogonal to each other.

The basic idea is to regard one of the objects as a "point of view object" (PVO) and then view the other object in four directions (north, east, south, west). Hence, at least one or at most four subparts of the other object can be "seen" from the PVO. The part of the object that actually is "seen" is in the interval where the two rectangles overlap, partly or completely. This is

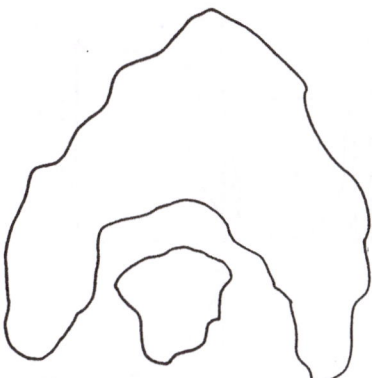

FIGURE 8. Two objects with overlapping MERs.

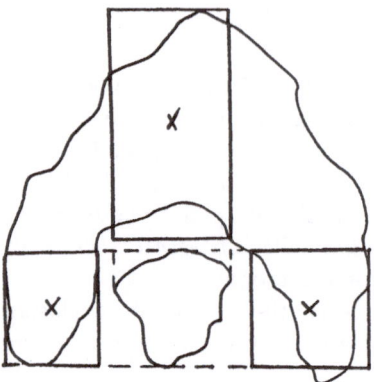

FIGURE 9. The PVO and its corresponding orthogonal relations.

illustrated in Figures 9 and 10. The subobjects can be regarded as point objects, which here correspond to the centroids of the rectangles that enclose each subobject. It is a fairly simple operation to identify and generate these points from the RLC. The next step is then to identify the relation between the objects by using the 2-D projection method described in Section 3.

Each one of the subobjects constitutes an orthogonal relational object of the original object, and, since the subobjects are regarded as points, a sparse vector description of the original object is generated. From this viewpoint, it does not matter whether the original object is of closed or linear type. This makes the methods powerful. However, it is of importance that the subobjects are interpreted correctly. Figure 11a shows a correct interpretation of a north and a west segment while the interpretation of the same element in

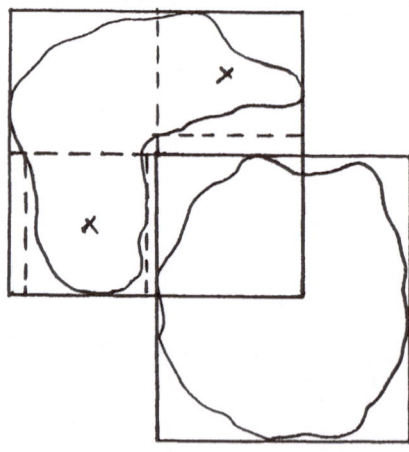

FIGURE 10. The PVO and its corresponding orthogonal relations for partly overlapping MERs.

Figure 11b is erroneous. The natural interpretation is to look clockwise. Hence, nine different combinations can be identified:

2 points: N–E, E–S, S–W, W–N
3 points: N–E–S, E–S–W, S–W–N, W–N–E
4 points: N–E–S–W

No other interpretations are allowed. It is also possible to regard the element in between the orthogonal ones. But this is not necessary since enough information is available anyway (see Section 5 for further discussions).

The technique of finding orthogonal relations is described in the following algorithm.

```
Procedure Ortho(x, y)
begin
      /*this procedure finds the orthogonal relations of object x with respect
       to object y*/
      /*find the minimum enclosing rectangle of x and y*/
      find Mer(x), find Mer(y);
      /*find the four relational objects of object y intersecting with the exten-
       sions of object x*/
      y–W = W-extension(Mer(x)), Mer(y);
      y–E = E-extension(Mer(x)), Mer(y);
      y–N = N-extension(Mer(x)), Mer(y);
      y–S = S-extension(Mer(x)), Mer(y);
      return({y–W, y–E, y–N, y–S});
end
```

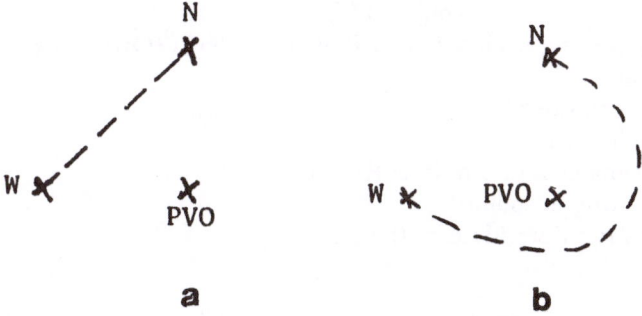

FIGURE 11. A correct (a) and an erroneous (b) interpretation of orthogonal relations.

6. *Segmentation by Orthogonal Relations*

The technique of finding orthogonal relations can be applied to segment objects in an image. First, we process the image and recognize the objects. Then, for each object x, we find its orthogonal relational objects with respect to object y. If the number of orthogonal relational objects is less than 2, the minimum enclosing rectangles (MERs) of objects x and y are disjoint. Therefore, we need not do further processing. If the number of orthogonal relational objects is greater than or equal to 2, then we will add them to the list Rel(y). After all object pairs have been processed, we have for each object y a list of orthogonal relational objects Rel(y). The object y can then be segmented into |Rel(y)| segments. The reference point of each segment is the center point of each orthogonal relational object. The symbolic projections (u, v) can then be obtained from this symbolic picture, where each segment is regarded as a separate object.

The algorithm now follows.

```
Procedure OrthoSegment(f, u, v)
begin
     /*object recognition*/
     recognize objects in the picture f;
     /*initialization*/
     for each object x
          Rel(x) is set to empty;
     /*find orthogonal relations*/
     for each pair of objects x and y
          begin
          find Ortho(x, y) /*orthogonal relations of object x with respect to
                         object y*/;
          if |Ortho(x, y)| > 1 then Rel(y) = Rel(y) ∪ Ortho(x, y);
          find Ortho(y, x) /*orthogonal relations of object y with respect to
                         object x*/;
          if |Ortho(y, x)| > 1 then Rel(x) = Rel(x) ∪ Ortho(y, x);
          end
     /*segmentation*/
     for each object x
          segment x into objects Rel(x);
     /*2D string encoding*/
     apply procedure 2Dstring(f, m, u, v, n);
end
```

An example is given below. The original image contains objects "a," "b," and "c," where "a" and "b" are point objects, as shown in Figure 12a.

After applying the procedure Ortho, we find that Ortho$(a, c) =$ $\{x, y, z\}$, and Ortho$(b, c) = \{w, y\}$. Therefore, object "c" contains four relational objects "x," "y," "z," and "w," as shown in Figure 12b.

The segmentation result is illustrated in Figure 12c. The object "c" is segmented into four segments, "x," "y," "z," and "w." To obtain this segmentation, we can "grow" each orthogonal relational object until it meets with another relational object. The center of each relational object is used as the reference point of each segment. In this way, all orthogonal spatial relations are preserved.

The 2-D string encoding of the picture is $(u, v) = (x < az < w < by,$ $z < bw < xy < a)$. To simplify the encoding, we can merge orthogonal relational objects that are adjacent and belong to the same object. For example, if we merge two orthogonal relational objects into one segment, we can use the reference point of either object, or the centroid of the merged object, as its new reference point, *provided that all orthogonal spatial relations are still valid.*

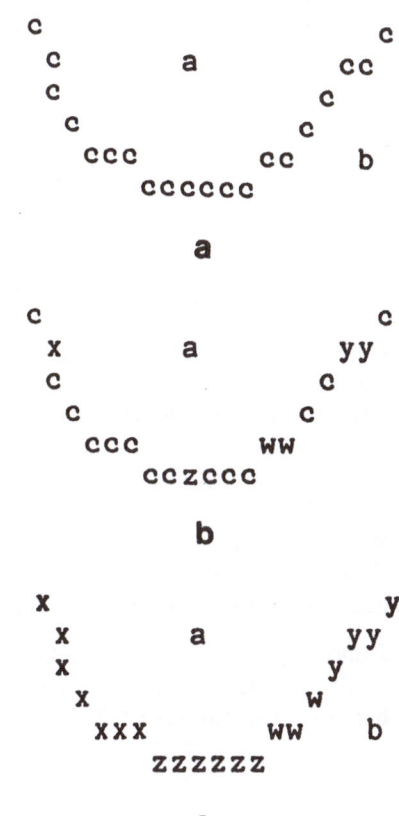

FIGURE 12. A segmentation example.

For example, if the objects "w" and "y" are merged into "y," the encoding becomes $(u, v) = (x < az < y < b, \; z < b < xy < a)$. All orthogonal spatial relations are preserved.

7. A Knowledge-Based Approach to Spatial Reasoning

Symbolic projections and their application to orthogonal relations provide a means that can be used as a basis for spatial reasoning. This will be illustrated in a number of examples below in this section and also in Sections 8 and 9. From the 2-D string representation, spatial relations can be derived without any loss of information. Furthermore, from these spatial relations, even more complex spatial relations can be derived. Therefore, by combining the 2-D string representation with a knowledge-based system, flexible means of spatial reasoning and image information retrieval and management can be provided.

The knowledge-based approach to spatial reasoning is illustrated by two examples below.

Example 1. An island outside a coastline.

Figure 13 illustrates the orthogonal relations. The 2-D symbolic projections are then

$$U: C_1 < C_2 i$$

$$V: C_2 < C_1 i$$

The following rule is now applied

if $U: r_1 < r_2 p$ and $V: r_2 < r_1 p$
then
facts(south r p)(west r p)
verbalization "The object $\langle p \rangle$ is partly surrounded by the object $\langle r \rangle$ on its south and west side."

When applying this rule to the example, r will be substituted by C and p by i, that is, (south C i) and (west C i). These facts are now stored in the fact database. The verbalization is sent to the user.

Example 2. A forest near a lake.

In Figure 14, L_1, L_2, and L_3 illustrate the orthogonal relational objects which are part of the lake. The 2-D symbolic projections are

$$U: L_3 < FL_1 < L_2$$

$$V: L_3 FL_2 < L_1$$

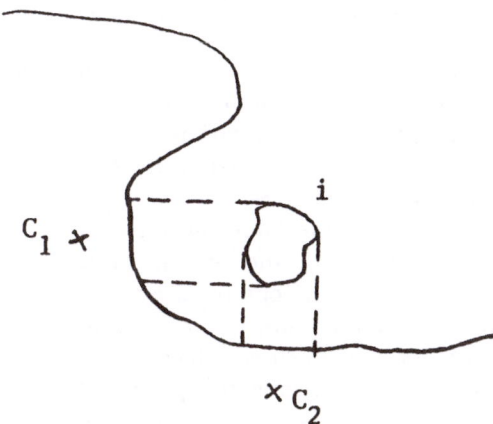

FIGURE 13. The orthogonal relations
between an island and a coastline.

This is matched with the following rule:

> if $U: r_1 < p\ r_2 < r_3$ and $V: r_1\ p\ r_3 < r_2$
> then
> **facts**(west $r\ p$)(north $r\ p$)(east $r\ p$)
> **verbalization** "The object $\langle p \rangle$ is partly surrounded by the object
> $\langle r \rangle$ or its west, north, and east side."

In this example, we will substitute p by the forest F and r by the lake L.

By successively applying rules that correspond to each one of the basic orthogonal relation types, it is possible to identify all object-to-object relations. For example, the fact identified in Example 2 is (west $L\ F$), (north $L\ F$), and (east $L\ F$).

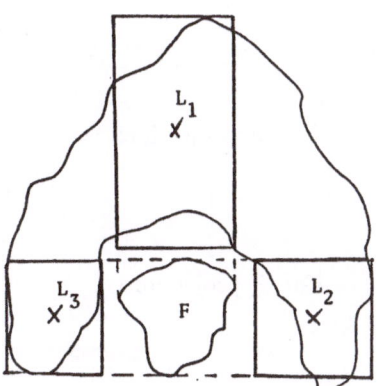

FIGURE 14. The orthogonal relations between
a forest F and a lake L.

8. Visualization of Symbolic Pictures

The knowledge-based approach to spatial reasoning can be expanded further. In the examples in Section 7, it was demonstrated how spatial relationships between various spatial objects can be inferred. In this section, we will show how spatial relationships can be inferred from symbolic descriptions of images.

Consider the following question: given the 2-D string representation, can we visualize the objects in the original picture? An algorithm to reconstruct a symbolic picture from its 2-D string representation is given in Ref. 2, where the objects are assumed to be point objects. If the objects are pieces of a segmented object, then we must somehow reconstruct (and reconnect) the segmented pieces. Of course, the RLC description can be retrieved from the image database and manipulated to visualize the objects. This is, however, time-consuming. An alternative is to apply *connection rules* to reconnect the segments from a reconstructed symbolic picture. Hence, by successively using the rules discussed in Section 7 on more complex structures, supplemented with some new rules, it will be possible to generate a sequence of facts that can be used for connection of orthogonal relational objects. This method is especially useful when the orthogonal relational objects are expanded into segments. The example below shows the rules used to generate all facts that are needed to reconstruct a description of the object.

Example 3. The problem is to describe an image and generate an approximate visualization. The image contains three objects, X, Y, and Z. X is a linear object, and Y and Z are point objects. From the image the following 2-D symbolic projections are generated using their corresponding orthogonal relations.

X-to-Y projections

$$U: X_2 < X_3 \, Y X_1$$
$$V: X_3 < X_2 \, Y < X_1$$

X-to-Z projections

$$U: X_5 < X_4 Z$$
$$V: X_4 < X_5 Z$$

Y-to-Z projections

$$U: Y < Z$$
$$V: Z < Y$$

In the X-to-Y projections, one of the basic rules that describe relations is applied:

if U: $r_2 < r_3\,pr_1$ and V: $r_3 < r_2\,p < r_1$
then
facts (south r p)(west r p)(north r p)
verbalization "The object $\langle p \rangle$ is surrounded by $\langle r \rangle$ on its south, west, and north side."

This gives the following facts:

$$\text{(south } X\ Y\text{), (west } X\ Y\text{), and (north } X\ Y\text{)}$$

The relation X to Z uses the same basic rule as in Section 7, Example 1. Hence the following facts are generated:

$$\text{(west } X\ Z\text{) and (south } X\ Z\text{)}$$

Finally, for the relation between Y and Z, none of the basic orthogonal relation rules are useful because this relation is even more primitive. The relations between Y and Z are of type nonoverlapping rectangles (see Section 5). Hence the following rule could be used:

if U: $r < p$ and V: $p < r$
then
fact (northwest r p)
verbalization "The object $\langle r \rangle$ is to the northwest of $\langle p \rangle$."

It is easy to see that eight rules of similar type must be available. The result of the execution of the rule above is the following fact:

$$\text{(northwest } Y\ Z\text{)}$$

The next step is to verify whether Y and Z are on the same side of X or whether they are on different sides. In the latter case, a fact of type

$$\text{(Between } X,\ Y,\ Z\text{)}$$

is general. However, this is not the case here. This is mentioned because

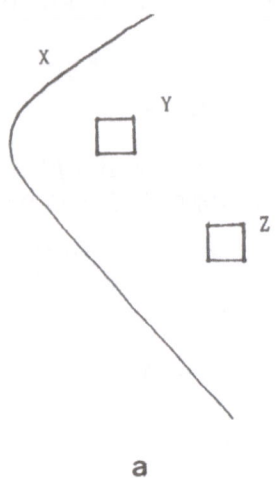

a

Symbolic Picture

```
--------------------
| B | F |   |   |
--------------------
| F |   |   |   |
--------------------
|   | F |   |   |
--------------------
| L |   | F |   |
--------------------
```

Projections

(LFB<FF<F , LF<F<F<BF)

b

FIGURE 15. The result of connecting orthogonal relational objects: (a) of the road X and the neighboring buildings Y and Z; (b) a building, a forest, and a lake; (c) a road, a forest, and a building.

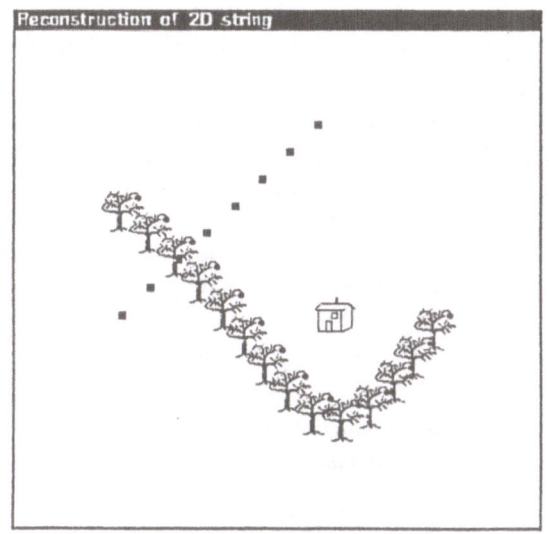

Symbolic Picture

			R		
F					
R	F	B	F	
			F		

Projections

(RF<F<FB R<F , F<RFBF<F<R)

c

FIGURE 15 (*continued*)

there must be some rules available that describe a relation of this kind. Instead, the following rule will be fired:

> if (west *r p*) and (west *r q*)
> then (west *r p q*)

from which the following fact is created:

$$(\text{west } X \, Y \, Z)$$

By using all available facts generated so far, it will be possible to describe the object *X*. However, it is obvious that also some general facts concerning the type of the objects and the distances between them must be used when describing the objects. The solution to this problem is illustrated in Figure 15. In Figure 15, it is assumed that *X* is a road and *Y* and *Z* are buildings.

9. Image Information Retrieval and Manipulation

The basic rules discussed above correspond to the relations discussed in Section 5. Hence, the following groups of rules can be identified:

- Rules corresponding to objects with nonoverlapping rectangles.
- Rules corresponding to objects with partly or completely overlapping rectangles.

In the first group, the rules must deal with the relative positions among objects. Therefore, at least eight directions must be identified, and more can be added if necessary to deal with more refined directions. In the second group, the rules correspond to orthogonal relations and must deal with partly or completely surrounded PVO objects. In this group there are nine rules, which correspond to the nine combinations of orthogonal relations discussed in Section 5.

Other rules that may be needed are rules that extract more complex relations, for example, for such objects as:

- An object situated to the east of a group of objects.
- An object between two groups of objects.

Even more rules can be added to deal with complex relations between groups of objects. Therefore, the knowledge base is extendable. However, a limited number of basic rules should be sufficient to take care of most common types of spatial relations. In what follows, we give more examples of image information retrieval/manipulation using symbolic projections.

Example 4. The problem is to retrieve crossing linear objects. Figure 16a illustrates a bridge crossing a river. By regarding the endpoints of the bridge object as PVO objects, the following orthogonal symbolic projections are obtained:

$$\text{PVO} = a_1 \qquad u{:}\ b_1 < a_1 b_2 \qquad v{:}\ b_1 a_1 < b_2$$

$$\text{PVO} = a_2 \qquad u{:}\ b_3 a_2 < b_1 \qquad v{:}\ b_3 < a_2 b_1$$

The above symbolic projections describe the crossing relationship. Therefore, the following rule can be formulated:

if $u{:}\ r_1 < p_1 r_2\ \wedge$
  $v{:}\ r_1 p_1 < r_2\ \wedge$
  $u{:}\ r_3 p_2 < r_4\ \wedge$
  $v{:}\ r_3 < p_2 r_4$
then
  (crossing $p\ r$)

When p is bound to a and r is bound to b, we obtain,

- (crossing $a\ b$)

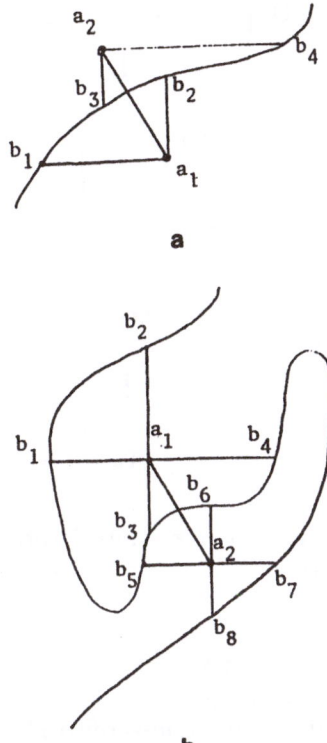

FIGURE 16. Crossing of a river and a bridge.   **b**

The above rule describes a "north-east and west-south" crossing relationship. Fourteen rules covering the standard types of crossing relationships are given in Figure 17. Although some rare cases are not covered by these standard rules (one such example is given in Figure 16b), most crossings can be retrieved using these rules.

Example 5. To retrieve coinciding objects, the following rule suffices:

if u: $pr \wedge v$: pr then (coincide—with p r)

Example 6. Rules using symbolic projections can be applied to terrain elevation data analysis in automated map data processing. Figure 18 illustrates how symbolic projections can be applied to map elevation data verification. The problem is to verify whether the point object p has the correct elevation level compared to the elevation lines in the map. The point object p must have an elevation in the interval

$$\text{height.} r_1 \leqslant \text{height.} p \leqslant \text{height.} r_2$$

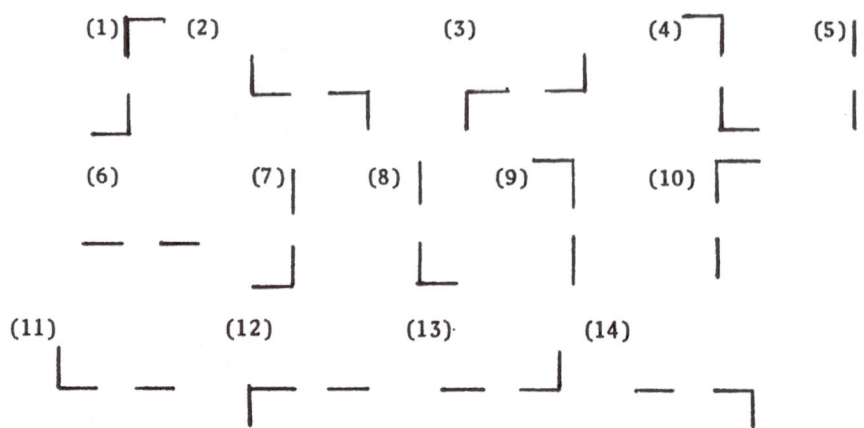

FIGURE 17. Fourteen crossing relationships.

Let w be the symbolic projection along the z-axis. The following rule can be applied to verify elevation data:

if w: $r_1 \, p < r_2$ $^{\vee}$
  w: $r_1 < p < r_2$ $^{\vee}$
  w: $r_1 < pr_2$
then (elevation-verified p)

When the point object p is on a hilltop, the following rule can be applied:

if w: $r_1 r_2 \, p < r_3$ $^{\vee}$
  w: $r_1 r_2 < p < r_3$
then (elevation-verified p)

where r_3 is an imaginary point object whose elevation is set to the value of the next higher elevation level. Similarly, for a point object at the bottom of a valley, the following rule can be applied:

if w: $r_3 < p < r_1 r_2$ $^{\vee}$
  w: $r_3 < pr_1 r_2$
then (elevation-verified p)

where r_3 is an imaginary point object whose elevation is set to the value of the next lower elevation level.

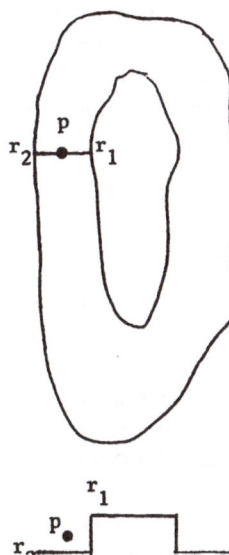

FIGURE 18. Verification of map elevation data.

Example 7. As illustrated in Figure 19, to verify that two linear objects are approximately parallel, we can use the following rule:

if u: $p_1 r_1 < r_2 \doteq u$: $p_2 r_3 < r_4 \wedge$
$\quad v$: $p_1 r_2 < r_1 \doteq v$: $p_2 r_4 < r_3$
then (parallel pr)

where $\doteq$ is a similarity operator between two strings. Two strings $x_1 \ldots x_n$

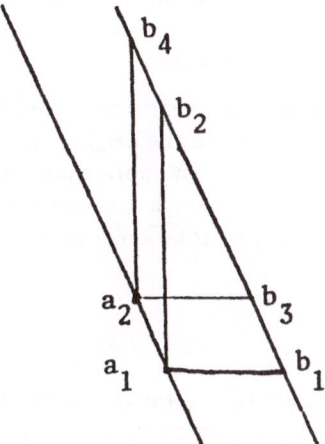

FIGURE 19. Verification of parallel linear objects.

and $y_1 \dots y_n$ are similar under the $\doteq$ operator if (a) x_i and y_i are either objects of the same type or $x_i = y_i = \text{“}<\text{”}$ and (b) the distance $d(x_i, x_j)$ between any two objects x_i, x_j of one string is equal to the distance $d(y_i, y_j)$ between the corresponding objects v_i, v_j of the second string.

10. Discussion

10.1. Matching

Image matching is often required in many applications. For example, matching satellite images with maps is important so that images can be used as overlays on the maps. Matching cannot be done unless the image has been properly registered. One problem is that the image might have a different orientation than the map, that is, it needs to be rotated. Assuming the rotation can be done, the matching procedure can be described as follows: we automatically or manually identify a number of characteristic orthogonal relations, from which the symbolic projections are generated. The matching of a map with an image is achieved by matching the symbolic projections. The steps in the procedure are as follows:

1. Find objects with orthogonal relations in the image.
2. Generate the orthogonal relations for both the map and the image.
3. Generate the 2-D symbolic projections for both the map and the image.
4. Match the map with the image, by matching the 2-D symbolic projections of the map and the image.
5. If the match is successful, then terminate. Otherwise rotate symbolic projections of the image 90 degrees and go to step 4. If the projections have been rotated 360 degrees, then choose a 45-degree direction from the original direction and go to step 2. Otherwise terminate.

As can be seen, the orthogonal relations and their projections are used to characterize the original image and the map. It is not necessary to generate the sketch for more than two original directions, 0 degree and 45 degrees, since the sketch can very simply be rotated 90 degrees. The algorithm for 90-degree rotation is recursive and can be described by:

$$U_i + 1 = V_i$$
$$V_i + 1 = \text{reverse}(U_i)$$

where (U_i, V_i) is the original symbolic projection, and $\text{reverse}(U_i)$ generates the reversed string of string U_i.

10.2. Query Processing

As mentioned in Section 1, an image information system should support both simple query processing and knowledge-based complex query processing. Complex query processing may involve the generation of objects using set-theoretic operators described in Section 3. For example, we can retrieve all type-1 and type-2 objects within a specified area and generate the union (or intersection) of these objects. As illustrated in Figure 20, the icon-oriented user interface is well adapted to this task. By searching the knowledge base and matching against the symbolic projections, we can answer complex queries such as:

"find all objects to the south of X"
"find all spatial relations between objects X and Y"

A pictorial example of such queries using an icon-oriented approach will provide the user a friendly and intuitively meaningful way to specify queries. The pictorial query can then be transformed into symbolic projections and used to retrieve matching pictures in the database.

10.3. Symbolic Reasoning

Generally speaking, expert systems are not particularly good at handling spatial data.[3] Symbolic reasoning is generally not possible because this type of data rquires a large amount of memory to keep track of the various spatial relations. Moreover, this process is normally slow when conventional methods are used. Orthogonal relations represented as chains of 2-D

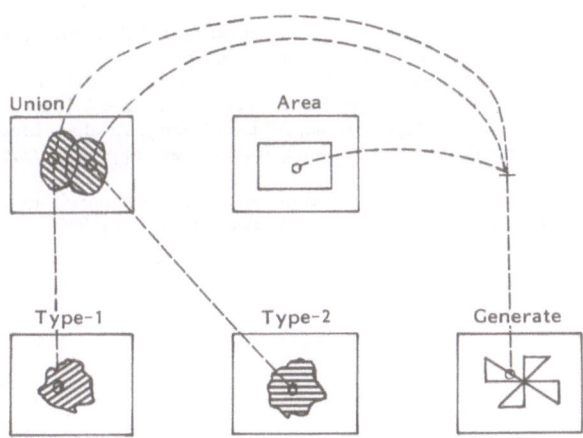

FIGURE 20. Icon-oriented user interface for image manipulation.

symbolic projections constitute a basis for efficient use of spatial knowledge. For example, another potential application is path finding in a map. The symbolic projections can be used by a planning expert system to generate an approximate route. The approximate route can then be algorithmically refined to a definite path using previously developed algorithms.[4,5]

In the above, we have demonstrated the orthogonal symbolic projections can be used for:

- deriving spatial relationships
- generating verbal descriptions
- direct visualization
- matching
- processing pictorial queries
- spatial reasoning

The proposed spatial knowledge structure therefore can be very useful in designing expert systems for spatial reasoning, as well as knowledge-based image information systems.

Acknowledgments

This research was supported in part by NSF Grant DMC-8510804 and NRL Contract N00014-86-C-2038.

References

1. E. JUNGERT, Run length code as an object-oriented spatial data structure, Proceedings of IEEE Workshop on Languages for Automation, Singapore, August 27–29, 1986.
2. S. K. CHANG, Q. Y. SHI, and C. W. YAN, Iconic indexing by 2D strings, Proceedings of IEEE Workshop on Visual Languages, Dallas, Texas, June 25–27, 1986.
3. D. A. WATERMAN, *A Guide to Expert Systems*, Addison-Wesley, Reading, Massachusetts, 1986.
4. T. LOZANO-PEREZ, Spatial planning a configuration space approach, *IEEE Trans. Comput.* C-32(2), 108–120 (1983).
5. E. K. WONG and K. S. FU, A hierarchical orthogonal space approach to three-dimensional path planning, *IEEE Trans. Robotics Automation* RA-2(1), 43–53 (1986).

15

THE USE OF VISUAL REPRESENTATIONS IN INFORMATION RETRIEVAL APPLICATIONS

Donald B. Crouch
and Robert R. Korfhage

1. Introduction

Information retrieval (IR) is concerned with the representation, storage, and retrieval of documents or document surrogates. The output of an IR system in response to a user's request consists of a set of references which are intended to provide the user with information relevant to his or her information needs as expressed by a query.[1] Conventional information retrieval systems operate on large-scale computing systems in an environment where direct access to system facilities is generally limited to search intermediaries and to a few researchers who have been trained to use somewhat complex user–system interfaces. However, poor query formulations and inadequate user–system interaction may still occur even with skilled users. For example, Cleverdon[2] has noted that "if two (trained) search intermediaries search the same question on the same database on the same host, only 40 percent of the output may be common to both searches." Since skilled users often find it difficult to formulate effective search requests and to interact usefully with document retrieval systems, less competent users may be faced with insurmountable problems. This situation is especially critical at the present time; a large number of casual users will soon obtain

DONALD B. CROUCH • Department of Computer Science, University of Minnesota—Duluth, Duluth, Minnesota 55812   ROBERT R. KORFHAGE • Department of Information Science, University of Pittsburgh, Pittsburgh, Pennsylvania 15260.

access to very large information resources through the combination of powerful microcomputers and optical storage technology. In these circumstances, it is essential to consider the use of visual representations in information retrieval systems as a means of simplifying the user–system interaction for both novice and experienced users.

In this chapter we analyze the primary information retrieval models utilized by automatic retrieval systems in order to determine how advanced user–system interfaces might enhance conventional approaches to document retrieval. We then review current research activities in the design of graphical user-oriented interfaces for information retrieval systems and examine the usefulness of visual interaction as an effective means of solving problems associated with the basic retrieval models. We characterize a pictorial representation of queries and documents which forms the basis for a graphical display that provides an interactive tool for visually assessing the similarity of multidimensional vectors in the document space. The tools and methodologies developed to support the exploration of document collections in a visual context are described, and results obtained from their use in an experimental information retrieval system are presented.

2. General Nature of the Retrieval Environment

To determine how visual representations might be used in an information retrieval environment to enhance current approaches to automatic information retrieval, it is useful to consider the four basic models of information retrieval: namely, the Boolean retrieval model, the vector space model, the probabilistic model, and the language processing model. Each of these models will be briefly described and examined.

2.1. Boolean Retrieval Model

Most conventional retrieval systems are based on the Boolean model. Queries are expressed as a set of terms interrelated by the Boolean operators *and, or,* and *not.* Such systems retrieve information by performing the Boolean operations on the corresponding sets of texts containing the query terms. The query operation is simple to perform in practice since most systems implement the model through inverted lists. Although the Boolean model can be used effectively in text retrieval (in fact, a query can be formulated to retrieve any particular subset of items), imprecise or broad requests utilizing the *or* relation can result in the retrieval of large numbers of irrelevant texts while narrow or precise queries consisting of term phrases created by the *and* relation can exclude many relevant items. In practice, a compromise is often obtained by the use of a query formulation that is neither too broad nor too narrow.[3]

Although the Boolean model has been widely accepted, it does have its problems:

- Boolean queries are difficult to construct; intermediaries are generally required to add terms not originally included, provide synonyms or alternate spellings, drop high-frequency terms, etc.[4]
- Boolean systems generally do not provide for the assignment of term weights.
- The size of the subset of documents to be returned is difficult to control.
- The retrieved documents are usually presented in a random order (no ranking based on an estimate of the query-document relevance is provided).

One author recently wrote that due to the difficulty in formulating a query, "research and development in information retrieval since the 1950s has concentrated on methods which can provide better retrieval without the need for Boolean queries."[5]

2.2. Vector Space Model

The vector space model is conceptually the simplest retrieval model. In this model, the content of each document or query is represented by a set of possibly weighted content terms. By term is meant some form of content identifier, such as a word extracted from the document text, a word phrase, or a concept class chosen from a thesaurus. A term's weight reflects its importance in relation to the meaning of the document or query. Each informational item may thus be considered a term vector, and the complete document collection becomes a vector space whose dimension is equal to the number of distinct terms used to identify the documents in the collection.[6, 7]

In the vector space model, it is assumed that similar or related documents or similar documents and queries are represented by similar multidimensional term vectors. Similarity is thus generally defined as a function of the magnitudes of the matching terms in the respective vectors. A frequently used similarity function is the cosine correlation function which measures the cosine of the angle between two vectors in the multidimensional vector space. In this case the similarity between two vectors is inversely related to the angle between them; a cosine value of 1 indicates that the two vectors are identical, and a value of 0, that the two are totally dissimilar.

A vector representation of documents and queries facilitates certain storage and retrieval operations, namely,

- the construction of a clustered document file (consisting of classes of documents such that documents within a given class exhibit substantial similarities with each other); in clustered collections, the search of a collection can be limited to the documents within those clusteres whose class vector representations are similar to the query vector.
- the ranking of retrieved documents in decreasing order of their similarity with the query; in this case, the retrieval of a document in response to a query is made to depend on either a minimum similarity value or a specific number of items to be retrieved. (For example, all documents which correlate with the query with a threshold value in excess of 0.5 are retrieved, or, alternatively, the top 20 items, say, which correlate the highest are returned in response to the query.)
- the automatic reformulation of the query based on relevance assessments supplied by the user for previously retrieved documents; the intent is to produce an alternative query whose similarity to the relevant documents is greater than that of the original query while its similarity to the nonrelevant items is smaller.

The vector processing model also exhibits certain disadvantages, namely,

- some model parameters, such as the query–document similarity function, are not derivable within the system but instead are chosen *a priori* by the system designer,
- terms are assumed to be independent of one another, and
- term relationships are not expressible within the model.

A recent characterization of the vector space model is contained in Ref. 8.

2.3. Probabilistic Model

A document is chosen for retrieval in the probabilistic model whenever its probability of being relevant to the query exceeds its probability of being nonrelevant.[6] Document relevance properties can be estimated by using the occurrence probabilities of the terms assigned to the document. Thus, $P(D\,|\,\text{rel})$, the probability that document D occurs in the set of relevant documents, can be expressed as $P(t_1, t_2,..., t_n\,|\,\text{rel})$ where the set of t_i's is the set of terms comprising D. $P(t_1, t_2,..., t_n\,|\,\text{rel})$ must be computed on the basis of the occurrence probabilities of the individual terms, say, $P(t_i\,|\,\text{rel})$. Factors could also be included for the occurrence probabilities for dependent term pairs, triplets, and so on. To provide estimates for these probabilities, either a known probability distribution can be assumed to characterize the occurrence characteristics of the terms or, alternatively, if the user has direct access to the retrieval system during the search operations, term occurrence statistics could be gathered during the searches based on user-supplied relevance information.

The probabilistic retrieval model is theoretically appealing since it allows for term dependency and produces ranked output in decreasing order of presumed importance of the documents. However, it is very difficult to estimate the probabilistic parameters needed by the model. Until viable methods appear for actually obtaining such estimates, simpler retrieval models will be used in practice.

2.4. Language Processing Model

Whereas the Boolean, vector, and probabilistic models discriminate among the documents based on preassigned document index terms, the language processing model distinguishes the documents based on a linguistic analysis of the actual document content. Complex linguistic units are associated with each document or query for content representations obtained by a linguistic analysis of the text of the informational item.[9] In theory, the linguistic model can include all kinds of linguistic relationships. However, in practice the linguistic tools needed for complete document analysis are still too weak, and the knowledge bases needed to cover the breadth of subject matter in document collections are difficult to build. In particular, there are no methods currently available for building usable structures that cover the common sense knowledge needed to analyze ordinary written texts. However, MCC's CYC project involving the building of a large knowledge base of real-world facts, heuristics, and methods for efficiently reasoning over the knowledge base may eventually lead to a solution to this major bottleneck.[10]

Any kind of language analysis raises issues of lexical, syntactic, and semantic ambiguity that cannot be dealt with in unrestricted texts. Efforts to incorporate syntactic phrase analysis routines, supplemented by the assignment of semantic markers, will continue in the future. However, the practical usefulness of such systems is not currently assured.

2.5. Limitations of Existing Retrieved Models

In summary, some of the problems associated with the four retrieval models are as follows:

- Boolean retrieval model: no ranking of retrieved documents, no weighting of terms, very difficult query formulation

- Vector space model: no term relations
- Probabilistic model: difficulty in estimating needed probabilistic parameters
- Language processing model: lack of effective operational methods to use the model

How may we overcome some of the existing limitations in these information retrieval models? We believe the solution lies in the development of advanced interface tools for user–system interaction which may be employed during the course of retrieval operations to resolve many problems that cannot be easily solved through automatic procedures. Specifically, since nearly all search and retrieval operations are currently conducted using on-line search strategies controlled from console terminal devices, it is possible to overcome some conceptual difficulties by using selected information judiciously supplied by the user population during the search process. The importance of user-supplied information has already been confirmed in practice through the success of relevance feedback operations where user relevance judgments serve automatically to enhance the search formulations.[7]

This study focuses on man–machine interfaces that are based on a visual representation of objects in an information retrieval environment. We limit our discussion to the vector space model since objects in this model have an inherent visual representation. Furthermore, the vector space model is the basis for most experimental information retrieval systems because of the advantages that it has over the Boolean model.

3. Graphical Interfaces and Information Retrieval

Computer graphics technology has advanced rapidly during the past few years. However, the graphics technology has not been fully incorporated into existing sophisticated information retrieval systems. Research in the application of graphics technology to on-line document retrieval has generally been limited to the enhancement of user–system interaction through the utilization of window management techniques and man–machine communication devices (such as the mouse).

User-oriented interfaces for information retrieval systems are generally based on *fancy* displays and are either menu-driven or use windowing as a communication medium. In menu-driven systems, the user is typically presented with a list of possible actions with appropriate instructions regarding the next activity; the primary goal of such systems is to facilitate the use of a system with computerized aids previously available only to the search intermediary in noncomputerized forms.

Interface systems based on windowing use graphic displays with multiple windows as an aid to user comprehension. One such system, Caliban,[11] uses an *information window* for the display of thesaurus portions or retrieved document information. In addition, a *command window* is used to list alternative future moves, supplemented by a *message window* which may be used to initiate additional search steps. This type of interface may be considered to be more flexible than a simple menu-driven system; its aims are an effortless learning process for the user and the matching of graphics technology to user capabilities and limitations.[12]

Regardless of the approach taken in the design of the interface system, fancy interfaces are primarily concerned with system functioning and convenience as it relates to the user. While these types of endeavors have produced interesting designs for information display, they have not necessarily enhanced retrieval effectiveness. Interface tools and methodologies for interaction are needed which permit the user to manipulate and access information in ways substantially different from those used to date.

Coinciding with the development of graphics technology has been a redirection of emphasis in the processing of multivariate statistical data from a purely mathematical analysis to one of visual examination.[13-20] Visual representation of data has long been regarded by statisticians as an extremely useful technique, and most now regard it as an essential prerequisite to a more formal analysis of the data. Emphasis of such techniques is on the review, display, and manipulation of multivariate data as a means by which one may readily assimilate its underlying structure. In this regard, graphics is viewed as an instrument for reasoning about quantitative data.[21] Since document collections may be represented as multidimensional vector spaces, it is appropriate to investigate the application of this aspect of graphics technology to the document retrieval process as a means of increasing retrieval effectiveness.

The information retrieval concepts of clustering and query reformulation have been effectively illustrated using graphics art. For example, document relationships may be graphically visualized by representing term vectors as points in the vector space where the distance between points is inversely related to vector similarity; that is, two points will appear close to each other when their vectors are similar. A typical example of a document vector space appears in Figure 1, where documents that are sufficiently similar have been included in a common query or cluster.[22]

Similarly, the query negotiation process may be represented graphically to illustrate how a reformulated query may actually move through the document space to new document areas. For example, the well-known relevance feedback procedure may be viewed graphically as shown in Figure 2. The

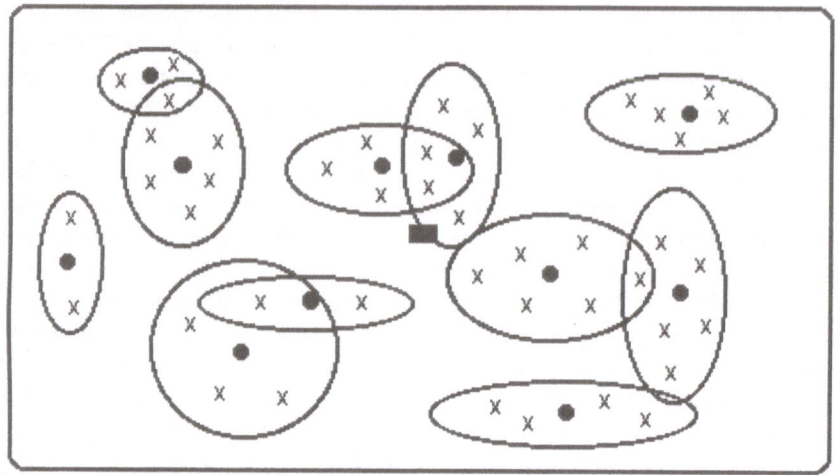

FIGURE 1. Typical clustered file organization: ×, stored document; •, cluster centroid; ■, centroid of document space.

initial query represented by △ in Figure 2a first retrieves one nonrelevant (N) item and one relevant (R) item; when information from the relevant document is incorporated into the query, the query *migrates* downward as shown in Figure 2b where new documents, not previously seen, are now retrievable.[7] One can envision the manner in which such displays could be used in an interactive retrieval environment if systems existed which could provide a visual representation of the document space.

The data being manipulated in an actual retrieval environment generally exhibits rather large dimensionality. A cursory review of the literature reveals that most statistically applied graphical techniques deal only with data of two or three dimensions. Yet, while many of these methods are applicable to higher dimensions, they often produce displays which are not particularly meaningful and which therefore convey little additional information about the data. In fact, some graphical approaches when extended to higher dimensions either "fail to improve the communication of the information or, worse still, misinform."[23] The following discussion is therefore limited to those techniques which have either been used in a document environment or appear to hold promise for such applications. A more detailed analysis of the applicability of existing graphical analysis methods to the document vector space model is contained in Ref. 24.

Two general methods have emerged from studies dealing with the visual representation of multidimensional data. Since a visual examination of multivariate data may be easily made when the data are functions of only

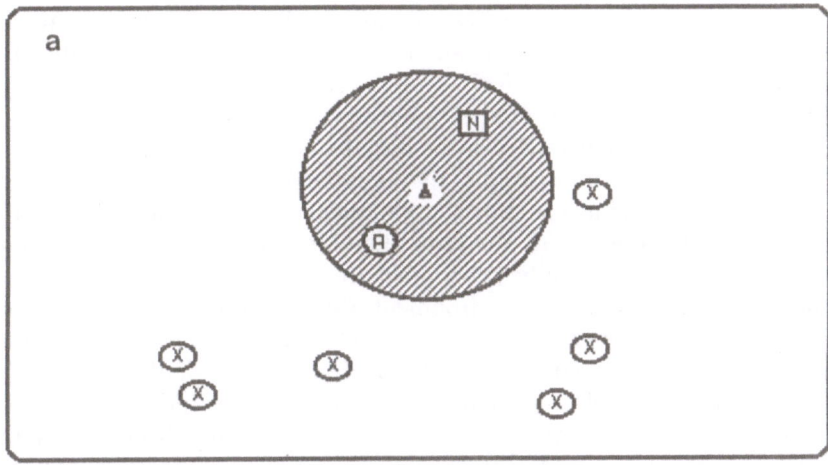

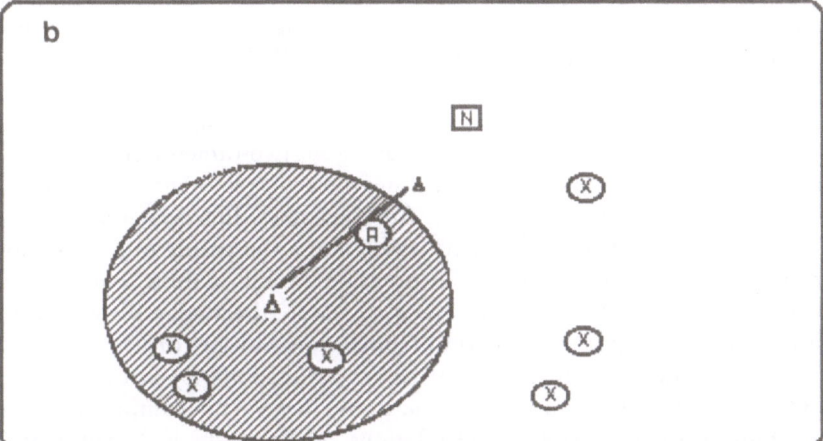

FIGURE 2. Relevance feedback illustration: (a) initial query; (b) reformulated query.

a few variables, several analytical techniques have been developed which seek to obtain a geometric representation of the original n-dimensional data in reduced dimensions.[25-28] Other graphical approaches represent the data points as icons, and the vector components as features of the icon; these methods are known as *multivariate point graphs*[29] and are predicated on the assumption that the psychological perception of the icons will follow closely the relations of the points in vector space. For detailed discussions of various mapping and iconic displays, the reader is referred to Refs. 13, 14, 16, 20, and 30.

Since our primary objective is to develop exploratory graphical methods which can be used in an interactive IR environment, the time required to generate a graphical representation of the document space is a critical factor in the design or selection of the graphics display to be used in this study. In document retrieval, the data being analyzed typically exhibits large dimensionality; for example, the moderately sized MEDLARS collection of 1,033 documents contains 6,927 significant terms, and the small ADI collection of 82 documents contains 886 identifying terms.[31] Mapping processes cannot realistically be applied to a collection of either of these dimensions in an interactive environment, since such methods involve time-intensive, iterative generation and analysis of geometric point configurations. Furthermore, for such data it is highly unlikely that the final spatial display would be indicative of any relationships present in the original document vector space. To overcome these problems, a document collection may first be reduced to a manageable size through clustering, and mapping may then be applied independently to each clustered set of documents. This combined approach has been successfully used in revealing the structure of scientific specialties based on author co-citation analysis.[32–37]

The geometric representation of multidimensional data produced by mapping techniques is particularly beneficial in locating clusters or outliers present within a set of data. By studying a two-dimensional display of points, one may quickly observe the nearness or remoteness of individual data points within the metric space. Such displays, however, do not reveal the characteristics of the data items which cause the points to be close to or far removed from other points. To obtain this information, one normally must analyze the data at a more detailed level. Alternative display techniques exist which not only permit conclusions to be drawn about the relations of data items in terms of nearness or dissimilarity but also in some cases make it possible to ascertain the individual vector components which contribute to the observed spatial relations. These methods do not generate a geometrical representation of the data vectors and therefore do not require any computational analysis of the vectors themselves or iterative refinement of spatial configurations. They are thus computationally more efficient than mappings.

The general objective of nongeometric *multivariate point graphs* is to represent multidimensional data in all its dimensionality. Each of the original *m* data vectors is translated into a curve or iconic representation in which each dimension of the vector space corresponds to a feature of the icon. The resulting *m pictures* are then displayed for visual analysis. It is assumed that the similarity or dissimilarity of the pictures is directly related to distances between corresponding points in the original multidimensional space. While the final display of the nongeometric graphical methods may be visually more complex than two-dimensional maps of m points, thereby necessitating more user analysis to determine the structure present within the data, other benefits may be derived from these approaches. Some of the well-known iconic displays are Andrews' function,[38] Chernoff faces,[39] and trees and castles.[40].

Most iconic representations, while computationally fast, are limited to multivariate data of relatively low dimensionality. However, this limitation poses fewer problems than those created by the fact that multivariate point graphs are inherently difficult to use in making definitive, numerical scale judgments about the relative distance between the data points generating the icons. While Andrews' method does produce displays with labeled vertical and horizontal axes, displays obtained from applying Andrews' method to document vectors were found to be too complex for detailed visual analysis.[41]

Visual representations based on existing graphical techniques do not appear to be especially applicable to document collections in the large. We desire graphical displays which coalesce and represent the document space in such a manner that the user may discover the information residing within the database (which is relevant to his or her needs) through visual analysis and exploration of the data.

4. Desired Characteristics of a Visual Representation

What are the features of a graphics display which will enable a user to conduct a visual, exploratory analysis of the document space during the retrieval process and thereby to produce a ranked set of documents based on perceived similarity with a query? Firstly, for global analysis, we need a graphical representation of documents that makes it possible for one to gain quickly a subjective feeling of the general relationship between the documents and the query. A cursory visual analysis of the graphics display of a query and a set of documents should allow one to classify the documents roughly into two categories—those documents which appear to be highly similar to the query and those which appear to be dissimilar to the query. Secondly, for more detailed analysis, the display should enable one to gain a feeling for the query–document relationships as reflected by a specific term or set of terms. In particular, for assessing the relative similarity of a document and a query, the display should assist the user in deriving the following information about the two entities:

- The number of terms with nonzero weights common to both the document and the query,

- The importance of each common term as reflected by the query term weights.
- The importance of each common term as reflected by the document term weights.

The importance attached to a term by both the query and the document is a primary factor in estimating query–document similarity. Thus, the graphics display must provide the means for one to assess visually the degree of importance attached to a term by both the query and each of its documents

A graphical interface based on these two features (along with supporting tools to mananipulate the data) should enable one to conduct a good visual analysis of a set of documents. With properly designed tools, the user should be able not only to increase the effectiveness of the retrieval process beyond that provided by more conventional information retrieval systems but also to gain a deeper understanding of the relationship between queries and relevant documents in the vector space model.

5. Pictorial Representation of Document Vectors

In order to design a grahics display which satisfies the requirements delineated above, we concentrated on the development of an *iconic display* which is computationally fast, enables one to make definitive judgments about the perceived similarity of documents and queries in a timely fashion, communicates with clarity and precision, and reveals the data at several levels of detail from a broad overview to a fine structure. Other approaches to the visual representation of multivariate data, such as mapping and ordination techniques, were found to be too inefficient for interactive use in an information retrieval environment.[24] As in any experimental graphics research, the final graphics display "came from an evolutionary process in which earlier versions were tried on many data sets and changed on the basis of their performance."[42]

5.1. Component Scale Drawing

Figure 3 contains an example of a pictorial display which may be used to establish the similarity between a query and a set of documents in the vector space model. In this so-called *component scale drawing*, data vectors are represented as line drawings with the horizontal axis representing the query terms, and the vertical axis, class values indicative of the importance of a term. Documents are reduced to the length of the query, since only terms in common with the query affect similarity judgments. An abscissa of 1

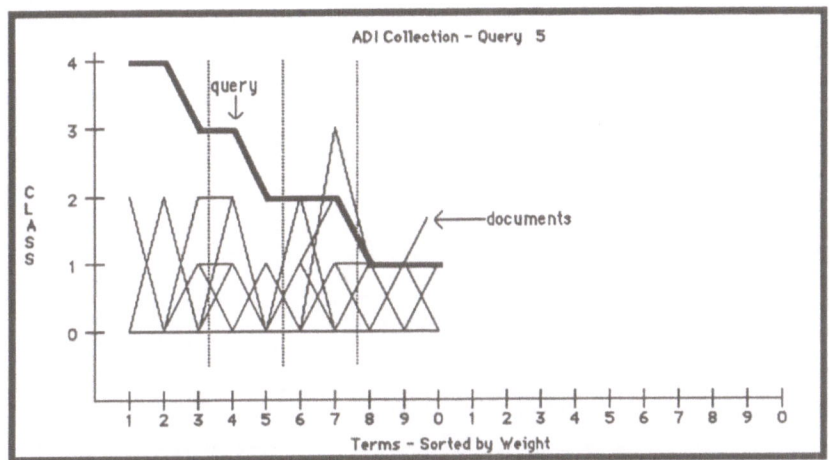

FIGURE 3. Component scale display of the document space.

corresponds to the query term which has the highest term weight, and an abscissa equal to the length of a query (that is, the number of terms in the query) represents the lowest-weighted query term. Thus, the query vector is displayed in decreasing term weight order, that is, in decreasing order of term importance as determined by the query. It should be noted that the document collection being displayed is the ADI collection containing 82 documents; the query consists of 10 weighted terms.

An ordinate of any point composing a document may have only one of five possible values (0–4). Each value represents a range of term weights, with class 0 signifying the absence of a query term in the document vector itself (a zero weight). In assessing similarities, one does not need to know the actual ranges of weight for the other ordinate classes; one needs only to know that for any class i, the weights of all classes with ordinate less than i are less than the weights of class i, and for any class with ordinate greater than i, the weights are greater than those of class i. Thus, a term corresponding to a point on the document whose ordinate is class 3 is considered to be more important than a term in that document with a lower ordinate and less important or indicative of a document's meaning than a term whose ordinate is class 4. It might be observed that this relationship between ordinate classes forces the query to be generally stairstepped downward from the point on the line representing the first query term.

During the analysis process, documents are being constantly moved to and from the display at the discretion of the user as he or she makes decisions about the similarity of documents with the query. (This feature is provided by the tools of the interface.) Depending on the subset of

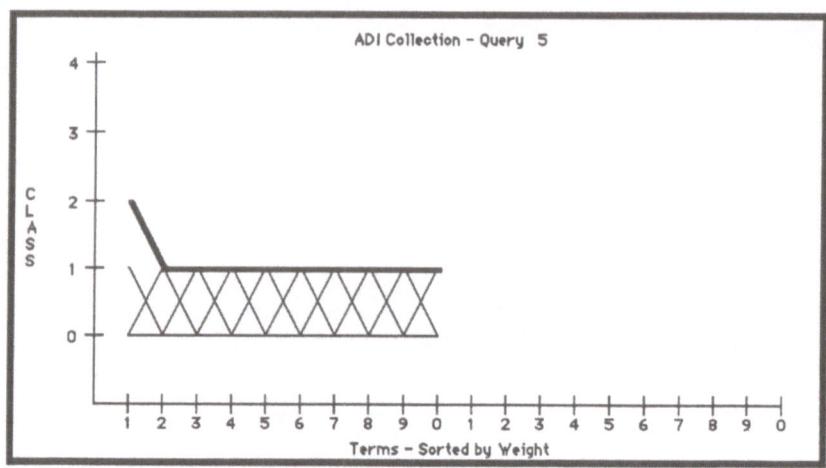

FIGURE 4. Effect of severe scaling.

documents being evaluated, the user may desire to see more or less
discrimination among the displayed documents. This desire is met by the
provision of a sliding class scale which the user can activate at will; one just
clicks on the desired scale and the documents are immediately displayed
using an alternate range of term weights for the class ordinates. If one
desires to suppress the less significant terms in the vectors, that is, give more
importance to the heavily weighted terms, then one can choose a more
severe scaling than that which the current display is using. Conversely, by

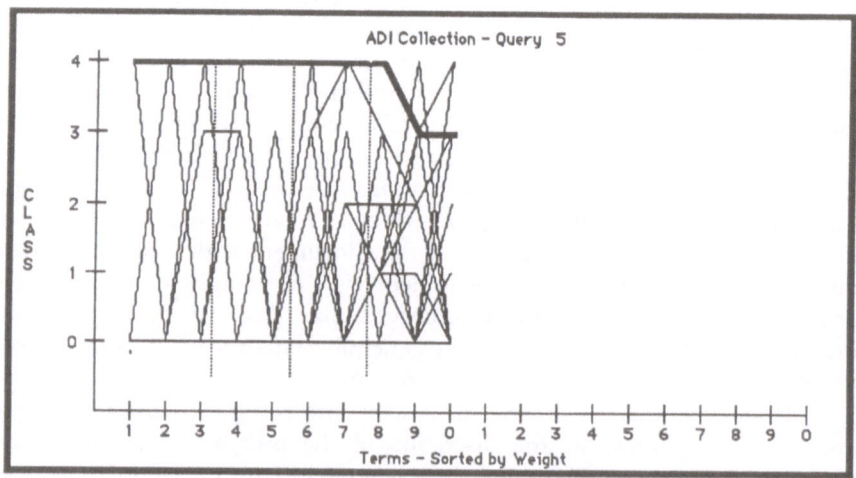

FIGURE 5. Effect of least restrictive scaling.

choosing a less restrictive scale, the lower-weighted terms are permitted to rise above the baseline of ordinate class 1 and to appear as peaks in the display. For example, the user can force the query vector and all documents to be flat at ordinate 1, with no discrimination between documents (Figure 4), or the user can force the query to be a flat line with ordinate class 4, in which case the document vectors will have many peaks (Figure 5). In general, one chooses a rather severe scaling when one is attempting to identify and rank those documents which are very similar to the query, and a less restrictive scale when only lower-ranked documents are being displayed and analyzed. In other words, one would not attempt to analyze all documents with a liberal scaling such as that used in Figure 5. Instead, one would begin with a display such as that in Figure 3 and gradually modify the scale as fewer documents remain to be analyzed. Through this dynamic scale control, one can easily determine the relationship between vectors.

What advantage does this approach have over the display of the actual vectors themselves? Remember that the primary objective is to rank the documents visually according to similarity with the query vector. A glance at Figure 6 will show how confusing it could be if one were to have to analyze a display of the actual documents and queries. In this figure the vector components are not arranged in sorted query term weight order and the term weights themselves are not scaled. The scale selection process is an effective means of simplifying the display while at the same time permitting one essentially to look at the relative effect of the raw weights on the similarity of vectors. Furthermore, the results of our experiments support our

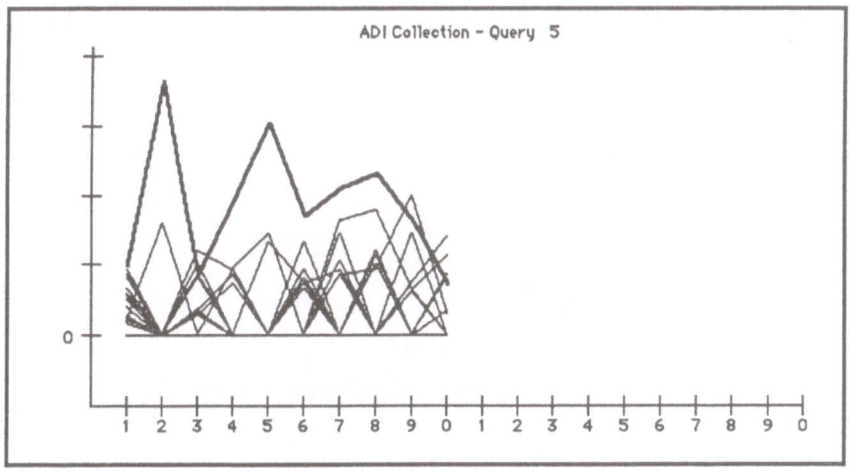

FIGURE 6. Display with actual vector term weights.

contention that the lack of knowledge of actual weights does not adversely affect one's ability to gauge the similarity of query and documents.

Before presenting the experimental results of ranking a set of documents through visual analysis of component scale drawings, we will describe the primary features of the user interface.

5.2. *The User Interface*

The tools provided by the interface enable one to compare query and document vectors visually in a readily comprehensible manner and to generate a ranked list of the documents in perceived order of similarity. All commands are selected and activated by pointing and clicking the console's mouse; the keyboard is not used.

Figure 7 contains the actual display of the beginning of a sample session. The user is initially presented with a highlighted query and the set of documents displayed in the manner described above. The document vectors are shortened to the query length, and the terms are sorted in descending order according to query term weight. The class weight scale is arbitrarily set at a midrange value of scales. The five buttons in the upper left-hand corner represent the class scales. If one were to click on the lowest button, the query vector would be displayed as relatively flat at the class weight of 1.

The dotted vertical lines in Figure 7 serve to separate the documents into four overlapping sets ranging from the first set, which contains those documents with nonzero weights corresponding to the most significant query

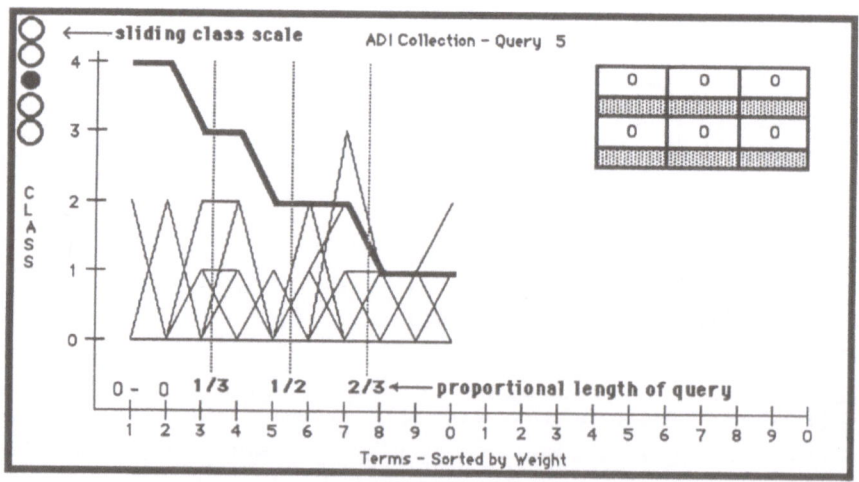

FIGURE 7. Display at the beginning of a session.

terms, to the last set, which contains those documents that have nonzero weights for the least significant terms. The abscissas of these three lines are values corresponding to one-third, one-half, and two-thirds of the length of the query vector. These indicators prove useful during the ranking process; for example, the documents that are most similar to the query tend to have peaks (non-zero-weighted terms) in the region to the left of the $\frac{1}{3}$ line.

The user may select a document by clicking on any point of the document. The chosen point is enlarged, and all documents passing through it are immediately highlighted. The number of highlighted documents and the total number of non-zero-weighted terms are automatically calculated for the user. The query is always highlighted and does not affect any of the quantitative values which are displayed by the system. The reason the user may want to know the number of points is perhaps readily obvious: the similarity of a document and a query is a function of the number of terms they have in common. Any time a set of documents is chosen in this fashion or through use of one of the options described below, document numbers (which uniquely identify the documents) are displayed for the chosen items.

If the user desires to extract a set of documents from among only those which are currently highlighted, he or she may do so by clicking on any point of any document which is highlighted. The system responds by highlighting only those documents passing through both points, the first point being the one which created the initial set of highlighted documents; the number of documents, total number of significant terms, and the actual document numbers are also displayed.

To facilitate the sorting of documents into groups, the user may initiate the transfer of all currently highlighted documents (query excluded) into one of six groups. The user does this by clicking on one of six shelves contained in the upper right portion of the display. The highlighted documents are immediately removed from the display and added to the list of documents which may have previously been inserted into the shelf. The number of documents in a shelf is displayed in the shelf itself. If the user clicks on a shelf when no documents are highlighted, the list of document numbers for those documents contained in the shelf are displayed. It should be noted that the order in which documents are entered into a shelf is retained by the system. At the conclusion of a query analysis session, the final ranking of the documents is determined by essentially concatenating the ordered lists of document entries contained within each of the six shelves, starting with shelf number 1.

Usually, only a single document is highlighted when the user invokes the transfer command. However, another option does exist which permits one to add to the current set of highlighted documents as successive points are clicked. This feature is useful if the user has completed an evaluation and desires to select a group of documents quickly for transfer. The system notes the order in which the documents are highlighted and transfers this knowledge to the shelf when the documents are removed from the display.

The interface system also permits one to return documents from a shelf to the active display. This feature lets the user use one or more shelves as temporary storage. One may thus move a group of documents out of the display area in order to simplify it, analyze the remaining documents and assign them to appropriate shelves, and then return the previously removed documents to the display for further analysis.

Another useful feature permits one to select documents on the basis of the number of nonzero terms contained therein, expressed as a function of the length of the query. When this option is exercised, the user chooses the percentage of the length desired (10–90%). In response, the system automatically highlights all documents which contain more than the number of terms represented by the designated percentage.

Once all documents have been removed from the display, the user may signal termination of the analysis process. A ranked listing of the documents is generated based on the user's analysis.

The basic set of tools provided by the interface permits the user to manipulate the active display in the manner that he or she finds most useful for ascertaining the similarity of vectors.

5.3. Basis of the Component Scale Display

Documents which are highly similar to a query possess certain characteristics which prove useful in visually assessing the similarity of documents and queries. The component scale display is designed to reveal these characteristics and thereby to enable a user to distinguish readily between those documents which are in general strongly related to a query and those which are not.

The characteristics of highly similar documents were discovered by performing a statistical analysis of the documents in the ADI and MEDLARS document test collections for each of 65 queries. We subdivided the documents into four sets: Set 1 represented the five documents most similar to the query and Set 4 represented the five documents which are ranked 16th through 20th in similarity to the query. The ADI collection had 175 documents in each set, and the MEDLARS collection had 150 documents. For ADI, 59% of the documents in Set 1 had a peak to the left of the $\frac{1}{3}$ line in the corresponding component scale drawings and only 7.4% of Set 4 had such a peak. For MEDLARS, the corresponding figures were 71% and 41%. The highest peak for Set 1 for ADI occurred to the left of the $\frac{1}{3}$ line in 45% of the cases and to the left of the $\frac{1}{2}$ line in 81% of the cases. For

Set 4, the corresponding figures were 5.7% and 29%. For MEDLARS, the figures are 51% and 85%, respectively, for Set 1 and 29% and 61% for Set 4. In general, the higher-ranked documents had more terms in common with the query than the lower-ranked documents, and they also had more of the *important* terms in common with the query.

As a result of this analysis, we have concluded that three major observations need to be made of a document when one is visually determining the relative similarity between it and a query:

- the location of its first nonzero term: Where does its leftmost peak occur in relation to the vertical lines representing one-third, one-half, and two-thirds of the length of the query?
- the location of its most significant nonzero term: Where is its highest point in relation to the three dotted vertical lines?
- the number of nonzero terms in common with the query: How many points does the document have?

The component scale display readily permits one to glean this information in an interactive manner.

This information must be evaluated for a set of documents with due consideration being given to the scale which is being applied to the actual term weights. If the scale is restrictive and few documents have points with ordinates greater than 1, then the peaks with an ordinate greater than class one are very significant even if they are not associated with the more significant terms (leftmost terms in the display). As the scale is relaxed, additional points occur with ordinates greater than 1. In this case, the number of points (terms) which a document possesses assumes more importance than the ordinates of the points. A complete methodology for visually assessing the similarity of objects using component scale drawings is contained in Ref. 43.

5.4. Experimental Results

To ascertain the power of this representation in making similarity judgments visually, a series of experiments were performed in which a query vector was displayed together with the set of documents in the database. The user, with the aid of the tools provided by the interface, ranked the documents in the order of perceived similarities with the query. Fifteen queries were evaluated. In order to establish the discriminatory power of the display, the perceived rank orderings for each query were compared with the known relevance rankings of the test collection. The average Spearman rank correlation coefficient for the 15 cases was 0.85. These results are encouraging and lend support to the validity of this pictorial representation as a graphics display in information retrieval. The component scale drawing is computationally fast, provides a quantitative scale by which relative distance judgments can be made, and does not become too complex when a large number of data points are displayed.

6. Summary

Information retrieval systems are not currently taking advantage of the immense power of visual displays for revealing the relationships existing among documents and queries in the document space. The results obtained from the use of the graphics display and interface tools introduced in this chapter demonstrate the feasibility of the use of visual representation of objects in an information retrieval environment.

Acknowledgments

This study was supported in part by the National Science Foundation under grants IST 84-05749 and IST 87-02735.

References

1. G. SALTON, *Automatic Information Organization Retrieval*, McGraw-Hill, New York, 1968.
2. C. W. CLEVERDON, Optimizing convenient on-line access to bibliographic databases, *Information Service Use* **4**, 37–47 (1984).
3. G. SALTON, Another look at automatic text-retrieval systems, *Commun. ACM* **29**(7), 648–656 (1986).
4. E. A. FOX, Information retrieval: Research into new capabilities, pp. 143–174 in *CD ROM*, S. Lambert and S. Ropiequet (Eds.), Microsoft Press, Redmond, Washington, 1986.
5. G. COLVIN, The current state of text retrieval, pp. 131–136 in *CD ROM*, S. Lambert and S. Ropiequet (Eds.), Microsoft Press, Redmond, Washington, 1986.
6. C. J. VAN RIJSBERGEN, *Information Retrieval*, Second Edition, Butterworths, London, 1979.
7. G. SALTON AND M. J. McGILL, *Introduction to Modern Information Retrieval*, McGraw-Hill, New York, 1983.
8. S. K. M. WONG AND V. V. RAGHAVAN, Vector space model of information retrieval: A reevaluation, pp. 167–186 in *Research and Development in Information Retrieval*, C. J. van Rijsbergen (Ed.), Cambridge University Press, London, 1984.
9. K. SPARCK JONES AND M. KAY, *Linguistics and Information Science*, Academic Press, New York, 1973.
10. D. LENAT, M. PRAKASH, AND M. SHEPHERD, CYC: Using common sense knowledge to overcome brittleness and knowledge acquisition bottlenecks, *The AI Magazine* **7**, 65–84 (1986).
11. H. P. FREI AND J. F. JAUSLIN, Two-dimensional representation of information retrieval services, pp. 383–396 in *Representation and Exchange of Knowledge as a Basis of Information Processes*, H. J. Dietschmann (Ed.), North-Holland, New York, 1984.

12. T. E. LINDQUIST, Assessing the useability of human-computer interfaces, *IEEE Software* **2**(1), 74–82 (1985).

13. B. EVERITT (Ed.), *Graphical Techniques for Multivariate Data*, North-Holland, New York, 1978.

14. P. WANG (Ed.), *Graphical Representation of Multivariate Data*, Academic Press, New York, 1978.

15. S. L. APPLEGATE, The use of interactive raster graphics in the display and manipulation of multidimensional data, Ph.D. thesis, Department of Mechanical Engineering, Purdue University, Lafayette, Indiana, 1981.

16. V. BARNETT (Ed.), *Interpreting Multivariate Data*, John Wiley and Sons, New York, 1981.

17. R. H. MYERS, Methods for Presentation and Display of Multivariate Data, Technical Report CR-165788, NASA Langley Research Center, Hampton, Virginia, 1981.

18. K. W. HEINER, R. S. SACHER, AND J. W. WILKINSON (Eds.), *Computer Science and Statistics: Proceedings of the 14th Symposium on the Interface*, Springer-Verlag, New York, 1983.

19. V. BARNETT AND T. LEWIS, *Outliers in Statistical Data*, 2nd Edition, John Wiley and Sons, New York, 1984.

20. P. G. N. DIGBY AND R. A. KEMPTON, Multivariate Analysis of Ecological Communities, Chapman and Hall, New York, 1987.

21. E. R. TUFTE, *The Visual Display of Quantitative Information*, Graphics Press, Cheshire, Connecticut, 1983.

22. G. SALTON AND A. WONG, Generation and search of clustered files, *ACM Trans. Database Syst.* **3**(4), 321–346 (1978).

23. H. HEFFERNAN, Computer graphics technology outpaces user skills, *Government Computer News* **4**(9, May 24), 6 (1985).

24. D. B. CROUCH, The visual display of information in an information retrieval environment, in *Proceedings of the International Conference on Research and Development in Information Retrieval*, Association for Computing Machinery, New York, 1986.

25. R. N. SHEPARD, The analysis of proximities: Multidimensional scaling with an unknown distance function. I, *Psychometrika* **27**(2), 125–140 (1962).

26. R. N. SHEPARD, The analysis of proximities: Multidimensional scaling with an unknown distance function. II, *Psychometrika* **27**(3), 219–246 (1962).

27. J. B. KRUSKAL, Multidimensional scaling by optimizing goodness of fit to a nonmetric hypothesis, *Psychometrika* **29**(1), 1–27 (1964).

28. J. B. KRUSKAL, Nonmetric multidimensional scaling: A numerical method, *Psychometrika* **29**(2), 115–129 (1964).

29. L. WILKINSON, An experimental evaluation of multivariate graphical point representations, pp. 202–209 in *Proceedings of the Conference on Human Factors in Computing Systems*, Association for Computing Machinery, New York, 1982.

30. J. M. CHAMBERS, W. S. CLEVELAND, B. KLEINER, AND P. TUKEY, *Graphical Methods for Data Analysis*, Duxbury Press, Boston, 1983.

31. E. VOORHEES, The cluster hypothesis revisited, pp. 188–196 in *Research and Development in Information Retrieval*, Association for Computing Machinery, New York, 1985.

32. H. SMALL AND B. C. GRIFFITH, The structure of scientific literatures I: Identifying and graphing specialties, *Social Stud.* **4**, 17–40 (1974).

33. B. C. GRIFFITH, H. G. SMALL, J. A. STONEHILL, AND S. DEY, The structure of scientific literatures II: Toward a macro- and microstructure for science, *Social Stud.* **4**, 339–365 (1974).

34. E. GARFIELD, *Citation Indexing: Its Theory and Application in Science, Technology, and Humanities*, John Wiley and Sons, New York, 1979.

35. H. D. WHITE AND B. C. GRIFFITH, Author cocitation: a literature measure of intellectual structure, *J. Am. Soc. Inf. Sci.* **32**, 163–171 (1981).

36. K. W. McCAIN, Longitudinal author cocitation mapping: the changing structure of macroeconomics, *J. Am. Soc. Inf. Sci.* **35**(6), 351–359 (1984).

37. P. DOREIAN AND T. J. FARARO, Structural equivalence in a journal network, *J. Am. Soc. Inf. Sci.* **36**(1), 28–37 (1985).

38. D. F. ANDREWS, Plots of high-dimensional data, *Biometrics* **28**(3), 125–136 (1972).
39. H. CHERNOFF, The use of faces to represent points in k-dimensional space graphically, *J. Am. Stat. Assoc.* **68**(6), 361–368 (1973).
40. B. KLEINER AND J. A. HARTIGAN, Representing points in many dimensions by trees and castles, *J. Am. Stat. Assoc.* **76**, 260–269 (1981).
41. A. J. MITTAL, The visual analysis of information in an information retrieval environment, Master's thesis, Department of Computer Science, Tulane University, New Orleans, 1986.
42. W. S. CLEVELAND AND I. J. TERPENNING, Graphical methods for seasonal adjustment, *J. Am. Stat. Assoc.* **77**(3), 52–62 (1982).
43. D. B. CROUCH, A graphical method for interactive visual analysis of data in an information retrieval environment, in *Data Analysis and Informatics*, E. Diday (Ed.), North-Holland, Paris, 1987.

GENERALIZING THE SHEET LANGUAGE PARADIGM

ALLEN L. AMBLER

1. Introduction

Spreadsheets offer a means of writing certain types of application programs quickly, interactively, and with minimum training. In fact, spreadsheet users probably do not consider their work as programming. Yet, they are expressing a computation, the process of which is programming, and the medium for such expression is a programming language.

As programming languages, spreadsheets are designed to solve a specific class of table-oriented computational problems. Their functionality is limited. Yet, for the specific class of problems they address, they are the language of choice.

As important for our purposes is the observation that there are a large number of users who, while intimidated by conventional programming languages, seem to have no difficulty learning to use spreadsheets and use them to develop quite complex programs. While the author knows of no empirical studies explaining this phenomenon, we can form some reasonable hypotheses:

1. The programming environment is nonmodal and interpretative. The editor is embedded into the environment in such a way that the user sees no separation of activities. Every cell entry produces an immediate parsing, semantic interpretation, and computation. Feedback is immediate.

2. Spreadsheets avoid the notion of variables. Conventional programming languages require the concept that a variable is a name bound to a cell (or cells) such that when a variable name appears as the

ALLEN L. AMBLER • Department of Computer Science, University of Kansas, Lawrence, Kansas 66045.

target of an assignment, the cell to which it is bound is assigned a new value. Spreadsheet programmers simply identify a cell by pointing at it and either directly entering the cell's value or entering an expression, the result of which becomes the cell's value. The notions of variables and names are not required.

3. Spreadsheets encourage the idea that a cell contains a single value throughout the computational process. Hence, avoided is the potentially confusing notion that the value of a cell varies over the execution of a program. "Encourage" is a key word because spreadsheets do allow the value of cells to be recomputed iteratively within a single computation of the program; however, few spreadsheets solutions need to make use of such facilities.

4. Spreadsheets are nondeclarative and typeless. Again because there are no variables, declarations are not required. Cell expressions are simply made to reference other cells (by pointing at them). In essence, all possible storage cells are predeclared. The only task the spreadsheet programmer has is to decide what value he or she wishes a given cell to contain. Furthermore, no type declaration is required. A given cell can contain a value of any type. Types are dynamically tested during expression evaluation, and reasonable type coercions are performed. The result is that spreadsheet programmers are for the most part unaware of the concepts of declarations and typing. (While spreadsheet display format options contain implicit typing information, this information is not binding, that is, it is not an error if the cell receives a value of a different type—the formatting information is simply ignored.)

5. The order of evaluation is derived, rather than specified. This is possibly the most significant aspect of spreadsheet programming. The user need not be concerned with control flow. Control flow is entirely derived based upon computational dependencies. For the inexperienced programmer, this is a tremendous simplification of required concepts, and even for the experienced programmer, it reduces in the extraneous non-problem-related information that must be supplied to obtain a solution. [However, it is not without consequences. Programs that do contain cyclic evaluations (loops) can be expressed. When inexperienced programmers accidentally express such a program, they may find it difficult to comprehend the nature of their problem. Fortunately, inexperienced programmers seemingly do not naturely construct cyclic programs and, hence, rarely face this problem.]

6. The spreadsheet is itself the output medium. There is no concept of external input/output. This is again a tremendous simplification for

the user. In essence, it creates a WYSIWYG (*what you see is what you get*) programming environment. (On the other hand, having no concept of external input/output is very limiting. More on this later.)

For each of the above observations, it can be argued that the visual and interactive aspects of spreadsheets play an important role. Clearly, the visual representation of the cell matrix allows the omission of the concepts of variables (item 2), declarations (item 4), and output formatting (item 6). In addition, it contributes to the visual image of a large cell matrix wherein each value is computed once per evaluation (item 3) and wherein the order of evaluation is not specified, but derived (item 5). The visual interface with its various operational areas contributes to the modeless operation (item 1). Hence, being visual contributes significantly to the success of spreadsheet languages.

But are spreadsheets visual languages? Chang[1] defines *visual programming languages* as languages for programming with visual expression objects that do not have an inherent visual representation. One problem with this definition is that the phrase "programming with visual expression" is ambiguous. It might be interpreted as programming visually, that is, with visual expression, or it might be interpreted as programming wherein the result is a visual expression, that is, an expression viewed visually. The distinction between these two interpretations is significant. The former represents in essence a *visual editor* that employs graphical interaction techniques to do language-specific editing of a language that may or may not have inherent visual qualities. The latter corresponds to a graphic representation of a language (which may or may not be otherwise conventional). Examples of a visual editor facility are pointing at an object to generate a reference to it and selecting an object from a menu and dragging it into a program context as a means of declaring the object. Clearly, visual editing techniques are an important aspect of visual languages, and spreadsheets employ visual editing techniques (perhaps not as much as they might), but visual editing is not our interest here and so little more will be said about visual editors.

From the discussion that follows Chang's definition of visual programming languages in his paper, it is clear that by this definition he means programming wherein the result is a visual expression (the latter interpretation). Chang goes on to further subdivide visual programming languages into two types: those that are inherently nonvisual but have imposed visual representation, and those that are inherently visual. The former he refers to as linearly represented and the latter as visually represented.

A similar classification is derived by Shu.[2] She distinguishes (1) languages that support visual interaction and (2) languages that allow programming with visual expressions (also, (3) languages that process visual information—which are not of interest here). This definition is less crisp. All category 2 languages would seem to be category 1 languages as well; whereas Chang's categories, distinguished by inherent visualness, are disjoint.

Nitpicking aside, what both of these authors are trying to say is that any conventional language can be expressed in a corresponding visual notation using a simple syntactic transformation. For example, Figure 1 illustrates a short program segment expressed both in Pascal and visually using a Nassi–Shneiderman structure diagram.[3] "Visual" Pascal is what Chang would categorize as a language that is inherently nonvisual but with imposed visual representation and Shu would refer to as a language that supports visual interaction. Without wishing to argue whether these visually transformed languages are visual languages at all, they are clearly different from languages whose inherent, natural expression is visual, and for which it may be somewhat difficult, or at least not as natural, to express the same program in a linear textual language. We will refer to these two categories as *visually transformed languages* and *naturally visual languages*. (We prefer the concept of "naturalness" to that of "inherentness" as being both closer to the intended meaning of the categorization and perhaps more decidable.)

Clearly, spreadsheets are not visually transformed languages, even though aspects of spreadsheet languages, expressions for instance, readily map into linear textural languages. Perhaps not as clear is the question of whether spreadsheets are naturally visual languages. At times, spreadsheets are definitely naturally visual, that is, the expression of certain problem solutions is simplistic, if not elegant, to an extent that we do not find in the

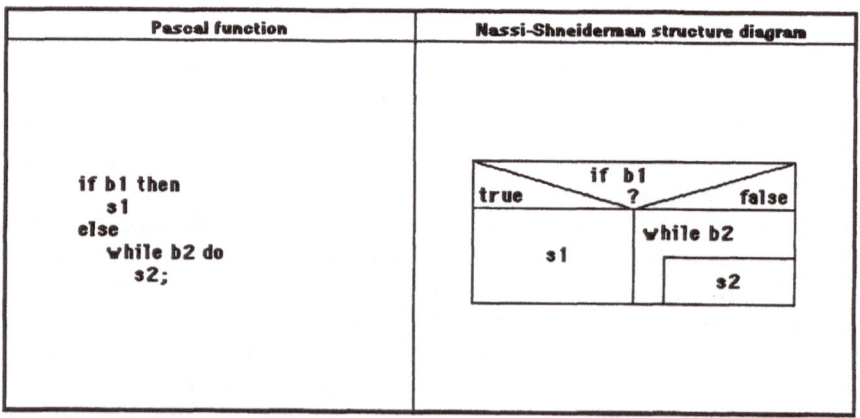

FIGURE 1. Short program segment expressed textually in Pascal and visually using Nassi–Shneiderman structure charts.

corresponding linear textual counterpart. For other problems, spreadsheet solutions become distinctly nonvisual and unnatural.

The sections that follow address by way of a series of examples the question of natural visualness and identify shortcomings of spreadsheets as naturally visual languages. This discussion is intended to motivate a possible generalization of spreadsheet languages. The remaining sections provide an overview of such a generalized spreadsheet language and relate it to the preceding discussion.

2. Spreadsheets

A spreadsheet is a visual representation of a worksheet as a two-dimensional matrix of cells. Each cell is specified by a computational expression and a visual presentation format. The computational expression provides an operational definition of the value of the cell. The visual presentation format specifies how the value is to be displayed when the matrix is viewed. A computational expression can be a simple value or a computed expression that may reference other cells as well as a set of predefined functions.

To illustrate many of the significant points of spreadsheet languages, we will consider a sequence of progressively expanded problem cases. The objective of this analysis is not to criticize spreadsheets (or Pascal) for their limitations, but rather to explore the positive characteristics of spreadsheets and to try to understand where spreadsheets fail in order that we can build upon their positive characteristics.

Case 1. Consider the following example problem: sum a column of 10 numbers, displaying the sum below the last in the same column. Assume that the 10 values are entered directly (i.e., it is not required that they be read from an input file) and that as a first pass we wish to avoid loops because they require extraneous variables. First, we consider the development of this program within the context of a spreadsheet. The steps are as follows:

s1. Select a column of 11 cells at the appropriate place within the visual image of the worksheet, and, for each of the first 10 cells, enter its value by simply typing it in the cell.

s2. Within the 11 cell enter the following formula:

$$= SUM(R[-10]C : R[-1]C)$$

This formula is interpreted as: sum the column of numbers beginning 10 numbers above the current cell (in the same column) and continuing down to the cell immediately above the current cell (in the same column). [Note that the above formula is entered by typing "= SUM (", followed by pointing at the first cell and dragging the pointer across all 10 cells to the last cell (which results in the expression R[-10] C : R[-1] C being automatically generated), and finally by entering")." This type of visual editing greatly facilitates the entry of cell references.]

s3. To adjust the presentation format, select the 11 cells and then select the appropriate presentation format from a display format menu.

The resulting spreadsheet is shown in Figure 2. Now, let us develop a similar program in Pascal. It requires the following steps:

p1. Definition of data structures to hold the 10 values and the resulting sum:

```
program compute(output);
var
    Numbers: array[1 .. 10] of integer;
    Sum : integer;
```

p2. Initialization of the cell structure, followed by printing the 10 values in a column:

```
begin
Numbers[1] :=1;
Numbers[2] :=2;
Numbers[3] :=3;
Numbers[4] :=4;
Numbers[5] :=5;
Numbers[6] :=6;
Numbers[7] :=7;
Numbers[8] :=8;
Numbers[9] :=9;
Numbers[10] :=10;
writeln('$', Numbers[1] : 8 : 2);
writeln('$', Numbers[2] : 8 : 2);
writeln('$', Numbers[3] : 8 : 2);
writeln('$', Numbers[4] : 8 : 2);
writeln('$', Numbers[5] : 8 : 2);
writeln('$', Numbers[6] : 8 : 2);
writeln('$', Numbers[7] : 8 : 2);
writeln('$', Numbers[8] : 8 : 2);
writeln('$', Numbers[9] : 8 : 2);
writeln('$', Numbers[10] : 8 : 2);
```

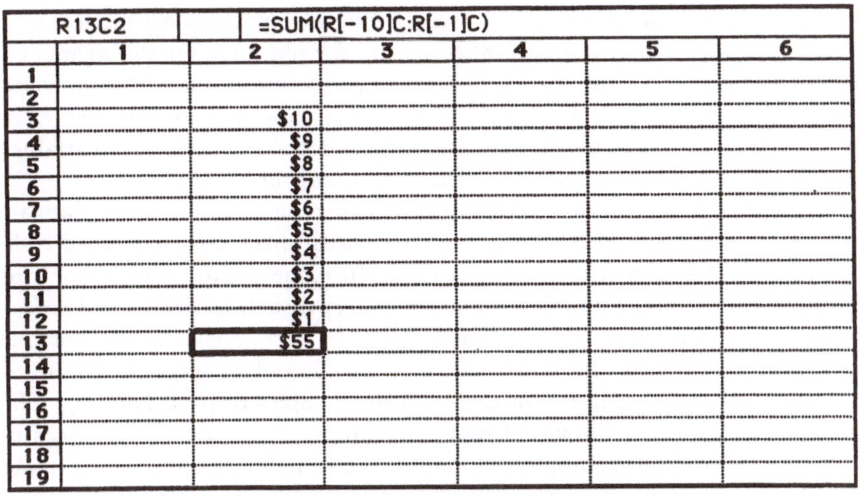

R13C2		=SUM(R[-10]C:R[-1]C)				
	1	2	3	4	5	6
1						
2						
3		$10				
4		$9				
5		$8				
6		$7				
7		$6				
8		$5				
9		$4				
10		$3				
11		$2				
12		$1				
13		$55				
14						
15						
16						
17						
18						
19						

FIGURE 2. Spreadsheet solution to Case 1.

p3. Computation of the sum:

```
Sum :=Numbers[1]+Numbers[2]+Numbers[3]+Numbers[4]
      +Numbers[5]+Numbers[6]+Numbers[7]+Numbers[8]
      +Numbers[9]+Numbers[10];
```

> (It might be argued that it is an unfair comparison to use the SUM function for the spreadsheet while forcing the Pascal program to perform a series of binary additions. There are two arguments in favor of this seeming disparity. First, spreadsheets provide a number of functions that take and return matrices as arguments. This is part of the power of these languages within their limited problem domain. Second, Pascal does not allow the construction of functions that take as arguments matrices of arbitrary size. Hence, one cannot construct an analogous function in Pascal.)

p4. Display result as a dollar amount with two decimals in a field width of 10 characters:

```
writeln('$', Sum : 8 : 2);
end.
```

p5. Compile, link, and execute this program.

> (Note that if the output format is important, this program may require considerable rework to arrive at an acceptable presentation format.)

The Pascal program is a travesty, and no experienced programmer would ever write such a program; however, the objective for the moment is not to write a program that experienced programmers would appreciate, but to introduce as few additional language concepts as possible while expressing a similar solution. As it is, we were forced to introduce variables, arrays, declarations, assignments, and stream output.

For this simple problem, using a spreadsheet has certain natural advantages over writing a Pascal program: the spreadsheet does not require the declaration of a data structure to hold the 10 values or the sum; there is no requirement for understanding semantic concepts such as names and assignment; the presentation format is easy to adjust; and no specification of control flow is required. In short, the user is allowed to express a solution without knowledge of many of the traditional topics in programming. This is possible because of the visual representation of a cell matrix and because of the visual editing techniques that allow one to point at, rather than name, objects. The idea of placing values into visual cells seems natural; binding names to storage locations one cannot see and then assigning them values takes considerably more understanding (particularly when we also introduce the idea that variables may be reassigned values during the course of evaluating the program).

While few problems of interest to even spreadsheet programmers are this simple, a great many problems require no additional concepts; that is, they can be solved within a cell matrix with the use of predefined functions that take as arguments expressions employing constants (entered directly) and cell references (entered by pointing).

Case 2. Suppose, to extend the above example, we want to write a program that will sum an arbitrary, but fixed, number, N, of numbers. Both the Pascal and the spreadsheet solutions assume a fixed number of cells, where each cell is individually assigned a value. If we change the number of values, then we must change the number of cells (and the number of assignments, etc.). This means in essence that we construct a new program each time we are given a different number of values.

For the spreadsheets this approach is not infeasible. One simply enters the numbers sequentially (hitting Return after each number). When all numbers are entered, the sum expression is entered and the range of numbers is pointed to as before. The whole process is not that different from using a calculator.

The Pascal solution can similarly be altered by changing the dimension of Numbers and adjusting the number of assignment statements and the number of terms in the sum expression. However, the process quickly becomes infeasible as N becomes larger.

Case 3. Suppose that we now want to construct a *single* solution that will sum an arbitrarily large, but fixed, number, N, of numbers. (Both Pascal and spreadsheets insist on fixed, static dimensions for all objects so we will consider this case first before looking at the general case of arbitrary N.)

The most straightforward solution is to allow for a sufficiently large, but not arbitrary, number, say, 1000. The spreadsheet can then be organized so that at the end of a column of 1000 empty cells, the 1001st cell has the formula $= \text{SUM}(R[-1000]\,C : R[-1]\,C)$. In short, we use the same solution as before except that we reserve 1000 cells, instead of 10. Whatever cells are not actually used (i.e., no value is entered into them) will be treated by the SUM function as though they were zero.

The Pascal solution could also be written as an extension of its original form, but it would contain in excess of 2000 statements and an expression with 1000 terms. Clearly, at this point the Pascal solution must be transformed to another form. To do so requires that we introduce new concepts (loops and index variables) and make some new assumptions about how values will be entered (from the keyboard). The revised solution is as follows:

p'1. Definition of data structures to hold up to 1000 values and the resulting sum (along with a loop index variable):

```
program compute(input, output);
var
    Numbers: array[1 .. 1000] of integer;
    Sum: integer;
    i: integer;
```

p'2. Initialization of the array by reading and echo printing values in a column. Note that to allow for entering less than 1000 values it is necessary to incorporate an extraneous "end-of-input" test. To simplify the example, we shall assume that end-of-input occurs when end-of-file occurs:

```
begin
for i :=1 to 1000 do
    if (not eof(input)) then
        begin
        readln(Numbers[i]);
        writeln('$', Numbers[i] : 8 : 2);
        end
    else
        Numbers[i] :=0;
```

p'3. Computation of the sum:

```
Sum :=0;
for i :=1 to 1000 do
    Sum :=Sum+Numbers[i];
```

p'4. Display result as a dollar amount with two decimals in a field
width of 10 characters:

```
writeln('$', Sum : 8 : 2);
end.
```

p'5. Compile, link, and execute the program, entering the values as
required.

This program begins to appeal to an experienced programmer, but to
the inexperienced programmer this is a rather complex program. The
spreadsheet is still simple and visually natural. It parallels the process we
might use if we were to approach the problem with only pen and paper.
The Pascal solution, however, while gaining on good textual form, bears no
resemblance to the manual process. It has lost all intuition. In addition,
having modified the program to read as input its value matrix each time the
program is run, it no longer allows that a single value might be changed
without reentering the entire value matrix. While this is not unlike a
calculator, it is clearly inferior to the spreadsheet solution.

To this point, the solutions analyzed provide spreadsheets their greatest
competitive edge. As we begin to extend the problem further to allow
greater flexibility, we will find that the spreadsheet solutions become less
naturally visual and more textual.

Case 4. Next, consider the case where N is arbitrary. The problem for
both languages is that both require fixed dimensions. The spreadsheet
matrix has a fixed maximum size. Pascal will only allow arrays that have
fixed dimensions. Possible solutions are to convert to a file input algorithm
that sums as it reads or to convert to a dynamic cell allocation algorithm.
Since spreadsheets allow only the former and since dynamic allocation
requires additional and complex language concepts, we will use the former
solution. (Many spreadsheets are unable to even attempt this problem. They
have no way to iteratively read and sum values. Excel[4] is one that does.)
The spreadsheet solution is considered first.

In Excel,[4] it is possible to define macros that behave similarly to
subroutines. They can be passed arguments and can return a value (which
may be a matrix). To solve this particular problem, we define a macro

SumForArbitraryN. This requires a macrosheet. A macrosheet is a new type of sheet similar to a spreadsheet except that it is evaluated as a sequence of statements with explicit control flow, rather than as a sequence of expressions with deduced evaluation ordering. This allows an extended set of operations, including operations to control branching—conditional and unconditional. The result is that it is now possible to construct algorithms of a rather conventional linear textual style. In the solution below, a simple loop is constructed. The process is as follows:

s'1. A macrosheet is selected. The macro statements will be entered one below another in a single column. The starting point and extent of the macro is determined through its name declaration. Figure 3 shows the window used for declaring the new macro name. (This window appeared in response to a menu command.) A new function SumForArbitraryN is being added. It is bound to the cell array beginning at A5 and extending to A12 (a column of eight cells). The macro will begin execution with the statement at A5 and will continue downward cell by cell until the end of the macro, unless either an explicit branch occurs or a RETURN is encountered. In the latter case, the function returns the value of the RETURN expression. Should the macro fall through the bottom without encountering a RETURN, an error is reported.

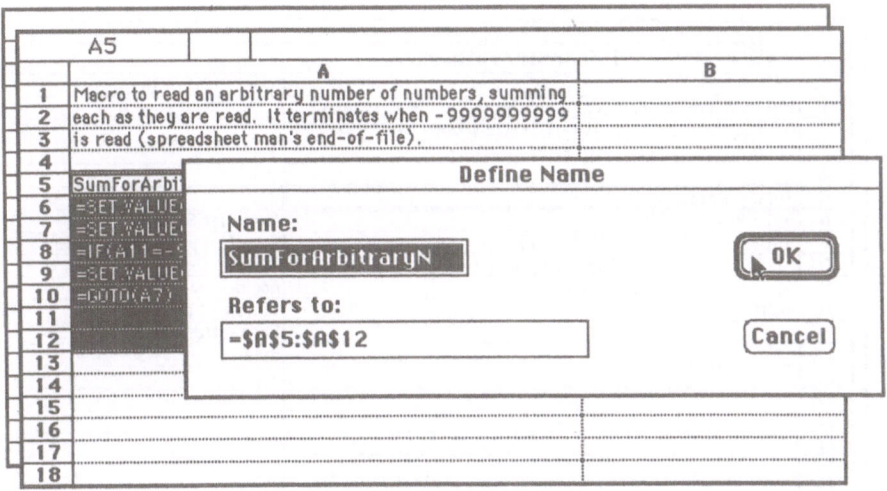

FIGURE 3. Naming a new macro.

s'2. The macro is shown in Figure 4. It is a simple loop that corresponds to the following Pascal code segment:

```
function SumForArbitraryN: integer;
   var
      temp, sum: integer;
   begin
      sum :=0;
Loop:
      readln(temp);
      if (temp=-9999999999) then return(temp);
      sum :=sum+temp;
      goto Loop;
   end;
```

Because we cannot test end-of-file in the macrosheet language, we must use some other termination convention. We use the convention that end-of-input occurs whenever the value −9999999999 is encountered. (More suitable terminations can be constructed which do not invalidate a potentially legal input value, but they increase the complexity of the solution without adding to our current discussion.)

Note that to allow repetitive assignments, the macrosheet language introduces an assignment statement that alters the value of another cell, rather than maintaining the spreadsheet convention

	A5		SumForArbitraryN	
	A			**B**
1	Macro to read an arbitrary number of numbers, summing			
2	each as they are read. It terminates when -9999999999			
3	is read (spreadsheet man's end-of-file).			
4				
5	SumForArbitraryN			
6	=SET.VALUE(A12,0)			Initialize Sum
7	=SET.VALUE(A11,INPUT(":",1))			Top of loop: Read next value
8	=IF(A11=-9999999999,RETURN(A12))			Test for loop termination
9	=SET.VALUE(A12,A12+A11)			Add new value to Sum
10	=GOTO(A7)			Bottom of loop
11				Currently read value
12				Sum
13				
14				
15				
16				
17				
18				

FIGURE 4. Macro code for SumForArbitraryN.

of associating with a given cell a formula that specifies its value. While macrosheets attempt to maintain the visual appearance of a spreadsheet, they have a significantly different semantic model.

s'3. The final step is to invoke the macro from a spreadsheet. This is done by entering the expression =SumForArbitraryN() in some cell. (There are menus available to assist in this process so that one need not type the function name.)

This solution leaves the realm of visual languages totally. In fact, it is not even a good linear textual expression of the problem. It requires all of the programming language concepts we have so far avoided: variables, iteration and control sequencing, order of evaluation, and input/output. Furthermore, it loses many of the properties we identified earlier as visual and beneficial, for example, each cell having a single value during the lifetime of a program evaluation and the order of evaluation being derived.

The corresponding Pascal program at least exhibits good linear textual form:

```
program compute(input, output);
var
    Sum: integer;
function SumForArbitraryN: integer;
    var
        temp, sum: integer;
    begin
    while(not eof(input)) then
        begin
        readln(temp);
        sum :=sum+temp;
        end;
    SumForArbitraryN :=sum;
    end;
begin
Sum :=SumForArbitraryN;
writeln('$', Sum : 8 : 2);
end.
```

As the generality of this problem has increased, the Pascal solution has improved in form, while the spreadsheet seems to have degenerated. This property suggests either that the original spreadsheet concepts are inadequate to support greater generality or that they have not been properly generalized. We contend that it is the latter rather than the former. The evolution of spreadsheets suggests that facilities such as macrosheets have been added ad hoc by programmers who quite naturally used a model with which they were already familiar. In the next section, we will look at how the original concepts might be generalized without the degeneration we have seen in macrosheets.

Case 5. Without belaboring the point much further, we simply note that were we to insist that the data be read from a data file, rather than the keyboard, a spreadsheet solution is impossible. Spreadsheet programs have a limited ability to read files created by programs of their own kind (other spreadsheets), but under strict fixed-size limitations. Essentially, the data file must map into some portion of a spreadsheet. This capability will not allow files of arbitrary length.

Comparisons with languages other than Pascal might be made of course; however, our purpose is not to evaluate Pascal or any of these other languages, but to illustrate where the spreadsheet model succeeds and where it fails. From the above discussion, it should be obvious that as we go from specific solutions to generic solutions, from fixed-size data to arbitrary-sized data, the spreadsheet model begins to lose its natural visualness. In the sections that follow, we discuss a possible means of generalizing the spreadsheet model such that this effect is reduced.

3. Objectives for a Generalized Sheet Language

As we have seen, the spreadsheet model works well as long as it builds on its visual representation. When it falls back on conventional language structures, it quickly degenerates. Its strengths are its evaluation model and its visual representation as a cell matrix for storing and displaying values.

The objective of the remaining sections is to motivate an understanding for an extended, conceptually consistent, spreadsheet model. This model relies heavily on a visual representation, generalized from the spreadsheet representation, to minimize required language concepts. Specific objectives are:

1. Each cell should be computed exactly once in any evaluation of a program.
2. Cells should be referenced by pointing and should not require names. (This is not to say that cells cannot be named.)
3. The "sheet" concept as both a computational scratch pad and a presentation medium should be preserved, but even greater flexibility to arrange sheets visually should be allowed.
4. The nonmodal, interpretative environment with extensive visual editing should be preserved.
5. The order of evaluation should be entirely derived.
6. The concept of sheets should be generalized to allow "subsheets."

7. The language should be able to accommodate matrices with arbitrary dimensions.

8. The language must support external files.

4. A Generalized Sheet Language

Let the basic "sheet" in a generalized form language be called a *form*. A form intuitively corresponds to a piece of paper (potentially a quite large piece of paper) on which can be pasted a variety of *objects*. A simple form is one on which a single large cell matrix is pasted covering the entire form. This simple form corresponds to a spreadsheet. However, multiple objects can be placed on a single form. Each object on a form can be referenced in one of three ways: by pointing at it (the most common way), by using a name (optionally assigned by the user), or by an automatically assigned default object number.

To create a form, each object is selected from an object template menu (visible in the upper right-hand corner of Figure 5), dragged to the appropriate position within the form, and stretched to the desired dimensions. The visual aspect of each can be independently controlled, including whether the grid lines and scales are to be visible, font selection, cell sizing, and so on. Each cell can contain only a single formula which must compute to one of a numeric value, a string (text), or a graphic image.

A cell expression can reference any cell (or cells) in any object within the containing form or within other forms, subject only to the restriction

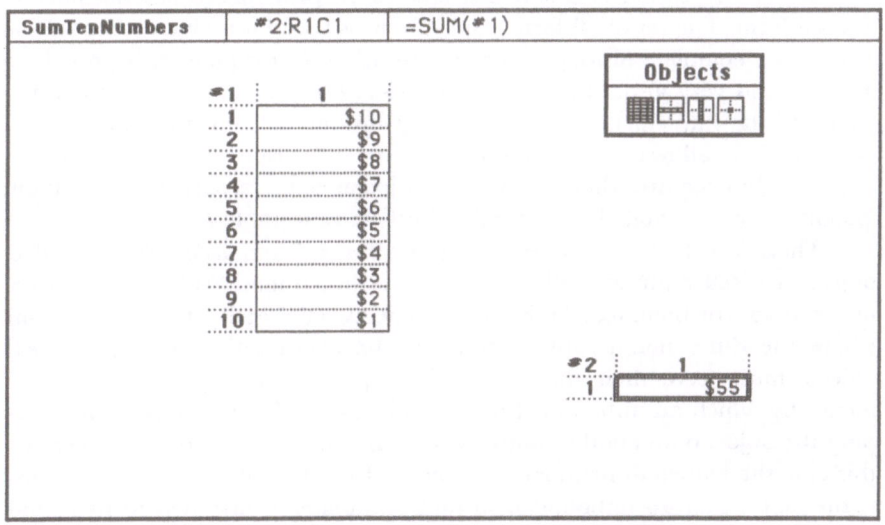

FIGURE 5. Generalized spreadsheet solution to Case 1.

that the resulting derived evaluation must not be made to be circular. Since order of evaluation is updated after each new cell formula is entered, if any circularity were to be induced, it could be determined immediately. Cell references are usually constructed by pointing at the desired cell(s) or by referencing previously assigned names. Internally, cell references consist of a sheet instance, an object reference, and a row–column reference.

A sample form providing a solution to Case 1 above is given in Figure 5. For this form, there are two, unnamed objects: #1 and #2. The first object, #1, contains the 10 values to be summed; the second, #2, contains the result of the sum. The expression used to compute the sum =SUM(#1) is interpreted as: sum the entire cell array of object #1. (Note that a user would not type #1, but rather would select the object by pointing at it; textually we record #1.)

The order of cell evaluation is entirely deduced based upon cell dependencies. The only means of influencing cell evaluation ordering is through references, direct or indirect.

A subform is similar in content to a form, but certain objects will inherit their values as parameters. These objects will initially be left blank. In addition, the value of one or more objects may be returned. How parameters and results are bound is discussed below. For each evaluation of a form or subform, each cell is evaluated only once, that is, cyclic evaluation is not allowed. One consequence of this rule is that no parameter can be altered (since parameters must have been evaluated prior to invoking a subform).

Every invocation of a subform creates, in principle, a new instance of the subform. The set of all forms and subforms used for a given computation provides a complete history of the computation. Consequently, it provides a natural and very visual means of debugging. (In practice, the only requirement of the implementation is that any instance of any subform may be viewed. This allows the possibility that not all instances will actually be retained, but requires that any discarded instance be reconstructible without potential loss of data; that is, results must be repeatable.)

There are two categories of objects: *bounded* and *unbounded*. Bounded objects are cell matrices with fixed, known dimensions. Both of the objects in Figure 5 are bounded. Unbounded objects have at least one dimension where the dimension is unknown when the computation is specified. All objects must have their dimensions fixed prior to evaluation. The usual means by which an unbounded object will have its bounds fixed is by mapping the object onto another object whose dimensions are already known. In this case the known dimensions are inherited by the unbounded object. This is the case when an unbounded formal parameter is matched to its actual parameter, which must have already been evaluated and therefore has fixed dimensions. Another method is through evaluation of an expression, the result of which fixes some previously unbound dimension(s). Figure 6 illustrates a subform that computes the binomial coefficients for an order $N-1$ equation. The main object, named Coeffs, is an unbounded matrix. Both dimensions are unknown and are specified to take the value of the single-cell object named N. Hence, the order of evaluation requires that N be evaluated prior to any aspect of Coeffs. The value of N will be supplied as a parameter whenever BiCoefficient is invoked. For instance, if BiCoefficient(5) is evaluated (via some other form), then N will receive the value 5, and the Coeffs matrix will be dimensioned 5×5. When the subform is completely evaluated, the resulting value of Coeffs will be returned as the value of BiCoefficient(N) (in this case, a 5×5 matrix is returned).

Values for unbounded objects are specified by generic cell specifications stated in terms of the ij th cell, combined with specific cell specifications for specific fixed cells. For example, in Figure 6, the formula for cells RiCj where $i > 1$ and $j > 1$ is =R[-1] C+RC[-1], for cells R1Cj where $j > 1$ the formula is =RC[-1], and so on. Such formulas are entered as a single formula for each selected submatrix.

"Mapping parameters" is a matter of referencing objects on other sub-sheets. To construct a subform that "calls" BiCoefficient(N), we would:

1. Create a new instance of BiCoefficient(N) by selecting it from a list of subsheets and requesting a new instance.

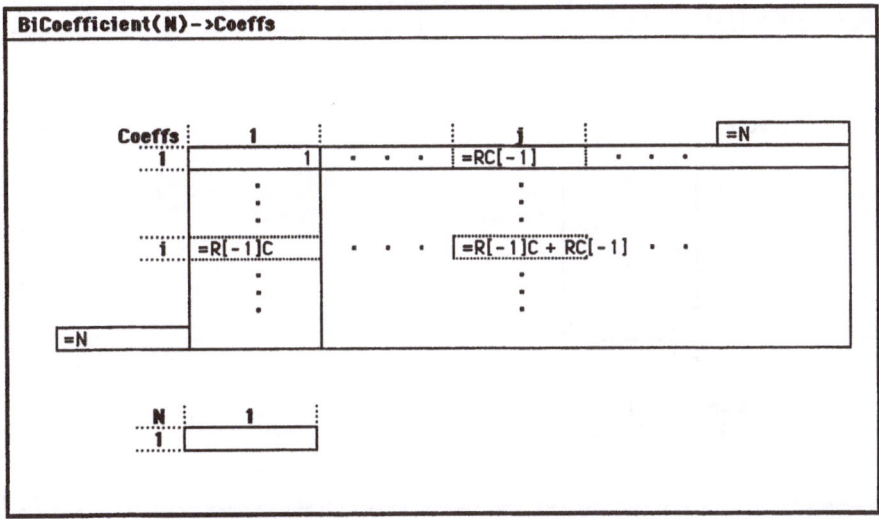

FIGURE 6. Subform that computes the binomial coefficients for an order $N-1$ equation.

2. For this new instance, select the object N which is expected to inherit its value and was previously left blank. This cell is now specified to be the value of a cell in the "calling" form which is known to contain the desired matrix dimension (5 in the above example). This has the effect of binding this instance of BiCoefficient(N) to its "input parameter" and, as a result, fixing the dimensions of the array Coeffs.

3. Select the matrix within the "calling" form that is to receive the results and indicate that the cells values are the same as those of the Coeffs object within the BiCoefficient(N) subform instance created above.

A recursively defined subform is accomplished similarly by allowing that the subform being defined is also simultaneously included on the list of existing subforms. Thus, in the process of defining a subform, one can select a new instance of the same subform and "map parameters." This new instance exists only for the purpose of "mapping parameters" and cannot be otherwise modified. This new instance will inherit the same relative relationship to any subsequent instance that it must create as that between the defining instance of the subform and its newly created instance. Since each recursive invocation creates a new instance of the subform, recursion provides a means of looping without needing to alter existing cell values.

Finally, the concept of a file maps naturally onto an unbounded matrix. Figure 7 shows the solution to Case 5 above, using a file for input. For this

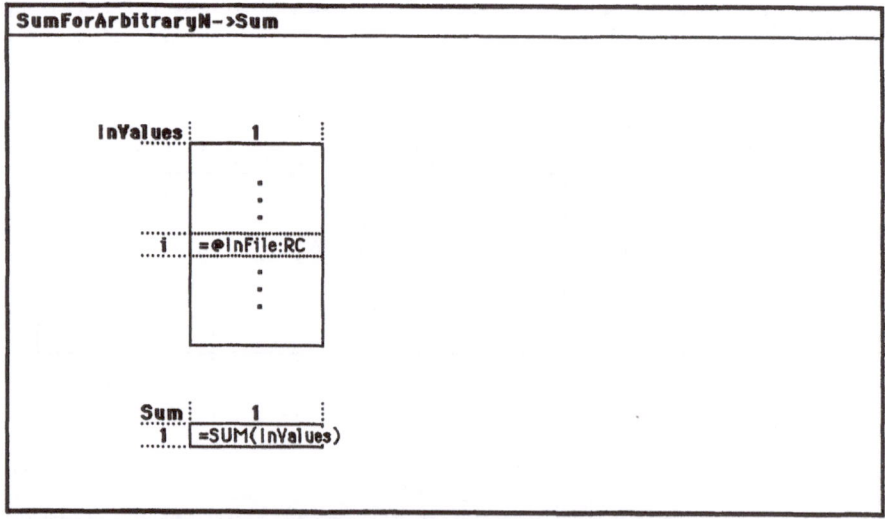

FIGURE 7. Generalized spreadsheet solution to Case 5.

solution, the unbounded object InValues is mapped onto the file InFile. The dimensions of InValues will be inherited from InFile and will be equal to $N \times 1$ where N is the number of records in InFile. The correspondence between InValues and InFile is specified by the expression $= @InFile:RC$ (@ signifies an external file). The rest of the subform specifies that the value of Sum is the sum of all cells of InValues (cell entry for Sum) and that Sum is to be returned as the value of SumForArbitraryN (from header declaration). (Note that we assume that the InFile consists of a sequence of records, each with a single numeric value. A more complex record structure could require that InValues contain more fields or apply a decoding function.)

We summarize the process of deriving this solution as follows:

f1. Select a new subform, name it SumForArbitraryN, and supply the name of the return object Sum. (It is not strictly necessary to name the object; it could be pointed at later.)

f2. Select from the objects menu a row-unbounded object, drag it to an appropriate place in the subform, and shrink the column dimension to 1. Specify the value correspondence with the input file by filling the formula $= @InFile:RC$ into cell RiC1. Finally, name the object InValues (again naming is optional).

f3. Again select an object from the object menu and drag it into place. This time, select the bounded matrix and redimension it to be 1×1. Name it Sum. Its value is computed by the expression $= SUM(InValues)$, entered by typing "=SUM(", pointing at the object InValues, and then typing")".

f4. To complete the solution, select a new form and a 1×1 bounded matrix. Its one cell value is computed by the expression $= SumForArbitraryN()$ [indicated by selecting the SUM object on subform SumForArbitraryN()].

It should be apparent that the generalized form solution to Case 5 provides the same conceptual advantage over the Pascal solution as the spreadsheet solutions to Case 1 and Case 2 did over the corresponding Pascal solutions.

5. Summary

We have discussed the strengths and weaknesses of spreadsheets as visual languages and have suggested how the spreadsheet paradigm might be generalized. Implementation issues are not discussed here, but an implementation of a language utilizing this generalized sheet language paradigm is in progress and such issues will be discussed later.

The concepts behind the proposed generalizations are extensions of the simple concepts already developed with spreadsheet languages. They depend heavily on the visual aspects of spreadsheet languages and attempt to minimize the number of conventional language concepts required, particularly for the inexperienced programmer.

The major concepts as viewed from a spreadsheet model can be summarized as follows. First, the concepts of the spreadsheet and the cell matrix are separated to provide forms and cell matrix objects which may be composed in a rich variety of ways. Second, a conceptually consistent procedure abstraction mechanism (a subform) is introduced to replace the misfit macro mechanism. Third, the concept of a bounded cell matrix is extended to an unbounded cell matrix. Unbounded cell matrices provide a convenient mechanism for matching parameters as well as for mapping naturally onto external files. Fourth, the evaluation mechanism is made even more strict by totally eliminating all forms of cyclic evaluation, except recursive evaluation (which creates a new instance with each invocation). This provides a complete computational history that can be viewed for debugging. In essence, the single-value-per-cell evaluation model parallels hand computation using paper and pen (with no eraser)—each subcalculation requires a fresh piece of paper.

It seems clear that for a larger set of problems than is the case for spreadsheet languages, this generalized paradigm provides a simplistic and highly visual approach. This simplistic visualness is the quality we are seeking in naturally visual languages. The graphic medium itself should allow us to simplify communication of information by exploiting the inherently high bandwidth of visual communication. In so doing, we should not be surprised if we are led to new language models or caused to think about problems differently. Clearly, we expect that "different" will also prove to be "better."

References

1. S. K. CHANG, Visual languages: a tutorial and survey, *IEEE Software* **4**(1), 29–39 (1987).
2. N. C. SHU, Visual programming languages: a perspective and a dimensional analysis, pp. 11–34 in *Visual Languages*, S. K. Chang, T. Ichikawa, and P. A. Ligomenides (Eds.), Plenum Press, New York, 1986.
3. I. NASSI and B. SHNEIDERMAN, Flowchart techniques for structured programming, *ACM SIGPLAN Notices* **8**(8), 12–26 (1973).
4. MICROSOFT CORPORATION, Microsoft Excel, Bellevue, Washington, 1985.

EPILOGUE

Research work in visual languages is maturing. We see in the work presented here a healthy combination of the development of visual languages for various specific purposes and an increasing discussion of the theoretical basis and design principles underlying this work. Already the ideas discussed here have spread. If the design principles are good for visual languages, how can they be extended to three-dimensional languages, or to "languages" involving other senses? Some researchers, for example, are discussing "earcons," the auditory analogue to icons. The objective of this type of work is to provide the user with a system interface that is as effective and easy to use as possible. Traditional textural interface elements have their place; but icons, animation, and other visual elements can be used effectively to enhance the interface, and thus make computer-based information systems more readily available to a wide group of users. The ideas that form the active research topics of today will influence tomorrow's standard interface elements; the ideas that are "pie in the sky" today, including appeals to the visual, auditory, and other senses, will evolve into serious research topics in the future.

INDEX